Literary History and Avant-Garde Poetics in the Antipodes

a hungry metaphor born, it breaches
somewhere out from Botany Bay
    – Alison Whittaker, "not one silent lamb", *Blakwork* (2018)

They who live at the centre of a circle think only of the centre. To those who are half-way removed from the centre to the circumference so much of the area of the circle is of importance as lies between their line and the centre,—to which they ever look wistfully. They who dwell on the outside, think much of the outside, but do so still with a consciousness that they are but outsiders.
    – Anthony Trollope, *Australia and New Zealand* (1873–4)

Does work provide you with most of your self-esteem? If not, where does that mainly come from?
The outdoors is sovereign (are sovereign?)!
    – Javant Biarujia, "Oneirodynia of the Masculine" (2002)

Literary History and Avant-Garde Poetics in the Antipodes

Languages of Invention

A. J. Carruthers

EDINBURGH
University Press

Edinburgh University Press is one of the leading university presses in the UK. We publish academic books and journals in our selected subject areas across the humanities and social sciences, combining cutting-edge scholarship with high editorial and production values to produce academic works of lasting importance. For more information visit our website: edinburghuniversitypress.com

© A. J. Carruthers 2024, 2025

Edinburgh University Press Ltd
13 Infirmary Street
Edinburgh EH1 1LT

First published in hardback by Edinburgh University Press 2024

Typeset in 11/13pt Adobe Sabon by
Cheshire Typesetting Ltd, Cuddington, Cheshire

A CIP record for this book is available from the British Library

ISBN 978 1 3995 2682 1 (hardback)
ISBN 978 1 3995 2683 8 (paperback)
ISBN 978 1 3995 2684 5 (webready PDF)
ISBN 978 1 3995 2685 2 (epub)

The right of A. J. Carruthers to be identified as the author of this work has been asserted in accordance with the Copyright, Designs and Patents Act 1988, and the Copyright and Related Rights Regulations 2003 (SI No. 2498).

Contents

List of Figures	vi
Acknowledgments	viii
Prologue	x
Dedication	xv

PART I Chronometries (Antiquity, 1897–1947)

1. Tzara's Chronometer: Literary History and the Antipodal Avant-Gardes	3
2. 1897 in 1981: Stéphane Mallarmé *avec* Christopher Brennan	47
3. New Order of the Line: W. C. Williams, Ern Malley, Harry Hooton and the 1940s Avant-Gardes	100

PART II: Aftershocks (1947–Vanishing Present)

4. The Dada Chronicles: Jas H. Duke and Barry Humphries	159
5. Expansive Geometries: Ania Walwicz's Polish	208
6. Lionel Fogarty's Historical Style	241
7. Traitorous Text: Amanda Stewart Off and On the Page	283
A Wáng Gă: an Epilogue	305
Index	340

Figures

2.1 Christopher Brennan, title page of *Musicopoematographoscope* (1897). 51
2.2 Christopher Brennan, second title page from *Musicopoematographoscope* (1897). 62
2.3 Christopher Brennan, interior pages from *Musicopoematographoscope* (1897). 66
2.4 Christopher Brennan, handwritten Celtic font; "the fair white page", from *Musicopoematographoscope* (1897). 69
2.5 Chris Edwards, from *A Fluke* (2004), presented lengthways to preserve spacing. 76
2.6 Anna Couani and Sneja Gunew, eds. *Telling Ways* (1988), showing cover and title page featuring a visual poem by Thalia. 78
2.7 Collective Effort production *Missing Forms* (1981); two variant covers for the anthology, featuring visual works by Jas H. Duke. 79
2.8 Alex Selenitsch, "Sonnet 1974/81" (left, as it appears in *Missing Forms*), and a page from the chapbook *Sonnets* (1975, right; this chapbook includes a version of the image on left). 82
3.1 Jean-Jacques Lecercle, "Diagram 1: Naive", *Interpretation as Pragmatics* (1999). 123
3.2 Jean-Jacques Lecercle, "Diagram 2: Anxious", *Interpretation as Pragmatics* (1999). 123
3.3 Jean-Jacques Lecercle, "Diagram 3: Clever", *Interpretation as Pragmatics* (1999). 123
3.4 Jean-Jacques Lecercle, "Diagram 4: Pretentious", *Interpretation as Pragmatics* (1999). 123
3.5 Jean-Jacques Lecercle, "Diagram 4: Pretentious", *Interpretation as Pragmatics* (1999). 123
4.1 Jas H. Duke, visual poem from *Destiny Wood* (1978). 182

4.2	Jas H. Duke, cover of posthumous artists' book *Dada Kampfen um Leben und Tod (Dada Fight for Life and Death)* (1996).	183
4.3	Jas H. Duke, excerpted page from *Dada Kampfen um Leben und Tod (Dada Fight for Life and Death)* (1996).	184
4.4	Jas H. Duke, cover for *Archduke 4* (1974).	193
4.5	Jas H. Duke, page from *Industrial Woman* (1986).	194
4.6	Jas H. Duke, visual poem in *Poems of War and Peace* (1989).	197
5.1	Ania Walwicz, "Self-Portrait" (2015 painting); courtesy of the Ania Walwicz Archive.	211
6.1	A. J. Carruthers, interpretive diagram for Fogarty's "Decipherer".	270
6.2	Natalie Harkin, slip cover containing the three volumes of *Archival-Poetics* (2019).	280
7.1	Amanda Stewart, performance score for "The Liberated Showroom" from *I/T: Selected Poems, 1980–1996* (1998), 38.	289
7.2	Amanda Stewart, "Haiku for Min Tanaka", from *I/T: Selected Poems* (1998), 12.	290
7.3	Amanda Stewart, visual pieces from "The Twentieth Century Never Happened" (2010), NZEPC site.	292
7.4	Amanda Stewart, ", No Person, speaks", from *I/T: Selected Poems* (1998), 8–9.	300
7.5	Amanda Stewart, "vice versa", from *I/T: Selected Poems* (1998), 60.	301
8.1	Georges Perec, from the Black Ring-file, folios 79/80; list of stations on the Sydney–Wollongong line, and names of the commando, in *53 Days* (2000, first published in 1989 by Editions P. O. L.), 223.	306

Acknowledgements

This was a long-haul book: it began long ago in the Antipodes and certainly among friends. Candid conversation is where it began. For this I first thank Amelia Dale, Pam Brown, Amanda Stewart and Chris Edwards for the best talk over these years. Sneja Gunew became an inspiration late in this project, encouraging avant-garde risk. The extraordinary Justin Clemens led me to Dada Humphries and many other things. I also feel grateful to Antipodal historiographers – Ann Vickery, Sam Moginie, Brendan Casey, Michael Farrell and Tim Wright. I thank Sam in particular for our mutual work on Duke very early on. I'm glad to share a friendship with film producer Margaret Fink, who was Hooton's publisher in the 1950s (plus lover, artist, avant-salon hostess) and her daughter Hannah. I feel through Margaret that I "know" Harry to some degree – as Margaret booms in a loud voice over lunch: "HARRY WAS *KIND*!" I thank Hannah and Margaret for granting permission for use of quotations from Hooton, and for carrying his spirit into the twenty-first century.

I thank Ross Digby and Elena Galimberti for their assistance and generosity in opening the Ania Walwicz Archive to me at a most difficult time for all who knew her. The organisers of the Ania Walwicz memorial, Marion Campbell, Sneja Gunew and Anna Gibbs, provided us a space to reflect; this will continue. Pi.O. has been an inspiration to multiple generations of avant-garde poets. I thank him for working with the Estate of Jas H. Duke to grant permission for the use of Duke's materials. Copyright is attributed to the Estate, and permission is granted for the purposes of Chapter 4. Amanda Stewart has become a dear friend and confidante. I am deeply grateful for her life's work, and for allowing me to quote from it. Cathy Vidler has graciously provided the cover image, which appeared first in *Wings* (Cordite, 2020). Alex Selenitsch kindly permitted use of "Sonnets". Jean-Jacques Lecercle has granted permission to reprint the Malley diagrams from *Interpretation as Pragmatics*. Permission to reproduce Georges Perec has been granted by David R. Godine

Publisher, who put out a 2000 edition of *53 Days*. Parts of Chapter 4 previously appeared as "Jas H. Duke and the Chronicle of Avant-Garde Poetics" in *JASAL* 18.2 (2018).

I thank my Chinese colleagues and friends at the Australian Studies Centre, through SUIBE (Shanghai), at which I held a very generous Oriental Scholar Fellowship while serving as a lecturer there. Ouyang Yu was there at the time, but also Zhou Xiaojun, a Lawsonist (and more, but he began with Henry Lawson), and a most generous soul. In Shanghai, Wang Guanglin was and continues to be my dearest mentor, and Beibei Chen a dear friend and heroic Antipodalist. At the English Department of Nanjing University I thank first and foremost Yang Jincai, as well as Xu Lei and Wang Shouren, for their accommodation, wide-ranging intelligence and welcome.

My American friends have shown much generosity from afar. Charles Bernstein, who I had the pleasure of meeting in China, always believed in this project. Joan Retallack, Rachel Blau DuPlessis and Lyn Hejinian have shown big-hearted interest in Antipodal poets and discussions concerning. I am stunned by the support afforded me from the editors of this series, Georgina Colby and Eric White. Their close attention to each aspect of the book and its production is crucial to its integrity. Without them, or the scrupulous copy-editors, this book would not have launched into this exciting international context.

Lastly, I am grateful to the Australian National University for a Visiting Fellowship with the School of Literature, Languages and Linguistics in 2023, in particular the Discipline of English and the Centre for Australian Literary Cultures.

A. J. Carruthers, The Australian National University, 2023

Prologue

Though the idea of an Antipodal avant-garde has been at the forefront of literary debates about Australian modernism, and though it has played a significant role in the development of modern Australian poetry and poetics, no account has yet been made for a narrative of Australian avant-garde poetry in the broader history of the global avant-gardes. This is that first account. My motive is twofold, two "expanding circles" of avant-garde literary history: one, an outer historiography of avant-gardes and its theoretical beginnings in Europe, and two, an inner one, the "local" and Antipodal context which speaks back to those first contexts. By no means does one "circle" overcome the other; rather, each bounces off or intersects with the other. This is a study that cuts across hemispheres – a resolutely hemispheric, transnational and geopolitical study. It connects with the avant-garde aftermath outside Europe and North America, thus also Eastern Europe, the Americas, post-colonial and post-Soviet contexts, the Global South and the Asia-Pacific.

"Avant-garde" did not simply mean one thing to an Australian poet. The idea or the existence of avant-gardes, and the way the term has been deployed varies widely over the literature. In these pages I have tried to put together both a dossier for the poetic avant-garde of the Antipodes ceaselessly in dialogue with the international avant-gardes, and move through debates in literary history and theory through an examination of key texts and events. Events that haunt Australian literary history have been cited as significant for understandings of modernism's relation to the avant-gardes: Christopher Brennan's version of Stéphane Mallarmé's *Un Coup de Dés* in his 1897 work, *Musicopoematographoscope*; Ern Malley and Harry Hooton; the moment Dada appeared in Australia through Barry Humphries in the 1950s with the Melbourne Dada Group, the Ubu-like character Tid, and Dame Edna Everage, a version of Duchamp's Rrose Sélavy, followed by the first Dada performances of poet Jas H. Duke in 1973; and sustained experimental practices in poetry and performances by Lionel Fogarty, Ania Walwicz, Amanda Stewart and Mez Breeze, all of whom were in dialogue with radical avant-garde poetics and its manifold practices. The Antipodal avant-garde notably interacted with African-American, North American, British, European, Eastern European (Bloc and after), Asia-Pacific and other Oceanic fellow-travellers. Thus I engage with a rich history of translation and multilingual crossing.

The first part of this book, *Chronometries*, concerns "avant-gardes" in general and at large; therefore the general reader will have a handle on its key foci and figures. Names like Tzara, Ern Malley, Stéphane Mallarmé, Jerome Rothenberg, Les Murray and Christopher Brennan need little or less introduction. But in the second part of this book, *Aftershocks*, there are names that come in and out, names that the reader may know and may have to look up, depending on their proximity to these contexts. I am aware that the nominal surface of this text may take time to process: contemporary names like John Tranter, who started *Jacket*; John Kinsella; poet and small press bookseller Kris Hemensley; Hazel Smith, a UK emigre and experimentalist who might sit beside Language Writers of both US coasts, or in the UK avant-garde, figures like Bob Cobbing and Maggie O'Sullivan. These are names in a category that might have general rather than specific currency in poetics-inflected criticism. They will be of interest to experts, poets and enthusiasts alike. The visual poetry of Alex Selenitsch and Pete Spence may be compared with counterparts like the Noigandres of Brazil or again a figure like Cobbing. Where the Aotearoa, New Zealand context is concerned, there may also open up an additional context to which this can all be compared in the most general sense (pedagogically perhaps, too, I hope that there can be comparative resonance across Te Tai-o-Rehua, the Tasman Sea); Hemensley might be compared with Alan Loney with regard to the work of letterpress and small press publication and distribution, and Michelle Leggott with examples here included that engage with North American contexts. As to the case study poets, these may be entirely unknown to some readers. If so, I hope fruitful connection and comparison can be made. Lionel Fogarty has been compared with Amiri Baraka, Sonia Sanchez and even US Language Writing. Manifold senses of Black radicalism and geopolitical anti-Imperialism here come into play; the poetics of African-American experimental writing as compared with Indigenous poetries in the Antipodes, the Americas, the African continent and elsewhere. By no means did any one of the figures I choose to focus on here, if they were based in the Australian mainland, "launch" the Antipodal avant-garde or the idea of an alternative Australian literature. It will be seen how this is not the case. I hope the reader can bear with names and that naming can both afford power to their referents and question that power, which once was theophanic, and doubtless could still be.

The rest is history; and yet, what precisely is or was an Australian literary history? How did it take up or resist the initial openings of the early twentieth-century avant-gardes, and what does this mean for the historical understanding of the reach of avant-gardes in relation to modernism, and in relation to the global – transatlantic, transpacific – constellation of literature and literary studies? How, as Robb Hernández shows in *Archiving an Epidemic: Art, AIDS, and Queer Chicanx Avant-Garde*, can one take from what is amorphous or "unknown" and make for it a vocabulary and an history? What is this "destruction" or "explosiveness" at the core of the conception of all avant-gardes? Drawing out the longer history of the avant-gardes, do we neutralise the effect of the original explosion or ignite it over and over? Joining other studies concerned with transnational perspectives of the avant-gardes, and taking critical poetics as a way in, this book is an intervention in literary histories of modernism and avant-gardism through the lens of Australian poetry. That it pertains to national literary culture goes without saying. That it resists the confinement of nation must be underlined. In the years since the fall of the Soviet Union and Yugoslavia, a period which saw the near-total collapse of the old Second World, a new horizon opened up and the financialisation of the globe took place. It was imposed across classes and nationalities, opening up new hemispheric and geopolitical lines of influence and oppression. The Antipodal continent fits uneasily within the North–South and East–West divides of the post-Soviet era. Antipodal and avant-Europe hardly coincide. It is this that Spivak in the *Critique of Postcolonial Reason* refers to with regard to Kant's "foreclosure" of Indigeneity. It would have been too much to call this book an *Antipodal Critique of North–South Judgment*, but it might eventually have come close to something like it. Perhaps it can be understood in the term *ostranenie*, used by the Russian Formalists, the making strange as restorative of true feeling – now *Austranenie*, defamiliarisation of avant-garde works of art. It's separation as much as coincidence.

The notion that avant-gardes in the Antipodes could not emerge because it was a "cultural desert", a cultural "backwater" of sub-imperial or secondary Europe, comes down both to complex entanglements of nation, colony and cosmopolis, and a misunderstanding of what I call the Antipodal City, the complex of a non-liberated country in the Southern hemisphere that is counted as part of the "Free" (or "First") World. This can be gauged already in a pioneering 2016 work by Jennifer Loureide Biddle, *Remote Avant-Garde: Aboriginal Art under Occupation*, which gives this some significant advance, it being the first in-depth study of an artistic avant-garde on the Aboriginal continent. Without a better sense of what the continent in question here means, in the configurations of geopolitical space, what we mean when we say "Australia" will not change resonance and this study will not move underneath our feet. But I hope it *can* move underneath our feet, so to speak, when what is called Australia becomes part of the global vocabulary of the achievements of national sovereignty and national liberation in a different key, meaning national sovereignty as *against* what we know about the continuations of empire in the new century. There is no argument here in favour of Australian literature as the achievement of a country in the Western Bloc. There is another "Australia" that opposes its position in such a bloc from within.

It should be tabled here that my use of archival and personal material is extensive. Word-of-mouth, oral history, interviews, anecdotal evidence, rare documents, one-offs: these have played a role in laying out the historical fabric of this book and determining its scope. This is history from the ground up. This is a contribution to the study of twentieth and twenty-first century poetics in a period-crossing and formation-crossing sense, through the lens of an unknown avant-garde, and in light of what it brings also to the avant-gardes of all times and places. It is relevant to everything that we call "poetics" today in the aftermath of modernism. What we know to be the avant-garde, and what we deem modernism, are sometimes given greater clarity when seen from without. Distance can also prove fatal. The Antipodal continent might also be the place where avant-gardists go to die, as when George Perec blamed the Antipodal continent for his own death, after *53 Days*, in 1982. In the time gap of writing this book too the avant-gardes of the Antipodes, and the world, have changed. The belatedness of this study is a consequence of distance and of proximity, gaps in time and leaps forward. It is a late appearance of an avant-garde comparatively speaking, but perhaps more importantly an avant-garde that was already there in the beginning.

A note on phraseology: I have tried to deploy the term "avant-garde" with clarity throughout by referring to it in the plural as "avant-gardes", given its international multiplicity and trans-temporal dimension – the extension of avant-gardes over time and space into the new century. I avoid generic use of "the" avant-garde, and instead refer to the "historical avant-garde" often in terms of its Eastern European, Romanian influence, or rather as the "early twentieth-century avant-garde". I have tended towards the indefinite, slightly hypothetical "an" avant-garde in other cases to foreground the national specificity of an Australian poetic avant-garde, which is crucial for Chapter 6 particularly. I am fairly sure, without reverting to blunt canon-making, that an Australian *poetry* avant-garde congeals into a loose count-as-One, yet still the plural is deployed to encompass multiple configurations of avant-gardes in Australian art and culture – "remote" avant-garde, First Nations/Aboriginal avant-garde, 1940s avant-garde, etc. – within the one pluralistic frame. I limit the use of "vanguard" and "vanguardist" to cases where the shock-troop or otherwise political semantic has appeared, as of its Leninist historical usage.

Lastly, we are a long way from envisaging an Antipodal literary studies for which the horizon is no longer colony, and therefrom one in which the "outer" readership sees in "Australian literature" something different than what is expected of a colony, but my modest hope is that through the power of poetics (and joining historiographical and theoretical analyses of the long aftermath of avant-garde modernism already showing the way), this is one small step in another direction.

Dedication

To Philip Mead

I acknowledge the sovereignty of the Indigenous lands upon which some of this writing took place: Budawang land, Bidjegal land and Ngunnawal land. None of these lands were ceded and custodianship was never given over.

The basis of revolution and liberation remains the Aboriginal sovereignty movement. This writing is dedicated to the past and the future of Indigenous sovereignty; to revolutionists and warriors of all Nations who have fought for it, died for it, and will fight for it in the future; to Treaty-minded republicans during the present era of Occupation; and to all those who envisioned liberation of the continent but will not live to experience it.

I would like to further dedicate this study to the memory of Ania Walwicz and Cathy Vidler, who both passed away during the writing of this book. I wish that they had been able to see it. I honour their contribution to the Antipodal avant-garde.

Part I

Chronometries
(Antiquity, 1897–1947)

Chapter 1

Tzara's Chronometer: Literary History and the Antipodal Avant-Gardes

Jerome Rothenberg's translation of Tristan Tzara's poem "Maison, pour Aragon" reads:

> arp & the barbered arbor
> reignite the open night
> in the special pocket edition made for australian kangaroos
>
> arp & the arc-shaped bark
> are framed by semirámis
> arp the arc & the arbored barbered bark
>
> o crisp chronometer[1]

Marginal histories, theoretical epicentres. Tzara beholds a crisp *chronomètre* to measure time – crisply historical, as if it were a moment ago – and already there we have a challenge to the conspective view expected of any history; these exhortations begin on a small scale and off-centre, literally in the margin. The poem, for that is what it is, appears faint red on a cluttered page from the sixth number of *Bulletin Dada*, published in Paris, March 1920. It isn't the only thing by Tzara on the cluttered page; there are all the sinister jokes and hermetic verses Dada became known for, but the "false" news of the poster page in the *Bulletin* is far more typographically pronounced than the other issues, so superimposed are its various elements.

Dada magazines made the movement. Emily Hage's recent study of Dada periodicals captures at various angles the motives (and

---

[1] This translation first appears in Rothenberg's *Writing Through: Translations and Variations* (47).

antics) of the evolution of collectives and their affiliates that we now know to be both saboteurist and transnationally connected. For Hage the early 1920s was a contested period for the magazine medium – the moment Dada became Dada-ism. From such micro-poetic lensing a latter-day enormity looms like a shadowy double over the avant-garde aftermath wherever it carried through, from its century to the next. This is the rhetorical dramatisation of a claim, or perhaps a necessary misreading. That an avant-garde poem has revealed its destiny in another hemisphere and another time (though we cannot curtail hasty assumptions about time) is to seek patterns of argumentation that can situate an avant-garde in a larger temporal and indeed theoretical framework. To be forthright: Tzara's pocketing of the "pocket edition" of Australian kangaroos, in the figural outer-scape of a poem motivated by a distinctly audial or temporally measured drive, here at the outset, begins a temporal hunch and merits spatial query. It isn't yet trans-nation, for reasons that need to be gone in to, but its content is exceptionally outwards-bound. Tzara does not imagine a kangaroo to be a reader for no reason. But what is Tzara saying, and who is listening? Time tells where this leads: the curiosity of history is its bidirectionality. The whole theoretical edifice may be put into dispute if we keep crossing temporal lines and take avant-garde time at its word. Crispness is freshness, but we cannot put all our faith in the vanishing present, nor all our faith in the margins.

In this book's opening evocations we shall remain on the ledge of theory before diving into the chasm of history. At this inaugural point, the idea of the avant-garde and idea of an Antipodal literature are two utterly incompatible things. I lodge here an hemispheric-localist disclaimer. What Tzara sought from the Antipodal continent concerns everything about the modernist avant-garde (scaled down a little, at least, to literary history), of much concern to literary theory (scaled up), and, through both, levelled on a more even plane to produce an example for literary criticism in its struggle with and against history. The hemisphere that Tzara would not come to experience first-hand is one articulation of how the avant-garde turns to points of crisis and uncertainty to articulate its situation in proximity to cultural centres. Texts lead the way, as criticism demands, but what an avant-garde text can say, whether removed or emergent from a resistant or stubborn literary culture, depends on where you are, who you are; which continent, in a city, at a university, at a poetry reading or on the street where the poets have been loitering. Divided attention picks up these "loiterly subjects" in time and space, as the Australian-born scholar Ross Chambers, who joined Oulipo in 1961, would say. Factoring in the vicissitudes of global position, plus belatedness, proximity and distance, patience becomes history's virtue. Texts wait a long period of time before being heard or seen, but even then, as with all revelation, that which is revealed must also be accepted by the one who receives it.

This is at core *literary history*, not *a* literary history, and yet still contextualist, as is protocol; ideas have been dragged over the gravel of facts and counter-facts, historical ideas and counter-ideas, pitted against some legitimately bad reflection, all the gravel of doubt and misunderstanding on the levels of history and historical context. I hope not to have caused disappointment where texts have seemed to exhaust themselves upon analysis. This work is not finished. Key characters live on. The best readers are yet to come. If this disclaimer hides an interior motive, it is the sheer extranational, educational nature of this pursuit. A hemispheric understanding of what the avant-gardes were, in general, begins in the present, with what it has now become. It gives insight into what avant-garde poets wanted, for themselves, for their peers and for their future, for a place in history. What they thought about history matters.

Recuperativity is literary history's temptation, and when the idea for this project first came to light it was largely recuperative, but recuperative frameworks were not the only frameworks later deployed. The timestamp for this first direction should remain visible, but as time went along and the documents accumulated I realised that, doing both literary history on the one hand, and hurriedly revising frameworks of literary theory on the other, was the kind of double act that required simultaneous attention, and thrived off it. I very quickly wanted to avoid the pitfalls of a purely recuperative project while examining recuperativity from a literary-theoretical and historiographic standpoint. It was not as simple as that top-down way of doing things: bringing those who have been neglected into the limelight. I began to re-examine certain key debates in literary history, not just questions of canon and canonicity, but more the stressed dynamics between literary history and literary theory in light of works from Antipodal poetics and its resonant contexts. Much of this found its way also into the classroom, debates and interpersonal disputes. The notion, if not the historical existence, of an avant-garde has not been concealed from the study of "Australian literature" in general. It concerns the legacies of nineteenth-century Antipodal literature, fictive modernisms up to the time of Patrick White and David Malouf, and discussions pertaining the status of avant-gardes in relation to contemporary experimental tendencies, that is, its worth, emergent trends, turns, groupings and their opposing counterparts, real or imagined. It concerns figures whose poetics are well known who have neither claimed such notoriety as that of avant-gardism nor necessarily invited it, like Oodgeroo Noonuccal, Judith Wright, Les Murray, John Tranter, John Kinsella, poets who have elicited discussions of the "experimental", less avant-gardism. It connects with broader debates around global modernisms, associated modernities and the "historic" avant-garde broadly construed.² It concerns the origins of avant-gardes in antiquity. The principle concern: how avant-gardes engaged with, and sometimes contradicted modernism, is further troubled by these hemispheric quandaries. Key terms of use in this area, "experimental", "avant-garde", "inventive", "innovative", are put under pressure particularly where pivot points between modern and contemporary, early century versus late century, are concerned.³ I find these terms flexible because of the politics of hemisphere and its necessary cosmopolitanisms. Recent works like *Reading Experimental Poetry*, edited by Georgina Colby, bring questions of perplexity into the fray alongside social and political moves in and outside the bounds of empire; the focus is placed squarely on the problem of the reader, who reads and how, how difficult forms are read in difficult times, and how certain kinds of authorial "mastery" have been or can be repudiated (3). "Invention" is a rhetorical twist on experiment in these frames. Charles Bernstein, in the preface, riffs off W. C. Williams in *Paterson* – "Without invention nothing is well spaced" – by placing the slew of associated terms, "avant-garde, experimental, exploratory, innovative", in the context of "rootless cosmopolitanism", a broad resistance to lyric

---

² There has been a good amount of searching contemporary commentary regarding "experimental poetry", its worth or quality (Cassidy; Page), its prevalence and its political potential or political contradictoriness (Dunk), and the reactions it causes among detractors and sceptics, more so than in the case of card-carrying adherents (Alizadeh, "Battleground").

³ Another collection that is worth pursing in this direction is *The Fate of Difficulty in the Poetry of Our Time*, edited by Charles Altieri and Nicholas D. Nace. It focuses on problems of contemporary difficulty in relief against modernist predecessors, mostly in North America. Individual poems, cases of difficulty, are printed before each essay. Brian Reed's contribution is a decolonial reading of Sherwin Bitsui, born into the Tódích'ii'nii (Bitter Water Clan). In this extraordinary and provocative essay Reed raises a possible "trans-Indigenous" hermeneutics across literature of settler colonial states, like Australia, which Reed has before written on, and with reference to Lionel Fogarty. This seems to be also a question of criticism in general. Key here is the question of Enigma, which is one that criticism has always been confronted with at its divinatory edge, but as Reed also says, Indigenous readership as well.

containment (xi). The rootless cosmopolitanism that Bernstein can derive from *Paterson*, also a quintessentially *rooted* poem, embodies the contradiction of the avant-garde in global space-time. Williams's difficult relation with the early twentieth-century avant-garde gives us no easy access to the heterodoxy of canonical excess that produces the "supplement" of aesthetic invention; perhaps a new order of the line can only be a supplement because there is something else outside.

This is also to suggest that, although the problem of hemispheric lines of influence – North–South, East–West, continent and region – is now quite familiar to avant-garde studies, contexts don't always seep up to method, or to continue the groundwater analogy, we don't see sinkholes, we don't yet see how the context troubles method, as it should, nor how talking about it would raise questions not yet known to the discourse of the Crisis of the Humanities, and Literary Studies within. But if we don't have method we at least have critical modes and preliminary questions. This is a study of *how* certain poets responded to the early twentieth-century avant-garde in the Antipodal sphere from 1897 to the present day, and these lines of global response draw in the comparative context above all. Methodologies will shift and change. That's one angle, a noticeably comparative view to which we will be neither stranger nor informant; a difficult history of changing methods. But impasses to understanding the role of an avant-garde outside its European and American origins exist, I want to more principally maintain, because in its most formative moments avant-gardes have found themselves continually frozen before the spectre of historical time. We should recall that Dada, for instance, *nearly had no history*. Maria Stavrinaki's take on Dada encapsulates these sentiments. Dada cathected urgency into an imaginary present: "Only the present could allow another history to surge up, a history emancipated from servile obedience to the past and the chaste utopia of the future" (4). Frozen before an eternal present, Dada could offer no benedictory goodwill to the past or the future. It was Marcel Janco, though, who first warned us not to "trust anything that calls itself 'Dada history'; however much may be true of Dada, the historian qualified to write about it does not yet exist". On the inverse, Janco of course counter-claims that Dada was embedded "in the depths of human history" (35). Which history do we mean then? The avant-garde, as it were, nearly didn't have a history, in one sense, but in another sense, it could plumb the depths of human history.

I. Rhetorics of Scale: 1581, 1772, 1819

This is where our discussion of history begins, rent in two: history as *explicandum*, historiography as *explicans*. Two aspects of history in Janco's ambiguous negation of the word: the historiography of the qualified historian in the know and enough on the ground to know what went on in detail, and the ineffable thing of History. We may put it like this. If, much later, the spirit of negation anticipates the corporate uptake of avant-garde aesthetics – the "corruption" and neutralisation of its oppositional qualities in contemporary experimental art – on the other hand we have the long-lasting impact of Dada, precisely that "spirit of negation" within which the ferment of the future lives; two contrastive and painfully irreconcilable definitions of history. Our analysis risks on the one hand a constraining specificity that binds authorial energy and subjective agency to a socio-historical framework, and on the other reversions to an eternal constant that lies dormant and returns in some "primitive" manner to impel all historical figures of consequence toward a similar aim. It is of course the latter that Janco wants, and yet, in light of postcolonial theory and decolonial reading, it is possible to say that those primitivist strains remain a historically partisan negation. Though they lay the groundwork for History, they cannot bequeath us *histories*, histories that can be explained through the things that present themselves to us, whether persons, characters, cultures, economies, texts, events or archives. This is why the avant-garde of this era had to be called the "historic" avant-garde; not just because they were the seminal group, but because, theoretically speaking, they weren't historic enough.

Another Romanian, Matei Călinescu, draws attention to the metaphor of the avant-garde in the renaissance as a rhetorical figure. French humanist Étienne Pasquier (1529–1615), also a literary historian, uses the word in the environment of an attempt to write a national literary history using pugnaciously modern terms of superiority to the ancient masters. Pasquier also anthologises, "garlands" the examples to furnish his analysis, and to paint the picture of a generation of poets not in thrall of the ancients but in competition with them, which is to say "*contrecarre*"; seeking to counter, oppose, contradict. The agonistic analogy appears in the following passage:

> A glorious war was then being waged against ignorance, a war in which, I would say, Scève, Bèze, and Pelletier constituted the avant-garde; or, if you prefer, they were the fore-runners of the other poets.

> After them, Pierre de Ronsard of Vendôme and Joachim du Bellay of Anjou, both gentlemen of noblest ancestry, joined the ranks. The two of them fought valiantly, and Ronsard in the first place, so that several others entered the battle under their banners. (98)

Maurice Scève, Théodore de Bèze and Jacques Pelletier du Mans form a front line of a contemporary poetics of French Humanism. But not only was this the original or historic avant-garde of that part of the overall "development" of French poetry; they had aftershocks in subsequent generations: Pierre de Ronsard and the great poet-critic Joachim du Bellay. Thus it was not only the first literary avant-garde but the first avant-garde to have several waves in generations that followed, and the first to involve poets who actively participated in critique. The chapter, Călinescu stresses, is part of a "larger tableau of the overall development of French poetry, one of the first such attempts, in a European country, at "national literary history in the modern sense" (98). Literary criticism's attraction to the vital neoteric "valiance" of a war waged against ignorance (if it is not a challenge to criticism from the outside condition of literary history) takes up the language and indeed rhetoric of such history in Călinescu's reasoning to bring the vanguard/avant-garde metaphor into being:

> Pasquier, in trying to chronicle the growth of his country's poetry, felt entitled to transfer certain notions of the language of history (a language directly connected with the central reality of war, from which it derives much of its narrative structure and dramatic quality) to the language of an early and still very tentative kind of *literary history*. As a result, the metaphor of the avant-garde was coined. But the avant-garde analogy as used by Pasquier is just one among several elements that *together* form what might be called a rhetorical "constellation." No one of these elements is particularly emphasized in the context, and the reader is offered no criteria by which any one of them could be singled out. (100)

The way to make the avant-gardes seem historical is to chronicle its national emergence as metaphor or as an analogy. Thinking the avant-garde further as a rhetorical *constellation* of figures helps pull it out of the straitjacket of historiographies frozen before the recency of the expanded present that the avant-garde explosively opened up in the early twentieth century. The power of naming the avant-garde began in the *Recherches* of the Renaissance as part of the rhetoric of progress for the eternal present of the "moderns" – even the moderns of antiquity. But what does "Australia" do or mean to such a rhetoric of the avant-garde? Does it too come from war? Is an

Antipodal avant-garde only possible to describe as a national literary history? Can it intervene in the quarrel of the Ancients and Moderns? If it was a "subsequent" avant-garde, albeit in another hemisphere, is it not following the precedent set by Pasquier's literary genealogy? Returning to Tzara, it should be put on notice that one is called to validate one's reading with an exemplary poem, one from the first avant-garde, often called "historic", or early twentieth-century, even if later we abjure such historical leaps of faith and obligatory terms of reference. But perhaps we could look for an avant-garde as rhetorical figure of literary progress in any other century or literary tradition, like the Renaissance, or scenes of the long Frontier Wars in Australia, from the late eighteenth century to the first half of the twentieth. For what is more historic about those that get assigned the first of the avant-gardes, and any less historic about those that came after or predated them? What is an avant-garde poem and an avant-garde poetics as we understand it now? If "Aragon House" is an avant-garde poem, what scale of measurement should we use, what rhetorical constellation?

II. *The Chronometer*

We are right to be suspicious of exemplarities of this kind, especially ones that might "conscript or enslave particulars" (610), as Krishan Kumar and Herbert F. Tucker put it in introducing a 2017 issue of disciplinary scale in *New Literary History*. I don't mean, just yet, to say too much (who wants "megalophobia"?), but it does no good to say little or less with our particulars. Kumar and Tucker go upward from particulars in their movements through Percy Bysshe Shelley's "Ozymandias": the hour- or era-glass, sends us spinning into "delusions of grandeur" whereupon the colossal vastness of its longer vistas are outflanked by "superior orders of magnitude" at the sonnet's extremities. Magnitude, that is: "length of time in line 14 ("I met a traveller from an antique land"), length of space in line 14 ("The lone and level sands stretch far away"), where those "sands" may furthermore suggest an enormous chronometer, not an hour-glass but rather an "era-glass of continental dimensions" (609). The chronometer looms large as it melts history into theory.[4] The chro-

---

[4] The name of the thing, "chronometer", coined by watchmaker Jeremy Thacker in the eighteenth century, is in Switzerland reserved only for those timepieces certified by the Contrôle Officiel Suisse des Chronomètres (COSC).

nometer, for the editors, is an era-glass; its exactness not so much the issue as the magnitude of historical time that it can cover or uncover, in its dimensions.[5] There is a darker meaning for the chronometer in Australian history. The man who would lead the expedition to the Australian continent that would culminate in a devastating attack upon its First Nations peoples, leading to massacres, mass death, genocidal policies, destruction of land, widespread disease and a prolonged Frontier War, Captain James Cook (whose memorials are still scattered across the country), would acquire a marine chronometer for his second voyage from 1772 to 1775, following the "Possession" voyage (1768–71), in which Cook used lunar distances to determine longitude. The marine chronometer in the second voyage, Larcum Kendell's K1, a replica of H4, would more accurately determine longitude at the same time as cast into history an immense historic violence: the moment of invasion, followed by the longer events of dispossession, occupation and then resistance, the Frontier War and its cast of warriors, and ultimately the genocidal acts of settlement and settler society. This war, one of the longest in human history, and its legacies – including the dispossession, disruption, destruction and pilfering of land and its traditional governance and leadership structures in First Nations society – are not foreclosed by the Commonwealth (thus they remain foundational). But on the part of Cook, the act of mapping and measuring is not just a testament to a certain magnitude in a historical dimension; surveying, cartography, inventions in technology. It is an act with another dimension to it in the now well-known, but not widely enough circulated fact: struggling to get to shore because of some resistance, Cook shot at Gweagal people, in the territory of the Eora nation. It was "landing" by musket shot. No poetics of the Antipodes, let alone the avant-gardes therein, is possible without a sense of this first shot, without listening to it and its resonance through time. After the loss of America in 1783 and debates about the establishment of the penal colony in British politics, law and among the general public, the decision was one that emerged also on the cusp of British Romanticism.

---

[5] Another dimension to the word that can serve as a necessary diversion to edge us closer to modernism and war: it is worth noting that the word "chronometer" appears in Apollinaire's "Light Flaring" (*Selected Poems*, 237), a poem about war. A soldier measures the time between flash and bang of a shot fired with a chronometer; thereafter "The simple symphony of war begins." Apollinaire's thoughts on war frame the chronometer as a poetic concept: "And the poet is the observer of life and he invents the measureless light of mysteries we must train our sights on." The chronometer comes then to speak not just for the measurement of a moment of time but time itself considered in its "measureless" sublimity.

The American loyalist James Matra, in 23 August 1783 wrote "A Proposal for Establishing a Settlement in New South Wales", which would speak of "romantic views" of distance, advocating the colony not just as a solution to the fallout from America, but as a vital trade manoeuvre for its proximity to the Chinese Empire (40). Robert Southey would in the 1790s write in his "Botany-Bay Eclogues" of the "savage shore", surely there giving us the strains of a colonial-Romantic poem *par excellence*.⁶ In poetic terms, the question of Romanticism, even Romantic theory, a movement that Călinescu places among the first, after Pasquier, that can be called avant-garde, just as much as the significance of global trade routes, an empire in the Pacific, and a solution to the loss of the American colonies, might be key to any sense of Occupation and Invasion.

The image of the chronometer, therefore, is only the beginning of the metaphorical dimension that can shift theory into history, and vice versa. The scaling-up that places Invasion and Occupation at the very centre of a history of poetry in the Antipodes is based, *a priori*, on at least two fundamental theories pertaining to the land itself.

1. The theory of *terra australis incognita* (unknown Southern land), before it culminated in the historic doctrine and imperial policy of
2. *terra nullius* (nobody's land), a precursor to genocidal policy, not settled legal doctrine on the British side, actively and persistently resisted by Indigenous people before and after the Mabo v Queensland (No. 2) High Court ruling in 1992, which affirmed the legal concept of Native Title and rejected the notion.⁷

---

⁶ The significance of Romantic poems on the colony, including Southey's eclogues, are explored in the next chapter.

⁷ While no longer official doctrines or theories, these two are by no means absent, and not even in literary senses: one could argue that the Antipodes is still *terra incognita* in the sense of it being placed as an Anglophone literature difficult to place or "map" within global or comparative literature. In terms of *terra nullius*, Claire G. Coleman's 2017 apocalyptic novel, *Terra Nullius*, is a demonstration of this in a type of speculative fiction marked by various registers of estrangement. Citational headings to each chapter, fictive archival documentation, "colonial worldbuilding" as Alison Whittaker put it in a review, bends history with time and fragment to the point that "*Terra Nullius* is no longer familiar". And by book's end there's little resolve, and no expected reconciliatory gesture. The question here is who reads (Indigenous, non-Indigenous)? In "Australian history" popularly understood, Henry Reynolds's 1981 book *The Other Side of the Frontier: Aboriginal Resistance to the European Invasion of Australia*, set the scene, at least among literati and in mainstream discourse, for a greater acknowledgement of the Frontier Wars. Reynolds looked at the scale of the massacres, guerrilla tactics of the warriors, attempts at negotiation, and the motives and objectives of resistance. His most recent account of this history is *Forgotten War*.

Tzara's Chronometer: Literary History and the Antipodal Avant-Gardes

Theories of Antipodal poetry, for ultimately that is our subject, are underpinned by a historiographic element: the *ground*, or perhaps more precisely *Abgrund*, abyss, upon which a theory and a history is to be made, is *counter-historical* work. The shape of any ensuing literary history is underpinned by legal assumptions – a legal theory that precipitated genocidal policies, on the one hand – and the scales of resistance to it, on the other. Or, to put it more crudely, there is no stable ground from which an avant-garde emerges, as there is no stable ground from which the concept of Australia or the Antipodes emerges, suitable enough for a notion as unstable as the avant-garde. By shifting the historical purview to resistance, to take one particular element out of the above, we see how an Antipodal avant-garde emerges between a series of structural faultlines and contradictions; between settler consciousness and Indigenous ecological science, invasion and survival, invention and discovery, knowledge and unknowability, fullness and emptiness, and as nineteenth-century Australia made its way into the twentieth century, a century of industrial wars and mass disruption, more binaries would emerge, like that between socialism and labourism, between the notion of an "independent", Republican Australia and monarchy, or, as Humphrey McQueen put it in *A New Britannia*, between "radicalism" and "nationalism".

Another way of saying it is that the Antipodal avant-garde emerges from various dialectics in history. But before exploring these entrenched and powerful historical and political underpinnings of the Antipodal avant-garde, there is a fact that further confirms the centrality of mythographic and legislative foundations of Australian poetry in its settler and, later, Commonwealth constitutions. The first published book of poetry on the Australian continent in the period following Invasion was *First Fruits of Australian Poetry* (1819) by Barron Field, a poet and lawyer who, according to recent recuperative research, has a connection to the notion of *terra nullius*. Justin Clemens notes that Field's colonially transposed, transnational Romanticism would take a more sinister turn, from its Wordsworthian, and Miltonic intimations. Clemens argues that with Field,

> the publication of poetry in Australia begins as Romantic apparatchik satire, concatenating and compacting a sequence of literary allusions in order to turn *incognita* into *cognita*, and, in so doing, turning the Other, the monstrosity, into the norm and the priority. The very realisation of Australia as a real fiction, a state, turns out to be the consequence of the globalisation of European satire, which

sinks into the barren fields of itself as a time-capsule of disavowed invasion. (*First Fruits*, 33)

The time-capsule of disavowed invasion is both excavated by European satire and the barren field, mapped, by Romanticism, *on* to the burial site so that the real fiction of the Australian state can realise itself. Romanticism decides this Australian fiction through the *incognita*. Startling details. They will throw into relief the type of uncanny history we are willing to theoretically table. Neither theory nor history can alone do the work. Our theoretical cables are, will be, harnessed to history, but we release ourselves from the clutches of theory when history disrupts smooth passage. Conversely, *theories* of history, or ways of historicising, can fail to pass strength tests when placed against a historical catalogue other than that which those theories have been founded. I say this because to *map* a theory of a literary history, and especially with any spatio-temporal precision, as we may be accustomed to doing, has caused us to cling, clutch, loosen, let go of or even abandon certain theories throughout this book, to pull apart the maps, seek other shapes. The first fruits of an Australian avant-garde, I am trying to emphasise, cannot be mapped on to what already exists (an Aboriginal literary landscape), nor can it emerge in complete independence from European avant-garde formations (*cultures* of the Australian bourgeois state are not yet free of the Euro-US matrix by any means). I neither flee from spatial metaphors nor seek exceptional mapping in these pages. Antipodal literary history, like any other history, is subject to the machinations and distortions of time, but to measure, certify time with "chronometric" precision, means offering a history that makes sense of scale, discarding the maps we have by sheer default been given; to open up, through poetics, that which has been willfully obscured (*incognita*), or mistaken as void (*nullius*).

In the poems that appear before us we will see illustrated such complexities in the language and rhetoric of time and history, vacillating between official and oppositional *topoi*. I am not yet finished with what has, by necessity, become a speculative reading of "Maison Aragon", because another version of the penultimate line appears to offer a starkly different temporal sense that captures what we now know has scaled up the rhetoric of Antipodal time. The translation goes:

> arp and the barbered arbour
> in the free night resuscitate
> in the special australian kangaroo pocket edition

arp and the arc barque
are framed by semiramis
arp and the arc and the arbour-barbered barque
creak – Chronometer[8]

This time *creak* is placed beside the timepiece. The narrative strain might run as follows: Hans Arp and a trimmed tree are brought to life in a pocket edition for a certain pouched animal, the Australian kangaroo. This time the kangaroos are not translated as readers, contra Rothenberg's translation. We cannot forget here the reference to barbering and hair, which brings to our attention a later event, The Evening of the Bearded Heart, and the 1922 magazine *La Coeur à barbe*, that would mark the final break with the Surrealists. Arp and the boat are "framed" by Semirámis – prosodic responsibility shifts in that Rothenberg stresses the third syllable for us rather than the first in Tzara's original version – the legendary queen of Assyria. The correct stress for semīramis, oddly enough, is the second syllable. No matter, Arp's trimmed tree may have come from bark – bark displaces *barque* – but the roots don't join up: barque conjures a more ancient ship, but to us it would be the Imperial barque in the Antipodal imaginary, perhaps Cook's ship itself. The sonic duplicity in barque/bark, and croque/creak, that determines how the consonants clash and, ultimately, resolve. Creak seems to put us more in thrall of sound. So then there is no real narrative. If not narrative, what scene? The title indicates the poem's address: to the *house* of Louis Aragon. Perhaps it's something of a *tableau vivant*, then. Night has passed, the Cabaret Voltaire has already passed into history. "What's the time" seems the question, and chronometer the clue, to what passes, which in the original poem, printed and lineated like this

      MAISON
           pour Aragon
arp et l'arbre à barbe
ressuscitent dans la nuit libre
dans l'édition spéciale austra-
lienne pour les poches du kangourou
arp et la barque à l'arc
s'encadrent pour sémiramis
arp l'arc et la barque à barbe d'arbre
croque-chronomètre
              Tristan Tzara
       (*Bulletin Dada* No. 6, 4)

---

[8] This translation by Timothy Adès appears in Dawn Ades's *The Dada Reader*, 242.

finds itself leashed, or lashed, to the French verb *croque*, from *croquer*, meaning crunch, extending to Middle French *craquer*. Hence, cracker, or the crunch of *croque-monsieur*, meaning a grilled ham and cheese sandwich. Aside from the near sound-mimetic crackling and crunching (rather than creaking) of the word, it can also mean, colloquially, to squander wealth. In Galician it means a strike or bump on the head. Do we then hear "creak", or "o crisp"? Is the watch hitting Arp's head? Or is it merely mimetic: the sound of ticking, the creak of time? What causes the sudden shift from the alliterative, largely a vowelling of A, to the consonantal C?

The key, the truth, may be in the consonants. What the poem most acutely shows is how time abruptly sharpens to the shorter consonants, from the longer vowels. If it were not dashed with *croque*, creak, crisp, chronometer might resemble something of a holophrase.[9] If the holophrase measures time not just prosodically, which is to say if we look beyond the even stress of *croque* and *chronometre* toward a holophrastic concept (time) compacted into the word, the last line is less key change as last-minute shifting time signature. (We must use time signature figurally here.) To stretch the metaphor necessarily further, the longest line contains *kangourou*, the shortest, chronometer. Almost everything else, from the dactylic-trochaic run of "arp et la barque à l'arc" to "arp l'arc et la barque à barbe d'arbre", seems inexorably trained on that curt "croque-chronomètre"; something cuts us off, prosodically and ideationally, from the "antique" land with continental dimensions.

III. *1916: Songspirals in Zurich*

If being cut off from the "antique land" is indeed avant-garde to the max, no historical fact is more pertinent to the discussion here than Tristan Tzara's performance of three excerpts, translated into French, of Arrernte and Luritja Songlines or Songspirals (or, as forenamed, "Song Cycles"), taken from Carl Strehlow's 1907 thesis, *Die Aranda- und Loritja-Stämme in Zentral-Australien*, at the Cabaret Voltaire in 1917. We have, with this fairly well-documented event,

---

[9] The most extraordinary modernist use of the concept and the word "holophrase" is the opening to Hope Mirrlees's *Paris: A Poem* (1919), coming from the same year as "Maison Aragon". It begins "I want a holophrase"; a holophrase being a prelinguistic use of a single word to engender a complex idea. The term "holophrastic" might extend poetically, and to limit ourselves to modernism, to the agrammatical use of single words in Elsa von Freytag-Loringhoven.

one of the most concrete connections between the original avant-garde, its primitivistic tendencies, its sense of research, and appropriative practices we now call ethnopoetics. It occurs at the very point of avant-garde inception. Tzara's internationalist, European and modern-primitivist zeal, as Ann Stephen and Andrew McNamara would put it in a piece on modernism and primitivism in the Antipodes, or "Oceania", was not flippant, and in its approach anticipated the later connections between avant-gardes and ethnopoetics:

> Their route from remote Central Australia to the Cabaret Voltaire reveals a nuanced, culturally alert process of translation, quite different from the wild 'babble' of other dadaists ... Tzara had conducted ethnological studies across African, Aboriginal, Maori, and other South Pacific sources in Zurich's Technical University Library. (292)[10]

The importance of Tzara's lifelong project in ethnological study at the Zurich Technical University Library, from his examination of articles in *Anthropos* to the translation and compilation of poems from multiple sources, must be again underlined as a crucible in Tzara's poetics, and as Marius Hentea stresses this was a public, not just private, interest, in that

> Unlike Huelsenbeck, who presented primitive poems as his personal invention, Tzara was always careful, in public readings and in print, to make their provenance known. He wanted his first published poetry collection to be entitled *Mpala Garroo*, a clear sign of how important primitive poetry had become to him. He worked on a book of African and Oceanic poetry (he was among the first European artists to be interested in aboriginal Australian poetry), asking contacts in Italy if they could help him find a publisher for it. Having assembled over fifty primitive poems, he never found a publisher for the anthology, although a number of the poems were published in *Dada 1* and other reviews. (71)

The *Mpala Garoo* or *Npala / Garroo* cycle Tzara claims to have been only in proofs and later destroyed. The 1916 illustrated *La Première Aventure Céléste de Mr Antipyrine* then became Tzara's first

---

[10] I should footnote that the structure of this collection, with sections on Asia, Africa, Latin America and Oceania (Europe and the Middle East among these) is gratifying in its inclusion of the Antipodes as part of this world constellation of modernism. In their account of Tzara's appropriation of the Arrernte songs, Stephen and McNamara place it in the context of discourses of the "primitive" and the Antipodes both in world anthropological history and known provinces of High Modernism.

collection, and in it a short quatrain Npala Garroo appears. From those first translations in November 1916 to 1917 would therefore remain the years to which he was most dedicated in this interest, though as we have seen the impact upon poetic process was permanent. At the Cabaret Tzara chose for his French translation of the Poèmes Nègres, as Walter F. Veit reads it, a poetic solution between literal meaning and sound, in rhythm. For Stephen and McNamara, such "literalness borders on abstraction as the sounds and rhythms of the Aboriginal words rubbed against foreign tongues" (292), challenges Eurocentric distinctions of "civilized" and "primitive" (292). Their statement that Aboriginal cultures had "no written language or literature, science, architecture or sculpture – or anything recognisable as such in Western terms" has been tested in public debates surrounding Bruce Pascoe's *Dark Emu*, investigating Aboriginal invention in agriculture and aquaculture as evidence for a type of infrastructural, agricultural, technological and therefore social engagement with the continent's ecology, albeit yes, "non-Western" in kind. The debate continues.

Songlines have had a complex history of incorporation and estrangement from ethnographic knowledge. T. G. H. Strehlow, a descendent of Carl of the same missionary family, in his 1971 *Songs from Central Australia*, used anthropology, ethnology and linguistics to score the songs as recorded in the Central Desert, situating them in an oraliterary poetics of a global epical tradition in an intriguing final chapter. Although they are not museological items of interest, the linear musical score can only partially capture their whole sense; "musical notation of sung verse of this kind presents very considerable difficulties: for there is no fixed, invariable melody in our sense of this word" (40). The nature of tune and melody is unsettling for Strehlow, and the course of the analysis can be theoretically and critically unassuming particularly where the songs are compared to verse in the Western tradition. Various concepts emerge alongside an analysis of language and verse structure, from diction to parallelism and antithesis, syntactical and grammatical peculiarities, and rhetorical aspects, artifice in Aranda poetic diction as comparable to that of Anglo-Saxon verse, as removed from the "sober pedestrian march of the prose found in King Alfred's translations from Latin originals" (209). The "Hale River myth" of the kangaroo ancestor can be compared to parallelism in *The Tempest* (165); comparable compact compound words and kennings in Anglo-Saxon verse (185); subject matter with analyses of Norse skalds (248), Central Australian cloudbursts and duststorms with Chaucer's April showers (460).

The Greek Iliadic tradition leads to the most triumphal of claims for a comparison with the oral tradition since Homer (211–13), which easily overshadows the other comparisons. What Strehlow is most interested in is how poetics comes to disrupt a theory of the primitive, though it never leaves the discourse of the European sciences entirely, there is an unsettling sense to the analysis, including enormous slabs of quotation and textual assemblage: primitive, Strehlow says, does *not* mean "crude, backward, simply, undeveloped, or inconsequential" but rather "'original,' 'primary,' and 'radical,'" words which Strehlow retains in quotation marks. Central Australian literary matter is "not unsimilar to the raw material from which poets like Homer's predecessors hammered out poetry as an independent medium of artistic expression" and is therefore of universal interest (657). But unlike all the genres of verse to which it could be compared, these were, Strehlow claims, songs of the totemic ancestors and therefore had "*no human* authors" (659). In the final summary of the book Strehlow does not stop without moving to a theory of literary criticism to explain the apparent form and technicity of Central Australian poetry; Homeric and Romantic comparisons, including Blake, and possible future developments of the poetics were the Invasion not to have happened. "Radical" might apply to the mode of scholarship: at times its breadth is so epical that its scope reaches a kind of speculative and prophetic-critical mode.[11] Strehlow quotes from the lengthy passage of Sartre's 1948 *Qu'est-ce que la littérature?*, *What is Literature?*, concerning nineteenth-century poetry pushing to the limits of the very challenge it set for itself, and even its readability. It was the literature of adolescence that

> gives us a glimpse of a black silence beyond the massacre of words, and, beyond the spirit of seriousness, the bare and empty sky of equivalences; it invites us to emerge into nothingness by destruction of all myths and all scales of value; it discloses to us in man a close and secret relationship with the nothing, instead of the intimate relationship with the divine transcendence. (130)

---

[11] For further exploration in this area see Anna Kenny's *The Aranda's Pepa: An Introduction to Carl Strehlow's Masterpiece* Die Aranda- und Loritja-Stämme in Zentral-Australien *(1907–1920)*, an introduction to and critique of Carl's place in the wider history of German humanistic anthropology in Australia. For Kenny, Carl represents a "transitional" phase in modern anthropology, and yet also laments what has been lost to modern anthropology. In modern or postmodern Antipodal anthropology, Stephen Muecke has brought these questions across to continental theory, cultural studies, nomadology and philosophy, including "updated" Deleuzo-Guattarian, and more recently Latourian terms of reference. See in particular a representative work: *Ancient and Modern: Time, Culture and Indigenous Philosophy*.

We can have no doubt Strehlow is drawn to the passage because of the lines on "black silence" and the evocation of "massacre", although a close reading does not tease out how the fear of the animistic and the divinatory, or myth and "all scales of value", might be related more directly to such histories. We can keep in view the fact that Sartre's discourse concerns the identification of late nineteenth-century French poetry with a yearning for the "unproductive" past – with undertones of festival, initiation rite and the Prodigal Son – that ends with "Trotskyizing surrealism". These two, the late nineteenth century and its "belated fulfilment" in surrealism's permanent revolution, or permanent violence, though it joins arms with the Communist Party, cannot unite for the aim of a socialist total literature, the coming together of *praxis* and *exis*. It is quickly directed against the "Stalinism" that shut its doors to at least one kind of avant-garde. For Strehlow, Sartre provides us a glimmer of one theory of avant-garde production and its decline after 1940 (if not an indictment of our literatures as well), for if the question of the myth of literature is left wide open, after Breton, surrealism left literature nothing to do but to challenge itself (120). Comparing Étienne Léro with Aimé Césaire allows Sartre to measure "the abyss that prevents a black revolutionary from utilizing white surrealism" (310). But Strehlow rather drifts back to the analysis at hand, and enjoins us, in no straightforward way, to go back to old needs and longings, the "learning and singing of 'primitive verse'" that might still be "among us" even though curtailed by, in the Western terms used, science and material culture (717). Amid a searing critique of contemporary culture in the 1960s, Strehlow uses these fabrics to rail against obscurity in modern verse:

> Modern verse cannot afford obscurity to the same degree as 'primitive' verse. Central Australian aboriginal verse was, as we have seen, largely the handmaiden of religion; and religious formulae and magic charms have always gained much of their air of mystery, venerability, and authority from their dark and archaic language. But, as I have explained at length elsewhere, even the most obscure of the Central Australian couplets generally stimulated the interest of their audiences because of their fascinating rhythmic measures and tonal patterns; and the couplet or quatrain structure of aboriginal verse could be readily ascertained even when the words were completely baffling. Again, the obscurity of Central Australian poetry sprang almost entirely from its highly specialized vocabulary: the structure of the sentences themselves remained grammatically on a fairly simple level. Much of the obscurity in many modern English poems, on

the other hand, derives from deliberate acts of interference with the normal structure of English sentences. Often all the words in a sentence are well known to the reader; yet the meaning of the sentences still escapes the understanding. Smartness of this kind is probably resented much more than the use of new and strange words by the poet. Sometimes, too, the metres used are too fragmentary or too dull to fascinate the listener. (718–19)

Two obscurities to speak of: a true and real one and a modern obscurity which in the most basic sense is too deliberate, too artificial. That the regression (or progression) to clarity mirrors a conciliatory course in the 1930s away from an aesthetics of "interference" toward radical politics doesn't always hold up to historical scrutiny, yet evidence can be given to poets having given up experiments for what Sartre called "committed writing". To choose between politics and poetry – that is a problem that may never leave us. But the loose nexus of ethnopoetics later in the century would not suffer the consequences of obscurity because they activated the charm that chant and other "fascinating rhythmic measures" could stimulate in performance, while making appeals to visual interest in their anthologising, in the wake of a growing body of knowledge in poetics as to how to read apparently nonsemantic elements of poetry semantically. Strehlow's commentary also puts into view the problem of the performance and theatre of poetry as a way to offset the charge of obscurity or bring a specialised poetics – in his expression "deliberate acts of interference", of poetic "sentences" brought to life – and although Strehlow has an idea of meaning that is foreign to ours, Strehlow uses "primitive verse" to change modern verse in all its dimensions in a debate about ordinary readership and obscurity that has always dogged the outsider art of poetry. Modern poetry could not afford what Central Australian verse took as read: the necessity of obscurity.

Psychoanalysis, in a comparable analytic diction to Strehlow, too was troubled by First Nations ritual and totemic ancestors, not only Freud's *Totem and Taboo* but equally in Theodor Reik's *Mystery on the Mountain: The Drama of the Sinai Revelation*, from 1959. Freud had told Reik he was on to something with this research. Reik compares puberty rites and initiation festivals, which he gets second-hand from various resources (and various literary evocations at the close of most chapters), with the giving of the Torah on Mt Sinai. In the sound and the fury of dramatic theophany Reik perceives similarity to the festivals of initiation. In one moment in the long explication of the case Reik imagines an anthology of "Decalogues" of the First Nations to parallel the Ten Commandments, though a creative intuition here would have required a better understanding of Indigenous law. To do this Reik uses Carl Strehlow's "excellent report" on the Loritja to show that there may have been comparable "codes" to the Hebrew Decalogue. Then Reik contemporises:

> The governments of the world order their people to commit mass murders as though they had never heard of the Sixth Commandment. At this critical moment mankind is faced with a question of destiny. Will the swing upwards that starred in the initiation of neolithic Australian tribesmen, and was continued in the initiation of the Hebrews in the desert, be futile or will that inner demand prevail? The question is not what the future of mankind will be, but whether or not mankind will have any future. (87)

In another passage, Reik claims that "The tears shed by the Hebrew mothers when their boys were taken away from them have a prototype in the sorrow of the mothers in the Australian initiation" (108), which has unnerving significance given it was not the initiations but the Stolen Generations that were the cause of such sorrow at this very point in time. Reik inhabits a similar approbation of European discourses of savagery for shunning its own primitivity in the name of external "morality". But what makes Reik's thesis most astounding for our comparison here is his reading of revelation as a great leap backwards – the events at Sinai as not just an incorporation or rejection of Egyptian religion but innovation through return: gaining strength from an even more ancient cultural core through Yahweh in order to reinvent religion. Psychoanalysis, or psychoanalytic theory, in the Reikian or archaeological vein, which is only partially Freudian, would keep close to the enigma as the driving force of the case.

Tzara's own type of searching colonial primitivism in the short poem "COLONIAL SYLLOGISM", which ends "No more enigmas!" (*Seven Dada Manifestos*, 51), may compare; for to do away with enigmas is to advocate not revelatory reading but rather divinatory method, for a revelatory one leaves nothing concealed. The giving of the Torah, the giving of the Law as end of enigma is made all the more apparent by dwellings in the divinatory; refusing what in revelation would become rhetorical through the maintenance of the enigmatic. That is to say we have here not simply Tzara's assault on logic in the Dada passages, but the rhetoricisation of colonial syllogism as the doing away of enigmas; Tzara's repudiation of revelation. Or as he wrote in "A Note on Negro Poetry" in 1918, "we are God only for the country of our knowledge, in the laws according to which we live experience on this earth, on both sides of our equator, inside our borders ... Poetry lives first of all for the functions of dance, religion, music and work" (77).

Differences and disparities are only made clear by a further account of how these songs are still sung and play their role in living culture. The use of past tense in some of the above is not necessary. It amounts to not just a demystification of the enigma but a partial and continuous revelation of culture from generation to generation that cannot be reduced to the notion of "native informant" either. It produces effects in history that are not yet available to method. The word "Songspirals", as the Gay'wu Group of Women name it in a 2019 book, better describes (in their case for the Yolŋu people, far Northern Australia), the cyclical relationships of the generations and each moiety. The Gay'wu group present the Songspirals to the outsider in a restorative way, as one of generous opening up of knowledge to the outside (non-Indigenous) observer, but it is a poetic and dialectical undertaking; Songspirals "created our land" long ago, and continue to do so. Living culture as creation is singing to land, and land sings back – "twisting", "turning", "looping" describe the spiral movement of the songs. Margo Neale and Lynne Kelly in a dual-written account of their experience with Songlines extend it to "history":

> Songlines, related to Dreamings or Dreaming tracks, connect sites of knowledge embodied in the features of the land. It is along these routes that people travelled to learn from Country.
> Country holds information, innovations, stories and secrets – from medicine, engineering, ecology and astronomy to social mores on how to live, and social organisation, including moiety division and kinship systems. It is the wellspring from which all knowledge originates and gives rise to the expression "Our history is written in the land." By "history" we mean all knowledge: sciences, humanities and ancestral knowledge, not only what is compartmentalised as Western history. (ii)

History therefore means both the past and an evolving or expanded sense of the spatial present, and bringing history into the present as an intentional act produces a different sense of history to that of the museological or compartmentalising drives of "Western history". There are echoes of Reik's Israelite drama here in one sense: going back or returning to Country in order to find innovative knowledge after venturing out. Yet "First Knowledges" history is not Western history in part because the concept of time which takes the "enduring present" and "eternal time" to be paramount, and to some extent it is a constant attempt to remove obstacles to history *as knowing*, as the ability to know or see "history written in the land". Western divisions of "past, present and future, or historical and contemporary, are not particularly relevant, though they are useful at times" (iii). Lynne Kelly describes the retroactive process, synonymous in some aspects with research, of reactivating the sense of beginning with the oraliterary universe of Walter J. Ong, coming through silence, and finally regaining memory through the process of "experimenting":

> As I gained more insight into the way Songlines work, even at this superficial level, the more horrified I became about the past. If I was becoming so engrossed in my landscape after only a year or two of experimenting, how intense must it be for people who have lived their entire lives this way, as did their parents and grandparents, as have their forebears and ancestors for all of time? How traumatic must it have been to witness invaders build fences across Country and shoot anyone who tried to visit their sacred sites? (4)

The last sentence here refers to the mass atrocities that stemmed from a state-sanctioned and mostly top-down genocidal policy dedicated to an attempted eradication of First Nations people during the long Frontier Wars (1788–1930s). Sites of the massacres have been better documented in research the last several years, especially through research spearheaded by Lyndall Ryan and corroborated by Indigenous testimony. Over a period of almost one and a half centuries, at least 311 massacres of an untold number have been documented. Massacre, slavery, war, poisonings and genocide precede the long twentieth-century history of assimilation, incarceration and deaths in custody, specific cases of which, like the death of Julieka Ivanna Dhu in 2014, were compared to those in the United States that precipitated the various waves of the Black Lives Matter movement a year before. These two recent accounts of Songline history, part of an evolving movement of knowledge, represent "celestial adventures" Tzara could never have had, but certainly sought after.

The catastrophic failure and frenzied violence of Australian settler-colonies at war gave rise to warrior histories, histories of resistance and struggles for cultural survival, the scale and magnitude of which Kelly testifies to in the passage above, and it is through this history of resistance that a First Nations avant-garde comes into view. Bringing these facts back into circulation in a manner that is in dialogue with its "unrecognisability", in Western terms, more than just a revival of existing scholarship on the matter, retroactively revises the historiography of modernist primitivism and Tzara's avant-garde internationalism. For the fact that Songspirals continue, long after Tzara performed them, is a key point of recognition for our scaping of avant-garde time. Yes it becomes more than the "wild babble" of other Dadaists, as Stephen and McNamara say, but better than this, it tells us what the apparently nonsemantic babble might actually have been meant to mean. To fully listen to Tzara, however, requires that we listen to the sounds that came from the other side, voices that spoke back from what for him could only have seemed an Archimedean Point. The sheer *scale* of a project like Strehlow's is invaluable in its own way, but its scale is also brought about by a pursuit of knowledge that is both in and outside experience. To *prevent* the foreclosure brought about by Tzara's colonial syllogism, we listen to First Nations avant-gardes. In the larger context of the Antipodal avant-gardes, the topic of this book, my argument is that the *recognisability* of an Antipodean consciousness to the international avant-gardes was clear and apparent, but remains for various reasons hidden or obscured. In a manner of speaking, it has been hiding in the pouch, or pocket of the avant-garde world system. It has been there all along. The French critic Émile Saillens, as early as 1910, could find an avant-garde in the Australian bush:

> The bush has its history, which is that of Australia ... the bush is not a fixed place, a country that one can inscribe on a map; it is a place in movement, almost a state of things: the meeting ground of unspoilt nature and modern men. And the bushmen are therefore the vanguard of Australia ... It is the bush, too, that the individual life of the Australian is most characteristic, and lends itself best to literary interpretation.[12]

The French "discovery" of Australia was for Saillens an alternate, preconscious "history" that never came to be; and now for us, a making-conscious in literary interpretation, in that he would read Henry Lawson's poetry as the key to the Francophone-Antipodal mystery, the colony that was almost to be, and that Georges Perec was no doubt troubled by in his last book, *53 Days* (or Jean-Jacques Lecercle in a discourse on Ern Malley). Lawson, we mean, not only of vanguard bush balladry in this eccentric, remotist sense but of the red, socialist-urban and engaged suburban voice. Yet the modern

---

[12] This translation appears with the original French in T. Inglis Moore's 1971 book *Social Patterns in Australian Literature*. Thus "Et les bushmen sont donc l'avant-garde de l'Australie ...".

pre-echo of an avant-garde again draws us to the point of colonial violence.[13] This point can either serve as an eclipse, a way of foreclosing any further inquiry, or we can simply say thus far that those outside spaces that defined the avant-garde and its distant aftershocks have meant that it's the *shape* of this historicity that evolves, moves, interacts differently. I have never doubted that there is a need to detour through Australian literary modernism, but Antipodal time, in its distortions of the shape of modernism, will give these discussions a flavour of caution even if the outcome will seem more brazen. The avant-garde's relation to the modern is further exposed to doubt. To draw from critical history: Harry Heseltine, Australian academic and anthologiser, would edit the 1972 *Penguin Book Of Modern Australian Verse* seeking a middle way that was "to find a meaning for 'modern' neither too deeply embedded in traditional values nor too grossly implicated in the shifting enthusiasms of current polemics and the latest doctrine" (xv). Heseltine's attempt, however, to even-handedly describe a "Modern Australian Verse", takes the post-war moment as its starting point, when in the early 1950s Australians began to give way to a "new set of perceptions about themselves" (xv). Hence poets whose careers had been established before the 1950s, namely R. D. Fitzgerald and A. D. Hope, are not in this modern constellation. What should be apparent from this anthology, first of all, is that Modern Australian Verse, understood thus, and anthologised thus, does not require *per se* an avant-garde as integrated into the larger design of Modern Australian Verse.

IV. Critical Lag and the Captive Avant-Gardes

Modern, *not* avant. And still yet those critical takes on modernism in the Antipodes with their subtle degrees of caution need not be

---

[13] This is no attempt at a psychopolitical leap of theoretical faith. But a properly historical approach to the historic avant-gardes does show us more than the narrative assumption of that moment as a radical spark: avant-garde as *exception*. It is this which has led me to not so readily assume a "radical" impulse at the core of the avant-garde project. Here I welcome performance studies theorist Richard Schechner's situating phrase "conservative avant-garde", whereof each passing year (coming ever closer to the impossible present), Schechner says, "the historicity rather than the currency of the avant-garde is seen more clearly" (896). I too am convinced that the avant-garde aftermath was one of a conservatising and sanitising direction, or path, even though these arguments are much less applicable to the Antipodal context. I will also insist, however, that we need to remain alert to the fact that what happened to the avant-garde *afterwards* has, and will have, some retroactive impact on the meaning and composition of the earlier instances.

discarded here. This is a history of the many figuralities of avant-garde in Antipodal writing, and as the dossier of such a history was put together it became increasingly apparent that the avant-garde did not simply mean one thing for an Antipodal poet. So then caution remains. If not held captive by the apparent short circuit of Antipodal modernism, the avant-garde might have flourished, so when modernism conducted itself in the *absence* of an avant-garde I have perked up. But for the most part, any mapping of an Antipodal modernism I will here do is within the bounds of exploring the impact this has had on the question of an avant-garde. The most substantial book of scholarship to date on the notion of an Antipodal avant-garde is Biddle's *Remote Avant-Garde: Aboriginal Art under Occupation*, which looks to Aboriginal art as a space for a decentred avant-garde in Occupation Australia, or what Biddle calls "an emergent body of aesthetics that I call remote avant-garde: new and experimental art of the Central and Western Desert of Australia, including the town camps of Alice Springs" (1).[14] Biddle reads across a range of media,

> from the stop-motion animation and still-life sculpture of Yarrenyty Arlterer to the digital landscape portraiture of Tjala Arts artist Rhonda Unurupa Dick and the Desart Photography Award, the grass and fiber artistry of Tjanpi Desert Weavers, the ochre experimentations

---

[14] The topic of avant-gardism within or without modernism has become nothing short of an academic "growth area" this century, with books on avant-gardes of almost every major literary tradition and across the major art forms. In 2019 major publications included *Archiving an Epidemic: Art, AIDS, and the Queer Chinanx Avant-Garde* by Robb Hernández, several assessments of Northern European avant-gardes, including *The Danish Avant-Garde and World War II: The Helhesten Collective*, by Kerry Greaves. Sophie Seita's *Provisional Avant-Gardes: Little Magazine Communities from Dada to Digital* shares a similar historical arc to this book. Kurt Beals's *Wireless Dada: Telegraphic Poetics in the Avant-Garde* continues and updates theories and histories of media in avant-garde studies. Titles other than Biddle's that look at the Antipodal avant-gardes have tended toward the gallery arts, and include *Permanent Revolution: Mike Brown and the Australian Avant-Garde 1953–1997* by Richard Haese, an assessment of the collage, assemblage and installation artist Brown, whose decades-long career included frank depictions of sexuality and involvement in the Australian politicised counter-cultures of the 1960s and 1970s. For Haese, Brown's concept of "Imitation Realism", which arguably unites Brown's diverse array of practices, including an interest in "Oceanic Primitivism", speaks to a universal aspect of the avant-garde artist as one committed to "often violent, unscripted and undisciplined change" (9). Much of Brown's visualism engages language in the manner of global conceptualism. A 2017 exhibition at the Heide Museum of Modern Art in Victoria, curated by Sue Cramer and Lesley Harding, produced a catalogue, *Call of the Avant-Garde: Constructivism and Australian Art*, examining Australian responses to Constructivism from mid-century (Ralph Balson, Frank Hinder, George Johnson) to contemporary (Rose Nolan, Zoë Croggon).

of Warnayaka Art, the biliterary poetics of Tangentyere Artists' town camp artists, and the acrylic witness paintings of June Walkutjukurr Richards. (1)

Examples offered here of the "imperative to experiment", or simply "experimentation", are multimedial; each example is prefaced with a phrase that encapsulates its experimentality, by way of media. But they do not so obviously intervene in avant-garde history, conventionally understood: "Experimental arts of the desert are not, in this sense, an obvious avant-garde but are more subtle, dispersed, antispectacular even" (10). Rather we see, in the spirit of the first avant-gardes of the early twentieth century, refusals of containment, stubborn provisionality. In the case of June Walkutjukurr Richards's canvases, which are, also, in cross-mediatic terms, writing surfaces, Biddle reads them as works of "biliterary dexterity"; that is, painterly yet poetics-oriented and multilingual by cultural necessity. In Richards, language fights back against the institutions that try to contain it. "Carpetbagger", a 2008 painting by Richards, consists of an acrylic, cursive rendering of the title word – "Carpetbagger" – in white upon a black canvas, the word being a pejorative term for art dealers who profit from Aboriginal art and undercut returns to artists (Biddle, 82–3). Biddle's analysis brings the complexity of the word "avant-garde" to the works in a way that asks us to look further into the spaces – bounded and unbounded – of language opened up by these works; to use the word, that is, to go back to the literal sense without naïveté. Not roundabout, the *remote* frontline is where the temporal, spatial and national contradiction of an Antipodal avant-garde begins.

The notion of a remote avant-garde again reduces our reliance on an assumed belatedness and futurity, or centre, periphery and margin, when it comes to the cultural influence and the timescape of any such avant-garde. Biddle's is an extraordinary and provocative inland history that could transfer back out from the Central Desert to uses of language in urban Aboriginal art, in the galleries of the major cities and ports of entry, or what Samuel Moginie has called the entrepôt.[15] In the broader history of contemporary Australian art, parallels can be drawn with the political-conceptual language work of Indigenous artist Vernon Ah Kee, where select phrases, often touching upon First Nations political struggle and Aboriginal subjectivity, are written in black sans serif font against a white back-

---

[15] I am grateful to Sam Moginie, poet, for raising the idea of the entrepôt (or "entrepoetics") early on in our friendship.

ground, with an often-exaggerated lack of kerning (spacing) between characters. The effect that Ah Kee's language works upon the viewer is to force a double reading. One never quite sees it right the first time – and the act of producing one's own kerning, separating or sorting the words apart from one another is a type of reading that is both uncomfortable and an allegory of language acquisition; a type of linguistic defamiliarisation crucial also in the poetry of Lionel Fogarty.

These can be compared too with the work of conceptual artist Ian Burn, a member of the 1970s Art & Language group, memorialised by American conceptual artist Adrian Piper upon his death in 1993 (both shared an interest in Hume). Burn would take interest in the complex treatment of Western art forms in Indigenous art practice in ways that concern gaze theory – relations between the observer and the observed – and interactions of Western modernism, naturalism and primitivism. With Ann Stephen, Ian Burn would co-write an article on Albert Namatjira, arguing that Namatjira's application of mimicry and counter-appropriation in his landscape and woomera-paintings are, in a manner, parallel

> with the tradition of the readymade in Western art for "double-coded" objects like the woomera-painting. The strategy of the readymade centred on the contradiction between the art object as commodity and the pre-industrial craft basis of its production, thus implicating the art object in different and contradictory economies ... The parallels lie with the ability of Namatjira's art to articulate "oppositions" between the modern and the primitive in Western culture. (254)

The contradiction of conceptualism, in its art-historical instance, and differently in its later poetic reprisal in late twentieth- and early twenty-first-century Conceptual Writing, is not only Duchampian unoriginality but what those moves meant in terms given by economics, production, labour and the commodity (254). Burn's works extend these questions, through language and perception, but at another frame of remove altogether again, responding *antipodally* to conceptualism as made institutional through the larger context of successive historical waves of the international avant-gardes. Reach, antipodal reach and reach-back, defines Burn's art-practice. Two instances of that are *Cubist Reversal* (1966–7) which annotates a Cubist painting by pointing out the different elements you might be seeing (shoulder, chair, eye, pipe, moustache), and *A Thread from a Canvas of Jackson Pollock for Australia only 1951–1969* (1969), which presents the thread underneath which is the title description

(Burn, 81, 93). Late work involved medially reflexive language written over reproductions of landscape paintings, but even then, late career, Burn remained interested in the historical avant-garde, in works like *Concerning Léger's portrait of my mother* (1990), which, in a deadpan way, speculates how Léger could have gotten hold of a portrait of his mother in order to do his 1932 work, including imagining that she had been taken by Margaret Preston's 1927 *Still Life*, which "used Léger's composition, again writing Australian art history into the history of the avant-garde through humour" (Stephen, 82).

These conceptualist excursions, with all their experimentation with language and media, make concerted connections with poetics even if they seem more invested in the gallery arts. From these examples I have come to share such historical imperatives that experiment matters – whether emergent from art-historical cultural centres within which Indigenous and non-Indigenous artists have been participating, or from remote Indigenous language and culture – in ways that synthesise interior and exterior modes of reflection, as well as conceptual and political approaches to mediated language. The way Antipodal avant-gardes have felt compelled to interrogate language and media I will treat seriously here in that it has not always been so obvious; not obvious as to the way such language art came to find itself happily ensconced in a contemporary art gallery, whether regional or city-central, privately or publicly funded. These works antipodally flip the notion of avant-garde from front-line to off-centre, even off-grid. The idea of remote comes to question the constitution of cultural value; for a certain kind of "remote" Indigenous art is figured as more authentic by the art market, yet only a certain kind of remote art is deemed of value. If the contemporary gallery has become a space which contains the avant-garde to the point of, in some analyses, emptying it of an originary radical purpose, here the proximity of artmaking to the threat of state violence renders these works resistant in the most urgent of ways, resistant indeed to the contexts in which they appear. Biddle is quick to remind us that "remoteness", if not reclaimed, as an aesthetic or poetic category, retains sinister connotations: it has been used to justify acts of state intervention and land acquisition, most notably the Northern Territory National Emergency Response Act 2007 (2007–12), introduced by the John Howard government.[16] Biddle's

---

[16] The Northern Territory Emergency Response, or "The Intervention", of 2007, which involved the forced acquisition of Aboriginal towns, the deployment of the army, under the pretense of restoring order to Northern Territory Indigenous communities, has further destroyed the relationship nationwide between First Nations people and

analysis consequently becomes not so much "metatheoretical" as historical, concerned with "history in the making" (17); a historical poetics in which the centrality of the desert, and the mission, needs to be emphasised.[17] To account for the remote not as a space of decay and state neglect (though it has been the latter) but rather of cultural sustenance and continuation, and to make such an account with a view to poetics and aesthetics emerging critically from Indigenous communal locales, a sense of "remote" comes to oppose forms of white nationalism. The "remote avant-garde", Biddle notes, stands for a continuity of earlier art practices as much as a break: novelty emergent from tradition, tradition remade, in the paintings of June Walkutjukurr Richards and the Warburton Arts Project, and it is, no less, a poetic, or poetics tradition.

"Tradition" here is the essential term. Reading antipodally, I want to emphasise that Tzara's primitivist avant-gardism emerges from a modern, and certainly transnational horizon, but one pointed crucially towards a *tradition*, and that it was this tradition that Tzara saw as beneficial to the avant-garde enterprise, if not purely "interesting" in and of itself, motive alone for an exploratory poetics. English writer Bruce Chatwin would also find interest in Central Desert culture. In 1987 he wrote *The Songlines*, an influential work that, combining fiction and non-fiction, looked, through an English lens, to the Central Desert for personal and spiritual affirmation. Like Tzara, Chatwin's curiosity remained that of an outsider, with a sometimes ill-informed yet ever-restless mind. It has been well recounted that, originally Samueli Rosenștok, Tzara coined his own name from the Romanian *trist în țară* (sad in one's country). As Marius Hentea points out in his biography of Tzara, the expression more correctly would be trist la țară, a little fact which made Tzara smirk: "His pseudonym is an incomplete effacement of his origins, the seemingly cosmopolitan name turning out to have a

---

governance on the national level since its implementation, and through aspects of its present continuation in the derivative Stronger Futures in the Northern Territory Act 2012 by the Julia Gillard government.

[17] Biddle notes the historical link between remote-based community art centres and the founding of missions (16). Beginning in the late eighteenth century, reserves, missions and stations in Australia were three kinds of sites of forced habitation for Indigenous people as part of the policy of Segregation, denying Aboriginal people access to traditional land and sacred sites. In the twentieth century, missions and reserves were sites for the eugenics policy that resulted in the Stolen Generations, over a period spanning most of the century. Lionel Fogarty grew up on a "punishment reserve" in Cherbourg, Queensland, an experience that would drive his political resistance and inform his poetics.

particular ancestry, and perhaps even a particular meaning, but it can all be denied" (2). Later, in the United States of America, a loose nexus of "ethnopoets", particularly the prominent poet, translator and anthologist Jerome Rothenberg, somewhat a neo-Dadaist, would carry this interest in Antipodal and global Indigenous culture further into the twentieth century. Edited by Dennis Tedlock and Rothenberg, the journal *Alcheringa*, which ran through thirteen issues and two series throughout the 1970s, took its name from the Arrernte word for Dreamtime. It was dedicated to the translation of "tribal" poetries, its relevance to the activity and value of experimental forms, orality and performance, and to enlarging "our understanding of what a poem may be".[18]

It's time to say this: the global avant-gardes, so it would seem, never forgot Dada internationalism, or at the very least the legacies of Tzara's avant-garde primitivism never forgot the Antipodes. In saying all this, I am still refusing one-way origin narratives that begin with an avant-European-American-ethnographic legacy, for the reason of balance; primarily this is because I am going to show that the Antipodal avant-garde is also a tradition that, not solely due to the market imperative in the arts, sought the kind of internationalism Tzara sought. I am going to specify precisely how Antipodal poetry spoke back to the avant-garde, but it must first be noted that twentieth-century Australian poets, especially poets coming out of extended white settler strains into the modern period, could feel "sad in one's country" enough to seek national affirmation, or perhaps a kind of consolation, in Indigenous culture. It is well known that Modern Australian Verse had its cultural nationalists, the Adelaide-based Jindyworobak Movement, a group that would wield some influence of considerable note. The Jindyworobaks would build a brand of appropriative modernism in the 1940s, and as one of its most active members, Reginald Charles, or Rex Ingamells, would claim, they were the first to openly explore a nationalist desideratum, through the modern settler context, by calling to mind First Nations cultures.[19] Perhaps their most famous claimed adherent was not

---

[18] This dot-point appears as part of a text titled "Statement of Intention" (1) by the editors Tedlock and Rothenberg, introducing the new series, which would run four volumes up to 1980. By way of pre-emptive response, the first lines of Lionel Fogarty's poem "Alcheringa", in *Yoogum Yoogum*, read: "We learnt to love you in that / historical jail" (48).

[19] The major Jindyworobak poets in Brian Elliot's edited anthology, for reference, are as follows: Rex Ingamells, W. Flexmore Hudson, Ian Mudie, William Hart-Smith and Roland Robinson, with Hudson being one of Ingamells's earliest supporters. The question of an accommodation, or embrace of intercultural nationalism, or transna-

actually an original member, Les Murray, self-styled the "last of the Jindyworobaks", which gave Brian Elliot, in his introduction to *The Jindyworobaks*, a detailed, chrestomathic (form-led) anthology of Jindyworobak poetics, the idea that they were, as a movement, a "completed form" as such (Elliot, "Introduction", xvii). According to Elliot, Ingamells would use the term "Alcheringa" to mean "*total* Australian identity . . . the national identity viewed *sub specie aeternitatis*" (xxviii), before and after 1788. For Murray, however, to be the last of the Jindyworobaks meant also to be opposed to the very idea of an avant-garde, and institutions of experiment in general. And yet, no matter how opposed to experiment the original Jindyworobaks may ultimately have been, the operation of an Antipodal avant-garde has for some critics come to be as synonymous with the Jindyworobaks as it was synonymous later with Ern Malley. Like Tzara, it was to Indigenous aesthetics and Indigenous narrative that the Jindyworobaks would turn to seek such rootedness, and to an extent linguistic exploration. They would also take it to be a spiritual quest, as Peter Kirkpatrick wrote: "When the avant-garde finally arrived in Australia . . . it did not speak in an Indigenous tongue, nor in a white male vernacular, but in the language of the subconscious" ("New word come tripping slowly", 219). Kirkpatrick appends the name "vanguard" to the group, or Club, particularly Ingamells, Wilfred Flexmore Hudson and Ian Mudie, and he associates Jindyworobak "Aboriginalism" with those incantations of the primitive that attempt to critique and provide a solution to the problems of modernity, reading their primitive poetics alongside Picasso's interest in African tribal art and Hugo Ball's Dadaist sound poems. Kirkpatrick can even cite "Karawane", a key poem of the sound poetry canon, as a significant example in comparison (219).[20] This association makes sense but only in light of the sometimes macaronic, and in Kirkpatrick's words, "baffling" incorporation of Indigenous

tionalism, or, at least, of cosmopolitanism, has been made complex by Jayne Regan who claims that one of its key members, Flexmore Hudson, was a "cosmopolitan Jindyworobak". The same may be said for the concerted ethnopoets of *Alcheringa*, working from cultural centres (the United States) with a concern for the peripheries, in Regan's phraseology, "world-mindedness" for poetries of the cultural margins. But for the latter the purpose involved less nationalism and more formal interrogations of poeticity itself: "what a poem may be". The same could not be said for the Jindyworobaks.

[20] To this we could add, prior to 1917, Aleksei Kruschenykh of the Russian avant-garde, who would take the Georgian vocabulary and Armenian alphabet as sources for his "transrational" poems. There is an account of this in Maria Tsantsanoglou's "'The Fantastic Tavern' and Other Caucasian Stories" included in the collection *The Russian Avant-garde, Siberia and the East*, based on an 2013 exhibition.

words in Jindyworobak poems. Rather than careful use, and done with Indigenous permission or in collaboration as is protocol, their poetic uptake would approach "nonsense", hence the comparison with the history of Sound Poetry. Kirkpatrick nonetheless adds that "the need to assert national identity tended to constrain innovation at the same time as inviting it" (219), and on the level of poetics we do not see the kind of invention that Picasso, Ball or indeed Dada engaged. This was admitted by the Jindyworobaks themselves, and revealed in their own self-historicising impulses. Elliot admits the Jindyworobaks "never set out to write Aboriginal poetry in English words ... they always retained their white character, shown in the most unmistakable way in their continuation in the European tradition of lyrical styles" despite the fact that their use of Arrernte "ceremonial and ritual epics" which were oral, communal rather than individual, might have called for formal break with those traditions (Introduction, xxviii). This is in contrast, we may say, to the uptake of such forms by strains of Dada appropriation from Tzara to Rothenberg. We could outline several exceptions, if time permitted, through some of the poems of Ian Mudie, Rex Ingamells and Max Harris, who was up until 1939 associated with the Jindyworobaks – the Jindyworobak Club published his first book in 1940, *The Gift of Blood*, with unusually punctuated poems, alongside the surrealist play that is the book's title piece. Harris was associated more famously with Ern Malley as the editor of *Angry Penguins*, and being the one supposedly duped by the hoaxers, Harris would write poems that offered an unusual, if not formally experimental syntax. Regard "The Traveller", dedicated to Giorgio de Chirico, the Italian protosurrealist. One of its stanzas, a quintain, reads:

> Antipodes refute, lassitude overbears
> the waiting foot: no ticket to procure
> the full stretch of body is secure
> crumpled on the board of lowest stair
> where never foot stood voice screamed
>   (*The Angry Penguin*, 25)

The connection with the previous and following stanza here I need not quote, though it might add context, because there is an unusual syntactic discontinuity with the stanza breaks; I cannot help but think this is the very "waiting foot" Harris seeks, a foreign foot that travels and arrives at, in a later stanza, the "ghost platform of/ Antipodes" (26), and the dedication to de Chirico in itself is curious if not typically Jindyworobak. First published in 1942, this poem may by emblematic of the 1940s, a decade in which poets enthusiastic about literary upheaval knew about the changes that had taken place in modernity but were still trying to find a way out of such Antipodal refutations, or refusals of the modern, the modernist or the claim to be modern.

The Jindyworobaks were not an avant-garde, even if it was quite clear they were modern, staking out a rare claim for literary grouphood under the sign of a national culture not yet, and still not emancipated from its settler past. Their "politics", if cosmopolitanist, well-travelled, would be weary of foreigners seeking to "set foot" on settled territory, and settled poetic territory as well. Further to this, they were doing this without, to any significant extent, the wholesale questioning of poetic forms. The only other group that might have constituted a factionalist avant-garde occurred later, in the form of the Anarcho-Libertarian Push of Sydney, which was not entirely literary nor poetry-focused (1940s–1970s), and of which Harry Hooton was a member, discussed in an upcoming chapter, in light of the modernist and avant-garde ultimatum that was or became Ern Malley. This interlinguistic as well as cultural compulsion to cite, incorporate or appropriate in Malley bears some similarity to the Jindyworobaks in that they were exoticising an interiorised Other from the selfsame continent in which they made their art, but the results were not the same. If the Jindyworobaks were Antipodal modernists without an avant-garde sensibility, the inverse notion, of an avant-garde without modernism, is no more or no less unusual.[21] And as will become more palpable from here, the politics of the Australian avant-garde is defined by such contradictions, for there is on the one hand resistance, stubborn refusals to engage with avant-garde forms, and on the other hand a stultification, fascination with, even awkwardness before the spectre of the European purveyors of cultural modernity. The Antipodes becomes a space not only of

---

[21] For one instance, the Indian avant-garde, with which I find it curious to make some Antipodal comparison, would find itself oddly situated. For Partha Mitter, it could not partake of the triumphalism of its origins, even if Indian modernists would look to peasant culture, or, also, towards the discourse of primitivism (which Hal Foster also would reprise as a reference for Modern Art). Mitter argues that the "heroic age of primitivism" ended in 1941 (226), but what the reception of Indian modernists showed was a certain "Picasso-Manque Syndrome", meaning that it would be read or viewed as derivative, imitative, even where critics failed to read subversive intent, or skipped over *affinity* to find only *emulation*. I am indebted to Mitter for this illumination, applicable to Antipodal modernism by (incomplete) comparison: if there was any parallel in the colonial modernities of both Indian and Australian modernism, it would invite the notion of avant-garde *manqué*. Read *again*, as I am doing and as Mitter has done, derivation is seen as only part of the story in most of the cases I present here.

vanguard reiteration, but of an engagement with vanguard poetics and aesthetics that can involve at once critique, resistance and enthusiastic participation.

This book is about literary history as much as it is, by deed, *a* literary history, a catalogue behind a claim. Literary history, seen through the lens of Australian poetry, encapsulates both responses and resistances to power and the *labour*, we might say, if not simply "work", of poetics. What is, what was the Australian avant-garde? My argument has become this: the Australian avant-garde is, was, not only historical; it is, was, or became unusually interested *in* history. It's not so straightforward however if we examine at once the way Australian modernism seems to *want* to operate without the need of the "historic" avant-gardes, but also the way it responded on the odd occasion to them. We need not draw too hasty a conclusion that some vital core or impetus, missing from Australian modernism and therefore from Australian poetry, would trace us back to politics alone, and yet the flavour and formation of the society and modern nation of Australia in all its manifest forms (including the structure and history of Federation, debates around Republicanism from the beginning of the European settlement and even before, to the tug-of-war between nationalism, radicalism, socialism and labourism in nascent modern Australia, alongside the manifold contradictions of settler society – the Frontier Wars, convicts, the Squattocracy, bushranger histories – and of course governance, the politics of economy, and no less importantly, public policy) affect the Antipodal avant-gardes at every slight warning of their emergence or existence. It is a fact that commentators have noticed certain absences – revolution, a Republic, a Treaty – that certainly gave a sense, a cultural sense too, of stagnation while leaving a potential modernism up for grabs in a society that never quite became modern.[22] The perception, then, is

---

[22] The relation between Republicanism and the avant-garde is a topic of its own, but there have been suggestions of such tensions in scholarship on the 1919–33 Weimar Republic. In *The Captive Republic*, an account of the various historic strands of Australian Republican thought, Mark McKenna argues that the Australian republic was held "captive" because of the "fluidity of political language, a notion of political change which is both propelled and impeded by its own historical baggage" (5). The very signification of a republic, in Latin *respublica*, gave it impetus and prevented its realisation. In the twentieth century, McKenna argues that as policy the "end of the affair" with Republicanism was between 1863 and 1995, given the book was published before the failed Republican Referendum of 1999. In this period, however, Gough Whitlam (Prime Minister, 1972–5) would begin the handback of land to the Gurindji and introduce the Australian Land Rights Bill, before issuing a call for a Republic in the final pages of *The Truth of the Matter*, Whitlam's rebuke of Sir John Kerr (the Governor-General who dismissed him). My contention is that, regardless

that the field of Australian poetry became something of an entrepôt: "Australian received foreign poetries but did not export its own," as Nicholas Birns put it in "Australian Poetry from Kenneth Slessor to Jennifer Strauss" (173), yet that lack of stocks on the world market, and as a result the import-only model, of the received, gets further entrenched again through the absence of Revolution, despite significant resistance either in settler society or during the Frontier Wars, because of the "captive" Republic, and the absence of a Treaty or constitutional recognition of First Nations Australians, absences that underpin the collective psyche, nay, even "unconscious" of modern Australia insofar as it remains an unspoken element in world as well as Antipodal discourses, particularly those discourses concerning the modern literary landscape.[23] Birns writes that because Australia was "not a 'hotspot' of political crisis" and given "Australia's perceived rejection of modernism" (173), whatever risk we might take in presenting a cutting-edge Australian modernism to a global audience would be neutralised by a potential forfeiture of "multiple centres of literary production" (173). No vanguard then, which comes at the cultural centres from the cultural margins, but Birns harbours no intention to surmount this problem, taking this to readings of the poet Kenneth Slessor (1901–1971). A "Slessor-centric" approach is the only one we have to contend with, if simply because only one kind of modernism was permitted to flourish in the conditions we have above outlined, for whereas Australian poetry

> was marginalized within the old modernism, the modernism that saw itself as the avant-garde and the cutting-edge, the reckoning of Australian poetry that flourished in the modernist era was produced to seek the worldwide modernist approval it did not get. (174)

of policy, the notion of a Republic needs now to be viewed as not only an issue of policy structure but rather one entangled with Land Rights and the Frontier Wars (1788–1939) (See note 5).

[23] What McKenna would call the radical, socialist strand of interpretation arguably does not encapsulate the spirit of Republican sentiment or policy interest in Australia: a republic does not always emerge from revolution. But it concerns modern Australian literature in the sense that a "Republic of Letters" would find no historical justification in any Antipodal notion of nation. The question of what to do with a modernism without revolution, as a modernism without the avant-garde, is one of modernity itself. It is of course true that revolutionary defence and resistance, from the long Frontier Wars to the Indigenous Tent Embassy, the Murrawarri Republic, the Eureka Stockade, an 1854 gold miner rebellion, or the Darwin Rebellion led by the Australian Worker's Union in 1918, did not congeal into a change in the official definition or official discourse of national sovereignty. Thus if we are to speak in a strong rather than weak sense of a "Republic of Letters" we would be including within the phrase this historical train of events.

Such reckoning, then, in the context of this writing, less for modernist approval than for explanatory gain, would seem to have found its day if we consider what modernism means *now* – the role of institutions like the Modernist Studies Association and other like bodies that represent or purport to represent the worldwide flourishing of modernist studies – but even in these environs, Birns indicates still that it is better to stay on the "safe side"; the critical scale would "remain largely within the accepted canon of Australian poetry of this period" (174). There are undoubtedly "core margins" (margins in close proximity to cultural centres), and "peripheral margins" (margins of margins); yet our argument is that literary criticism in league with literary history can and must make sense of both. Our charge is that Birns does not dialectise the canon in arguing for it. If the task of the critic is simply to broadcast it and accept it, the collateral damage from this approach is a sidelining of poetics. What results is a criticism with no recourse to a corpus considered in apposition with matters of poetics, of what affords some general importance outside the scale of consensus critical worth when that consensus is clearly uncertain. I say this also because, in any constellation of literary history properly theorised, "safety" is neither the utmost priority nor the foundation for a study, conspective or not, and because what "cutting edge" means, in avant-garde studies, is theoretically and historically up for grabs. The problem of canonicity here cannot then be done away with by a sheer statement of position: we may remain on the safe side; but the safest bet is to ask questions: what "dangers" lurk on the other side and what is (on) the other side? What critical attitude, what critical demeanor, can be deemed "safe" or "unsafe"; and which attitude or demeanour should a critic adopt? In presenting an "adequate worldwide airing" without first coming through Slessor – much the case here – in the world corner of literary studies, can an *unsafe* picture do better in upping the stakes or garnering approval?

V. Literary History as a Challenge to the Avant-Garde

To give answers to these questions we must reframe the question. It seems natural, to a critic formally trained in the study of poetics, to ground poetics *in theory*. But re-envisaging theoretical accounts of experimental poetry when history comes into the fray becomes a juggling act. A prepared *definition* of poetics won't do! Various "unsafe" definitions crop up. Philip Mead's is one to work off:

"Broadly speaking, poetics is the name we give to the fractal geometry of textual meanings" (*Networked Language*, 2). But what would a fractal geometry be? First, a metaphor: such "fractal geometries" that lead to, or are simply and complexly "of", textual meanings, *mean* poetics, or the unpredictable shapings that the study of making shows up. We come to it in the midst of Mead's discussion about the need to confront the whole vexed question of poetic difficulty:

> The consensus about how poetic meanings are generated, though, hasn't been able to produce any simple equation that can adduce the meanings of even fairly straightforward instances of poetic language. It doesn't dispel the unease about the difficult limit cases that some poetic expression presents . . . What does lyric poetry have to do with "society"? More worrying still, it seems, are the instances of poetic language that appear schizophrenically disordered. What's the point of the textual embodiment of a (deliberate) deficit of "meaning"? . . . Thus, in the Australian context the critical discourse on poetry lags seriously behind, or is out of sync with, the formal innovativeness and linguistic range of historical and contemporary poetic production. It's as if literary theory and criticism can't envisage ways forward. (*Networked Language*, 2–3)

It is possible to talk comfortably and in some restrained way about difficult limit cases. They can be presented as proof indeed that criticism lags behind the linguistic inventiveness of neglected textual objects, but, on the other hand, my intention in this book has, over time and in the course of examining the documents, not been to cut the lag or play catch-up. It has been, rather, to *theorise lag and historicise catch-up*, to match a literary-critical and theoretical discourse with those texts in Australian poetry that have gained significant attention for their difficulty, or that have been ignored because of their difficulty, in order to present the problem as informed by literary theory and literary history at once, and to present this historical problem as intimate to literary criticism broadly speaking. In a sense, we must *envisage* a way forward, but I remain cautious in making this overt at every turn simply because I have held out on the possibility that authority is shared between text and critic, and that the critic, more than deficient host, has left house, and for good reason: criticism takes on an almost prophetic task at this juncture in its search for a new framework.

To go further, then, or to get ahead, we need to calibrate our critical discourse in accordance with the fact that we are about to find ostensive points of contact between literary theory and literary history. I have said that in the very deepest way these problems are literary-historical some time before they become literary-theoretical questions, and one of the most pressing confrontations in this regard is found in those ruminations on the subject by Hans Robert Jauss. The leading problem in "Literary History as a Challenge to Literary Theory" and the Konstanz school of *Rezeptionästhetik* at large, was not so much the irrevocable parting of ways between Marxist historicism and pure formalism, but rather the way an aesthetics of reception – otherwise, we may say, histories of reading – would question the history of literature as canon, and what the didactic application of this would be. The canon comes into play when Jauss pursues issues of historical objectivism, and this problem has an analog in literary-critical reading itself: it poses a problem for anyone who would like to stick to some modicum of judgement or taste.

If it is all about reception, can we guarantee that a reception history is a history of what readers should or could be finding of worth, or of interest, in a text or historical set of texts? Literary history in such a new key, Jauss tells us, puts reading in context, context closer to the historical, and "more like an orchestration which strikes ever new chords among its readers and which frees the text from the substance of the words and makes it meaningful for the time" (10).

Familiar as it may sound, we don't have a clear path around these orchestrations yet. The reception and recuperative model for reading avant-garde texts introduces another set of issues to this schema. Avant-garde literature has a complex reception history. At once it is rejected by an apparently "mainstream" audience and celebrated in some specific academy or set of academies. At other times the avant-garde is celebrated as a bulwark against the academy and academic reading. Outside of academies altogether, avant-garde literature is at some points taken up by an imagined "mainstream" readership as an alternative to the market-driven texts they are encouraged to access, in cases where a popular readership has found itself at odds with those texts that have been deemed popular for it. Then, as we know from Janco's denialist reading of Dada history and Stavrinski's analysis of Dada presentism, both avant-garde discourses and "practitioners" alike find history threatening. An historian alone cannot read the avant-garde text, but this failure to read might be itself the impetus that keeps driving along the desire to keep reading. The question of "who reads" is for Bob Perelman institutional: modernist genius invites and demands rereading, a handy fact for the institutions built around reading them – writer, critics and graduate students – precisely because certain modernist texts are so difficult to read (*The Trouble with Genius*, 5).

Presentism is, on the one hand, the syllabus. But the status of the avant-garde within modernism at large has itself produced a readership that goes beyond modernist genius. Preferring to take matters into their own hands, poets and performers might want to remove the avant-garde from the classroom and the syllabus in order to put it back into daily life. *Ulysses* has demanded readings and commanded many an intensive Unit of Study, and the same can increasingly be said (I hope) for Gertrude Stein, though the irony could not be lost on, say, courses in appreciation of Italian Futurism or some such other avant-garde mainstay. The question might become more urgent when presentism is literalised, when one takes avant-garde instruction or practice quite literally. But here we are talking mostly within the ambit of modernism studies proper. In the case of Language Writing in the United States on both coasts, which Perelman admits as, or assigns the name, avant-garde, legacies of institutional incorporation had occurred in a manner not widespread in other literary cultures. From an avant-garde poet's perspective, to flash one's *avant-garde card*, as Perelman has put it, is also to admit one doesn't know what it exactly is, which is to say that it rarely acts its age; which is also to say any avant-garde is "catching up" with the present, whereas a "critical concept" of the avant-garde in effect sequentialises and transhistoricises it as "tokens of a single process" (Perelman, "My Avant-Garde Card", 881, 893). In each of these cases, regardless of outcome or consensus as to worth, readability or teachability, the avant-garde has produced crises *in readership*, crises which make it, of course, fascinating subjects for literary-historical inquiry if one tries to draw from this a sequential narrative. It culminates in this:

> What does a literary world look like in which the avant-garde acts its age? A world in which the avant-garde is not ahead in some crucial sense but only historical? Is it a world that is all that different? (Perelman, "My Avant-Garde Card", 893)

Picture this: a critic, any critic, has found themselves well within sight of an avant/modern horizon, but as they find themselves aggrieved before questions of historical aftermath, it soon dawns upon them that they too are contributing to critical orthodoxy around an avant-garde. This is not to say those reading effects *are not real*. To use terms from Jauss, we may say that the "orchestration" avant-garde texts have produced strikes not so much chords, harmonies, as sows discord among readers, freeing some and baffling others, bringing some into newly formed substances of words and their meanings, and alienating others from the idea of substance or meaning altogether.

Deciphering the meaning of an avant-garde text, therefore, may not have much to do with how we define a text as avant-garde. Paul de Man's assessment of the Konstanz school sheds further light on Jauss's original problem, and if we can see here at least a slither of an opening towards a history of avant-garde reception, it does not mean leaving meaning behind or letting lag set in. Lag, or the deferral of disparate nexuses dedicated to the examination of how meaning is made. For de Man, the boldness of the school was in their bid to bring poeticians and hermeneuts together, tying the "knot" between them that has, at various points, since Aristotle, become disentangled. On the one hand, the hermeneutic enterprise which belongs to a theological tradition is occupied with the meaning of texts, and as such "the ultimate aim of a hermeneutically successful reading is to do away with reading altogether" (56). On the other hand poetics, in its scientific sense and in its historical usage, concerns the "taxonomy and interaction of poetic structures", and in the case of the Prague linguistic circle, poetics (*Werkstructur*) is then further distinguished from hermeneutics proper (*Interpretationssystem*). Yet, crucially, as de Man stresses, Jauss turns against historical positivism in that his interest becomes no longer directed toward the "definition of an actual canon but toward the dynamic and dialectical process of canon formation" (58). The lesson we learnt, from the oft-misapplied phrase "horizon of expectation", derived from Husserlian phenomenology, was therefore that we have a horizon of consciousness that, like perception, only appears when there is focus against a horizon of *distraction*. And de Man is right in pointing out that this is a model redolent of the psychoanalytic preconscious, and the scene of the analyst and analysand, precisely given its role in mediating the silhouetted "private inception" and "public reception" that revolves ultimately around the dialectic of knowing and not-knowing. This may be easily circumvented in literary history because it stresses reading rather than knowing, but Jauss's innovation is in his pitting this against canonical essentialism: "At the moment of its inception, the individual work of art stands out as unintelligible with regard to the prevailing conventions. The only relation it has to them is that of contemporaneity or of synchrony" (de Man, 60). This then turns into "an entirely contingent and syntagmatic relationship between two elements that happen to coincide in time but are otherwise entirely alien to each other" (60). In such a move we then begin to see how the history of reading emerges from this synchronic arrangement in that the differentiation "that separates the work from its setting is then inscribed in the historical, diachronic motion of its understanding (*Horizontswandel*), which ends in the discovery of properties held in common between the work and its projected history" (60).

So we have now some remote yet not insignificant linkage between reception and semiotics. And yet, despite these highly perceptive readings, what for de Man is missing in Jauss is precisely the play of the signifier. In de Man's final analysis, and this is the crux of his critique, the play of the signifier is missing from Jauss's reading of one of Baudelaire's *Spleen* poems and so it gets lost in the style of his reading; an inattention to the rhyming of Boucher / débouché (66), and, as a result, "For reasons of decorum, the gap that Jauss opened, by his own observation, in the aesthetic texture of the language is at once reclosed, as if the commentator felt that he might betray the integrity of the text with which he is dealing" (66). We are to expect, then, that the critic, when placed before the play, the coarseness and the violence of the signifier, will respond in kind with a kind of aesthetic restraint. There will be something that remains, not wholly given over. This is a critical resistance to the fulsomeness of the text: what criticism reserves for itself, what is held in reserve, is not a theoretical suspicion of history, nor a historical suspicion of theory as such.

The Antipodal avant-garde is curious, if not atypical, in this respect because if it induces any horizon of expectation, what occurs is a kind of *Horizontswandel* that is unusually refractive: it is at once unintelligible to prevailing conventions, resoundingly intelligible to the logic of the group or groupings, and at certain points, either transformative for critical readings or leading to an impasse in readings themselves, the kind of impasse de Man saw in Jauss's reading of Baudelaire with regard to the chorality of punning and verbal play. Critics have, on the whole, struggled to read such work and to deduce meaningful observations from much avant-garde literature, regardless of its "integrity" (on multiple levels), or the generally perceived seriousness of the work, either in terms of literary history or literary theory. When criticism is caught between theory and history, or if it fails to negotiate these two exterior situations as part of a larger composite, it may have no way out but some path to the future, a prophetic mode. And it is this that makes the "lag" of Antipodal poetics-inflected criticism (or any criticism) all the more curious and worth further meditation. Whether a reading is synchronous, of its time, or ahead of its time, or behind the times (not up with the sheer urgency and pull of the present), neither means a critic has been too caught up in history, for history may enlighten a path to the future, nor does it mean the critic has been too caught up in the present, for the present too is a good indicator of potential future critical paths. A critic may use an old critical method for new literature, or a new critical method for old literature, or present method for present texts; there are degrees of a/synchronicity. Antipodal avant-garde works have been, and continue to be, read, and read *now*, but as Mead pointed out with his several senses of "critical lag", and as de Man noticed with respect to Jauss's reading of Baudelaire, criticism may have shown too much restraint. Poetic restraint, and historical restraint, which is to be expected, has been met with Jaussian "aesthetic restraint". And we need to notice it. Our purpose is not to chastise anyone over this, suffice to say that the poems themselves have set the line of sight on our horizon of expectations. Literary history is a challenge to the very notion of an avant-garde because, in the very crudest of senses, the avant-garde has been captured by the theories (and institutions) that have attempted to, or succeeded in, containing it.

VI. *Impossible Histories*

Literary history is a challenge to the avant-garde, also, because we have not let it escape theories of historical change. For this we have before us a generous spread of historical morphologies to draw from. In their Introduction to an edited collection, *Impossible Histories: Historical Avant-gardes, Neo-avant-gardes, and Post-avant-gardes in Yugoslavia, 1918–1991*, poet Dubravka Djurić and art theorist Miško Šuvaković propose a tripartite periodicity for Yugoslavian avant-gardism: historical or "classical" avant-gardes, neo-avant-gardes and post-avant-gardes. Šuvaković defines the middle term using a further triad: "The term neo-avant-garde refers to the second wave of the avant-garde, which may be defined in a number of different ways: as a rehashing of the first avant-garde, as a maturation, or as something entirely distinct from the earlier movement" (26). In the Yugoslavian context, these are borne out in neo-avant-garde aesthetics in ways that both reflect upon and critique the historical ramifications for beleaguered state socialisms of the great period of Soviet decline, and attendant sociopolitical and geopolitical maladjustments in the broader region. These kinds of historical and transnational studies, studies in what I would like to term the "comparative" or "hemispheric" avant-gardes, I have found illuminating for how they talk back to theoretical debates like those between Hal Foster and Peter Bürger that interrogate the relation between an originary avant-garde and its subsequent neo-vanguardist iterations, whether post-war, or arising from the social and political tumult of the late 1960s and early 1970s. Scholarship knows this dispute well enough. Foster critiques Bürger's thesis by accusing him of forwarding the notion of a unified theory in which the historical avant-garde is projected as an "*absolute origin* whose aesthetic transformations are fully significant and historically effective in the first instance" ("What's Neo About the Neo-Avant-Garde", 11). In a more recent defence by Bürger he calls attention to the "deferred action" of the avant-gardes; awareness of the distance of a sequence of subsequent events from an originary point (the originary avant-garde) does not "devalue the construction from a fixed end-point but exposes it for what it is: a construction" ("Avant-Garde and Neo-Avant-Garde", 710). Without an absolute origin, and with a sense of constructedness in mind, the fate of the term "neo-avant-garde" is sealed. We are no longer theoretically well-equipped, and we no longer can imagine historical formations outside European cultural centres, synchronic points of advancement, negotiation, compromise, betrayal, exposing indeed the very *constructedness* of this originary point. Yet the object of the neo or the post is not so much to tether itself to assumptive origins as to find itself estranged, as it were, from vanguardist eventhood and vanguard objects. I don't even mean to suggest that hemispheric, non-European or non-American avant-garde formations automatically cancel out all other senses of "neo", of avant-garde historical continuity. Perhaps these problems are best summed up by Brian Reed in *Nobody's Business: Twenty-First Century Avant-Garde Poetics*, which, while troubled by the notion of avant-garde, deploys it for mainly US American poetics in the new century. Reed asks a series of theoretical questions about the avant-garde in the book's opening:

> Since the 1960s, avant-gardism has a mixed, complex history as a critical concept. Can an authentic avant-garde still exist? Or can there only be shallow effete echoes of past movements and achievements? Can an avant-garde ever actually succeed in bringing about revolutionary social transformation? Does an espousal of vanguardist aims amount to enslaving art to the logic of the marketplace, especially the constant demand for new products and new fashions?

Is avant-gardism inherently masculinist? Is it solely a Western phenomenon? (xiii)[24]

Most of these questions became all the more complicated the more I looked into them, and where they have remained unanswered, these are questions that I hope this book's proceedings can go some way to providing answers for. Yet we can also remain aware that they are difficult, if not impossible questions to answer in one fell (historical) swoop, unless we have a view of history that treats historical time as dynamic, rather than linear, or static. Take, as a momentous example, recent attention to Baroness Elsa von Freytag-Loringhoven (1874–1927). For all the historical work done on the Baroness so far, and a lot of it has been done, the sheer extent to which it all adds weight to theses of avant-garde constructedness along the lines of gender and histories of the avant-gardes in sculpture, poetics, performance, is yet to be seen. It will be in some future time.[25] For the German Baroness to enter into history, the story that must be told is of her body as a site of avant-garde performance, her body as foreign presence in the streets of New York, and of her role in the conceptualisation of the Duchampian readymade. They are specific histories, but with radical theoretical consequences. Less shallow, effete echo as transformative radical historicism, avant-garde poetry in this regard is written again as an impossible history, impossible in the sense that it finds itself frozen before its evental origins and in need of objects. The Antipodal avant-garde is one more puzzling piece in the mosaic of this impossible history.

---

[24] Tyrus Miller, concerning the neo-avant-garde in *Singular Examples*, places Jackson Mac Low in the spotlight as one of the most important actors in this history for many reasons, some of which include his reworkings of Kurt Schwitters and MERZ, as well Cagean procedure albeit through prosodic invention of a different kind. Miller and Reed are principle advocates of this contemporary-historicist position. In *Nobody's Business*, Reed explores the continuation of avant-garde poetics in *very* recent poetry, not without qualification, as my quotation of the Preface above shows. Hal Foster's art-historical argument, from *The Return of the Real* to *What Comes After Farce?* maintains a similar premise, arguing for improvement upon successive cycles.

[25] Several more conspective publications of Baroness Elsa's work, particularly *Body Sweats: The Uncensored Writings of Elsa von Freytag-Loringhoven*, and growing popular knowledge of the importance of her art practice and life to the Dada movement, have, I think, come to bring some change to the overall character of debates about avant-garde poetics in particular, and the way avant-garde events and objects are figured in general.

Chapter 2

1897 in 1981: Stéphane Mallarmé *avec* Christopher Brennan

> For it is surely not to be denied that a person often persuades others, and just as often himself, that he believes something when he simply has nothing against it and leaves it quietly in its place. Nearly all historical faith is of this kind, unless it happens to be based on a determination of the faculty of desire, such as the faith in the historical element in a revelation, or the faith of a professional historian, which is inseparable from respect for his occupation and from the importance that he is bound to place on his painstaking investigations, or the faith of a nation in an event that supports its national pride.
> – J. G. Fichte, *Attempt at a Critique of All Revelation*

It's the story both of distant kinship and revelation. When Christopher John Brennan wrote to Stéphane Mallarmé on 9 August 1897, it was to express literary revelation, marking gratitude to a poet "whose works have been to me the greatest renewal, the greatest revelation" (Hughes, "C. J. Brennan", 27).[1] In a powerful extended reading of Brennan's *Poems*, a collection that is also a sequence, and his relation to modernism, or Mallarméanism, through the trifold Esotericism, Romanticism and Symbolism, Katherine Barnes traces Brennan's

---

[1] Three letters from Brennan to Mallarmé were first published in *The Australian Quarterly* in 1947, edited by critic Randolph Hughes, shortly after the Ern Malley affair. Hughes is disparaging of the "stumbling and fumbling" of the letters: "Here the bush doesn't even begin to smoulder: there is no ignition of style. One gets the impression that Brennan was so nervous with reverence in approaching the Master that he was paralysed or at least anchylosed into a state where he could only stammer" (30). Hughes is troubled with its being "not at all English" but rather Brennan thinking in French (31).

study of German Romanticism, particularly Novalis, to a poetic theory of moods. The Absolute is never far from these divagations, and thus Brennan could participate in the extraordinary leap from the transcendental to that other side; from German philosophy's late phase, between Kant/Fichte and Hegel/Schelling to Mallarmé, taking with him the philo-poetic revelation that would be both divine and worldly (adequate to our dreams), ultimately harmonious (attempting or approaching the Higher Self), and capturing the dialectic of Romantic conception and Symbolist "form and strategy" – those "graphic techniques" of "expressive typography and careful attention to *mise en page*" (*The Higher Self*, 175). Mood itself can be studied; moodiness as the effect or in its affects can also be mood the technique. Mood plays a structural role, the union of inner and outer worlds, the situating of mind in Nature, leading then to the numinous sense of a Higher Self, Barnes's theoretical key phrase. But the study is also earnestly and in fact reciprocally historical: "It is time for Brennan's work to become known outside Australia, and it is time also for Australians to rediscover, or at least to re-evaluate, *Poems*. The result can only be an enrichment of our culture" (*The Higher Self*, 272).

To quote Fichte is on one level disingenuous here because it would take some by no means mild break in Schelling to move away from this kind of critique of revelation – but its purpose is to show just how much the question of history (and Nation) was there in the problem of revelation before it became in German Romanticism the return of religion in History and Myth. Who will read Brennan, and who in "our" culture would be enriched, depends much upon historical intervention. Professional historians, like philologists, possess a kind of historical faith. And faith still guides our path through the enigmas of history; but here we have radically modified our faith in senses of nation and as such our occupation has shifted. The earlier part of Brennan's letter to Mallarmé quoted above brings up the foreignness that such an attempt to reach Mallarmé and his language necessitates: "I should be almost entirely cut off from the legendary tradition of my Celtic ancestors" (Hughes, "C. J. Brennan", 27). It is a revelation from outside, a kinship from within. But if the question of a national revelation comes again to tug at our historical faith, historical unity could only be found in a reappraisal of the Songspirals, Indigenous poetries, or amongst the Celtic ancestors themselves, the Jindyworobaks of the 1940s (of which more will be said in the following chapter) could give senses of rootedness, of an enriched cultural *arts* of sovereignty. Therefore and for this precise reason the best avenue of reappraisal that seems adequate for Brennan is his place in the long history of the Antipodal avant-gardes and the heritage of experimental poetics stemming from Mallarmé, an enrichment of rootlessness. The mood of Brennan's poetics might repeat in Antipodal (or Celtic-Antipodal) poets from the 1940s and even after, in tone, in senses of staleness, flatness or dagginess of affect or effect, a straining to be heard, an intellectual earnestness beating back ceaselessly against the threat or the reality of a cultural cringe. There is no sense of constricted access here: the collection *Australian Divagations*, edited by Jill Anderson at the beginning of this century, works its way around a phrase Mallarmé uses in a letter back to Brennan, "a kinship of dream"; kinship, an anthropological term, opens up the Antipodal axis we might expect – but the collection shows that Mallarmé's influence could reach further than Brennan, with poets as important as A. D. Hope and John Forbes, in Australia, among the key inheritances, just as it could continue in France with poets like Anne-Marie Albiach. In the case of Albiach we again see how experimental poetics, that question of graphic technique, shows up in the long aftershocks brought about by the typographic experiment of *Un Coup de Dés*. If Brennan's enigmatic poetics follows the history dictated to us from Malley in Antipodal modernism, the history of failure, Brennan would set sail over the seas and reverse it, stop the failure before it came about. To speak about this relation I use *avec*, with, doubling with, twinning in sync, to keep the sense of kinship in mind throughout, and to move the theoretical fabric over to revelation, a byword in this instance, and perhaps only this instance, of divagation, a forcing by chance, an account of how in Mallarmé Brennan saw genius in the riddle and saw time compressed to such an extent as to open up a space in an expanded present. Something was revealed to Brennan from Mallarmé. Time stood still. But for something to be revealed it must be *accepted* as a revelation. Not just blind worship of a Master, for as Jill Anderson has pointed out Brennan had to actively read Mallarmé and Mallarmé read Brennan for the kinship to operate.

1. *Full Score Malahrrmay*

The notational element in poetics ceases to be merely an analogy to music when it becomes prosodically scorewise. Mallarmé prefaces *Un Coup de Dés* as if he knew that what looked like a break with tradition was not meant to be anything more than an extension of this kind of prosody: the "stripped down mode of thought, with its retreats, prolongations, flights" comes to be in spoken air "a musical score" (*Collected*, 122). It is a strange invocation of the future present when Mallarmé adds that "Today, or at least without presuming upon the future that will emerge from this", this attempt "participates, in a way that could not be foreseen, in a number of pursuits" dear to his present – "*le vers libre et le poëme en prose*" (*Collected*, 122–3). Those two, then, became in the presumed and then consummated future, the foundation of the twentieth-century notational poetics in prosody "joined under a strange influence, that of Music, as it is heard at a concert; several of its methods, which seemed to me to apply to Literature, are to be found here" (*Collected*, 123). The ancient technique of Poetry, and its unique source, remain intact. But that it is an *application* of technique and method is the crucial point that Mallarmé makes for the old relation.

That the influence of Music upon prosodic senses of the (poetic) Page is strange for Mallarmé should cause us to defamiliarise the facts of poetry in relation to music. The musico-poetic relation, though it is sometimes disappointing to emphasise this in classrooms and enthusiastic spaces that call for mediatic and disciplinary relations to be made, is very uncertain and always has been. Influence more than confluence, tension more than unity, describe the relation. Emphasising "synthesis" of the arts can sometimes obscure the formal relations between music and poetry – scores might be visually interposed, as graphic objects so to say, but they might also be used as structuring devices. In Mallarmé the status of the *blanc*, the white blank space, meaning or indicating pause, or silence, is "musical" in the counter-prosodic sense, and therefore might resemble a score but remain clear of structure. Readings of encrypted code rarely go so far as to find in the poetic text the structure of a score, though this has been claimed of Plato's dialogues (J. B. Kennedy). Musical form can also be openly declared and followed through, as is the case with Langston Hughes's *Ask Your Mama: 12 Moods for Jazz*.[2]

The problem of the "music of poetry", therefore, remains between its performative function and its visual or graphic instantiation. The text at the centre of this discourse, better known now than ever before, contains all the same elements of notationality, scorewise and prosodic reinvention and invocations of uncanny time and temporal presence. Its general name is *Musicopoematographoscope*, but includes another, the *Pocket Musicopoematographoscope*, and it

---

[2] This I discuss in *Stave Sightings*, 1–39.

Figure 2.1 Christopher Brennan, title page of *Musicopoematographoscope* (1897).

is Brennan's 1897 handwritten version of Stéphane Mallarmé's *Un Coup de Dés Jamais N'Abolira Le Hasard* (see Figure 2.1). Brennan had come across Mallarmé in his travels to Berlin only several years prior, having been awarded a travelling scholarship at the University of Berlin from 1892 to 1894. So when the 1897 edition of the Paris journal *Cosmopolis*, aptly titled, arrived in Australia that year with excerpts from *Coup de Dés* within, Brennan, who was working in the New South Wales Public Library, took special notice of it, and promptly decided to do his own version. The 1981 publication, by Hale and Iremonger, comes with a dust jacket which tells us the two works "represent a unique flowering of European avant-garde art in colonial Australia". It is the poetry of an "Australia" not yet Federated (Federation is 1901). The title page begins with the question of time coming right in at the top, as if a border-frame: "THE RAGE OF THE PRESENT!!" – "PERFECTION OF THE PAST!" – "THE ART OF THE FUTURE" (9).

"Paree" and "Malahrrmay" could set off a strain of reading of Antipodalist larrikinisation, a translation into colonial vernacular, the audience for which would be mostly, then, local. The most significant guiding fact is that both *Un Coup de Dés* and *Musicopoematographoscope* were published posthumously as books. The appearance of *Un Coup de Dés* in the journal *Cosmopolis*, where Brennan saw it, was prior to its full presentation as a book in 1914 at the eve of the first avant-garde showings. We ought to keep in mind that the use of *font*, or typeface experimentation occurs in the *Cosmopolis* version, not the 1914 versions – had Brennan only seen the latter, or Mallarmé's own handwriting which he closely mimics, he might not have had the idea of reforming the poem by hand. The discrepancies of the *Cosmopolis* setting are such that I consider it a different poem in some respects, as Mallarmé did (he saw it as insufficient, a "compromise" there), and yet in some ways more instructive even if less structurally sound. That it is framed as an "Observation Relative au Poème" gives it a sense of artefactual and critical scrutiny that the book version does not; it is introduced as a novelty of music in words. It was too, of course, cosmopolitan – a cosmopolitan transmission event for an Antipodal avant-garde also because the journal, which only ran from 1896 to 1898, would allow Brennan to catch in a narrow window the last year of Mallarmé's life, his late work. Brennan's interest would not have skewed this way had he not been given the opportunity to travel. It was in 1893 that Brennan first encountered Mallarmé, and their correspondence began the year after.

The question for this study is whether Brennan's version did the same as what Mallarmé's did: *spurn an avant-garde*, as Trevor Stark notes in *Total Expansion of the Letter: Avant-Garde Art and Language After Mallarmé*, such that the influence of the posthumous publication of *Un Coup de Dés* "from the birth of cubism to the diffusion of Dada" could become the subject "of intense identifications, rapidly proliferating readings and misreadings, and acrimonious internecine debate" (4). We would be setting out far too narrowly if that was just the aim, given the argument that *Musicopoematographoscope* should be read alongside all of Brennan's verse brings in the first contradiction: is this 1897 experiment an avant-garde *anomaly*, or a typical modernist occurrence; an odd avant-garde experiment encased within an modern oeuvre? Can we figure Brennan's Mallarmé simply in the terms of Modern Australian Verse rather than the global avant-garde? Barnes reads it as ironic that the enthusiastic response from Mallarmé to *XXI Poems* was on the back of its just having been disparaged by Australian critics. Yet this is not an unusual historical occurrence, apart from a polemic on the matter, particularly if we take Malley into account, and the later contradictions of Australian Dada, and in one sense it is the foundation of the *Musicopoematographoscope* works. Brennan's life was tragic. Setbacks in his institutional and personal life – removed from his position at the University of Sydney in 1925, the same year that his lover Violet Singer died – would mean he spent the remainder of his life in poverty. It is tempting to write this narrative of declension into the whole of Antipodal modernism itself. Doing this, the "solution" to Antipodal hopelessness seems either to *re*-historicise it into an alternate history of Antipodal avant-garde poetics, on the one hand, or *re*-globalise it into the course of transnational modernism. To resolve or solve the enigma of Brennan we can simultaneously expand contexts and localise poetic origins.

Lloyd Austin, another Brennan critic, gives an account of a curious moment perusing an exchange between Henry Davray and Mallarmé regarding Brennan. Davray is mildly affronted about a lack of capitals and full stops in an "Australian poet" he had been reading (confounding as a "Chinese puzzle"), and Davray recounts Mallarmé taking immense trouble, before replying to the Australian, trying to solve the enigmas, before protesting (to Davray) "that he had succeeded" (100). The passage, Austin says, "seemed worthy to be quoted *in extenso* for several reasons" – if nothing else "it tells us that Brennan's poetry was discussed and defended by Mallarmé himself at a *Mardi* attended by Paul Valéry" (100). Brennan's Mallarmé, and Mallarmé's defence of Brennan's difficulty at the famous Tuesday evenings, captures the most pressing question of avant-gardes in modern and modernist historiography because it is a problem concerning critical reading as much as poetic invention. Indeed in our time, Mallarmé commentary and criticism, which we want to keep in view with all this, has taken strange turns in the face of enduring questions of difficulty. On the one hand there is Mallarmé *scholarship*, which proceeds as usual, as all or most scholarship should, with its proper use of historical document and theoretical measure to produce continual revelations upon Mallarmé's life and situation in order to dispel false leads (spurious enigmas, unworthy emendations), yet on the other hand another world has opened up in philosophical treatments, like those of Jacques Ranciére, Alain Badiou and Quentin Meillassoux. In those there is less reliance upon documentary and textual methods, but their employment has struck philosophy, especially French, a veritable blow that has jolted it into entirely new conditions of thinking. It would seem impossible to resolve the two kinds of Mallarmé reading. In one sense those philosophical readings are nothing but challenges to critical reading. Critical readings of Mallarmé, that is to say, will both find itself challenged or nonplussed by this philosophical reading, while philosophical reading will occasionally draw upon the work of scholarship in order to find itself before the Void or the precipice of truth. Meillassoux, for instance, embarks upon an "unfashionable" reading by code:

> It is no longer fashionable to believe that behind Mallarmé's most opaque poems there is a hidden secret that, once revealed, would ultimately and definitively clarify their deep meaning: neither a personal (or even obscene) "little secret," nor a "great secret" drawn from the wisdom of a religion from whose resources Mallarmé took his lead. The only secret involved, we like to repeat, is that there is no secret.
>
> We can happily concede the disqualification of this type of psychoanalytic, biographical or esoteric decryption. Nevertheless, not all coding is necessarily of this type; and one need only attend to Mallarmé's writings to guess that they contain another. For there are indeed serious reasons to suppose the existence, in the case of the *Coup de dés*, of an *endogenous* code – decryptable solely by means of clues disseminated throughout the work itself – rather than an *exogenous* one, whose key would be located outside Mallarmé's writings, in the life of the poet or in some ancestral doctrine. (4–5)

Though Meillassoux's thrilling decipherment comes close to the question of music, it is a pity that code remains numerical and not also notational, metrical but not prosodical. What Meillassoux is doing throughout is what Frank Kermode called divinatory criticism (endogenous, internal, rather than exogenous, which would be revelatory), which has a history that goes back not only to Schleiermacher but to the whole German hermeneutic tradition. While it has a history, it is not historiographic. Its history is in fact closer to philosophy than Meillassoux allows: it is just as strongly there in Boeckh as Schelling and Schlegel (Hermes Trismegistus, Newton, Bloom fit into the mould too) but of course for Meillassoux it is strictly speaking philosophy conditioned by a literary masterpiece. There is no doubt that in the face of such reading the critical reading of the more recent kind can seem weak, ineffectual, ineffective even as a mode of address that we might have lost or be losing. Yet there is no use in resisting philosophical readings from the point of view of criticism. There is no use defending our reading from theirs. We have our critical modes and we think them strong, with their combinations of literary history and literary theory and their senses of the whole course of literature going into the future, and we can happily learn from the philosophical reading even though it is not ours by type or method.

Literary history gives us our kind of revelation, which must culminate in a comparison between two versions of the same poem, or, more correctly, a type and a token. The later version is also not without its riddles, though we may have to look to a different method to find them. It concerns, also, not just originals, but dates of emergence and contextual climates. It is an odd concinnity of dates that leads us from Brennan and Mallarmé to the 1980s in Australian poetry. Here we open Mallarmé to a thought from the Antipodal outside, to the uncertainty of history and historiography, and to the avant-garde discontents of the other side of an evanescent kinship. No ancestral doctrine leads the way. Rather, the enigma of the avant-garde itself seems to live within Mallarmé, the figure who comes before it all; for without Mallarmé the fount of avant-garde revelation and its divagations – Antipodal included – might never have happened.

II. *1897: Chronometries in southland*

IV
L'ère d'autorité se trouble
Lorsque, sans nul motif, on dit
De ce climat que notre double
Inconscience aprofondit,

V
Que, sol des cent iris, son site,
Ils savent s'il a, certe, été,
Ne porte pas de nom que cite
Entre tous ses fastes, l'Été.

These are two stanzas from the first version of the poem that would become "Prose, *pour des Esseintes*", and it perhaps cannot suffer any more interpretation; Lloyd Austin professes in 1963 to have studied forty commentaries on it before offering his own, in *Poetic Principles and Practice* (79). For Austin the poem is Mallarmé's most difficult, a critical mirror of projection and a critical joint effort. This reading does not add to those readings, nor to the enigmatic criticism of divination and rhetorically heightened revelatory reading, but it goes to a reading of its translation. The first curiosity is that it is a "long" poem, his last, and of course, secondarily, that it is prose (and therefore not fully a poem), but in the poetic and liturgical sense of "sequence". Austin looks at the handwritten draft of a first version and can barely make out its date of composition. It might have been 1884. Austin then goes after variant readings of the two versions (A and B), a conjectural or divinatory reading at that, and determines a good deal of *varia lectio*, but none radical. The narrative concern is largely the character of the poet and his sister. Our interest however must jump over many of these details to get to the key line under translation, but to give a clear picture of the equivalent stanzas of the second version which then gets its full title *Prose pour des Esseintes*, they ought to be set side by side:

IV	IV
The age of certainty wears thin	L'ère d'autorité se trouble
When, without reason, it is stated	Lorsque, sans nul motif, on dit
Of this southland which our twin	De ce midi que notre double
Unconsciousness has penetrated	Inconscience approfundit
V	V
That, soil of an iris bed, its site,	Que, sol des cent iris, son site,
They know if it was really born:	Ils savent s'il a bien été,
It bears no name that one could cite,	Ne porte pas de nom que cite
Sounded by Summer's golden horn.	L'or de la trompette d'Été.

A structural reading of the poem, which Austin reproduces in its entirety, leads to architectural unity on par with Meillassoux; a three-stage unity of ecstasy, silence and artifice. All three make up a kind of reading of the very poetic act itself (83). It's a reading that captures invocations of the liturgy, the Idea, in various structuralising sections: Introduction (I–II), the Narrative (Island, III–V), the Idea-Flowers (VI–VII), the Poetic Vocation (VIII–IX), the Existence of the Island (X–XII) and the Conclusion, the Poetic Ritual (XIII–XIV). All of these make for scintillating analysis, but we must confine ourselves to Austin's reading of the two stanzas that are our concern, falling within the Narrative (*a*) The Island, stanzas four and five:

> The next two quatrains are difficult. The poet pauses for a moment to consider the disturbing fact that despite its indubitable existence the island is said to be nameless. The tense here reverts to the present. The two quatrains should probably be taken as a kind of parenthetical comment by the poet who momentarily suspends his narrative in order to debate this point. The syntax is rather complicated but is coherent. The main clause is: "L'ère d'autorité se trouble ... lorsqu' on dit ... que son site ne porte pas de nom ..." The age of authority ("L'ère d'infinité" in A) is disturbed when, quite groundlessly, it is

> said of this land of the South ("midi" in B, "climat" in A), at which the poet and his sister, both as yet intellectually unaware of the nature of their ecstasy, were gazing intently, that its site, the ground where the hundred irises grew, bears no name quoted by Summer's golden trumpet. The main difficulties here are the identity of the "ère d'autorité," or "d'infinité," and what is meant by the reference to Summer. What is important is the suggestion that although this land may have no name, its existence is attested by the flowers it brings forth: the poet says of the irises: "Ils savent s'il a bien été." (87–8)

Let us break the reading before returning to its last part. The rest of the poem can be read more straightforwardly, but the disturbance of tense and time creates a suspension. It is an interlude, a break, a pause, a difficulty or parenthetical comment. To consider it apart from the poem is to isolate it (it is an island). Some coherence can still be found, but when the South or southland comes in, Austin is quite right to notice that it is said "groundlessly". It comes as a surprise. Though the land has no name it is known not directly but indirectly, by what it brings forth: its flowers, its flowering. It continues:

> Critics generally regard the "ère d'autorité" as referring to the dogmatic criticism of the time. But it is perhaps more likely, in the light of the variant in A ("L'ère d'infinité"), that this is a metaphysical question. Both "infinité" and "autorité" would fit very well the idea of religious dogma and discipline. We would then have here a reflection of Mallarmé's realisation of the illusory character of his former beliefs, and his recognition that the domain of the Ideal does not materially exist, or is not known to recorded history, is not mentioned in the annals of Summer ("fastes" in A), or by the trumpet of Fame with its golden sound. There is still much room for discussion here. (88)

The "double unconscious" evades Austin's grasp, given that it can be confined, in a less suspicious reading, to the sister: but the problem here is a dogmatic criticism, a mirror in the poem back to criticism itself, and that which *does not materially exist, or is not known to recorded history*. It is hard not to read these two together, the problem of criticism and what is not historically on record. No longer are we in an age of critical certainty (nor authority, just more trouble), in part because of the challenge of literary history. But Austin's reading gives us more "room for discussion". Do we quarrel no longer with reason? What is the meaning of the translation of *southland*? When the double unconscious gives birth in southland, what Mallarmé called in his letter to Brennan "une parentée de songe", dream-kinship, the site has a name but what is born does not, it cannot be cited. It bears no name. Born in that southland, some quantum leap from the penetrative unconscious, only *they* know "it" has been born. And what was it that was born? There is of course no suggestion, given this poem was probably composed in the early 1870s (published in 1885), that it could possibly refer to any foreknowledge of Brennan, but it certainly concerns the annals of history, perhaps the annals of an avant-garde, the "trumpet of Fame" more of course meaning what is put in and left out of history.

The problem of southland returns in the next, most confounding section, the "Existence of the Island" (X–XII). Again some strange disturbance in tense throws it back to the present. For Austin now it might be "that the present is not the poet's present, but the reader's, the future reader, who will read the poem when the poet and his sister are both dead and therefore definitively silent" (91). The distant shore again comes in and out of view, existence and inexistence:

> In B, the poet stresses the powerlessness of the shore-dwellers to attain the amplitude of the poetic vision ... But the shore-dwellers also contest the existence of the ideal realm. The young poet is amazed to hear wherever he goes the sky and the map eternally called to bear witness that this land did not exist. Even the water which divides as it goes round the island and therefore proves its existence, calls upon the sky and the map to testify that the island was never there ... The country that does not exist is the only real country, the true dwelling-place of the poet. (92–4)

There is no use trying to rehearse the long history of imaginations of the Antipodal continent, *Terra Australis*, this far forward into history, though the hemispheric understanding of the Antipodal position remains obscure in multiple senses, as we have well seen. Austin's reading in no way goes in this direction (except that the next chapter in his book concerns Brennan).[3] What the poem means, or what it shows, is the transition from unconscious ecstasy to conscious labour in poetic expression. It is a tension of temporal climates, Beauty from the Void, a poetry free of allusions (apart

---

[3] That such an account could include to Dante Alighieri is suggested by Alex Selenitsch's *Purgatorio Re-Placed* which rewrites Dante's *Purgatorio*, rendering Dante's purgatorial mountain as Australia. Selenitsch explains in an interview: '*Purgatorio* is antipodal because Dante sets it there. Mount Purgatory is the displacement of earth on the southern side of the globe, caused by the impact that made the huge pit that is Hell on the northern side' (Dale, 136).

from one to the Byzantine Empire), of tombs, cyclical return, and ultimately a haunting enigma. Curious then that Alain Badiou also finds those two stanzas Austin pauses upon exemplary in a reading from *Conditions*:

> The danger is that a truth, errant and incomplete as it may be, takes itself, in the words of the poet, as an "age of authority." It thus desires for everything to be triumphantly named, in the Summer of revelation. But the core of what is, the "southland" of our unconsciousness of being, does not and must not have a name. The site of the true, subtractively edified, or again, as the poet says, "the flower that a contour of absence has separated from every garden," itself remains in its intimate depth, subtracted from the proper name. The sky and the map reveal that this country did not exist. But it does exist, and that is what troubles authoritarian truth, for which only that which is named in the power of the generic exists. This trouble must be made more profound in safeguarding the proper and the nameless. Let us conclude, then, with the following, in which everything I've said is said as a scintillation. (128)

The two stanzas are then quoted. This is clearly not some critical or literary divination, it is rather a revelatory reading in the philosophic style; although Badiou himself does not name the country that is not named, we have above hinted at what we brutishly believe that name to be. I must confess to have read the poem having consulted no commentaries before querying these two particular stanzas, which seem to confound most readers of the poem as much as it did me. Yet whatever that nameless country is, let us say that it does exist, and it troubles the "authoritarian truth" of the early twentieth-century avant-garde. Brennan in *Musicopoematographoscope* speaks of an "inexistent desert isle" amid its extended critique of the Australian reading public. Thus we are going to extend the metaphor of the country that is inexistent to the problem of a literary historiography of the avant-gardes, and without delay, because the fact that Mallarmé troubles textual history has been or has become a question of the distortions of the avant-gardes in history. These are, most crucially, revelations about time. If there is ever an example of progressive influence, or a better passage to a full historicisation of the avant-garde and its causes, that example is Mallarmé. And yet Trevor Stark is adamant that the historiographic and methodological challenge is to provide a genealogy of the (*so-called*, as often now used off-hand) "historical avant-gardes" without simply "displacing their point of origin backward in time along a temporal axis that remains resolutely progressivist" (13). That phrase establishes, nay imposes a vector from a vanguard orientation toward a future from a singular point in the past, so to be truly historical about those first vanguards one should bring in senses of "belatedness" (via Theodor Adorno), and "anxious anticipation" of future "reconciliation" for key contradictions. It is a thought of time based upon withdrawal, deferral and a "resolutely nonlinear and indeterminate temporality" (14). The consequences of rehistoricisation extend to our arts of reading. And it could not be more momentous for our reading of Mallarmé. Stark well describes and captures the dynamism of historical time, but we add to it space. We are drawn toward the power of events, and events demand of us an object: texts. But when texts are compared – with their expanding circles of outgoing influence and effects – they appear not just in belated time, but in odd concinnity and immediacy across vast swathes of global space, perhaps something like the "twin unconsciousness" epigraphed from "Prose, *pour des Esseintes*'. Strange concinnities of space and time will be described, but they also concern those acts of responsible historiography Stark promotes. Making of Brennan a relevance that extends forwards to the '70s, '80s, '90s and the new century (decades in which avant-garde practices continue under vastly different global and geopolitical circumstances) takes us *back* to origins while contesting the very notion of an originary point. We are waging a war against the singularity of "the" avant-garde by submitting it to the transcultural and aesthetic nexus of a hemisphere without a name. The *site* from which we cite is how we now sight such temporal magnitude. It initiates what in rhetorical poststructuralism we call double reading.

None of this means we should ignore the immediate and local pressures that drove Brennan's experiment. Axel Clark's Introduction to the latter publication reveals just how much the hostile reaction to his *XXI Poems: MDCCCXCIII–MDCCCXCVII Towards the Source*, published also in 1897 by Angus and Robertson, already bearing the Mallarméan influence, convinced Brennan to turn to extreme invention. Before the *Pocket Musicopoematographoscope* one of the "Press Notices of XXI Poems" Brennan includes, defiantly, is from the *Bulletin*, which disparagingly refers to his "foam of words" – a sly comment that otherwise Brennan could interpret, following Mallarmé, as the highest praise. Clark in the Introduction records Brennan's fiercest argument:

> As it happened, Brennan had for some time been arguing with his closest friend, Dowell O'Reilly, about the proper relation between a

poet and his public. O'Reilly, who at that time was Labour[4] member for Parramatta in the New South Wales Legislative Assembly, felt that an Australian poet should write for his public: his poetry should be commercially successful, recognisably Australian, and intelligible to Australian readers. Through 1896 and 1897 the two friends argued hectically about the relation between a poet and his public, and about their own work. Though each admired the other's poetry, O'Reilly attacked Brennan for obscurity; Brennan replied firstly by defending his poetry as necessarily complex, and secondly by attacking O'Reilly for hardly writing any poetry at all. (4)

Brennan wanted most to show the "big MS" to O'Reilly. The negative and oppositional impetus here is paramount, and characteristic of avant-garde poets to come who would likewise show defiance against a literary community suspicious of its unusual elements and unwilling to embrace complexity. Brennan shows some hostility to the Australian general readership as an enterprise, hostility to the idea of a popular reader whose tastes were necessarily shaped and directed by an establishment (which could also include critics), and has decided to go all out against it. Brennan was clear about the dialectic of an Antipodal poet and the public. To the office of Australian poetry and its readership Brennan was saying precisely this: if you are offended by those works of mine that bear the influence of the European Symbolistes, let me show you an extreme example of it.

Brennan was born on 1 November 1870 in what is now virtually the centre of the modern city of Sydney, attending the University of Sydney in 1888. He would have a difficult relationship with the university throughout his life. Brennan was a prototypically urban poet in a poetic environment that already fashioned for itself a mythos of the bush. Michael Farrell in the 2015 book *Writing Australian Unsettlement* has offered a rare reading of the work as part of a longer history of "modes of invention", tracing a heritage of invention to nineteenth-century writing in the Antipodes. Farrell places it in a history of neglected texts, describing it as a poem which takes on "the diverse institutions of typography, the page, the audience, and poetry reviewing, in explicit, indecorous and avant-garde fashion" (141).

Like the Mallarméan original, the poem is, as we have stressed, a notational experiment in poetics. Brennan well understood what

---

[4] Clark spells Labour with a "u", and in the early twentieth century the spelling for the Australian Labor Party (ALP) would alternate between Labour and Labor, the latter distinguishing it from the British Labour Party.

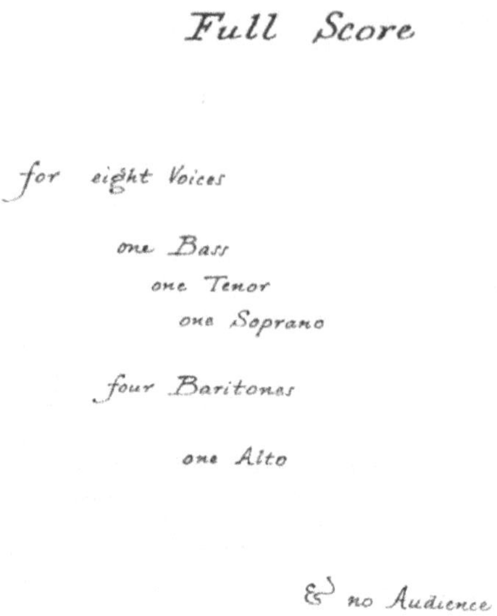

Full Score

for eight Voices

one Bass
one Tenor
one Soprano

four Baritones

one Alto

& no Audience

Figure 2.2 Christopher Brennan, second title page from *Musicopoematographoscope* (1897).

Stark called the Mallarméan use of the space of the poem *as score*. For the opening page (Figure 2.2), the "full score" for eight voices makes the work notionally choral, with an expanded role for the baritones. But it is equal parts serious and cheeky-critical. It includes its critique (reviews of Brennan), and, similar in kind to Mallarmé's *The Book*, published in French posthumously in 1957 and translated into English in 2018, there is a sense of totality to the experiment in that it presents itself as an interrogation of book form and book reception. As Clark puts it, "Brennan is replying to charges that his poetry is too obscure, too unorthodox and exotic, not sufficiently directed to his Australian public, by writing a work which is unashamedly *more* obscure, unorthodox and exotic, a work avowedly addressed to 'no Audience' at all" (5). The lack of audience is our crucial historical frame – that it is a choral joke about the Australian literary condition is only the beginning. Farrell argues that it changes our picture of Brennan's canonical verse oeuvre and unsettles perceptions of the origins of twentieth-century Australian modernism jumping forward to Malley, further noting that, quite unlike

> the hoax poetry of McAuley and Stewart's Ern Malley, it seems that the creator of the *Musicopoematographoscope* has been taken at his word: because Brennan appears not to take it seriously, neither have his critics, largely ignoring the *Musicopoematographoscope*

in favor of his normative verse oeuvre ... The innovation of the *Musicopoematographoscope* goes beyond that of a pastiche or parody of Mallarmé, though this is how it has been seen ... The *Musicopoematographoscopes* (plural, if we include the "Pocket" version) unsettle Brennan's own canon (as well as the critical canon that has constructed the creative one), changing our picture of him as a poet, of his poetry, and of the history and possibilities of practice and range in Australian poetry generally (139–140)[5]

Farrell is not so concerned with Brennan's distance or proximity from an avant-garde in a larger sense, but nonetheless we can take up Farrell's challenge through a comparable term, "invention" and its heritage, to show how historical canons are unsettled often by single works that double as insight-giving test cases. I've no doubt that Brennan's work fits into, in fact, spearheads an Australian tradition of "one-off" experiments, but there is enough seriousness in what occurs in Brennan's poetics here that can render it closer in kind to Malley.[6] It is a serious intervention into comparative styles of being modern, and as the opening page shows it is meant to be an experiment in authorship as much as readership. The effect, however, is different. That critical and self-critical doubt, sarcasm, being up front about reflexivity and the critical implications of a work, puts straight into view the counter-public attitude of Brennan's piece. He sends up his critics while at the same time questioning his own practice, and in a manner that resurfaces in Malley and others, he does so by doing history in the work, by bringing confrontative debates on modernism, Symbolism and what could be called the *theosophicalisation* of modernist poetics together in the one work. We could add too that the delay of publication renders it similar in kind to Malley, but whatever the comparison might show, we can treat it seriously as a case of inventive poetics, and there is no doubt that we are not duped to think so.

Given it was after encountering Mallarmé's work in Berlin that Brennan was inspired to become a poet and write poetry, it should

---

[5] The structure of the work, Farrell notes, is akin to assemblage. As he writes: "The *Musicopoematographoscope* is an assemblage of three works, with an attendant mini-work titled *Pocket Musicopoematographoscope*. The former three works comprise a parodic poster poem; the ostensible pastiche; and a collage of critics' quotes of Brennan's work" (140). Its careful construction in the manner of assemblage invites us to draw similarities with Malley.

[6] Or indeed an international tradition of one-off experiments done on the sly out of an oeuvre. An example, from modernism, that has gained more critical attention in recent years, is Hope Mirrlees's *Paris: A Poem*. Mirrlees would not return to these inventive visualist and spatial modes in later work.

be noted that several avant-garde poets studied herein, from Duke to Stewart, likewise found breakthroughs in poetic method after periods of travel. These are undoubtedly stories of initiation and return. Brennan corresponded with Mallarmé between 1894 and 1898, and had written on Mallarmé, with lamplights toward the Idea, monism, esoterism and neoplatonism, revelation, the unknowable and the sacristic, and it is the outwardgoing and learned curiosity of these writings that John Hawke puts on notice as a significant case of engagement with Symbolist influence. Most intriguing for the argument of this book are the temporal contradictions that came with this engagement:

> If Brennan's dating of the birth of Symbolism at 1886 is true, there is a lapse of at least a decade before the writings under discussion. The situation is in many ways analogous to what was happening in Australian art at the time: Brennan's contemporaries were painting in an Impressionist style in the 1890s, but painting in France had already moved on. (27)

Missing: that expected temporal lapse. *Musicopoematographoscope* is exceptional on the level of style and how it thinks through and against Symbolist aesthetics, but most of all, what makes it so curious is how in Antipodal terms it could so cut the (critical) lag we spoke of in the previous chapter. It was quick work, as needed for a poem to either catch up to, or be "of" its day (and not lag behind, as Antipodal Impressionists would). The fleetness of exacting and direct engagement is palpable. Note again: there was no gap between Brennan's sighting of Mallarmé's in *Cosmopolis* in May of 1897 and his reworking of it just a few months later. As Hawke suggests and as most analyses of the Malley affair show, this example seems in defiance of any sense of belatedness that seems to have haunted the Australian vanguard throughout the century and into the next. Defiance might be too strong a word, but as we know in hindsight, what happened to Brennan in 1897 happened to the avant-garde: Mallarmé's influence would pave the way for its various movements. Brennan's other verse also comes into consideration here, but put side by side, there are continuities between that verse and the 1897 experiment. If Brennan had realised, as Hawke suggests, the problem of belatedness, there is some strange sense that the experiment was a way of getting ahead of history, perhaps intervening in the dynamics of time and history, preventing belatedness by being on the ball in the vanishing present in some way that could flesh it out, or thicken it on either end *into* an expanded present. The content of the poem carries these concepts. Its commentary quality is perhaps most similar in tone to Harry Hooton (Chapter 3), and like Hooton it is replete with temporal reflection; upon the disjointed nature of historical time, novelty, belatedness, timeliness and untimeliness (Figure 2.3).

Not "giving a tinker's damn" for public response was the strategy that the avant-garde would have to take by necessity, a level of scorn worthy of G. Ribemont-Dessaignes's 1920 Dada manifesto to the public. This first part of the longer clause tends to play the same mighty role as "A throw of the dice" in the through-lining of its majesty, but of course as a sarcastic line in Australian slang – or as it appears across several pages "I DON'T GIVE IN SPITE OF MY CHARITABLE DISPOSITION ... A TINKER'S ... DAMN ... FOR ... THE ... PUBLIC ... *and* ... THEY RETURN ... THE COMPLIMENT"[7] ("the" and "public" appearing across two pages opposite each other) – we are tempted to read it simply as reactive rather than philosophical searching (that, we maintain, is also true). But the despair is palpable: the day may never come; an avant-garde procrastinates, its age has not been appointed by History. The text is graphically slanted both ways. "THIS TIME IS AGHOST" (which one first hears as "aghast"), and likely because of that, if "you're always late" (as this poem was not), what appears would find not only no audience but no place in history, taken as it were from a "heavily foxed" text, "blotched" with age, as Clark puts it in his Introduction (5). Clark too seems to know something is up with the timing of it all. Even where we might find ourselves more chronometrically misaligned, and even if to say this is to turn up late to the deliberation, there is a sense in Brennan's framework that the zeal for the conceptual and the enframing of its paradigms as sheer oddity contains a streak of sarcasm more than a dose of irony, and that like the later Malley affair, and true to an avant-garde "larrikinesque" attitude, the work was a bit of a trick, aware of its status-to-be as historical document, one whose notational elements demand different, perhaps even graphoanalytic or graphological readings. The trick as it were was to keep bringing up time in ways that would both

---

[7] Clark adds in the Introduction that though this is the basic text, "Against this basic text subordinate words are balanced like notes in musical harmony" (5). Though Clark might have added that the unification of notes into harmony requires the further distinction of harmony against moments of dissonance. This is a common problem with musical analogies to poetry, something Northrop Frye well knew, in that more often than not the critical reader assumes the main relation between music and poetry is one of harmony, whereas its closest analog is in fact the interplay of something like harmony *and* something like dissonance in the prosodic field of the poem.

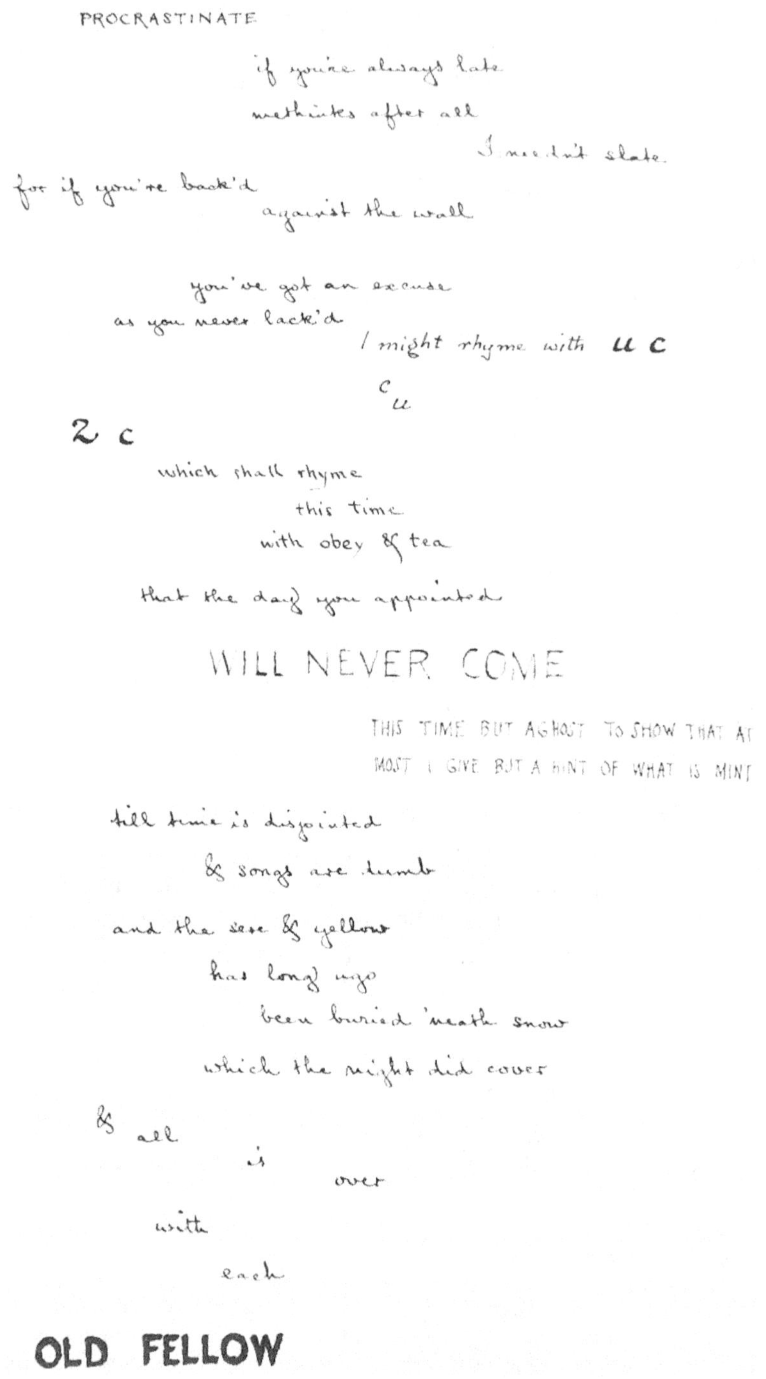

PROCRASTINATE

if you're always late
methinks after all
I needn't slate.
for if you're back'd
against the wall

you've got an excuse
as you never lack'd
I might rhyme with U C
C
U
2 C
which shall rhyme
this time
with obey & tea
that the day you appointed

WILL NEVER COME

THIS TIME BUT AGHOST TO SHOW THAT AT
MOST I GIVE BUT A HINT OF WHAT IS MINT

till time is disjointed
& songs are dumb
and the sere & yellow
has long ago
been buried 'neath snow
which the night did cover
& all
is
over
with
each

OLD FELLOW

Figure 2.3 Christopher Brennan, last interior page of *Musicopoematographoscope* (1897).

astonish and confound future readers. What are we to make of the critical *discussion* of rhyme in the above passage (itself an aporia to its onward drift)? Surely "till time is disjointed / & songs are dumb" (in the future, we are "2 c"), as the bibliotic and graphic distortions certainly are, will be heard in at least two different ways. It is, of course, a chronometric, as well as reflexive discussion, cryptically embedded. To take it historically, we can subject these historical meanings to scrutiny on several levels. Brennan's masterwork seems in so many ways an impossible historical oddity, and given how long it took for it to come to light and enter critical debates, it remains a "chronometric" outlier in Australian modernist or avant-garde poetics. And yet chronometrics, as I want to call it, is capable of taking the sheer consequence of parallel appearances (a consequence of exact dates), into the field of critical readership. It is "critical" in the deepest sense because those demanding outliers that get signposted as halting progress or severely belated rip-offs (avant-garde manqué) have come to restructure our debates. For as Farrell shows, the history of poetic invention in Australia doesn't begin with Brennan. The history of "unsettled" forms, inventive forms, is a history that can be traced back to the nineteenth century in examples like Ned Kelly's *Jerilderie Letter*. Invention also implies reinvention on the level of form. For this we could include works like A. D. Hope's *Dunciad Minor: An Heroick Poem* (published 1970) or Justin Clemens's *Mundiad* (in several volumes since 2004), mock works, or self-conscious "antipodalisations" of received forms, "reprisals", rather than hoaxes *per se*. I therefore have permitted some fluidity with the phrase "languages of invention" in a way that serves a historical purpose, no less. Rather than making an absolute claim to "the new" we are stressing the rhetoricity of newness.[8] Permit then a triple-thesis for the inventions or reinventions of *Musicopoematographoscope*?

1. The fuller literalisation of the musico-poetic analogy, the bringing down-to-earth of the analogy to a fuller score while in no sense removing it from prosodic bases, nor subtracting it from the symbols of Number and Siren, or encoding and encryption, nor

---

[8] The phrase "languages of invention" has been used by Hyejin Youn, Deborah Strumsky, Luis M. A. Bettencourt and José Lobo in an article entitled "Invention as a Combinatorial Process: Evidence from US Patents". It argues that invention involves refinements and combinations of existing technologies, in US patents, rather than the creation of new building blocks. In a more familiar way, Loy D. Martin uses the phrase "literary invention", and I would like to think the phrase can be taken in both literary and nonliterary senses, particularly in its use outside the Humanities.

relinquishing riddle and its opposite in revelation. Retaining the structure of a broken clause by having two separate books making up the larger work, it moves the poetic line onto the larger system of a choral-orchestral score in a serious way that, while still analogous in the field of the poem, presents a different type of notationality to poetic prosody. The full score therefore means also a "free use of counterpoint" which can mean nothing more and nothing less than the freer use of the musical analogy – one of the "many improvements" Brennan makes to the Mallarmé original, as stated on the title page. Evidence for this analogy at work is the splitting of the page into up to three registers, opening the vertical and horizontal movement of the text in a way more pronounced than Mallarmé, and setting up a "counter"—"point" – contrasting prosodies simultaneously operating and countering one another. For instance, "THE . . . PUBLIC" divides across pages 12 and 13, as one of several instances where one reads not only the diagonally down and left to right but simultaneously parallel (down) *and* left to right, as the multiple systems of an orchestral or choral, rather than single-system, score, but within this, one can see how the opening of registers sets parts against one another. More precisely, this is to say that the single unit, for Brennan, is not the two-page spread, left to right, but the *simultaneity* of a two-page spread going down vertically at the same time as horizontally, sometimes even within the registers of a single page. The chorastic realisation of the score is incipient in Mallarmé but more pronounced in Brennan. Rather than a flowing back-and-forth between the pages, it is also a channelling within the page.

2. The detechnologisation of the word through a contradictory scoping (the "-scope" of telescope, the clarifying instrument, machine, in short technology of writing) and simultaneous presentation of some "regression" to the graphological: handwritten notation. It is in this sense a pre-historicisation of the avant-garde, a scoping, a vision of it. Where Mallarmé anticipates the typographic explosion of the Dada avant-garde letter, Brennan sees it back, so to speak (a visionary move *in reverse*) to the time without typeface, exposing its status as experiment. It seeks a forward and backward movement in time. Brennan therefore uses various different graphological techniques of his own, writ by hand, including forward and backward slanted cursive, serif and sans-serif fonts (one Celtic). It is in part a Celtification and colouration of its field of reference, with figures like Ollamh, or sections like:

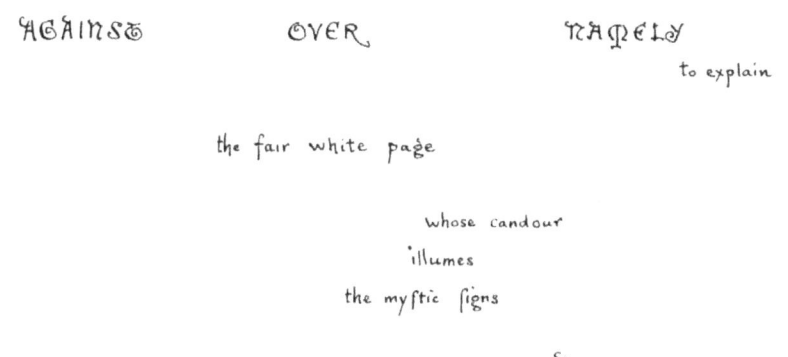

Figure 2.4 Christopher Brennan, handwritten Celtic font; "the fair white page", from *Musicopoematographoscope* (1897).

Perhaps the variable slant or slope of the text is a realisation of what Walter Benjamin recognised in Mallarmé as the construction with, and alongside, the economics of the present that had come crashing down upon his otherwise traditional, crystalline structures; that is, the slow *horizontalisation* of the Book. In the short piece "Attested Auditor of Books":

> Now every thing indicates that the book in this traditional form is nearing its end. Mallarmé, who in the crystalline structure of his manifestly traditionalist writing saw the true image of what was to come, was in the *Coup de dés* the first to incorporate the graphic tensions of the advertisement in the printed page. The typographic experiments later undertaken by the Dadaists stemmed, it is true, not from constructive principles but from the precise nervous reactions of these literati, and were therefore far less enduring than Mallarmé's, which grew out of the inner nature of his style. But for this very reason they show the contemporary relevance of what Mallarmé, monadically, in his hermetic room, had discovered through a preestablished harmony with all the decisive events of our times in economics, technology, and public life. Script—having found, in the book, a refuge in which it can lead an autonomous existence—is pitilessly dragged out into the street by advertisements and subjected to the brutal heteronomies of economic chaos. This is the hard schooling of its new form. If centuries ago it began gradually to lie down, passing from the upright inscription to the manuscript resting on sloping desks before finally taking itself to bed in the printed book, it now begins just as slowly to rise again from the ground. The newspaper is read more in the vertical than in the horizontal plane, while film and advertisement force the

printed word entirely into the dictatorial perpendicular. (*One-Way Street*, 42–3)

Slanting and sloping back and forth across the page for Brennan moves the angling of the book up and down its scales, from its Press Notices and title pages to its traditional station on the flat desk as a book-text. The meaning of its angling is within all these metaphoric circles, and if the "nervous reactions" of the Dada literati is the later consequence of this move against constructivism, Brennan's move anticipates this; perhaps it is more Dada than Mallarmé in this respect. The size of the 1981 edition is enormous (close to A5 in our measurement), and it is, as the title page says, from its original intention, a poem and a Poster; more "shamelessly" an advertisement.

3. Its unity with Mallarmé rests finally with its sense of time and contemporaneity. Even through its irony, sarcasm, jest and occasional mocking tonality, the seriousness of it remains its refusal to move in line with the expectations of commerce and the "public" while remaining committed to a philo-poetic course, to poetic thinking. In the last moments of the *Pocket Musicopoematographoscope*, a haunting evocation of history, belatedness, anticipation and invention embodies the contradictions of the pre-avant-garde, and in this moment we witness Brennan setting up the dialectic of wit and negativity that informs both the Antipodal avant-garde and the historical aftershocks of Mallarméan influence in Western modernity, literary theory and twentieth-century philosophy. That Brennan does it immediately is "on purpose" and an accident – its contemporaneity is an anticipatory critique of Antipodal belatedness.

III. *2005, 1981: From Chance to Fluke*

Mallarmé would continue to fascinate Antipodal poets well after Brennan. It would have been a prime case of influence if it was not a fluke, an accident, a throw of the dice, another odd historical coincidence to add to the parts of our score: the contemporary experimental poet and visualist Chris Edwards, in 2004, writes what he calls "mistranslation" of Mallarmé, called *A Fluke: A Mistranslation of Stéphane Mallarmé's 'Un Coup De Dés...' With Parallel French Pretext*, which, he has said, was composed independently of *Musicopoematographoscope*. It's a remarkable "fluke" because, as Edwards claims, he did not yet know about Brennan's 1897 version before composing his own. First published as a small-press production from the town of Thirroul, south of Sydney (Monogene), it then finds its way to *Jacket* number 29 (April 2006), before ending up in a later collection *People of Earth* under the restored title "A FLUKE? [N]EVER!" John Tranter sold *Jacket* to the University of Pennsylvania after its fortieth issue in 2010, whereupon it was managed by the Kelly Writer's House. Edwards's poem thus appears in the Australian phase of *Jacket*, before Tranter brokered its trans-Pacific crossing. "Fluke" is given full meaning as a homonym; it can mean a whale's tale, the tail end of an anchor, a fish, a flatworm or, in a more laconically "Australian" sense, a stroke of luck; thus the Antipodeanisation of Mallarméan chance. Edwards follows the spacing of the Mallarmé original, homophonically translating "LE HASARD" into "BIO-HAZARD" and "CE SERAIR" into "QUE SERA", and so on (Figure 2.5). In a piece on *A Fluke*, Kate Fagan returns to the Brennanist roots of the mistranslation, placing Edwards's Brennan alongside Brennan's Mallarmé in a historical coincidence with Derrida:

> Brennan identified with Mallarmé as a serious intellectual whose writings were undertaken literally avant-garde, in advance of public watch on the limits of ontology and meaning. In the same year that Brennan's *Musicopoematographoscope* finally appeared in print, Jacques Derrida published in *Dissemination* an extensive reading of Mallarmé's short prose work "Mimique." Reading through Mallarmé's mime, the silent *comedie noir* icon of French theatre, Derrida argues for a diacritical philosophy of language in which the "blanks" of a page give meaning to the letters inscribed upon it, since they delineate the borders of every sign and confer "a certain inexhaustibility" or excess of potential energy to the glyphs and morphemes of written language. (Fagan)

Barbara Johnson's English translation of *Dissemination*, published in 1981, is a key historical point in the transport of Derridean theory to the Anglosphere, and as Johnson says, the mimicking, or acting out of spacing is a counterpoint to *Un Coup de Dés* in the section Derrida calls "The Double Session'. Johnson calls these moves "provocative":

> 3. *A Practice of spacing*. One of the first things one notices about "The Double Session" is its provocative use of typographic spacing. From the insertion of *Mimique* into an L-shaped quotation from Plato to the quotations in boxes, the passages from *Un Coup de dés* and

> *Le Livre*, the reproduction of Mallarme's handwriting, and the pages bottom-heavy with footnotes, it is clear that an effort is being made to call the reader's attention to the syntactical function of spacing in the act of reading. Through such supplementary syntactical effects, Derrida duplicates and analyzes the ways in which Mallarme's texts mime their own articulation, include their own blank spaces among their referents, and deploy themselves consistently with one textual fold too many or too few to be accounted for by a reading that would seek only the text's "message" or "meaning." (xxviii)

That it is provocative also means it is analysis, a calling-attention-to. Derrida's reading of *Un Coup de Dés* happens in the section "wriTing, encAsIng, screeNing", as a re-arrangement of Mallarmé's setting (320–1). As a meditation on the practice of poetic spacing this section is perhaps only surpassed by *Glas*. Edwards's *Fluke* therefore comes at a point of convergence of multiple temporal and theoretical markers, if not indeed coincidences, of this history. We will attend more to these eventual coincidences as they come. But Fagan's commentary upon it follows this with historical and indeed historicist placing, by situating Edwards in either the early twentieth-century avant-garde or post-avant-gardes, with all the complexities of coloniality and modernism (or colonial modernism) in stark relief. Brennan's description of Mallarmé

> as a "Hieratico-byzantaegyptic-Obscurantist" hints at a specialised reading of Mallarmé's centrality to the emergence of poetic Symbolism, while its maverick flamboyance—or perhaps its feral nature—suggests a deeper unease about the legitimacy of antipodean takes on cultural internationalism. There is a finely nuanced critique to unwrap here about late nineteenth and early twentieth century colonial Australia on the cusp of modernism, and the larger-than-life or monstrous artistic objects generated over subsequent decades by that tension—including for example the poems of Ern Malley, and more perversely, the Jindyworobak Movement. For now, I simply want to propose that "innovation" in non-Indigenous Australian poetry is marked historically by strong international identifications and sporadic refusals, and to observe that the twentieth century manifestations of these dialogues are strikingly evident in the avant-garde (or post-avant-garde) alignments of Chris Edwards' poetry. (Fagan)

We may add that 1981 is also the year Eddie Koiko Mabo addressed the Land Rights Conference in a landmark moment in Land Rights history. Though convergences upon 1981 are accumulating, the immediate impact of Edwards's poetics comes out of a longer

Antipodean heritage that would spurn "monstrous artistic objects" generated by the tension of a barred avant-garde, or with greater critical nuance, an avant-garde on the cusp and wedged between times and hemispheric spacing – between colonial and modern versemaking, between the non-Indigenous Antipodal intellectual and cultural internationalism. Ern Malley and the Jindyworobaks, subjects of our next chapter, embody this tension (as does the polymorphous comedic perverse of Barry Humphries). These produce the dialectics and the tension that lays the foundation for the humour of the mistranslation. Mistranslation, as historical work, doesn't escape history. It captures it as it remakes it. We see this in another amusing mistranslation of *Un Coup de Dés* by John Tranter, from 2006, the same year as Edwards, "Desmond's Coupé".[9] It has lines like these:

> A dance, in the garage full of vague parables,
> and which reality is dissolved?
> Except where the altitude peters out
> and an Aussie's loins are right on.
>
> A few swans, a vector dealer and
> a horse of interest —
> and a quantity of signals in general sell on,
> tell obliquities, part Elle's declivities —
> the furs, poems, see what theatre
> a septuagenarian from the far north of Australia
> see in the stars — freezing, oblique and full of suet —
> pass the aunt —
> a killer from Noumea —
> and this vacant surface is superior
> to any successive hurt.
>   (*Distant Voices*, 19)

It's a poetry of the humour of humour, in a tone more wry than Edwards's version, though Edwards can be just as wry, or dry.[10] Australia, wherever it is referenced, takes its place as part of a microscopic registering of the larrikin voice that signals both the opening of distance and the funny collapse of it as proximities to the original

---

[9] In his thesis for his Doctorate of Creative Arts, *Distant Voices*, Tranter describes how Edwards's poem predated Tranter's, and Edwards encouraged Tranter to finish his own homophonic translation of the poem "as a kind of friendly rival to his own" (117–18). "Desmond's Coupé" was first published in 2006, in *Rhizome*, a journal dedicated to postgraduate research at the University of Wollongong, where Tranter completed his Doctorate. The poem is included in his thesis.

[10] I have witnessed first-hand several readings by Edwards of mistranslations that had the audience in stitches.

come in and out of audibility. There lies the humour, but I don't hear it from the outside, or not fully, so I hear it partially. We can make of it specialised reading too: the aspect of "play" in Edwards is in a way both subject to an analysis of a Derridean kind and, historically, theories of the avant-garde. The Antipodal dialectic of the avant-garde is exposed perhaps in further senses of history, from Hegel, and Schelling, that posit history as a principle of freedom. That *Dissemination* could present here a positive sense of freedom in analytic play leads us to the negative freedom also of Marcuse's reading of Mallarmé in "A Note on Dialectic" (1960) presenting a historical dialectic which, as Fagan says of dissemination's Mallarmé, moves also to the "limits" of ontology, yet in Marcuse the move from ontology to history, from dialectical analysis to historical analysis, is the liberation of negation in philosophical thought: "Reason is the negation of the negative." Therein comes the question of Mallarmé and the question of his peculiar relation to the avant-gardes:

> The liberating function of negation in philosophical thought depends upon the recognition that the negation is a positive act: that-which-is *repels* that which is-not and, in doing so, repels its own real possibilities. Consequently, to express and define that-which-is on its own terms is to distort and falsify reality. Reality is other and more than that codified in the logic and language of facts. Here is the inner link between dialectical thought and the effort of avant-garde literature: the effort to break the power of facts over the word, and to speak a language which is not the language of those who establish, enforce and benefit from the facts. As the power of the given facts tend to become totalitarian, to absorb all opposition and to define the entire universe of discourse, the effort to speak the language of contradiction appears increasingly irrational, obscure, artificial. The question is not that of a direct or indirect influence of Hegel on the genuine avant-garde, though this is evident in Mallarmé and Villiers de l'Isle-Adam, in surrealism, in Brecht. Dialectic and poetic language meet, rather, on common ground. (Marcuse)

Doing then a reading of Mallarmé's common search for an authentic language means the language of negation is a "Great Refusal to accept the rules of a game in which the dice are loaded", and the greater part of truth is not that which is present but that which is absent. Badiou would find in Mallarmé a void out of which philosophy is challenged to truth. For Marcuse, theory, more than philosophy, prepares the ground of Reason and action, against the oppressive power of facts. It becomes a question of nonpolitical language: it is quite often the case that poetry that encases within itself a politically overt language ceases to be political. The avant-garde avoids this at all costs: the politics of avant-garde language is not its strains of pious or positive agreement with the status quo, but rather the dialectical and reasonable destruction of unfreedom. It is evident how the long legacy of Mallarmé's *Un Coup de Dés* in the Antipodes extends the language of contradiction in this direction; looking obscurity in the face, refusing the establishment of the facts of an avant-garde; a retaining or restitution of an avant-garde between the dialectic and poetic language. Brennan's and later Edwards's games find what is "awkward in the original" and further show that a fact is a fluke, rules are out, and "sporadic refusals" are in.

IV. *Facts of the Catalogue: 1975, 1981*

That Brennan's reinvention of Mallarmé became a critique of Antipodean literature of that period – and its reading publics – might ascend further to the fact that it could become, at more levels of remove, the foundation for *subsequent* critiques of Antipodean literature as canonical tradition. If we go by the negative, looking at what Antipodal literature was not, or what it refused, does this help us toward a determination of what it was? What is an Antipodal reading public? What did it mean for Brennan to turn his back on the reading public (apart from failure, later despair)? Is the depopularisation of one's writing, producing *deliberate obscurity*, an innately avant-garde gesture? Is it an inevitability for a poet confronted with a critical philistinism in a culture not yet used to philo-poetic invention? Is Brennan not launching polemics on two fronts: against Australian literature on the one hand, and challenging the avant-garde on the other, thereby writing himself into a kind of "no man's land" of the literary maverick who resists everything? And can there be an avant-garde without a historical sense of the "Group"? Are these coincidences not also consequences? Does this all then evolve into a dialectic of avant-garde historical change?

These are necessary questions, but to get a better sense of them we will scale it back a little – in an age less critical and more networked – by looking at the period into which Brennan's experiment appeared: the 1980s. The full score of history, we are told, are the facts that constitute the catalogue. The notion that there is no history without a critical revelation is troubling because if we accept that revelation is taken from the catalogue, we must also accept that the catalogue is giving us the *there* of things, the *facthood* of the irrational, obscure

CERTAINLY

a
disused
lair

LONE NUMBER

EXI(S)T STILL
other than as an hallucination outré going gone

COMMENCE STILL AND CEASE STILL
sour when demented up close a lot like Quasimodo
awful
park rangers rapidly quelled the profusion a rarity
SHIPWRECK STILL

the evident sum of improper poking
ELIMINATE STILL

QUE SERA

a pure   no

more or less
indifferently equals

BIO-HAZARD

Chaste
plumage
rhythmic suspension of the sinister
enslavement
awkward in the original
whose doubts and nagging susurrations justify the crime
fleeting
parallelised neutralities identify as the gaffe

Figure 2.5 Chris Edwards, from *A Fluke* (2004), presented lengthways to preserve spacing.

or artificial that seems to obscure the totalitarian sense of fact itself. Still the name of the bounded lot of documents is total in our word, catalogue. But in production, and indeed dissemination, and thereafter the *cataloguing* of experimental forms, one of those areas most vital to literary history at work, those very attempts to collate, anthologise, make manifest and collectively argue for an avant-garde poetics, taking a significant place in twentieth-century Antipodal poetry, allow us to claim that things are missing. It would not be until the late twentieth and twenty-first centuries that experimental, and explicitly avant-garde anthologisation took place in Australian literature. The anthologisers could make such claims. Equally parts provocative as defensive, aware indeed of the need to locate historical and social context, and issuing aesthetic and sometimes poetics-based justifications for the manifesting of experimental writing alongside (a) politics, anthologisers of Antipodal avant-garde poetry did not simply cast aside the question of the relation between the avant-garde and institutions or establishment circles: rather they are very concerned about them, either rejecting them forthright, making pleas for inclusion within them, pleas for the transformation of those spheres, or pleas for the interactivity of poetics and politics.

In 1975 *Mother I'm Rooted: An Anthology of Australian Women Poets* was published by Outback Press, and its editor Kate Jennings recounts in the introduction how it "metamorphosed into a political statement" about the position of women in Australia, and yet crucially "became, unabashedly, on my part, an attempt to question the standards of what is supposed to be good and bad poetry in the prevailing literary hegemony". In the year of the Bicentennial celebrations, 1988, another experimental anthology would emerge, bearing the title *Telling Ways: Australian Women's Experimental Writing*, edited by Anna Couani and Sneja Gunew. Couani in her introductory remarks claims experimental women's writing is "synonymous" with small press (9), and catalogues small press "infrastructure", meaning small presses, feminist "small mags", bookshops, workshops and the like (12–14). Gunew in her introduction brings forth the contradiction of literary ambiguity in experimental (women's) writing and the political imperative, stressing that perhaps by its very nature

> explicitly experimental writing does not yet proliferate in writing produced by women, at least in the English-speaking world. Experimental writing is dedicated to changing the ways which texts generate meanings, to transforming the signifying process itself. This enterprise is obviously and intrinsically open to misinterpretation.

 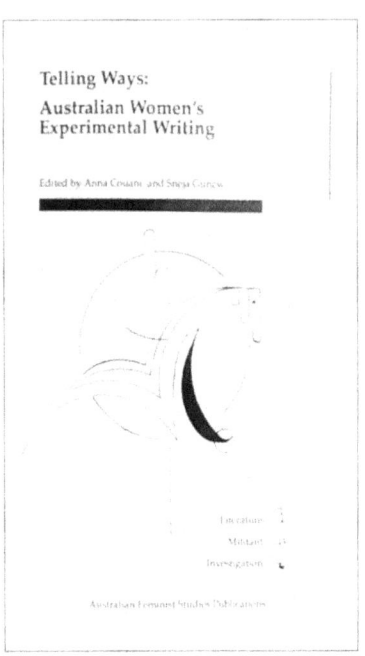

Figure 2.6 Anna Couani and Sneja Gunew, eds, *Telling Ways* (1988), showing cover and title page featuring a visual poem by Thalia.

> It is founded on ambiguity, irony, contradiction, shifting positions (including the inscription of gender) in writing and reading. For writing which offers itself as part of a political movement for change, this is dangerous territory. Political programs eschew ambiguity. ("Women's Experimental Writing", 6)

To answer the contradiction between form and politics put forth by Gunew, the cover and frontispiece feature a visual piece by the Melbourne-based visual poet Thalia, from a series that culminated in the 2015 volume *A Loose Thread*. It uses Isaac Pitman's phonetic markers for the words "Literature", "Militant" and "Investigation" (Figure 2.6).

Dada poetry would arrive in Australia in the 1970s, though it appeared in the comedic body of Barry Humphries two decades before (of this more in a later chapter), and it was in the 1970s that Thalia began writing. A significant figure in this enterprise was Jas H. Duke, the topic of Chapter 4, through an origin story told largely by Duke's peers. There would be, to use his neologism, "Dadaustralia". Duke would involve himself with the Melbourne-based Collective Effort Press, and their publication of *Missing Forms*, read here alongside

Figure 2.7 Collective Effort production *Missing Forms* (1981); two variant covers for the anthology, featuring visual works by Jas H. Duke.

Telling Ways, confirms that in the 1980s an avant-garde of discernible proportions, and a degree of self-consciousness, had emerged.[11] The year 1981 was chronometrically confounding, a year which would again misalign our critical and historical expectations, for as if by some quantum leap, Brennan's 1897 anomaly would join *Missing Forms* in starting the decade off on a vanguard footing (Figure 2.7).

Ingeniously, in neo-Dadaist manner, on several alternative covers by Duke the names of the featured poets are woven across the cover in a variety of fonts. The pieces within were jointly catalogued by Peter Murphy, Π.O., Alex Selenitsch, Thalia, Duke, Tony Figallo and Sweeney Reed, and the volume styles itself as a manifesto for avant-garde poetry and poets. "<u>WE DO EXIST</u>", so blasts the "Forward!" (as the editors decided to call it), and that blast of utterance, comparable to Harry Hooton's "I am alive", investigated in the next chapter, demands something fundamentally subjective: simply an insistence upon the existence of an Antipodal vanguard. This is one of several moments that the Antipodal avant-garde went

---

[11] I thank Hazel Smith for gifting me a copy of *Missing Forms* and for illuminating some of these concepts for me in conversation.

from being a programme detectable *in reverse* from its detractors (from those who resisted it, or simply in the realm of influence) to subjective utterance, a full-scale announcement of vanguardist intent. The "Forward!" is at pains to point out the difficulty in financing and then producing an anthology of this kind, sharing Couani's concern for production. "Missing forms" are presented as historically neglected, forms omitted from the catalogue, but also stubborn forms, as the anarchist Greek-Australian poet Π.O. would note. Although planning began for the anthology in 1975, its origins are in the earlier magazines *Fizrot*, *Born to Concrete* and *925*. In an Australian Broadcasting Commission radio presentation "9-2-5: the poetry of work", Mike Ladd recounts:

> Digging back through my own collection of Australian poetry magazines from the 70s and 80s I find a clutch of 925s. They had a great handmade look, put together before PCs when choice of font was determined by whatever your manual typewriter came with. The covers could have been designed by Malevich or one of the other Russian Constructivists. Next to the poets' names was always what job they did. Π.O., draughtsman. Jeltje, clerk ... As well as poetry, there were items from the press ... concrete poetry by Jas H. Duke, Π.O., and others ... 925 came out of a time of high unemployment in Australia, and the magazine was proudly left-wing. It was us and them. (6:05–6:55)

Published from 1978 to 1983, *925* would come to feature as avant-garde commonplace, if now an archival curiosity, comparable to the twelve issues of *291* edited by Alfred Stieglitz (1915–16) and the nineteen issues of *391*, edited by Francis Picabia (1917–24), the former being known as bringing concrete poetics to North America. In that sense *925* would be something of an adjourned reversioning of vanguard interchange across time and space, pitching unambiguously a radical poetics *in* politics, localist and anti-nationalist.[12] If *925* got to the insubordinate core of poetic writing as labouring against the conservative constitution of Australian poetry and an Australian nation, the aims of *Missing Forms* were equally insurrectionary. To again use their language, the purpose of *Missing Forms* was none other than "TO PREPARE THE GROUND FOR ANOTHER WAVE OF POETS AND ARTISTS".[13] Yet still it is

---

[12] *925* references the eight-hour working day, achieved nationally in the 1920s but the result of union strikes and agitation from the 1850s.

[13] When the ABC broadcast readings from *925* poets in 1981 they censored Duke's reading of "Shit Poem". Avant-garde subversion, vulgarity or profanity, which plays

hard to read *Missing Forms* so readily now, particularly its content, in an anticipatory light, given the way I have been trying to proceed. Those who engaged visual forms, some of whom appear in this anthology, like Duke, Thalia, Π. O. and Alex Selenitsch, and who do not, like Amanda Stewart, Pete Spence, Lê Văn Tài and Catherine Vidler, and the continuing tradition of visualist poetics in Australia, may or may not be linked to the insurrectionary strivings of *Missing Forms*. The question appears in discussions of Dada Paris and Dada New York and avant-gardes generally construed: what role its key members had in granting authority to themselves and their works, above and over the scholarly canonisation of their works. How they projected themselves into the future as a group, a generation or as part of a continuous tradition like an avant-garde, how their poetics "prepared ground", suggests a synchronic historicity because (though it would show us just how much marginal practices become cultural forms quaking to or against faultlines from multiple, and other, cultural centres) for the time being we actually know more about where these forms emerged than where they ended up, or who they influenced. Poems included in *Missing Forms* are documents in themselves of a generation of avant-garde poets pushing the limits of form, frame and poeticity. Take the "Sonnet" series by Selenitsch (Figure 2.3).

The utter conceptual 2.0 character of this work, in the manner of artist Marcel Broodthaers's 1969 reworking of *Un Coup de Dés*, where Broodthaers less erases as blacks over, or in effect "censors" the entire thing to give us some underlying geometric shape or ontic insight, manifests less as cryptic puzzle as solution (=).[14] The sonnet's octave (if we should call it that) forms two blocks, followed by the sestet custom-fit as two tercet-triangles such that you can see, that you only see, the sonnet turn. What's missing? Not so much forms as, if the shapes of the lines didn't already demonstrate it, words. But it isn't that lack of words that remains the puzzle of the work. The reader is given a solution. The solution seems to be something like

---

a significant role in the Antipodal avant-gardes (in Ania Walwicz, who was born in Communist Poland, and also the poetry of Ouyang Yu, or the paintings of Juan Davila), can be read in several ways. In this historical period it could push the limits of liberal-democratic tolerance. Such are the complexities of subversive intent when measured against contrastive social systems in the late twentieth-century avant-gardes. In the chapter on Walwicz I consider the importance not only of cultural background and heritage in modern Australia, after it had adopted multiculturalism as policy in the 1970s, but also the role of migrant experience of a social system other than that to which they were originally accustomed.

[14] It is worth noting that the 1975 chapbook does not include the equals sign.

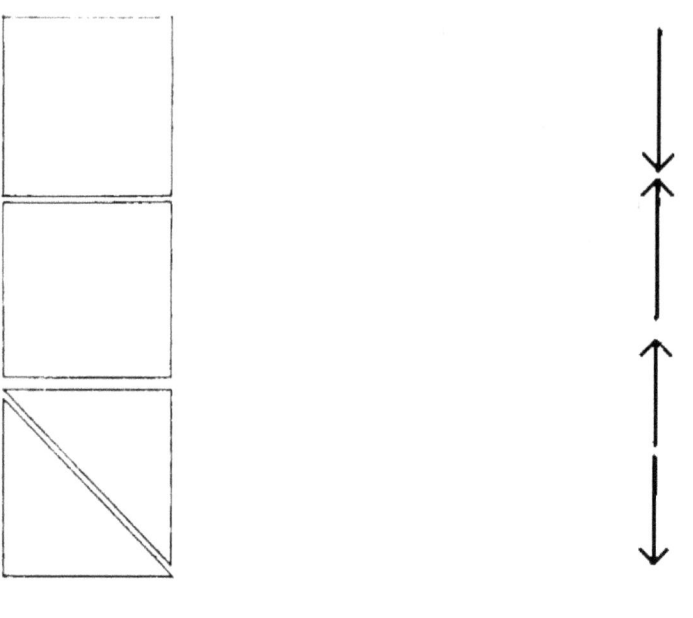

Figure 2.8 Alex Selenitsch, "Sonnet 1974/81" (left, as it appears in *Missing Forms*), and a page from the chapbook Sonnets (1975, right; this chapbook includes a version of the image on left).

this: we are not so sure about forms; we are not yet certain the name of a form equates to the transmission of its *temporal* characteristics. In that one sense it is like a musical score, a notational poetics, a reduction. In the arrows version we see different vectors; the octave "quatrains" are bound together, while the "sestets" are pointing out. These are traditional forms redrawn within another tradition. The verbicovisual vectors and visual planes of these and like works draw into the discussion key players and quiet forces outside the usual running of things, bringing to the fore new poetic geometries, other modes of conceptual questioning, and alternative understandings of what an avant-garde heritage did for the material and formal aspects of verbal art. Lines and shapes of transmission – placed in the context of the missing form(s) – are scaled up to relations of influence and trajectory in Australian poetics.

At core we have to think the line anew. What does it mean, or, from the above, what did it mean to be a concrete poet in Australia, to be working through missing forms? The literary-historical quandary is discomforting again because the chronometry seems botched; time frozen before an avant-garde past without an avant-garde future. The title "Missing Forms" is no accident if one thinks how historically what goes missing is that which gets shunted aside, what time lays off.[15] There is very little by way of direct link between the singularity of Brennan's work and the flourishing of visual poetry in the 1970s, except that the central anthology to emerge from a collocation of visual practices, *Missing Forms*, would construct a certain belatedness whose, for lack of a better word, *chronometricities*, might shed light on parallel strands, like appearances. Despite its obscurity, *Missing Forms* is a kind of "chrestomathy", an anthology of developing forms, doing the kind of historical work we have been looking for. It catalogues, in lines and shapes, the types of forms that might not have appeared in history if the literary avant-garde did not speak. If interventions of this kind reshape history and cast doubt on our image of time, such doubt was no less palpable a century earlier.

V. *27 July 1897 . . . 9 September 1898*

Dead in Valvins. D. M. *To the spirits of the dead*. Brennan was deeply moved by Mallarmé's death. In Brennan's long sequence *Poems 1913*, comprising 105 poems in total in five parts, Part II "The Forest of Night" (1898–1902) begins with this dedicatory forepiece, all in italics:

D. M.
STÉPHANE MALLARMÉ
DEAD IN VALVINS
9th September 1898

31 *Red autumn in Valvins around thy bed*
    was watchful flame or yet thy spirit induced
    might vanish away in magic gold diffused
    and kingdom o'er the dreaming forest shed.

---

[15] It is worth noting that the front matter of the anthology puts the title as "Missing Form" in the singular.

> *What god now claims thee priest, O chosen head,*
> *most humble here that wast, for that thou knew'st*
> *thro' what waste nights thy lucid gaze was used*
> *to spell our glory in blazon'd ether spread?*
>
> *Silence alone, that o'er the lonely song*
> *impends, old night, or, known to thee and near,*
> *long autumn afternoon o'er stirless leaves*
>
> *suspended fulgent haze, the smouldering throng*
> *staying its rapt assumption-pyre to hear*
> *what strain the faun's enamour'd leisure weaves.*

This would not be the only dedicatory poem. Lloyd Austin, examining the edition sent to Mallarmé, finds that Brennan has left "On the half title page, beneath the large title XXI POEMS a poetic dedication" in Brennan's calligraphy (102–5). It is headed "To Stéphane Mallarmé's homage" and dated 27 July 1897 and signed off 8 August:

> *A ſacred horror holds the place,*
> *hardly the leaves upon its hem*
> *may liſp the ſong that ſtirs in them*
> *but fails before the hidden face.*
> *The lucid gaze of ſilence there*
>
> *viſions in one auroral gem*
> *the ſecret of our diadem,*
> *the mortal pageantry of air.*
>
> *O fear'd beſide this Auſtral foam*
> *dim leaves that flit withouten home*
> *fain there to fall an offering,*
>
> *O'er you perchance a reſting-ſpace*
> *ſome ſhadow of that light may fling*
> *the autumn of a fleeting grace*
>
> August 8th

(Austin, 105)

The archaic use of the long s, ſ, had gone into decline a century before. One cannot help but hear fails in sails – and Austral foam takes that most integral Mallarméan metaphor, *écume*, to another shore, one that Brennan has left behind (again archaically, using the obsolete Middle English *withouten*). More than anything else, it is a poem that senses a coming death, a parting with time; and the promise to retain the amplitude of poetic vision seems to have been kept.

Thus *chrono* (time) *metrics* (measure). Time aligns, misaligns, hits and misses. Space induces time-lag, too. Cuts to lag seem miraculous, per the timepiece that got us noticing, in Brennan, confounding collocations and displacements of time. Yet this is literary history at its best: not driven by expectation, nor always given to follow a theoretical pattern or prediction. We are concerned not only with speculative avant-gardes at the fringes or hidden from view, but also direct engagements with the history of avant-garde poetics. On the level of poetics in theory, the inscription is perhaps the most timeless and most outscaped of forms: Brennan's diction does not so much shift from its more gruff vernacular in 1897 to the dulcet sibylline tonality of this poetic inscription, as freeze in the image of time. Though themes from this poem affect the rest of the sequence, thy and thee vanish; it serves as an interlude or interleaf, of which others exist in the 105-poem sequence. Mallarmé's grave breaks the sequence. What the European avant-garde would take from Mallarmé was no doubt the total expansion of the letter, especially the Mallarmé of *Un Coup de Dés*. But for Brennan, particularly the Brennan of this public-facing 1898 forepiece, Mallarmé seems more priest than prophet. Mallarmé may have meant double for Brennan; both modern and avant-garde, a means for defiance against one's own detractors and a deep spiritual connection to an outside. Hope Mirrlees and T. S. Eliot would not suffer the same fate, but for the legacy of avant-garde *poetics*, *Paris* and *The Waste Land* could give precedent for future works, particularly the modern long poem (despite how relatively short those two works are). Brennan here does not publicise *Musicopoematographoscope*, knowing that it would not be wise, as the later Malley affair either proves or disproves. It lay dormant in 1898.

Frozen before the time of the inscriptive letter (1898) and the graphological cursive (1897), Brennan's Mallarmé was far more private than the Mallarmé of Edwards. By the twenty-first century one did not need to hide one's experiments. Between Brennan and the experimental anthologies of the '70s and '80s the capacities of the poetic line and measure did not have to be suppressed to the same degree, but that does not necessarily mean "progress". Mikhail Bakhtin's "chronotope", which brought the inseparability of space and time into a historical poetics of the novel, would here show forth a slow shift in poetry, a chronotopics in which Australian poets would find different things to like or memorialise in Mallarmé. Bakhtin is often aware that what he says of novels does not automatically apply to poetry. Chronometric readings take questions of literary history to be questions of the nature of time. For the novel a chronotope, for a poem chronometrics; my deployment of the term simply demands that we take chronometric criticality into literary time, conscious too of how these analyses might be overshadowed by future events, match-ups or mismatches between similar texts in undisclosed futures.

An understanding of chronometric reading could take the place of already entrenched understandings of how successive waves of avant-garde poets across literary cultures evolved. The contrast, or contest, between "avant-garde" and "experimental" comes into play in narratives of evolution and continuation. Charles Bernstein and Tracie Morris, introducing *BAX 2016: Best American Experimental Writing*, write "America is an experiment" (as John Cage too proclaimed), and *Experiment* comes to suggest a focus on "work-product or test results" in contrast with *Avant-garde*, which often "evokes a hermetically sealed tradition hobbled by its own triumphalism" (ix). From this they declaim: "we may say *en garde*: wake up, poetry is about to begin!" (x). The American experiment is the American poetic century, the poetry of a Republic of Letters that participated in its vitality from the Objectivist nexus in the Depression years through to the end of the Cold War and the time of Language Writing in the 1970s and its long aftermath of contemporary experimental and conceptual poetry, with ramifications for the thought and practice of poetics all around the globe, a cultural and geopolitical power in ways complexly buttressed by the strength of the US military, historical intervention and interventionism across continents. Experimentation did not end in the new century, though its discourses of critical sustenance or controversy might have become exhausted or exhausted it. And although poetry has never been stranger to anti-traditional challenges to anti-traditional precedents, it might be possible that the word "experiment" for our time captures an expanded present in a way "avant-garde" cannot. Avant-gardes remain of a vanishing present: most of all, a historical tradition. Did Brennan "found" an avant-garde tradition in Australian poetry? Does Australian verse follow such patterns of nationhood, experiment, tradition, regeneration, renewal or even continuation? And is it only possible to extract a theory of the avant-garde from these senses of experimental opposition, or the move from long dormancy into quickened awakening? Has Australian poetry sprung to *en garde*? Can it ever? Are those cries by the anthologisers of *Missing Forms* not doing the same with WE DO EXIST?

The problem is there is no triumphalism that an avant-garde could resist or partake in. From the first printed verse in Australia, Barron Field, a sense of its proximity to failure even on the level of technique was palpable. Yet not just in the discourse of colonial triumph and failure: the lack of triumphalism in Indigenous verse before Occupation has strong legal and sacred foundation. Strehlow on the Songlines would claim "There were no national songs of triumph, and there was no real heroic verse" (658). Power and promise might prevail over passion and upheaval. If Antipodal literature is based firmly upon tradition in an Aboriginal sense, before a modern and colonial one, for non-Aboriginal Australians the spectre of a barred Republic casts a shadow over the Australian verse tradition. The most globally recognised poet to have written in the continent, Les Murray, could imagine a "Vernacular Republic" while privately opposing *both* the avant-garde and the failure to achieve a Republic ("How did it taste, our poor / three-quarters-sovereign flag?"), yet sharing in lyric language an affinity with a certain prosody that has invited comparison with Hopkins, as with the final verse of "Bat's Ultrasound", a poem that appeared first in the 1987 collection *The Daylight Moon*:

> *ah, eyrie-ire, aero hour, eh?*
> *O'er our ur-area (our era aye*
> *ere your raw row) we air our array,*
> *err, yaw, row wry – aura our orrery,*
> *our eerie ü our ray, our arrow.*
> A rare ear, our aery Yahweh.

The convergence upon Yahweh, whose spirit Theodor Reik reads back to an animistic past that aligns it with some elements of Indigenous religion, is Murray's catholic phenomenology, a sense of the Israelite spirit that listens. To that Murray could hear things few poets could, but Murray could not embrace the placement of First Nations at the core of any sense of Nation; Murray's own bewilderingly vast sense of experiment could only go so far, and his gruff but sensitive regional voice would remain dammed up in the problems that remain the First ones. Murray's voice remained, in no simple way, both the unique voice of a Middle Australia that would have fashioned for itself a "sovereignty" removed from Black/Blak cultures, and a dying voice amid a conservatising Middle that drove even Republican voices, like Murray's, to the periphery. The contradictions of Murray's voice began, of course, in eighteenth-century England. Modern Australia was not an experiment even if the state of Australia was a test for the capacity of a convict colony to survive, if not make up for the loss of the American one. It was more expense than experiment. Debates raged in public opinion in the British late eighteenth century along these lines, as one quatrain from John Freeth's 1786 poem "Botany Bay" more than adequately shows:

> Let no one think much of a trifling expense,
> Who knows what may happen a hundred years hence;
> The loss of America what can repay?
> New colonies seek for at Botany Bay.[16]

Freeth would publish under the name "John Free". Freeth's poem was written in the year the decision was made to establish a colony, or two years before Invasion, in 1788. Robert Southey's "Botany-Bay Eclogues", a series of four dramatic poems written in 1794, including a final fifth poem published in 1798 (therefore late poems on the matter given the broadside tradition of transportation balladry, to which Southey's poem can be contrasted), acknowledges by default and by accident the oncoming cultural and ecological calamity: "all the perils of a world unknown", "marshy heaths" and "pathless woods", all these remain "Unbroken by the plough". There is no joylessness in the continent that Southey couldn't imagine, "Where the rude native rests his drowsy frame" – and even the kangaroo seems to sing a "sad note'. It is an immature bleakness that drives the scenography of the poem to the conclusion that its remoteness was a curse when it was of course the opposite, yet Robert W. Rix can read social and political criticism in Southey's eclogues against the background of Godwin's political radicalism, his Pantisocratist fantasy, Foucault/Bentham and the panopticon, and its chosen Virgilian form. It is, so Rix says, a "poetics of penal transportation", but Southey's projective politics of disenchantment risked being self-marginalisation, so we get, oddly, a "romanticisation" of the convict, but at the same time a theoretical geography of banishment formed from afar: a "literary vehicle" for an argument of political philosophy (442). Rix stresses that these were (through lines of poetry) "theoretical speculations" rather than based upon

---

[16] John Freeth's poem is collected in *The New Oxford Book of Eighteenth-Century Verse*. Freeth's *The Political Songster* had been going since 1771 and had virtually become an annual by the late 1780s. For a synoptic account of the Antipodal myth in this period see Ruth Scobie's *Celebrity Culture and the Myth of Oceania, 1770–1823*.

direct experience (Southey never goes to Australia), that remained idealist notion of transportation to a "young and pristine" place of renascence. But of the harshness of the Australian desert, experienced by the poem's speaker Elinor, for this Rix deploys the discourse of Nature as an index for the psyche to explain how Southey can see "such harsh conditions as productive of virtues" (442). Yet in Rix's reading nothing is said of the poem's invocations of agricultural failure, which, by its inability to see potential productivity in the dry regions, was the very misinterpretation of the productive potential of the land that led to bad reports about the colony in its early years. Moreover, this epistemological and ecological blindspot on the level of agricultural, aquacultural and material production would become one of the chief precipitants of the protracted Frontier Wars, beginning in 1788. Rix also does not mention the poem's late evocation of fear – "And what if in my wanderings I should rouse / The savage from his thicket! / Hark! the gun!" – which closes the sequence (118).

Romantic poetics would respond to the Antipodes in a way already unthinkable in Tzara's sense of the colonial syllogism as he surmised it from afar. Like James Cook, Romanticism would reach for the gun. Tzara's distance was not the same as Southey's: Southey is, if anything, too close to see anything at all, let alone experiment with the distortions of distant observation, even though Southey's capacity for linguistic experimentation was otherwise profound. The calamity of colonisation was not the only thing that prevented it from being an "experiment" in the same way as the American colonies, or put another way, it was an experiment that quickly had to turn into an invention. No mass transportation had yet occurred on that level, and yet the lurking fact of oncoming nationhood or brotherhood was that it too needed to be invented as a fiction, a fiction designed not to cover the loss of America but to cover up genocide.

VI. *Experiri: 1940s–1970s*

Southey's blindness is our insight, perhaps, into why the botched birth of a nation was both unprecedented and unexperimental. But we seek in the chapters that follow a definition of "experimental" that can take literary interpretation into account. Historical meanings of the word "experimental" change as the word travels across space; there may be a way that the word "experiment", as it changes under our feet, has come to resonate with the problem of an avant-garde in the Antipodes because of its currency in the digital era. Friedrich Block in "Eight Digits of Digital Poetics" notes that this separation hinges on the notion that avant-garde (as producing the new at the cutting edge of history) is not reducible then to experimental (as doing something that is not necessarily either new or cutting edge but tests its materials). In an email I received from Justin Clemens on this matter he writes:

> This is where we might revisit the sense of what the experimental is today. Its etymology is extremely suggestive: literally, a coming out of danger (*periculum*). Experiment is of course also closely related to the modern English words experience and expert. They all derive from the Latin verb *experiri*, 'to try.' That verb is itself a composite, from *ex,-* out of, and *periri*, the present passive infinitive of *pereo*; *pereo* means to pass away, to vanish, to perish. Experiment (and experience) is therefore a coming-out-of or a passing-through-danger. On this basis, we could then define an experiment as something like: the emergent inscription and transmission of an artificially-produced hazardous event at the limits of the known ... Perhaps even more bizarrely, through the bizarre destinies of linguistic transmission, it turns out that the words experiment and pirate share the same root: 'classical Latin *pirate* < Hellenistic Greek *peirates* < ancient Greek *peiran* to attempt, to attack, assault (<*peira* trial, attempt, endeavour: see *peirameter*, n.) + *-tes*, suffix forming agent nouns).' OED ... An experimenter is therefore literally also an ex-pirate — which may also make us think of *expirate* (a 17th century word for breathing-out) and expire (a contemporary word for dying).

The most intriguing thing about such a "bizarre" etymological trip is that it ends with expiration of breath, either *periri* or expirate, finally, death, but it's through "pirate" we get similar semes to the senses of avant-garde an assault force, or attack-line. Accordingly the problem of linguistic derivativeness implies that if experiment is derivative, a "pirate" of the avant-gardes, and whether we speak of the originals in Tzara's Romanian ethnopoetics or the copies, as with Brennan's full score, this question will return to bother us where transcultural contexts, especially in the 1940s, were seen as an impediment to the construction of a local or nationalist literature less culturally derivative or deviant. Whether it's some kind of experimental piracy or a deathward-bound expiry of the expert, senses of the new are as troubling in "experiment" as they are in "avant-garde".

More historically evocative, then, the term "avant-garde" sticks, but the word "experiment", with its hints at piracy, death and danger, retain appropriate semes for the settler-colonial context. In the chapters that follow I treat the term "experimental" as every bit as historical as "avant-gardist", in the specific contexts in which it arises.[17] The exactness with which we can measure what ultimately would become *abstracted* puts the chronometric drive to test against a global horizon. A crucial aspect of this book, then, is born out of these openings: I want to recalibrate questions of "derivation" and so-called second-hand "receivedness" when it comes to experimental writing based on avant-garde poetic practices, and to instead argue that such histories operate according to logics of exteriority and interiority.[18] The stakes are high, to use images from economics (stake and stock), not only for history but for theory: What's a literary exterior? At what point is interiority achieved? Is political urgency subtracted in an avant-garde that enacts its politics outside cultural centres? Doubtless a literary-historical approach has allowed us to draw connections across avant-garde phases – in poetics, aesthetics, political and geopolitical situations – and we have been able to take stock of how an Antipodal avant-garde has expanded its reach across time and hemispheric space, and after 1970 lurched toward transcultural horizons. Neither a regressive nor a progressive political teleology alone can explain these transformations and continuations of the European early twentieth-century avant-garde in this hemisphere. As noted: literary history itself has been read as a challenge to the avant-garde, so much so that the avant-garde is seen to

---

[17] Peter Dear distinguishes the use of the word "experiment" from "experience" while noting the constructivist link through the history of science in *Discipline and Experience*, which begins in the seventeenth century. But Dear argues that "experiment" meant an array of things during the Scientific Revolution: "dictionary definition of an experiment as a test of a theory fails to capture the meaning and diversity of new practices of the seventeenth century" (22). In the study of poetry and poetics, we have often pitted tradition against experiment, to bad effect. Yet there are better exceptions. In his 1979 book *Tradition and Experiment in English Poetry*, Philip Hobsbaum argues that the great dialectic of English poetry is that between tradition and experiment, with experiment often stemming from external, and in the case of Spenser and Elizabethan sonneteers, Italianising tendencies to the "central line" of English verse (xii). I have thought this to be in part a dynamic also relevant to the avant-garde poets in this book, many of whom would encounter a "foreign" influence that sparked and enriched the work. Despite this, I have abandoned the theoretical descriptor "experiment" for the historical term "avant-garde".
[18] Hazel Smith, in an email exchange regarding histories of avant-garde and experimental poetry dually considered, noted the tension between "the wish to forge an Australian poetic identity at the time and international influences which were sometimes moving in other directions" (personal correspondence, 25 February 2017). It seems to me that this is the key tension in Antipodal avant-garde poetics after 1970, when the lines of contact (and sheer volume of international visits) both opened up new avenues of invention and asked deep questions of what would then constitute an "Australian-specific" response to these disparate poetics.

exist far outside literary history itself: an "impossible history". Such an exterior mode is an attitude of reading. *All* poetry is, to an extent, received, but how this term affects ensuing social, cultural and historical texturing (filling in) is the question. And we do not yet have answers.

If Brennan "covers" the story of the emergence of a pre-avant-garde from the late nineteenth century to the early decades of the twentieth (taking us to 1932, the year of his death), the period after 1940 and before 1970 is our next concern. This historical period is the most important for understanding the place of the avant-garde in Australian modernity, and how an Antipodal avant-garde emerges from it or responds to avant-gardism in poetry. This is the period known mostly for the Ern Malley affair, and debates that are as much about the break from Colonial to Modern, or Romantic to Symboliste Australian literature, as about the agons of modern verse itself. We can turn again to Kirkpatrick, who finds Slessor's reappraisal to be due in large part to the global academy and the "global reappraisal of modernism" as a broader and "more culturally contingent set of artistic practices than it was once construed to be" ("1940s–1960s", 12), meaning:

> Before this, "modernism" was typically conflated with the historical avant-garde, and until the late 1960s in Australia when a set of experimental younger poets came to prominence – what John Tranter later called The New Australian Poetry or "the Generation of '68" – the absence of an avant-garde heritage meant that the local poetic scene could appear inward-looking and tame. ("1940s–1960s", 12)

Experimental poetry, we might add, appears where an avant-garde is found to be absent. If, in the shifting terms of Kirkpatrick's analysis, the absence of a "historical" avant-garde renders the Generation of '68 an event that marks the inception of a home-grown avant-garde, there is more work to be done to measure the scales of derivation *on all sides*; which is to say, precisely in the European avant-garde "itself", and those who "did" historical avant-garde (modernism) in Australia whether synchronically or belatedly, a point I emphasise when exploring the work of Duke. I remain doubtful as to whether it is possible to read New Australian Poetry, lain alongside the forms of New American Poetry, as a comparably momentous breakthrough. Kate Fagan and Peter Minter extrapolate, in somewhat an experimental-fragmentary essay on *The Alphabet Murders* (in the form of an alphabet), how Tranter's strides overseas (to Singapore) mirrors Ashbery's (Paris). Foreignness is even linked to a kind of reverse "Orientalist" move here, and the "innovative" strain produced is thus an antidote to the conservative modernism of Slessor and others. Yet then, as Fagan and Minter put it, "Advance-gardism, it would seem, is an anxious and inevitable cycle of hollow repeats and potentially colonising explorations." The purpose here is to historically situate New Australian Poetry as Tranter intended. I intend to take special interest in questions of historical siting such as these, viewing them with an eye to the transnational and international contexts they speak to, mirror, even mock. Given the place the Australian bourgeois state would play and continue to play in the geopolitical and military defence of US hegemony (America's role as meddler in international affairs over the past seventy years is astonishing, if not vanguardist in its own way), Tranter can barely get much past a primary stage "without guaranteed future returns" – a Generation of '68 which faced off contesting postmodern poetries on the same colonising campground, coordinates reset "by a newly imperial compass, its dial minted fresh in the factories of America". I view "being avant-garde" as a set of socially mandated and culturally oppositional stances, attitudes, reactions, practices and performances encompassing a wide range of things; historical reference, interventions-into or due rehearsings-of formal avant-garde traditions (international, regional, local), culturally mixed styles, performances, and acts of writing, socio-historical association, dissociation, tendency, weak and intense grouping, even individualist "maverick" proclamation or provocation (rejecting grouping and claiming inimitability). Like Fagan and Minter I do not propose an automatic anti-colonial or anti-imperial good in all or any advance-gardism, though nor does it shore up the bad. Some examples in the second half of this book muck things up to such an extent as to upset even a contemporary status quo. Avant-garde sensibility can be construed as self-nomination, but self-nomination very often only dialectically evident through social circumstance. Conceptualised this way, we can begin to think of being avant-garde not as a clearly defined anti-canonicism, but as a set of historically informed practices that are fully adopted by some, partially taken up by others, and for others still, questioned or rejected.

The historical detailing that get us from the post-war period's blunt and sometimes clumsy rhetoric of innovation, the subject of the next chapter, to the more flourishing period post-Dismissal, the subject of the one after, open complexities that cannot all be covered here. In the latter period we can trace a certain cultural offset of tumultuous party politics. Upon the death of Gough Whitlam in

2014, it was the Liberal Party Prime Minister who took his place, Malcolm Fraser, who noted that it was not only the arts in general that Whitlam transformed but "perhaps in literature more than anything else, people felt released, able to write what they might not have been able to write before". To what extent was this true? The scale of cultural impact Whitlam had is measurable in a political sense only when placed beside public policy, and in that regard it was the 1969 programme, launched in his own words, "Without bombast, without rhetoric" but nonetheless launched in such a manner that it would "take Australia into the 1970s", that shook the Australian cultural superstructure. In there was the rhetoric of innovation and ambition. Whitlam grandly pledged "three of the most constructive and purposeful years in Australia's history – years of innovation, renovation, reinvigoration" ("1969 Election Policy Speech").

It was his dismissal, known as the Dismissal, in 1975, by the then Governor General Sir John Kerr and with final consent of the Queen of England, that became a watershed moment not only for governance and constitutionality, then understood, but for culture, arts and letters. Indeed Whitlam's controversial purchase, in 1973, through the National Gallery of Australia, of the 1952 painting *Blue Poles* by the American abstract expressionist Jackson Pollock, was a controversy that for Richard Haese, in his book on Australian artist Mike Brown and the Australian avant-garde, amounted to a government-sanctioning of the avant-garde:

> Gough Whitlam's official acceptance of avant-gardism was announced by his sanctioning of the purchase of Jackson Pollock's quintessentially modernist painting *Blue Poles* for 1.3 million by James Mollison, the director of the Australian National Gallery in Canberra. More significant was the fact that the government also now set about transforming the existing arts-supporting infrastructure of the Australian Council for the Arts, by establishing a new council with specialised boards for the various arts. In the past the avant-garde had relied on the support of a few private sponsors: now it found itself the recipient of unprecedented government largess. (*Permanent Revolution*, 187)

The impact of public policy, and indeed governance, on cultural history, is profound, and particularly in this decade.[19] That is not

---

[19] For Lindsay Barrett in *The Prime Minister's Christmas Card:* Blue Poles *and Cultural Politics in the Whitlam Era*, a scintillating analysis, the affair virtually made Whitlam's government avant-garde in the pejorative – a symbol of its extravagance and excess.

to say however that we have found the locus of all of this in either poetic or aesthetic specifics. If we are simply talking about the works themselves, and we are never *just* talking about works, then the way in which works responded to the era and to policy will not always be apparent.[20] It is therefore not a recurrent trend in these chapters, even as literary history, to find contextual markers for everything. Poems do theoretical work *with* history, and "do poetics" for other things, other impetuses, whether philosophical, antiphilosophical or theosophical rumination or provocation, crossing to the other arts to examine or imagine origins, to articulate the wishes, cursory, recondite or otherwise, of an individual rather than that of a social subject *per se*, to make specific commentary without demanding general analysis. I have been careful where and when to have recourse to sociocultural reasoning. Marking up the more exclusively literary half of a historical account is as much a question of the character of time, the chronometrics of it. This can be left to others who have made historical judgements upon Zeitgeist, like Harry Heseltine introducing the *Penguin Book of Modern Australian Verse* in 1981: "If any single quality pervades Australian poetry from about the middle 1960s on, it might be described as a sense of urgency ... an urgency to make poems unsoftened by the usages and pieties of the past. Substantively, our recent poetry has more consistently addressed itself to socio-political fact than perhaps any other period of our history" ("Introduction", xxxii–xxxiii).

VII. *Between the Centuries: 1980–Now*

The 1980s in Australia was a decade of contradictions, with 1988 being the year of the Bicentennial celebrations, on the cusp of the great geopolitical earthquake across the Eastern Bloc. Though it cannot be disputed that Australian poetry of the 1960s shows forth

---

[20] Doubtless the impact was material, because upon the election of the Whitlam government in 1972, funding for the arts increased 100 per cent. After Whitlam, funding for the arts stagnated. I remain sceptical of the extent to which public policy and governance on a state and national level defines point-blank the whole trajectory of an Antipodal avant-garde, even though I remain thoroughly contextualist. I provide this footnote because I deem it possible only that the impact of Whitlam was a special case, and that its occurrence coincided with some of the key turns of this book. Jenny Hocking's *The Dismissal Dossier*, published in several editions from 2015 to 2018, and ongoing research into 1975, illuminates not only the often underplayed role of the Crown in Australian political affairs, but also the broader cultural impact of the Whitlam era.

a certain social and political urgency reflected in poetics, we need not cathect that decade at the expense of others, as for instance the 1950s, the decade in which, to the best of our historical knowledge, Antipodal Dada first appeared, nor the 1970s as above, the decade of the Dismissal. That decade, just before the restructuring of unions and the advent of neoliberalism in the 1980s, spawned a new kind of politics more Green than Red. Anarchism doubtless drove the avant-gardes of the late '70s. Decadal assessments of poetics in literary history will therefore prevail in the ways we make it prevail. Decades are not static, no matter how much they may mark time so, or be seen to, in hindsight. They fold, overlap, contradict. Late in the century, new technologies would give rise to digital poetics, but by the 1980s, the global network of avant-garde poetry was wide enough to spawn a greater array of linguistic inventions not altogether dependent on technology as such. They could turn back to history. What Antipodal avant-gardists were "opposed" to no longer made them who and what they were. Invention would have its negative characteristics in these earlier experiments, but could transform from acts of refusal (of publics, of commercial attitudes) into games played according to new rules (new publics, communal sensibilities), in the register of small press and global conversation.

By book's end we will have a better sense of the range of inventive tactics of the Australian avant-garde in this decade, the decade that begins (again) with Brennan's Mallarmé. Javant Biarujia begins releasing work in the 1980s, though the foundations for Biarujia's poetics were lain well before. Biarujia's private language, Taneraic, which he began inventing in 1968, is cited by Charles Bernstein as "the most systematically and literally ideolectical poetry of which I am aware" (*My Way: Speeches and Poems*, 135). Biarujia describes Taneraic on a website dedicated to the language as "after the style of Mallarmé or Stefan George: a private pact negotiated between the world at large and the world within me" ("Introduction to Taneraic"). In 2022 the complete version of Biarujia's Taneraic dictionary, titled *Nainougacyou*, was published and distributed as private copies only (not sold; I was sent one personally by mail). This private and direct dissemination of material marks Biarujia as an avant-garde poet in the most original manner, and indeed Biarujia would conjure Tzara and other early twentieth-century avant-garde figures in ways that extend their archaeopoetic impetus (or send it back) in several works. Take these stanzas from a mesostic sequence "Spelter to Pewter"

> M
> *En in Aïda*
> CentRifugist centre left
> onCe a Khlebnikov
> or a HokUsai   or an early
> Pickwick for an irRadiation
>   scare or polYmorphous theories in Leicester Sq
>
> [idolater...] in Herits metropolitan
> Kazimir Malevich ajar asYlum anyone aver lava from Java
>   quaDrant
>   quatRain avatar
> black velar tOfu
>   pyscholoGical discourse amplifed
>   Franz KlinEs parameters
> chiselling asiaN
>
>   Consider thus
> TristAn Tzara or
> Konrad LorEnzs
>   sloganS
>   confrontIng
>   brUtal
>   huMiliation

There they are: David J. Melnick (*Men in Aida*, the 1983 homo-erotophonic translation of the *Iliad*), Velimir Khlebnikov, Kazimir Malevich, Tristan Tzara, Katsushika Hokusai, Franz Kline, the ethologist Konrad Lorenz: these are the chosen historical referents (and the linguistic material) for an off-axis Antipodal avant-garde mesostic. Languages of invention, or invented language? Eremite, Trappist, avant-~~modern~~, avant-manqué, Tzaraesque, (Retro-) Futurist, processual, and most of all, Cagean, we add to our growing list of radical Antipodal inventive forms. This is, oddly enough, not so much a "remote" as a solo path fully engaged with the global avant-garde and its histories. For Corey Wakeling, the matter of history in Biarujia is not straightforward:

> Biarujia's work marks out its own historical forebears and familiars in a way that I believe – although absolutely in association with contemporary histories of poetry such as American Language poetry, Australian bricolage, and European surrealism – happens to hybridise baroque linguistic ingenuity with deconstructive collage and games of poetic reality that defy straightforward historical alignment. ("Interview")

Another account, from Geraldine McKenzie, a poet of the late twentieth-century Australian avant-garde whose poetics could sit beside Language Writing in the US, compares Biarujia's techniques, or processes, in his 2002 book *Calques*, to Khlebnikov's, for the manner in which Biarujia's sound play "sets up connections between words, a process of selection that doesn't necessarily derive from philological correctness". We have said "referent", but the historical misalignment that feeds into, or tangles up, straighter lines of influence can reveal not only just how much Biarujia sought to make language outside reference and referent – a tendency shared by the avant-garde tradition at the time, most obviously the Language Writers – but equally show how hard it is to "pin down" any one influence in such a hybrid poetics.

To invent a language is to operate as fringe-garde or engage in escapage, to delve into or outscape onto an archaeopoetics. Biarujia's Taneraic is as good an example of a language of invention in this guise as we are going to get.

It goes deeper than this. Avant-garde poems and poets of the Antipodes – Brennan, Malley and Malley's detractors, Hooton, Fogarty, Duke, Walwicz and Stewart, and the many more that follow, all seek an oppositional position through the work of reinventing poetic language, yet in the most overt ways, the historical poetics of the poems is the ground of this work. They too seek a place in history. Antipodal avant-garde poetries would resist, in slight and sometimes momentous ways, the givens of language in processes of making. And yet, disparate as these documents of Antipodal experiment are, whether they come in the guise of invented languages, or languages of invention, from wild interlopers or monastic individualists, urban modernists or from the remote centre, from an interior intensity in First Nations vanguard languages, or blasts from outside, they all traffic excitable forms through visual or verbal extremity. Perhaps, with some exception, they are *all* accidents. To pick them up requires marginal historiographies tuned in to theoretical epicentres, whether the Euro-American imports of the first vanguard tradition in the early twentieth century, as is the case with Brennan, or whether emerging from linguistic invention within regionally specific contexts, as is the case with the First Nations and Blak avant-gardes.

Yet we can never be sure about time. Brennan's experiment was not belated but immediate. Perhaps his later verse lost the spark of that original inspiration and found itself at a distance again from that short participation in Symbolism. But a historically reflective look at avant-garde poems in the Antipodes show an array of attitudes to time, revealed in the chronometrics of the poems, an array of alignments and misalignments presented as literary history without linear progression. It will go this way. Examples to come in Part II, after our intermission, are no less confounding, no less accidental than the texts of 1897.

Tzara's Australophilic drives can now be set beside the Mallarmé-Brennan kinship. Was Mallarmé a shock event and founding figure of the Antipodal avant-gardes? Yes. But there remains much complexity in the interim. If it is not possible to read Antipodal literature without the avant-gardes, and neither the avant-gardes without the Antipodal cosmopolis, the intervening years between 1897 and the 1980s and after – the time of Biarujia, Murray, Edwards and the avant-aftershocks of the new century – is a whole period of experiment that tells another story. We cannot skip over mid-century, even if some skipping is necessary to tell the nonlinear history of the avant-gardes, as Stark noted of Mallarmé. The inexistence of the *southland* – its climate, its noon and its axial orientation – could be as remote as bits of Austral foam on another shore not yet common, or as close as the perfect concinnity of time we find with *Un Coup de Dés* and *Musicopoematographoscope*. No longer can we expect belated time to do the work of avant-garde history.

Again: we are in no hurry to appear with the key that unlocks the impossible history and lets us in to confirm everything that has been so far said, but what has been held captive is about to be let out. In poetry, the matter is language, language *scored* in prosodic time. Time bequeaths measure, discernible and imperceptible in the page-appearance of poems. Let us zone these histories more acutely (with deeper chronometricity), for Antipodal musings on time are about to usher in (so far as basic gestures to texts can get us) a new order of the line.

Chapter 3

New Order of the Line: W. C. Williams, Ern Malley, Harry Hooton and the 1940s Avant-Gardes

> New sign-posts stretch out the road that lingers
> Yet on the spool. New images distort
> Our creeping disjunct minds to incredible patterns
> – Ern Malley, "Young Prince of Tyre"

> Have a good look at me!
> I'm an idiot, I'm a practical joker, I'm a hoaxer.
> – Tristan Tzara, Dada Manifesto (V)

In December 1947, the twenty-fifth and last number of *The Australian International Quarterly of Verse*, a magazine that had been running since December 1941, was published with a Preface by William Carlos Williams, written in the form of a letter to the then editor Flexmore Hudson, associated with the Jindyworobaks. Its purpose was loosely adapted to these trans-Pacific circumstances and for this Williams was boldly Whitmanian: "What I presume for us here touching the writing of modern verse should equally well apply to you there across the world" (7). He adds that he can presume the reader knows "our poet Ezra Pound's dilemma" (7) – by that time he was admitted to St Elizabeths in Washington, D.C. upon extradition under the charge of treason for his illegal broadcasts, and would soon publish *The Pisan Cantos* LXXIV–LXXXIV – and, as a result, Williams wants to make clear the extent to which he opposes Pound: "Practically then, what I say to you, as an Australian, in an attempt to explain what my attitude may be toward writing, is that I am diametrically opposed (in my work) to such a writer as Ezra Pound—whom I love and deeply admire" (10). There is no doubt this was one of his most important literary relationships, as he would recount in autobiographical writings on his work "Before meeting Ezra Pound is like B.C. and A.D." (*I Wanted to Write a Poem*, 5), but even here the roots of tension are apparent; "I liked him but I didn't want to be like him" (9), writes Williams while recounting the moment his father asked Ezra what one of his poems meant.

What would the Antipodal reader learn? On the face of it, more about Williams's poetics than anything conducive of trans-Pacific dialogue. Antipodal readers would be perfectly aware of the importance of Williams's disagreements and the gravity of them to his context, even if they wouldn't quite know how to respond or connect it back. Here on impassioned display (and for public consumption) is that diametrical opposition to Pound, and the tragedy of a friendship interrupted by a public row around a legitimate political issue. Now that we have the means to historicise it, this lends insight still deeper into Williams's poetics, because Williams's "practical" desire to project a clear distinction within that dyad is intricate and revolves in part around questions of male friendship and the drive to patrilinearity in, or indeed as translation. Pound, the greatest of the translators, brings down the "riches of the ages" even as he divagates (7). The engendering of culture is patrilineal through diversion or swerve because it is bred "androgynetically" and "androgynously": "Newton begat Einstein just as Newton himself was got androgynously out of Archimedes" (7), an engendering that combines Williams's work as a physician and Aristophanes's birth myth. From this we can read Williams's long discomfort around Pound, who remained for him the paternal genius, and all dynamics thereof, as intersecting closely with the cultural politics of art in America: precisely its relations with the external world and internally with itself. Negating America would be an American matter, but in the postwar world, art (or poetry) as a social act bequeaths forms emerging from modern turmoil as the *material* of turmoil itself: "I look for direct expression of the turmoils of today in the arts. Not *about* today in classical forms but in forms generated, invented, today direct from the turmoil itself – or the quietude or whatever it might be so long as it is generated in *form* directly from the form society itself takes in its struggles" (10). That year, 1947, his poem "The United States" would be published, a poem that was the sum of thoughts brewing since 1945, in which he issued a defence of his place as an American subject: "The government of your body, sweet, / shall be my model for the world" (*Collected Poems Volume II*, 111). A year before, in 1946, the first book of *Paterson* had finally appeared, and his embarking upon that writing meant the long poem had gone from planning to fruition. It would be his biggest attempt in poetry at encapsulating, even erotising the body of the States, and one whose growing capacity after Book 1 would lead to the disjunction of later books, a disjunction that Randall Jarrell saw as a decline rather than an advancement, and that later critics would celebrate.[1]

We can read Williams's offering in the Australian issue as commentary within the bounds of his present thought on statehood, on the United States and of reverse exile. To find a route around Pound hinged on the issue of US American politics in its specific, and distorted modalities of exile and the politics of (dis)placement, or (il)locality, things that would define *Paterson*, and as such he is, through an unsettled preconscious, aware of the Australian context to which he writes, even if we know a lot more now about how much he was "assuming". I want to read it in such a way so as to get to the crux of this chapter's claim that what Williams was saying about the state of his context has bearing for what was happening squarely at this point in an Australian modernism on its global cusp. He is indeed quick to remind Australian readers that exile was no option: "So you see, when my friends went abroad I stayed here pitting myself against a chaos in my attempts to do what to me was the artist's greatest and most difficult task, to wrest from society, the politics and the economic phantasm before me new worlds of art. New forms" (10). Which is to say that the Destrudo and Mortido of or in form, evolving generatively out of the raw material of society and politics, informs and more so enforces literal patrilinearity: "father to father, no mother necessary" (11). Pound cut himself off from the motherland in order to become globally fertile, in a way that, as Williams would have it, led to literary sterility.

No desirable path, you could say. But what this engenders for us now – these notions of potency, fertility and nationhood, of America and its governing body, *ergo* the American body – are gender-concepts, concepts that Williams brought up to the Australian reader almost without prompt. How are we to read through the psychosocial thicket he weaves? These are personal, national and transnational threads, and tangled as they already are, all the more difficult does it then become when he ravels this with the question of poetic form and the line. These "severances", whether from genealogies or from national localities, were intimate to creative production. So much so that it would also mean a path towards invention: what

---

[1] For a detailed discussion of Jarrell's various critiques and critical appraisals, and the ambiguous stakes of Jarrell's various positions on Williams, see Margaret Glynne Lloyd's *William Carlos Williams's* Paterson: *A Critical Reappraisal*, 43–6.

Williams chose not to "abandon" was that which, in a more-than-metaphoric association of politics and aesthetics, came to urge him, and us, towards "Whatever inventions (discoveries) an artist can make lie in the forms of his art", inventions being primarily formal; "For the poet this means new modes of poetic form." "Form" takes us down, then, in a final step that encapsulates Williams's enjoinder, to foot and reinvention of the line. The status of form Williams is able to make resoundingly clear:

> To me the battle lodges for us as poets in the poetic line, something has got to be done with the line—it's got to be opened up, not left hanging as Whitman left it and knew he left it that way—but newly ordered, after some new order which the greatest poets, Australian or American, of our day must discover. ("Preface", 10)

The battle lines are drawn on the line itself. The line, for Williams, we know from other writings, had evolved from a nervous nature and an avowed "violent mood". It was cut short not drawn long, as it was for Whitman (*I Wanted to Write a Poem*, 4–5). If we read retroactively from later accounts, like Robert Grenier's, where he scrutinises in Williams the marks of a prosodist who in his specific phrasing has invented an "organic prosody", a new measure in variable foot, we might be tempted to conclude that Williams had indeed discovered a new order of the line. As Grenier reads it, "order" becomes for Williams, especially after 1940, the vital element in an organic American prosody and in the breathwork of an American line (10). One could not expect both Australian and American poets to take their rhythmic units from "American" speech, but the extent to which a reader can grasp the link between the variable foot as it tags the line and American speech, that gap, between the line, breath, and the national in speech, would be the challenge to close. We would do well to recall G. M. Hopkins's sprung rhythm here, which, less from an attempt to bring British speech into prosodic line as to fulfil his various theorisations of Inscaped verse, is precisely a type of prosody that one has to really work at and work with to hear (or indeed feel) what it is that gives it "naturalness". Such advice to the Australian reader, if it is really advice, and if Williams really thought it would apply across contexts (and once more, there's no reason to believe he didn't), at the very least offers a severance along one line of rhythmic fathers; a seminal line which, if extended further as Williams instructs, applies across contexts, and transects hemispheres. We will come back to the literal line later, however, when the examples arrive.

Extraordinary here are the implications for the gendered line. We can now read along or against the grain of the patrilineal as Rachel Blau DuPlessis does of Pound, Williams and Zukofsky and other male poets in her 2001 book *Genders, Races and Religious Cultures in Modern American Poetry, 1908–1934*, which uses correspondence to uncover an intricate web of bigendered congruities and incongruities at once individual, historical and philological: a "social philology" able to excavate stances and states of "manhood", masculinity or masculine effeminacy on the level of expression, therefore in poetics, "the line" and words. Pound and Williams would differ upon the subject of Elsa von Freytag-Loringhoven, Pound supportive on a poetics register and of her "non-acquiescence", whereas Williams would despise and praise her in contradictory terms; at once emotive, bitter, liberal, violent, misogynistic, mystical, mystified, sexual and "sexual-tropic" ("The Baroness", 284). Eric White has noted of their transatlantic encounter a distinctly national racialisation of Europe and America, especially evident in the fourth issue of *Contact*, "Sample Prose Piece – Three Letters", in which Williams calls Elsa "La Baronne" and the white porcelain table between them morphs into the Atlantic Ocean (White, 132–3). Thus a "new order of the line" might not simply be a new line of fathers, nor even differences (with women, against or for women), but a new seminal order of masculinity as Oceanic encounter. What was left hanging, the looseness or sagginess of the Whitmanian patrilineations against which Williams here calls a new generation to arms, is where he comes closest to drawing a parallel across the Pacific Ocean dividing two literary cultures. The difficulty of this passage lies in his assuredness on the sociality of art and poetic practice, because Williams then insists, with an undertone of heavy impact given the circumstances of Pound's dilemma, "the poet's very life but also his forms originate in the political social and economic maelstrom on which he rides" ("Preface", 11). Meaning: great poets need great audiences, and the audience of that great society would be underwritten as feminine (the thing, too, that would be "ridden", need we say more). In this regard he had castrated himself: "cut himself off from that supplying female, he dries up his sources" (11). Pound, in the end, would head "straight for literary sterility" (11).

1. *Williams and the Modern Antipodal Reader*

Let literary sterility in the Antipodes hold off till the discourse on Malley. I begin with these displaced arguments not just to show how much the avant-garde found itself outside the dictates of the modern, that we know, but also to show how much the moderns could differ on the question of formal invention and the role and status of avant-gardism. I begin here moreover to stress just how much an articulation of the Antipodal avant-garde can both widen and sharpen the discussion at hand. In Australia, as I have noted previously, avant-gardes could feel captive to the sheer weight of historical debates about modernism such that they felt bereft of any clear answer to it. If there was a response to such a new order of the poetic line in an Australian modernist context, mitigating factors intervene: the turmoil, in fact the battle, in Australia, was the Frontier Wars, and yet the absence of points of resolve or rupture – or more *total* opposition, in a Republic (of Letters), a Revolution or a Treaty – produce manifold contradictions that heavily bear upon literary history. This chapter is an answer to the question of whether these contradictions transmogrified enough to threaten the order, or induce a neoteric disorder, of the line. My answer, ultimately, is yes, but with a great deal of complexity in between. Australian modernists would hustle over how much an avant-garde should play a role in the modern enterprise, just as in the 1970s, postmodern poets would negotiate the role of the avant-garde in a challenge both to the literary establishment and the avant-garde tradition itself. Pitched in this way, the language of gender, generativity and fertility as a societal birth-mythography did not, in Australia, impel the postmodern or "neo"-avant-gardes, but neither did it impel modernists sceptical of avant-gardes, a dynamic that Williams could not have yet imagined. This is going to be in part a response to an alleged miscarriage of modernism in the Antipodes. But we are left to wonder if Pound and Australia came to mind for him because they meant similar things. Poundian modernism – and its mythography – prevails because Pound was not an American poet, even if Pound too suffered from and was interpolated by a US American maelstrom of social effects and energies (as Williams reminds us, he stayed; Pound and others were "exiled", or exiled themselves). And it is worth noting that the younger Pound, though "unmetrical" for Rupert Brooke's ears, is unsettlingly out of time too with the avant-garde even as he brands Imagism and Vorticism.[2] How Pound came to be *associated*, then, with formal modes of poetic invention brings in other struggles,

---

[2] Rupert Brooke's critique of Pound in the *Cambridge Review* finds Pound falling dangerously under the influence of Whitman with (to use the full phrase) the "unmetrical sprawling lengths" of his lines (166–7).

particularly between localised modernity and globality, opening new hemispheric lines in the early twentieth century.

To grasp a sense of what was at stake between avant-gardes and the modernist poet, we would delve further into Williams's account of the Baroness and of Dada, now that we know what role her life and work played in the avant-garde on two fronts.[3] This episode is incomplete without her response to "Dr Williams" as person and poet in her poem "Hamlet of Wedding Ring", published in *The Little Review* in 1921, a "brilliantly experimental prose poem" that would have given Williams an "electric jolt", as Irene Gammel puts it in a book on the Baroness (270). The poem doubles as a review of William's 1920 *Kora in Hell* (Gammel, 269), and if we give equal weight to this response, we see how an avant-garde acts when it is cut off from the supply-sources of modernism, and how the avant-garde New Woman, operating in transnational and erotic contexts (or in "Decadence", as Daniel Tiffany would frame it through the cryptaesthetic of Pound's Imagism), could *respond* to modernist men. What concerned modernists pitched against the avant-garde was the sterility, or fertility of these patrilineal or matrilineal chains of supply, amounting to nothing less and nothing more than critique of the avant-garde. In Williams's case it was not just a fathering-in-reverse, that could look with frustration upon those more non-acquiescent elements, but an inability to respond, effectively, in poetics. In the 1947 issue of the *International Quarterly of Verse*, the translation of Indonesian poetry and the inclusion of Irish poetry, placed seamlessly as it were alongside Australian poetry, is intriguing enough, and shows in Hudson's editorial work an internationalist intent, notwithstanding the frame Williams gives it. But "poetics" isn't the whole story here. One can imagine what kind of bafflement would then have ensued if excerpts of *Paterson* were to be included beside these and other poems within, or excerpts from the poems of the Baroness. Both the citational capaciousness of documentarian poetics, and the Baroness's extreme, unruly, frankly sexual lines, would have no Australian audience at all (so we might think). Better

---

[3] Amelia Jones, in *Irrational Modernism: A Neurasthenic History of New York Dada*, begins with Williams's scatological account of the Baroness in *Contact*, centring thereafter the Baroness as, to some historical degree, the seminal figure of New York Dada. Jones concludes that "From the Baroness's point of view", both Williams and Marcel Duchamp "exemplified the tendency among male avant-gardists to make radical art in their free time, while living more or less bourgeois lives, driven by neurasthenic fears of the modern challenges to their coherence as male subjects" (8). I will return below to the idea of neurasthenic modernism in reading Hooton.

at this distance, a respectful note of position and notoriety rather than a close integration of real poetics, one can suspect, in having Williams frame this final issue.

The problem with Williams's "social" reading is therefore that it serves only as *one kind* of social reading. It isn't the same kind of social-historical reading that we rather find in Ann Vickery's landmark text, *Stressing the Modern: Cultural Politics in Australian Women's Writing*. Vickery's study is locally granular, because it takes into account what modern Australian poetry had by that time become, and has the beneficial hindsight of all the work of modernist historiography to place it (plus the will to seek it). Williams of course would not have had enough ready access to poetry across the Pacific to have considered how women writers, early in the century, and into the middle of the century, like (Dame) Mary Gilmore, Zora Cross, Lesbia Harford and Nettie Palmer, would negotiate career, and negotiate the paternity of modernity, to fashion noteworthy bodies of work. How could he have known too how women writers would find ways to differentiate and negotiate the effects of social and historical reading and reception? Modern Australian women poets might not have disrupted "hierarchical syntax", as the Imagists would, but "experimentation happened in less obvious ways" (Vickery, 11). It was not just the Jindyworobaks, nor Malley, who bore all the weight for the moderns in the 1940s, not the least because, as I read it in the previous chapter, certain poets pivotal to the composition of Australian modernism, like Brennan, could do social reading, but the way that new forms of writing would emerge in "settler modernity", readable in a comparative sense (say, in contrast with Imagism), and in a specific localist sense, were singed with ongoing turmoil, attached to the dynamics of settler modern locales: a war-torn, genocidal colony competing for resources, a Federated nation in a continent, and throughout each phase of its history, insuperable contradictions. To use Williams's schema, these new forms would take the place of "struggle", but as Vickery notes, not one necessarily familiar to American or European modernists. If modern Australian poetry failed to find a Vernacular Republic, or failed to draw an appropriate prosody from Australian speech, it may be because we *didn't read closely enough*, if not also because Australian poetry had slackened into literary sterility. For what explicitly or implicitly avant-garde poetry, and other resistant or non-acquiescent poetries did was invent, and present, a diverse array of prosodic approaches, practices, praxes (aural, visual, conceptual) that speak directly to these global dynamics of the modern, in more, and sometimes less obvious ways.

Antipodal readers, whatever such a construction may mean in detail, with their own paternal-colonial impetus firmly lodged in place, would therefore not only be regionalist but peripherally aware of modern openings as framed through the shock therapy of external modernism and its discontents. That its history was "favorable" to modernism is no inveterate point. The decade of the 1940s, from wartime disruption to postwar reconstruction, saw strong Labor Party leadership throughout, from the Prime Ministership of John Curtin (1941–5) to the immediately post-war government of Ben Chifley (1945–9). By 1947, Chifley had led a ruling Labor government for two years in a period of reconstruction after the war that historian Stuart Macintyre has called "Australia's boldest experiment". The Chifley era, Macintyre argues, saw gender play a big part in the reconstruction of labour and economy, nothing short of a "new order for women" (185–90). One cannot help, of course, hearing double a new order of the line. The decade was a strong literary decade notwithstanding the presence or absence of an avant-garde. In 1946 Judith Wright's first book, *The Moving Image*, was published. Rosemary Dobson's first collection *In a Convex Mirror*, came out in 1944, and Kenneth Slessor's *Five Bells* was published on the eve of the decade in 1939, a collection which clearly engages modernism. Most of Slessor's work was published before the end of the war, and "Five Bells", the collection's title poem, dedicated to a friend who drowned in Sydney harbour, is distinctly modern in sound if not structure, with its heavily marked refrain – the five bells "coldly ringing out" – and its meditation on time and world, a clear break from Henry Lawson and the poetry of the late nineteenth century. Kate Lilley has described the poem's "allegorical refrain" as "masculine elegy" (263–4), synthesising Early Modern scholarship with existing scholarship on Australian modernism to draw such a conclusion.

The rebirth of Australian literary culture would seem an allegory for those gendered dynamics Williams inadvertently opened up: women writers, like Wright and Dobson, began their writing in the 1940s, so the "androgynous" birth could take place. But Williams's quandary, and his moment of writing through the chaos of modernism and its crises of sterility against provinces of modernity, is answered too in the tolling of Slessor's urbanite bells: there but for Slessor modernism might have died. I will not be claiming that before our eyes an Antipodal avant-garde would appear, as if a mirage, out of the desert. I will not claim the desert empty, yet nor can I claim that Malley, Hooton and the 1940s avant-garde were prophets of a poetic revolution to come. Drawing lines of connection between social forms and poetic forms, and most specifically, a new order of the poetic line, is not a critical habit exclusive to the Australian literary condition: what is most at stake here, I will stress, is the status of an avant-garde within and against modernism.

II. *The Neoteric Line*

Before situating Malley and Harry Hooton in these literary, political and ideological constellations, permit me one more clarification with regard to the avant-garde in theory. If the historical function of the avant-garde is, as Julia Kristeva would have it, to foment revolution in poetic language that in the semiotic realm cannot but disrupt the symbolic register, or, as Rosalind Krauss managed to convince us, if the avant-garde was born out of the discourse (and then the myth) of originality, then to what extent is it possible to pry our way out of twentieth-century revolutionary political culture without succumbing as it were to such excessive interiorisation encapsulated in the Surrealist flight from the political? What is the price of that modicum of aloofness required for the literary historian? How far can we go? Can we speak of ancient, even romantic, avant-gardes? The term *enters* history unobliged to the gelidity and the exceptionalism of twentieth-century historicism. Historicism releases the excess that, for scholarship, enfleshes the essay, but where the metabolism of modernism has sped up it is rarely allowed to go out, too far, or back, right back. Jed Rasula's adroit move from Dada narrative in *Destruction Was My Beatrice: Dada and the Unmaking of the Twentieth Century* to a theory of change itself in *Acrobatic Modernism, from the Avant-Garde to Prehistory*, seems enough to coax the discipline to embrace, rather than frame and neutralise, the frantic "metabolism" of modernism's avant-gardes.

History doesn't concur with our discipline, necessarily. Under such conditions, the first avant-garde in the dynamic we can understand today, even before Pasquier and the French Humanists, were the Neoteric poets (Neoterikoi) of the Hellenistic period, from the death of Alexander in 323 BC to the emergence of the Roman Empire. R. O. A. M. Lyne, in a 1978 work on the Neoterics, begins with Cicero's "humorously concocted" Grecising line which all but reveals that he "must in fact be *parodying* what he regards as a typical 'neoteric' line" (60). Lyne is specific about what makes Cicero's hexameter parodic of Catullus; "The autonomasia, the euphonic sibilance, and the mannered rhythm (the five-word line with fourth foot homodyne; the spondaic fifth foot)" (60). If it sounds to us like layers of parodic Antipodal modernism, Lyne is also concerned to draw parallels. Lyne sees an Alexandrian tendency or a reactive tendency to the Horatian epic; from this we begin to ascertain a "neoteric programme" (69, 76, 80–4). That history hears about a vanguard group (movement, school) from its detractors first (and that we know this from how we read their exemplary or typical line) is the lesson we might learn not only from the Greek neoterics but also the Malley affair, which I will place in a different imagining of literary history. I suspect, as Lyne did of the neoterics, that behind the affair something else lies, but the history I found does not confine itself to the 1940s. It rather becomes a beacon for modern and specifically avant-garde Australian poetry *erga omnes*. The dynamic is curious. Just as Cicero's parody of Catullus sets off this evidentiary hunch, and hunt, for a neoteric school, and just as it was the parody of the neoteric line that very plausibly identified the existence of a whole school, the Malley affair defined the modernism we came to understand as Antipodal. It did so in commentary and in the critical sphere with comparative rigour. We are in the position now to ask what characterises the Malleyan line and what precisely differentiates Australian modernist and avant-garde poetics at core. No loss at all: for even if an avant-garde *identity* appears neoteric from the negative, out of the framework of its detractors; a *reconstructive vanguard*, to move through the provenance of the avant-garde in the 1940s, the Malley-Hooton era (keeping an eye on what it became) allows us to put behind us some of the hopelessness of the pseudonymous infamity that envelops it.

The 2017 North American Green Integer republication of Ernest Lalor Malley's *The Darkening Ecliptic*, the partly citational hoax created with the use of various source-texts, and self-confessed "literary experiment" of Harold Stewart and James McAuley concocted to dupe Max Harris, editor of the *Angry Penguins*, confirms its status as one of, if not the literary *cause célèbre* of its century. For we have before us newly built contexts, hemispherically aslant and transatlantically realigned, contexts now glued to the global domain, a domain that, as Pablo Capra, the editor of the new edition points out, retemporalises *a posteriori*: "Newspapers carried front-page stories ridiculing the avant-garde for finding merit in Malley's poems. Chagrined, the avant-garde stood by their assessment" (n.pag.). Whether *all* avant-gardists stood by their assessment, I can dispute (Harry Hooton did not). It is, rather, a work that tells us something about three things: 1. Modernism in a global sense in and of itself, how it was perceived and what critical blockages to modernism there were in a certain place (Australia); 2. Citation as method peculiar to both modernism and the avant-garde; 3. *The place of avant-gardism in modernism* – that if there was anything new to signpost, it was the status of the avant-garde as a component of modernism that led to the obscure patterning of contexts that neutralised both. Few would doubt that the politics and poetics of Australian modernist poetry in the 1940s concerned itself not simply with the activity of the new. Malley was not an attempt at modernist genius, as Bob Perelman would phrase it, and Malley could not do what Williams demanded of Antipodal poetry. Models of impasse (literary sterility) and androgynetic passage define not the parturition of poetic genius but the genus of a cultural creativity itself. The way Antipodal modernism had run itself off the map then, and onto it now, through the figure of Malley, has to be read as historically conflictual: although, as Harris would later recount to the famous Australian art historian Robert Hughes, the affair changed the whole map, the entire history of Australian poetry (Heyward, xv), few knew what in *poetics*, in language, and in theory, it was all about. The fuss, as it were, was a fuss first, before it became a contest of ideas. And in debates about modern Australian poetry – other than some comprehension of the status of verbal experimentation as against "academic" formalism that came back in the 1950s in Australia, and, albeit differently, America too, or some such other reduction of the decadal turns of Australian literary culture – it's still up for grabs as to what Malley was about in theory. Obscurations – or claims of obscuration – aside, we can at least map the principle players in this game of modernist conspiracy. Perhaps, as Kirkpatrick reads it, the knee-jerk reaction to Malley was the very thing that created Australian modernism:

> Philistine laughter at the avant-garde overlooks the extent to which Malley's poems might have been an argument not so much against modernism as *about* it, and specifically about the fashionable authority of surrealism to speak the modern world compared to that of an older Symbolist heritage. (13–14)

Philistinic laughter at the avant-garde it was. But in no way did it spell the end of the conversation. John Hawke's study on the Symboliste influence on Australian modernist poetry, looking at Slessor, Hope, Wright, McAuley and Brennan, demonstrates in history, if not in theory, the extent of these negotiations. Occasionally the modernist ramifications of the Symboliste are writ large onto an avant-garde postscript. It was, after all, McAuley himself, who, in his 1975 anthology *Map of Australian Verse*, described the prose-poems of Frank Le Mesurier, in Patrick White's 1957 novel *Voss*, as "more avant-garde than anything else in Australian writing of that period" (6). McAuley's poem "Catherine Hill Bay 1942" has as its final quatrain:

> Not yet rotted by artists,
> Or some poetic tout,
> That day it just existed
> In time turned inside out.
>   (*Collected Poems*, 206)

Not yet, but very soon, time would turn inside out. And as Michael Heyward, author of *The Ern Malley Affair*, would note, the hoax was "however improbably, the conduit across the Pacific between the New York avant-garde and the Australian poets who began to write under its spell" (233). They took to Malley very quickly. John Ashbery in 1945 had shown interest in Malley's poetics as surrealist exemplar, as well as Harry Mathews, the American Oulipean, along with Kenneth Koch, James Schuyler, and a good proportion of the New York School. Koch included Malley in the 1961 edition of *Locus Solus*.

The crossed lines of global modernism after the 1940s have come to define how we read Malley: a careering route from negation to affirmation and back. For at once the Malley question puts up blockages and blindspots against any recovery of an Australian avant-garde. Yet on another level altogether its reappearance in a global context opens it up to new critical concepts and histories. Modernism guides debates about the Antipodal avant-garde in the international sphere, yet holds it hostage. It would seem, also, that in the context of comparative poetics, the crossed temporalities that mark the multiple births and rebirths of modernism between 1950 and 1970 cannot be retold through Malley alone. That's where we begin. For an Australian critical and poetics heritage, it remains unclear as to just how much we can play Malley alone against these currents, against the moderns, or with the antimoderns. Know then the *contest* from which these poems arose, and we'll find the light. Know the *context* and the poetics will sort itself out when the time comes to shift focus.

The light dims on this historical arc. What we've come to historicise as Antipodal vanguardism needs more or else. Our argument is therefore both simple and complex: Malley becomes part of the question not only of modernism but also the avant-garde, so a critical poetics of the Antipodal avant-garde robust enough to recontextualise the Malley poems in this kind of light becomes our priority. We can read the Malley poems, and the affair as a whole, not as stopgap, a comico-tragic nail in the coffin of Australian modernism, or symptom, but integral to a series of debates that followed it around and about avant-garde poetics. This moved them, and will move us away from the fatalistic notion of Malley as a dead end. Rather, we see how it becomes part of larger constellations of historical processes and contradictions that arose between modernism and vanguardism in the 1940s.

III. *Pseudo Avant-Gardes, or, Two Ways of Being Historical*

The story is too simple: the Malley affair *forestalled* the avant-garde, and it even forestalled a generalised modernism (how defined?). No matter: it did not recover. The situation was never resolved, and so thereafter Australian poetry would potter along without an avant-garde, and consign itself to that fate. This would not be wholly wrong. But if it was such a tragedy, exactly what *kind* of poetics was it that Australian poetry missed out on getting, or making? How did Australian poetry find itself in such a historically confounding position that critics would have to lament the poetry that *didn't* get written? It is true that the status of the poetic avant-garde in 1940s Australian poetry was, on the surface of it, determined by certain insurmountable historical events that have given critics cause to cite modernism as a lost cause. As above, the net "loss", I claim, that we must bear at the outset, is how to situate these lost or prohibited modernisms without an overt consensus around a birth mythography; it was not the case that what applied for Williams applied for the period in focus here. But in the absence of such myth we can see just how a situation of perceived sterility came to halt the goings on of modernism and therefore the avant-garde. It is here that we begin to conjure fantasies of temporal capture, of literary-historical time-capsules and belated timescapes. Paul Kane notes that the Malley affair "set modernism back twenty years" (142), but we need not necessarily read exhaustion as stemming from this one cause. What is "needed" in this case is an attention to literary history, and as Kane puts it, literary history in a subtler key. For literary history,

> however insular, is still inscribed within "history" or intersects with other "histories." We could argue, however jejunely, that the profound and traumatic changes that World War II enforced upon Australia provoked a conservative entrenchment not unlike the one experienced in America at the same time; that the postwar "Age of Anxiety" was a period of consolidation leading to the conformism of the 1950s, and that Australia followed suit; that the defeat of the Labor Party in 1949, and with it the advent of the Menzies government, was indicative of a broad social conservatism. In the more formal terms of literary history, we might argue that the avant-garde movement in Europe was played out and exhausted, that some reaction was inevitable. But, however we think of this period, it is unlikely that the adversary role modernist writers in Australia found themselves in would have been substantially altered if Ern Malley had not occurred. Nor would the modernist ranks necessarily have been swollen with flocks of "Angry Penguins," even though there were certainly some who felt betrayed, bewildered or put upon by the hoax. In sum, Ern Malley was an effect, not a cause; or rather, it became a "cause" because it was a symptom. The question then arises, of what was it symptomatic? (151)

Literary history as Kane reads it can contain the key to the question: of what was it symptomatic? Kane opts to read the symptom in a uniquely Antipodal negation of romanticism, alongside attendant contradictions between surrealism and romanticism. It is a convincing thesis, that not only allows us to make sense of just how much the literary-historical image becomes distorted across these Antipodal temporalities, but takes us closer to the driving vortex that lay behind the curtailed swelling of the betrayed modernist corps. The symptomatisation of Malley enforces a certain punctum from which we announce the voiding, even just "absenting" of either romanticism or a vanguard that refuses to face us. On the other hand, even if the Malley poems are in a parodic "tradition" of sorts, this doesn't get us really to what seems to be missing in Kane's identification of romanticism as an Antipodal blind spot, for the more glaring blind spot seems to be the absence of an avant-garde as a constituent part of Antipodean modernism. The crisis here can just as easily be framed as one of the status of avant-gardism as anything else. Equally a matter for the formal terms of literary history, the *character* of Malley's parodical negativity, we would be amiss not to point out, is continuous with Antipodal tradition. Read then some continuation of the Brennan-Malley effect in A. D. Hope's *Dunciad Minor: An heroick poem*, completed in 1950 and published in 1970, which he prefaces by saying "it began partly as a private joke never meant for publication and partly as an exercise in a form of literary criticism" (v). Not merely dismissive; Hope's literary-critical jokiness has been noted. In a 1969 lecture to the Sydney Association, Harry Heseltine reads A. D. Hope's parodic poem "On First Looking into Gerard Manley Hopkins" as serious jest, but also to a degree, a dismissal of Hopkins's prosody: hearing "foot-rot-feet". Rather than dismissing the poem as a bit of humour Heseltine marks deeper dynamics at play, the fact, for instance, that Hope feels "uncomfortably aware" that there is something more going on in rhythm (*Unspeakable Stress*, 9–10). In 1944, W. H. Gardner would publish his work on poetic idiosyncrasy and the tradition in Hopkins, and it was F. R. Leavis himself who most strongly warned against overlooking his prosodic originality for charges of "oddity" and "obscurity" in the reception of Hopkins, and appreciated that most radically dissonant of poems, "Spelt from Sibyl's Leaves" (*New Bearings*, 161–5). By contrasting Leavis's, and Hope's ear for Hopkins's prosody (for the latter, the "prosodic (even neurotic) strain" of it was too much to bear), Heseltine seeks a "third position" between, pre-echoing Hooton's view on Malley further below (*Unspeakable Stress*, 10). However difficult it was for Antipodal modernists to accept language-centredness in poetry, whether Hope, Stewart or McAuley, or whether Malleyan poetics mounts an argument either way, Heseltine seems to prefigure change in the critical industries themselves. Heseltine pleads for a refrain from blank dismissals of Hopkins's poetry. In a magnificent critical moment, he asks us to listen again, and listen openly to Hopkins "in its stressful way of happening" for its "unique combination of drama, declamation and song" and so "bid us attend to a rare spirit whose nature might otherwise have remained unspoken" (*Unspeakable Stress*, 22).

Drop back to the bunker and now we find ourselves searching for degrees of reflexivity in the act. Was the work of Corporal Harold Stewart and Lieutenant James McAuley (both were Australian military servicemen) undertaken at Victoria Barracks, the work of an avant-garde in disguise, or, as Philip Mead put it, a "pseudo-avant-garde"? Was it "unashamedly" avant-garde, as the Angry Penguins had apparently become (Mead, "1944, Melbourne and Adelaide", 113)? McAuley's early fascination with Gérard de Nerval, Guillaume Apollinaire and Mallarmé, like Brennan, seems to prove that it took a disaffected radical, one who *knew* the poetics he was sending up, to effectively concoct a reactionary text. On the other side, it was the mantra of the Angry Penguins to not stand for anything "pseudo-modern". Yet there is nothing more literally vanguardist than the fact that Stewart and McAuley wrote the poems in military barracks. Being not so up front about one's poetics, backing up one's "ribald interventions" ("Palinode"), obscuring one's person, not putting one's body on the front line, not being, as Macintyre puts it with regard to postwar reconstruction in the 1940s, quite up for "Australia's boldest experiment" – all this might be no coincidence when considered as a corporeal-temporal poetics, and on a "Corporal" register. An odd polarity beckons here, placing Malley in comparison with Harry Hooton. For all his proto-posthuman, or inhuman leanings – unseating the body to the mind, that readers might recall from Futurism – Hooton idolises, and ironises the irrationality of the modern body, and looks for justifications in the poetics of specific poets, like Whitman, Stein, Eliot, but not in a way that results in a negating of all aesthetic possibilities from these engagements. Hooton too was certainly "suspicious", if not intrigued, by modern form, but in a manner both reactive and openly participatory.

"Neurasthenic modernism", as Amelia Jones calls it in light of the Baroness, plays on these Antipodal nerves. Rethinking the conflicting bodies of moderns and vanguardists (the Baroness vs. Duchamp, Baroness vs Williams, to the more recent critical example), it is of course possible to conceive of the fact (should we not be again deceived) that McAuley and Stewart may have been avant-gardists *critiquing* the avant-garde – within global modernism, bringing in discourses on Hopkins, Eliot – but with negotiations of the modern at the core of their concerns. There are critiques that make a claim for the Malley poems as an intervention in poetics, as Brian Lloyd puts it in an article that grapples directly with the question of avant-gardes in light of what it means to "be modern":

> It would seem then that in some sense the Sydney group's platform of ideals and practices conformed to the category "avant-garde," despite their apparent objections to the very concept itself, and an acute ambivalence to the kind of environment in which avant-gardes operate. Conformation to the classic pattern of making attacks on other formations within the same milieu supports this view. This leads us to a new perspective from which to review the Ern Malley poems: as, in some senses, an avant-garde text, attacking another avant-garde text (thus satisfying the requirements of the *cause célèbre*), and proposing, through its criticism of Angry Penguins, a log of claims of its own: that is, a manifesto. Increasingly, this begins to be not the textual manifestation of a dispute between "ancients and moderns," but simply between two different ways of being modern. (31)

So convincing is the possibility of a manifesto at work that we would only have to go back to Malley's "Young Prince of Tyre" to see a layer of sincerity beneath the train of images:

> The magpie's carol has dried upon his tongue
> To a flaky spittle of contempt. The loyalists
> Clank their armour. We are no longer young,
> And our rusty coat fares badly in the lists.
> Poor Thaisa has a red wound in the groin
> That ill advises our concupiscence to foin.
> Yet there is one that stands i' the gaps to teach us
> The stages of our story. He the dark hero
> Moistens his finger in iguana's blood to beseech us
> (Siegfried-like) to renew the language. Nero
> And the botched tribe of imperial poets burn
> Like the rafters. The new men are cool as spreading fern.
> (1988 edition, 87)

The ridicule is the frame. Should any critic, any reader, be duped by their perception of language being renewed, that the new men against the imperial poets might be a riddle whose allegorical outworking would be Antipodal poetry itself, then the meaning of the riddle has remained obscure. That *Pericles, Prince of Tyre* was only half-written by Shakespeare (most likely written with George Wilkins some time between 1607 and 1608) and that the play is about ambiguity, about riddles, extractive meaning, should be enough to convince us that this is more than a mere reactionary slight on authorship and originality (we will see more about this in the next section on the Malley reader). Yet even if there is no manifesto at work, we need then to ask what it was they were poking fun at: What poetics? What type of ambiguity? What aspect of modernism and what aspect of the avant-garde? Lloyd's two ways of being modern pertain also to the issue of the rational. Two ways of being modern had to do with the question of surrealism; how in the Australian context, it had severed its ties with romanticism. For as Kane well points out, at the core of the Malley poems lies a desire for the modern (within this, but not reducible to it, the more extreme forms of experiment an avant-garde engaged) that both confronts and represses the dilemma of a constructedness in irrationality, or as Jones on the Baroness put it, the "neurasthenic" in modernity. For Kane again it was the question of what rationality they could get behind that was at stake:

> What we begin to suspect, then, is a division and tension within these two poets over the issue of unconscious inspiration . . . Increasingly,

especially as one investigates the early writings of the hoaxers, it appears that two aspiring mystics attempted to demystify an avant-garde with which they had affinities, in the name of a rationality in which they did not wholly concur. And if this language of paradox and tension calls to mind New Critical shibboleths, all the better, for the poems themselves deserve closer reading. (147)

The New Critical shibboleths get caught in the matrix of assumptions that the poems bring up and tempt us towards: what kind of close reading would uncover rationality and subjectivity at work? As to value in the modernist enterprise, could it be the irrationality in neurasthenic modernism, especially attributed to the radical body of the Baroness, that was enticing to the male hoaxers (the new men?), or was the citational element the sole cause of the poem's syntactic uncertainty? What rationale, what structure, in other words, did their unconscious minds take (split affinities assumed)? Here the theoretical aspect can come into sharper focus. Questions of the historicity of the avant-garde are pertinent to theoretical quandaries we have touched upon; namely how literary history poses a challenge to the avant-garde *as* theoretical in the environment of institutions. Tyrus Miller's 1999 work on the misunderstood relation of the avant-garde and theory exposes just how much 1. We rely on theory to get to an understanding of unrelentingly difficult avant-garde works, and 2. How theories are so often inadequately "applied" over the works, especially when they intentionally resist interpretation. A historiographical theory of the avant-garde would, on the other hand, take the *history of historical accounts* as a basis for theories. Theories of what? To a large extent, in this analysis, time. Also style, culture, politics. I will not treat the theory of an avant-garde as tantamount to a "politics of" the avant-garde, just as I will not imagine theory to mean a series of conspiracies that explain the root cause of an (or the) avant-garde. Theory can help with poetics, especially with difficulty, not only understanding reasons for difficulty but the changing historical meaning of difficulty. Neither am I emptying theory of politics. Hooton, more than Malley, was a theorist. Hooton too would pursue a very specific, and rationalist politics, "anarcho-technocracy", a machinic theory of materialism. But his was a species of rationalism not in accordance with the discourse of historical materialism. For all the irrationality of the corporeally wired vanguard wedged in neurasthenic modernity, being committed to a politics and political aesthetics could regulate Hooton's tetchy nerves, relinquish some egoic verve so to weather tricky social and philosophical crosswinds. It could also put his poetics into overdrive. Balancing, or playing off these tensions against each other in poems, and in close theorisations of 1940s Australian poetry: that is the critical choice ahead. The fuller this history becomes, the nearer we get, in theory, to the politics of an Antipodal avant-garde, but there are markedly contrastive ways of being historical about politics, and always two (or more) ways about it (but often two). Vanguardist politics emerges glutted with theoretical and historical dualities: rationalism as against irrationality, culture vs class, anarchism vs communism, fascism vs communism, anarchism vs libertarianism, humans vs machines, utopians vs realists, vectors vs returns, and so on.

Literary history squares with theory. It allows us to arrange before us the objects and subjects that compose the totality of an avant-garde, insofar as we can match texts to subjects. The pseudo, or pseudonymous avant-garde, as Mead put it, does after all imply the existence of a truer avant-garde on the other end. The Malley discourse, or narrative, made it easier to imagine that a vanguard poet was dead, or a hoax, than living and alive. Another narrative of the 1940s, especially one ready to take into account the works of Hooton, can reveal that the avant-garde poet very much could be a living participant: "listen to me: I am alive".[4] A living participant, that is, engaging explicitly, not pseudonymously, with theories intimate to global modernism, issues of poetics, aesthetics, authors, psychoanalytic and philosophical discourses, and with political cultures of the era. To add context yet again, let me be clear about the political situation the Angry Penguins faced: they operated within a limited framework. It was a time in which it was all too easy to pitch libertarianism against populism, modernist aesthetics against "people-centred" aesthetics. Taking Stewart and McAuley's

---

[4] From "It Is Great To Be Alive" (Hooton, *Collected*, 102), a closer reading further below. The critic Herbert Read, anarchist, and strident supporter of the avant-gardes and criticism thereof, weighed in on the Malley affair saying that the hoaxes themselves had been exposed. Read's critical approach very obviously leads to this, given his uses of Jungian psychoanalysis and interest in the psychical layers of artistic and literary objects. Robert Hughes, Australian art critic, celebrated and contentious in world terms, was, like Hooton, part of the anarchist Push movement. For Hughes, the wound to Australian literary modernism was so deep that it would engulf Australian participants in the debate (before Heyward), many of whom remained so much *parti pris* as to not get a full view (Introduction, xx). Hughes also reminds us that Malley's middle name, *Lalor*, recalls Peter Lalor, a leader of the Eureka Stockade miner's revolt in 1854. In criticism the affair renders literary modernism dead, or abidingly *undead*. Hooton's curious "I am alive" could also be an Antipodal avant-garde catch-cry pitched against deadness.

side, Australian communists were firmly united against the Angry Penguins, and in their schema it was anarchist individualism and reactionary nationalism pitched against Soviet realism and Soviet internationalism: the people-centred, "constructive", "right" and "correct" way to develop and advance modern literature, a line typical of communist parties and their adherents of this period.[5] Readers not accustomed to early twentieth-century analyses of class politics might find it some surprise that a major conflict was between the Leninist view that proletarian culture could indeed source Great Art, against the Trotskyist notion not only of a disjunct between Marxism and artistic method, but that the proletariat would have to learn from the creative intelligentsia (for as much as art would play a role), this as much as the Freudo-Surrealism versus realism binary. It was a time when it was possible for communists to argue that the proletariat couldn't produce good art. For the Australian communist, the Angry Penguins were the worst of the intelligentsia, not simply philistinic, but prohibitors of a free society. For a sense of this line, it is worth quoting at length Katherine Susannah Prichard's 1945 response to the affair:

> Fortunately, the "Angry Penguins" do not represent a trend of any importance in Australian affairs. The Ern Malley hoax has brought them more publicity than they ever enjoyed: but it has not enhanced their prestige. The rising tide of the national and international struggle for realism and sanity to direct plans affecting the future welfare of mankind will sweep past all such "slim, gilt souls," ignoring their futile gestures and megalomania.
>
> Australian communists are guided by the same principles as have guided Russian and Chinese communists, and will continue to guide the communists of the world. We can say, as did the Commanders-in-Chief of the Red Army of China, General Chu Teh [Zhu De], in an interview with a correspondent of the "Sydney Morning Herald," recently: "We are believers in the Marxist and Leninist principles, no matter how we were compelled by circumstances to diverge temporarily in matters of detail. Our main job is to stay on the locomotive of history and guide it in the right direction."
>
> Many able writers and artists in Australia will be stoking that locomotive. A literary hoax may not be a very significant contribution to our war effort, but it has cleared the way for development of modern poetry and prose on a sound basis. (457)

---

[5] The Malley episode was not enough of an issue to split the Party. A long history of splits within the Party pertain mainly to the status of Ted Hill and the complexities of the Sino-Soviet split.

Stridently positivistic in tone, and unflinchingly in the imperative, a sound which would solidify in the Brezhnev era and become part of long-term socialist diction, the Australian communists would affirm its "principled" line: its role in the historical locomotive. It is of course palpable to the modern Marxist reader just how much the Marxist-anarchist debates had persisted in these times, remembering that in the Chinese context, especially before Mao, these debates were foundational to the formation of Party ideology. I will return to these political questions in Hooton, an anarchist with individualist leanings. For now, let us pause to reflect upon another mode of future operative criticality: less focus on the hoax *qua* hoax as the question of what the Malley poems did in or to a poetics, and a sense of what those who have done readings *of* Malley (Malley readers) have offered up as a plurality of poetics. I will then do readings of Harry Hooton's poetics, from the 1940s to the 1960s, a significant instance of avant-garde poetics in these decades, thereafter expanding the horizon of discussions pertaining to the Australian avant-garde. A curt summary of this process would be to keep tab of the move from pseudo-avant-garde to Antipodal avant-garde proper: to pay some regard to those other participants and poetics of the period. The 1940s would be a period when avant-garde practices could still touch the surface of an Australian poetry even while still besotted with, and torn apart by, the vicissitudes of modernism. To this, Hooton is the key figure. So what proceeds here is a twofold agenda. First: to read global Malley readers from other hemispheres, and take stock of what they gained or lost in their readings of the poems. Second: to read this cycle of disputes and counterpoints in poetics in light of Hooton, who happened to be a Malley reader and an exemplary vanguardist, as our culminating example and final passage away from the Malley impasse.

IV. *The Malley Reader*

David Brooks, in *Sons of Clovis: Adoré Floupette and a Secret History of Australian Poetry*, connects Malley to another 1885 hoaxing work, *Les Déliquescences d'Adoré Floupette*, a send-up of the Symbolistes. Perpetrated by Henri Beauclair and Gabriel Vicaire, they are the "Sons of Clovis" because they revolted against their father, Clovis II. For punishment their vitality is removed and their muscles given to entropy. They remain inert, neutralised, impotent, robbed of life. This is a parable then of what Malley is believed to have done to

Australian modernism: left it inert, unable to do anything but surrender to a lifeless life-in-death, adrift. Malley readers could take the muscle out of modernism, yet we can also take the Malley reader to be an exemplary modern: the Malley reader claims to know, or claims Malley as the subject-supposed-to-know (in Lacanian parlance), and know something about poetics, style and the politics of Australian literary culture. The Malley reader is supposed to know, of course, something about global modernism and modernity, perhaps something about the avant-garde, and why the poetics of the poems can put modernism or the avant-garde to shame. Malley readers could be opinionated, grandiose, glib, depressive, opportunistic, short-sighted, eccentric, pedantic or confused. The latter, being confused, was probably the main outcome and for that the hoaxers succeeded. But by putting the question of the avant-garde back into the equation, some of these uncertainties are given unusual clarity.

Modernism might have lost its way because of this affair, but the avant-garde may not have felt the same historical jolt that the modernists did. Consequently it is the internationalism of Malley readers that I read as vital. In *Interpretation as Pragmatics*, Jean-Jacques Lecercle, French literary theorist and philosopher of language, includes a section subtitled "Australian Modernism", as part of "The Author, or: Intention'. He decides to do a close interpretation of "Dürer: Innsbruck, 1495'. "The poem is worthy," Lecercle implores, for "that is the first task of the interpreter – of a close commentary, of the kind of *explication de textes* the French educational system takes pride" (137). Lecercle's fivefold and remarkably long reading of the poem is unmistakably close, getting down to grammar, tense, what it is *about* (Dürer, Eliot, representation, Romantic imagination, illusion, the image of the black swan, repetition, alienation, "inanimation", anticipatory postmodernism, paradoxes of the modern, structures of feeling). Some preliminaries: the Australian poet, for Lecercle, is exiled

> because of his dependence on a European tradition (this is not the production of a "bush poet") that allows him to write, but rejects his poetry as marginal. The black swan mourns for an irretrievably lost original Australian voice. But it is also, *rara avis*, the incarnation of the Romantic genius whose exotic song, even if only at the moment of his death, will inform delighted Europeans that Australia at last exists on the map of world poetry. (140)

Most intriguing are the diagrams, or mappings, that Lecercle then provides to explain what is happening between Author (A),

New Order of the Line: the 1940s Avant-Gardes   123

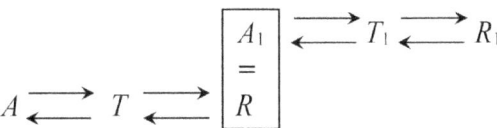

Figure 3.1 Jean-Jacques Lecercle, "Diagram 1: Naive", *Interpretation as Pragmatics* (1999).

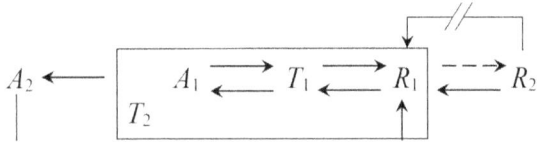

Figure 3.2 Jean-Jacques Lecercle, "Diagram 2: Anxious", *Interpretation as Pragmatics* (1999).

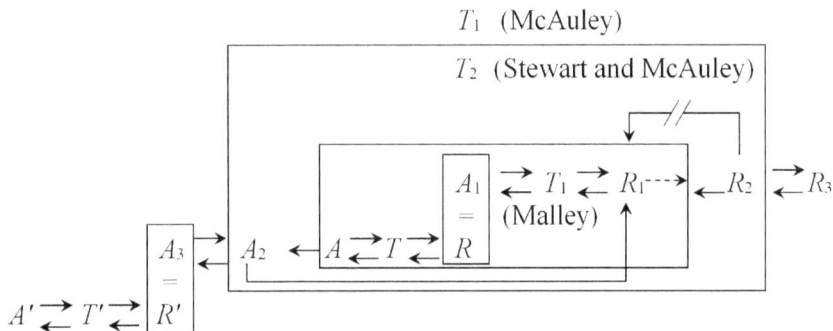

Figure 3.3 Jean-Jacques Lecercle, "Diagram 3: Clever", *Interpretation as Pragmatics* (1999).

Figure 3.4 Jean-Jacques Lecercle, "Diagram 4: Pretentious", *Interpretation as Pragmatics* (1999).

$\boxed{T'} \leftarrow (A_n\ A_3\ A_2\ A_1) \leftarrow \boxed{T_4\ \text{(Anthology)}} \rightarrow (R_n\ R_2\ R_3\ R_n) \rightarrow \boxed{T''}$

Figure 3.5 Jean-Jacques Lecercle, "Diagram 4: Pretentious", *Interpretation as Pragmatics* (1999).

Reader (R) and Text (T) once the hoax is revealed, and once it began being used by the Australian press to "demolish" avant-garde art.

The complexity and circularity is illustrated in stages, as is customary with philosophy of language (Figures 3.1 to 3.5). The five diagrams represent five situations, or successive stages that the Malley affair induces in Lecercle's reading of the poem. I have extracted them from the readings in which they are encased for expediency. The lay reader need not know any more than that the mathematical function of transformation, a type of mapping, produces operations. When an operation goes one way it produces sets. "A" becomes a set of Authors. "R" in these schemas are Readings, and are too operations or vectors: they operate on the text, and are too transformations.

This explication verbally unravels each reading. The first is a "Naive" and all too illusory one in that it reveals a chain of transmission (as a flow chart) where the reading is the circuit of Author and Reader through Text. In the second reading Lecercle is anxious, or in an anxious situation, because an equivalence between Author and Reader has opened new relations (Malley is an Author *and* a Reader; of what? Of Dürer). This chain of reading – Malley reading Dürer – rides infinitely leftward because Dürer too is a reader in the history of painting. Change in intention deceives the reader, makes Lecercle "look foolish", yet still requires this new, second, perhaps better reading, but it isn't as enjoyable, given the level of awareness of fabrication inherent in "*poietics*", and *techne*, itself. Whereas the first reading shows a simple circular transmission between Author, Text and Reader, in the second the sets lead to the Text itself.

Following this Lecercle embarks upon a third reading, revealing that the first was not as naive as was supposed. This is the "Clever" reading in that, newly enlightened as to the fact it was a hoax, a short-circuit of Freudian denial takes place. The two hoaxers are outside the Naive box, so to speak, and so is Lecercle (let me break protocol and say A_2 in Diagram 3 is the hoaxers). To summarise:

> My first reading constructed an author who was so modern as to be post-modern, and a poem that was a kind of pastiche. The second constructed another bent upon burlesque, and a poem that was a parody. The third constructs a modernist author and a poem engaged both in and with modernism. (145)

Now we have made it to modernism. But this is where it gets most "complicated", so Lecercle tells us, in that while it could amount to commentary on the issue of tradition and the individual talent (Eliotic modernism), his "megalomaniac" reading has departed from the text, now, through "a sort of metalepsis, or contractual Gricean [Paul Grice] implicature, so once it is understood that the whole thing is a hoax the contents of the poem, the poem itself, in fact, become immaterial: all that is of interest is the ingenuity of the author and the gullibility, or astuteness, of the reader" (147).

In the fourth reading (should McAuley here be T_3?) the naive reader (R_1) might not have been so stupid because McAuley's seriousness as a modernist (he has been pulled away from Stewart) and the fact that this was a serious poem, means he is a reader of Eliot and of (global) modernism. Another level of deception is unveiled because, as Lecercle admits, he has read Michael Heywood's book on the matter, and therefore knows that this poem, though later included in *The Darkening Ecliptic*, was written beforehand by McAuley. The whole situation, not just exclusive parties within, is pretentious, meaning that the accusation of the Angry Penguins is pretentious, even that the Reader has come to it pretentiously and is part of the frame. To identify the target: *being pretentious*. Pretentiousness, as a term not so much of interpretation as dismissal, is more curious as a literary trope than we may think, especially given, as a term of dismissal, rarely do we go further than dismissal: such a text is pretentious, as that is what it is. But what makes it pretentious? Are we reading on the level of class, or just hunch? More than irony, a theory of avant-garde pretentiousness in general, outside this reading alone, could take into account Lecercle's *"generalised imposture"* (148).

Thus far we have several expanding rectangles that present different reading ecologies or situations: the naive-postmodern, burlesque and full modernist engagement. But it is the final, and fifth diagram, "Ironic", that is unique, and the most illuminating for our purposes. Lecercle reminds us that *The Darkening Ecliptic* enters into the canon, and into the tradition, through its anthologisation in the 1991 *Penguin Book of Modern Australian Poetry*, edited by John Tranter and Philip Mead, which omits Max Harris and Harold Stewart while including the Malley poems in its entirety. This anthologisation has made Malley into a monument. In this diagram the arrows don't loop around: they are more hierarchical in this sublime monumentality. With Malley at the centre, going leftwards from the anthology is a T'-prime, which is a chain of Authors moving through towards an exemplary Eliotic modernism, bracketed because they are too numerous to be individuated. Going rightward are the chains of generic readers "$(R_1/R_2/R_3/R_4/)$" bracketed and deindividuated (now, it becomes apparent, they are more legion than Lecercle thought). But here the T'' double prime is something of a mystery. Lecercle seems to be saying that *The Darkening Ecliptic*, for all that it means for readers, is in this set anticipating something. Anticipating what? Something of a spectre, or monstrosity, a "Frankenstein".

The spectre that Malley anticipates, I read, is nothing but the avant-garde. What is missing in Lecercle's reading of Australian modernism is, of course, the avant-garde. It is a Frankenstein, a monster, because it has created something bigger than itself. I take this further than Lecercle to be *theory in the prophetic mode*, as Geoffrey Serle theorised it in 1972 with his nationalist history of the "creative spirit" in Australia, titled *From Deserts the Prophets Come*, as much as an external reflection upon the internal origins of an Australian "cultural cringe", as A. A. Phillips phrased it in 1950. Cringe here would be a combination of effects locally experienced, as opposed to naïveté, cleverness, pretention, anxiousness, experienced by the external critic. Prophetic of what? Literary revolution? What are we to make of the final assessment by Michael Heyward: "As poet and cipher he represents, with whatever perversity or futility, the definitive moment in Australian literary modernism. Malley is the exception that proves the rule: he is the only genuinely avant-garde writer in a country which has never sponsored a literary revolution" (237). Heyward's biographical portrait of Malley as exception, then exemplar of Australian modernism's contradictions is both beneficial for, and an impediment to, literary history. It risks a freezing-up, a stupefaction before the spectre of Malley, preventing a clear-minded contextualisation of the event as part of a longer poetics history of the avant-garde in Australian poetry. Lecercle is able to circumvent some of these literary-historical flaws in the fifth diagram. For this book, nevertheless, I am interested in how detractors of the avant-garde, even if internationally networked, shared a tendency to exceptionalise or totalise the affair in order to avoid, sidestep or downplay a greater range of approaches to the avant-garde in the Antipodes. Malley readers have not lacked clarity in exploring these issues, yet the narrative of exceptionality underpins a good many commentaries, as Guy Rundle had put it:

> Ern Malley was not the only artistic hoax to occur in modernity, but the others are all but forgotten. Ern persisted because the Australian avant-garde was so small that a hyperkinetic 22-year-old could be the editor of one of the nation's leading modernist publications, and was so eager to find a great Australian poet, that he could talk in the same letter of both the possibility that the poems were a hoax and also of his certainty that they were works of genius. (n.pag.)

The irony, Rundle suggests, is that it was precisely the smallness of the avant-garde, its weakness in context, that was the key to its global success and its persistence in modernity. We find the "forgotten" here suspicious, though; for reading the avant-garde as a series of historically mediated constructions, of examples and exceptions, not given but something unfixed, debatably uncertain in most of its coordinates – aesthetic, spatial, poetic – the *pretentions* of the Malley affair might say less about poetics as how in Australia "anything" could take centre stage. The question is now not *whether* an avant-garde existed, but which kind of avant-garde survived. What was this eagerness to take up anything and make it heroic? What lay behind such enthusiasm? Excitability, of course, more than blast, because an avant-garde will so often announce itself as a singularity: *an ism* within contested modernisms, not *the* avant-garde.

I find all this less confounding, though, than the fact that the use of *citational* elements, citational poetics, is so far "advanced", and attuned, in the Malley poems. I use this phrase, which entered the critical poetics lexicon through conceptual writing, and Marjorie Perloff's study on its longer history in modernism with *Unoriginal Genius* (which begins with Benjamin's *Passagenwerk*), and which found apotheosis in Charles Reznikoff's two-volume *Testimony* and *Holocaust* volumes, given Malley's demonstrably inventive and well-chosen spread of source-texts: dictionaries, the Concise Oxford, rhyming dictionaries, Dictionary of Quotations, a Collected Shakespeare and, most curiously, a US Army report on mosquito control. These produced the offbeat and, indeed, "surreal" gamut of literary effects that constitute its poetics. The mosquito report appears right at the beginning of "Culture as Exhibit", in quotation marks:

> "Swamps, marshes, borrow-pits and other
> Areas of stagnant water serve
> As breeding-grounds . . ." Now
> Have I found you, my Anopheles!
> (There is a meaning for the circumspect)
> Come, we will dance sedate quadrilles,
> A pallid polka or a yelping shimmy
> Over these sunken sodden breeding-grounds!
>   (1988 edition, 85)

The quotation marks don't make it any more obvious. Before the Internet it was not so easy to track down quotations as it is now. Despite this, they would state that "no care was taken with verse technique" (Heyward, 173). Here, I feel, as Lecercle did but for different reasons, duped. On the Antipodal continent it would have been difficult to imagine that the use of US government records of the

Holocaust in Reznikoff, Objectivist and modernist rather than avant-garde *per se*, could bring narrative epic and documentarian practice together in a manner that broke from collage and laid the foundations for conceptual writing in a juridical and political vein (much later M. NourbeSe Philip's *Zong!* would do the same with political and geo-political purpose). The obscenity trial against Max Harris, successful for the prosecutors and the first in Australian poetry, again confirms this odd association with law, state, nation and citation. If citation is the key to the poems, we shall have to begin all over again. Is it not the act of texturing, or peppering the citational text with both the Western Canon and eccentric source-texts like the US army mosquito control report, that gives poems like "Culture as Exhibit" (in hindsight) that scintillatingly Ashberyan affect of entering the talk-scape of a poem *in medias res*? Ashbery proffers a notably surreal, off-beat prosodics on the poems as we historically encounter them, and if we are to properly close-read, we would have to consider citation as technique, a type of poetics the prosodic result of which needs good ears. It's no New Critical shibboleth for the contemporary critic's critical toolbox. Perloff, who has been explicit about the influence of the New Critics in her style of close-reading, has shown that it is possible, with conceptual writing, to submit it to a kind of close reading. Robert Hughes, art critic, made the pun on the "well-wrought Ern" (Heyward, xix). Contrast Malley then with Cleanth Brooks's rejection of the notion that a poem could be the (over-)wrought product of a "formula" or "blueprint". Malley's recalcitrant deliberation is subtle because the conceits, and process, are both elaborately conceived (or "wrought") *and* spontaneously executed. The hoaxers raise a question critics have yet to contend with: the speed of composition itself, a factor sometimes known and often not, even when the date and time of composition is given. An approach to the language and literary effects of Malley poetics, if not evidence of Surrealist theories and techniques, becomes a kind of *underreading*, or, from the perspective of conceptual-citational poetics, an *overreading*, retroactive in the most historical of senses. And if the conceptualist toolbox does not amount to "technique", then how good were the hoaxers at doing citational poetics? With Ashberyan hindsight, very.

The Los Angeles-based, Australian-born conceptual poet, curator and performer Christine Wertheim, whose explorations in sound and visual poetry as well as sculptural/gallery work places her in the twenty-first century avant-garde, turns the critical gaze back on the American reader. Wertheim asks why it took Ashbery to send

Malley's star "streaking through the great blue vault of the Ozzie cultural sky", for when "passed through the transforming lens of the American avant-garde, Ern Malley's work did not only move from being derided to being admired; it also went from being fake to 'real.' For the Americans, who were hip to the hoax, the fictitious origins in no way detracted from the quality of the poems – perhaps those origins even enhanced it." Those attuned to an American cultural jouissance of the arras, like Wertheim, whose work in the gallery and performance context involves targeted engagements with 'pataphysics, ecology and literary science, would read Malley as a case of "literary experimentalism" in that more Oulipean of senses. For Wertheim, Lecercle's "pretentious" (not hip) diagram is especially useful for its interpolation of the author as an operation in a structure – R, A, T – letters that are *personae*, that are neither linguistic nor philosophical by default.

The final poem of *The Darkening Ecliptic* is "Petit Testament", after François Villon, and the final line of the whole sequence is "I have split the infinitive. Beyond is anything." David Brooks has considered the splitting of the infinitive, versus the split infinite, in philosophical as well as literary terms – it was misprinted in the Angry Penguins as "I have split the infinite" – but Brooks doesn't take the hoaxers at their word. Instead, subtending from a philosophico-literary angle, this slippage is read as the cause of their projection of their singular conflicts and emotions onto the Infinite, a projection despite the fact that McAuley, at least, could have distinguished the Infinite and the Absolute. The Australian literary-critical context, from the reductive judgement-based élitism of New Criticism and Leavisism (where one had to rely on the superior taste and sharper discernment of the Great Reader), to reactive, metaphysical and radical nationalists, New Left critiquers, semioticians with their enclosed vocabulary, sociological "Leninists", or even belated anti-deconstructionists, set a strange scene for the longer reception of the affair. In 1984, cultural critic John Docker (who, incidentally, could not place Hooton) issued a significant assessment of the Australian academic establishment, from Manning Clark to Leonie Kramer, Humphrey McQueen and Vincent Buckley, making a lively case for critical reading attentive to text and context, dually along national and international lines. Of Australian semioticians Docker would say that "like all colonial servants of an overseas cultural dominance (the theoretical majesty of Paris, France) local semioticians such as these are more enthusiastic about doing the work of intellectual imperialism than their metropolitan heroes are themselves" (218–19). On the one hand an intelligentsia is never an intelligentsia in one country alone, yet the Australian one could do the imperial voice better than the imperialists. It would be hard for anybody to see clearly. The importance, I want to strongly emphasise, of taking an internationalist view, lensing in and out from a distance, has practical purpose because measuring – in critical contexts, and in institutions – how and what methods were used to read texts, is a way of figuring out how certain conclusions were drawn about history and in this case about modernism and the avant-garde. It was done either by using methods or trends from afar, or not done because of localist resistance. There too we have some serious chronometric disjunctions, and disciplinary fates (and within these, fields) could be decided on this plane. Yet again a new swarm of Malley readers could bring new methods to the poems. A contemporary example: think how little critical vocabulary we had just fifteen years ago to make sense of modernist citational practices, from Benjamin to Reznikoff to Eliot's citational poetics in *The Waste Land*. That we have found ourselves taking citation more seriously has had big critical consequence for how we theorise modernism or, in historical terms, which parts of modernism we choose to focus on.[6] We needn't sell this as progress, simply shift.

The Malley reader (R∞) *is the Malley affair*. Let me say that because I remain suitably sceptical of claims to avant-gardism in the Malley poems, even where vanguardism has been touted as its major issue. I doubt that the poems, not the contexts but the poems alone can transform our understanding of avant-garde poetics, but I acknowledge that, in critical readings, especially Lecercle's, the Malley affair became an affair of the avant-garde. Close reading, yes, in ways that bring rhythm, line and form out of the Malleyan language, can do more and much, but without associated critical traditions and a global context in view, isolated readings of the Malley poems might not turn up much more than what we already have. Whether looked at in light of the shorter conceptual, or longer citational tradition, or again through frameworks of Surrealism – in application or as tradition (for McAuley, a real possibility) – it is all well and good to know more about avant-garde detractors. But we will not refrain from taking the next step: to determine what it could mean, in the Antipodes, to be an avant-garde practitioner, and

---

[6] See two works about a decade apart: Marjorie Perloff's *Unoriginal Genius: Poetry by Other Means in the New Century* and Leonard Diepeveen's *Modernist Fraud: Hoax, Parody, Deception*.

to stand by that practice. No points of gloom, then. Having hauled debates around Malley, Williams and modernism into the arena of the avant-garde, we take again a historical look, in context, and slightly away from these points of tension, to some texts written by another figure writing at the time of the affair. Looking at Hooton on the back of all this, and therefore returning to Malley and Williams later, not as cause, but by way of theoretical procession, we ought not lose sight, however, of all these elements so far flung into ideational orbit, of citation as a point of clarification, history wired up to theory: point-and-line-to-plane, as Wassily Kandinsky would say, between a mobile vanguard and static modernism, a singular modernity.[7] To begin again, with history and theory, through strenuous locale-framing and a little speculation, I will put the stakes of modernism and the avant-gardes to work in Hooton, to steer, redirect, more than divert our attention as it is poised on Antipodal modernity's avant-garde blindspot, for it is possible now to claim that there was truly a new order of the line at play.

Exemplarity? No. Tools to theorise avant-garde poetry better out of all the fuss made? Yes. The Malley poems, and their addressee, the Angry Penguins, do not account for the totality of 1940s Australian poetry, nor do they give us a picture of what the avant-garde meant at this period. I hope not to have lain out any assumption of exemplarity in advance of the coming narrative. Foundations unsteadied, the fate of the avant-garde is now reversed

---

[7] I am struck here by something Fredric Jameson said in *The Modernist Papers* of Wallace Stevens with regard to the "autoreferentiality of modernism" that will have to be, for now, an aside. In a not so much anachronistic as chronometric account, Jameson reads in Stevens's "Notes Toward a Supreme Fiction" an anticipation of, in the 1960s, an "unusual permutation" taking place where theory emerges to supplant older categories of philosophy and criticism, becoming synonymous with the life of poetry: "a moment in which 'poetry' also, in its traditional sense, dies and is transformed into something historically new, something that will gradually (in opposition to philosophy or literature alike) come simply to be designated as theory" (222). I think of this as a problem with criticism in the high modernist paradigm. For Jameson to detect this in Stevens shows the critical, or theoretical act to be one that in a sense replaces reflection for *revelation*. That the critic can illumine a theory emerging *from* poetry differs with the critic who applies, in a process of reification, theory *to* poetry. Antipodal modernism, and its distinct critical heritage in European and American theory, seems to take this dynamic to an extreme: its poets, while opinionated in theoretical terms, give the critic so many theories that need to be unraveled, such that the distinction between poetry in its traditional sense and the "historically new" is refused. Yet criticism has struggled because any attempt at theoretical congealment of the kind critics of high-European modernism are attuned is refused, leaving the only passage that of the prophetic (revelation), or to reprise John Docker's "Gloom Thesis", a type of cultural cringe.

by returning to literary history: reductive freezing before the figure of Malley melts away to show us other forms. In theory: a new order of the line.

V. The Hooton Era: Retrodictions

Hooton I take to be a Malley reader *par excellence*. In a letter to Oliver Somerville dated 16 December 1944, Harry Hooton writes that critic "Herbert Read asked me what I thought of Ern Mallee. I said Stewart and McAuley were worth respect and Harris was worthless ... But here again I am in the third camp."[8] His understanding of being the third camp is cued in to a sarcasm around terms; an intentional misspelling that exposes another Malleyan meaning, the "Mallee" (a type of Australian bushy scrub), pointing also to how meaningfully various the word had already become. And Hooton weighed in again: "What literature is there, / When two men can write one man's immortal life-work in two hours?" he would ask in "I'll Tell You Something", a poem written sometime between 1940 and 1945 that is addressed to both "comrades" and "lovers" (*Collected*, 179, 180). The "something" that Hooton here tells reveals just how rankled poets could be in the wartime, and postwar Malleyan context. In moving away by increment from the void of romanticism alone to that of vanguardism, we see how Hooton can turn sarcasm, scrappy parody and witty baulking into something engendering nothing less than a desire for a new line. This is how we will finally place it in perspective; Malley-slash or Malley-with-Hooton; thereafter a historically situated poetics of the 1940s avant-garde.

"Hooton was never a modernist" wrote Sasha Soldatow introducing the 1990 Hooton *Collected*, and Hooton's "attack" on Pound and Joyce would serve as examples (18–19), even though, as we will see, these strong opinions could also mark strong interest in modernist poetics rather than outright dismissal. Hooton's wide-ranging views, negotiating the crossed lines or conflictual "directions" of surrealism's explorations of the unconscious, the Jindyworobaks, philosophy and his professed urban-anarchist politics, combined

---

[8] I found this quotation in correspondence collected in the Oliver M. Somerville Papers, 1936–46, 1954, collected by Harry Hooton, held at the State Library of New South Wales. I thank Margaret Fink, Hooton's publisher and later executor of the Hooton Estate, for her assistance and guidance with Hooton's materials and his historical associations.

for a complicated response to the Malley affair. Hooton would first side with the hoaxers, before becoming uncertain, and as Soldatow points out, the hoax

> marked for attack what little modernism there was in Australian literature and killed it. Both McAuley and Harold Stewart single-handedly determined the course that Australian writing would *not* take. Almost half a century later, the conservative consequences still reverberate. Ironically, Max Harris reviewed *Things You See When You Haven't Got A Gun* in one line in the Ern Malley issue of Angry Penguins, "Our anarchist bull careers madly through this intellectual fog." (17).

This is the type of argument I have been warning against. But Soldatow, writing in 1990, is careful to point out that Hooton's place in these locales was complex: at once he was "marginalised" and widely read, and although he might now be "unjustly neglected", and if this was a more recuperative framework (us picking up the works for no other reason than to advance the marginal voice), we would skip over the fact that Hooton was in his lifetime published in most of the major magazines, and was himself a major small-press publisher. After meeting Margaret Fink (then Elliott) in 1952, their house became a salon, an avant-garde milieu (Soldatow, 21). There are more reasons Hooton may have seen another side to the affair, given his international counter-cultural connections and correspondence. Yet Soldatow retains a good degree of critical doubt: "I have always mistrusted the explanation that someone was ahead of their time. It is an absurdity. I would rather argue that Hooton was of his time while the majority of progressive artists and thinkers in Australia lagged far behind" (23).

The deathbed tapes of Hooton, taped in 1961, feature in a 1988 documentary *The Death of Harry Hooton*, broadcast on Radio Helicon, Radio National on 18 December 1988, produced by Amanda Stewart (of this book's closing chapter). He was heavily medicated, and his voice by then had become increasingly frail, distant and reflective. Having just seen to fruition the publication of his book *It Is Great To Be Alive* by Fink in the year of his death, 1961, he muses:

> You know, nothing would give me greater pleasure, and I think a lot of others would get pleasure, if this last sickness, which is almost my first sickness really, turned out to be a hoax, that the publicity gag of issuing from a deathbed my book *It Is Great To Be Alive* which

I've released so fervently on the point of death, if it turned out to
be just another false alarm. (Stewart, *The Death of Harry Hooton*,
57:46–58:18)

Hooton then speaks of death as both comical and a physiological adventure; the thought, he muses, that he would be "as Whitman said, some of the soil that nourishes the grass, that if you want [*sic*] me look for me afterwards, you'll find me under your boot-soles" (59:41–59:58), quoting from part LII of *Song of Myself*. Turning to both the question of the hoax and to Whitman at these last moments, an Australian vanguardist could not go out of this life more antipodally; thoughts turned to the outside world and to those aspects of authorial exteriority and authenticity that hoaxing raises. The main title of his posthumous 1990 *Collected Poems*, "Poet of the 21st Century", a title determined by Soldatow, historiographer and scholar of Hooton, indicates interest in history, posterity and goading questions of literary worth. Which twentieth century? A modern Australian one. Soldatow notes that although Hooton would read Henry Lawson in a positive light, it brought him back to Whitman, who "proceeded to shatter for Hooton the traditional idea of well-made verse, poetry that obeyed rules" (6).

Turn to the productive operations of typography, papermaking and the little magazine, and we find more than curious asides to this history. Looking at profit margins, aesthetic stances and small press histories since the 1940s, David Carter and Roger Osborne have surveyed the publication landscape with an eye to what being modern meant. For instance, *Meanjin*, in the 1940s, "saw itself defining an Australian tradition but also a *modern* tradition" (244), becoming through the 1940s and by the 1950s the most culturally substantial and bulky literary journal. *Meanjin* in the 1940s, they say, "might better be paired with *Angry Penguins*" than with *Southerly*, despite their historical coincidence, given the latter's role in fostering a professionalisation of criticism going into the 1960s and 1970s (245). Despite the fact that, as they note, few "independent literary reviews or little magazines survived beyond the late 1940s", it was at this juncture that new attempts "to claim the middle ground and the avant-garde were made"; for this new splintering and confirmation of ground, "At the avant-garde edge were Harry Hooton's *Number Three* (1948), *MS* (1950–1) and *21st Century* (1955 & 1957)" (248), published with Fink. Throughout the 1940s and 1950s Hooton was something of a small press guru, involving himself in little magazine publications throughout these decades. Localist as these productions were, Hooton's publication history would also span the globe. "The connections are tantalising," Soldatow would write: "Japan, India, Greece, South Africa, England, France, New Zealand, the USA" (21). Transpacific threads are most obvious: the San Francisco-based Inferno Press published *Power Over Things* in 1955. Inferno published Gil Orlovitz too, but few other poets that would gain later renown. No other attempt to place Hooton in an advanced historical course, in America or Australia, would antedate the publisher's grandiose prefatorial remarks. Despite the inaccessibility of his works, Hooton, so the preface states, was a creative journalist of "controversial & courageous distinction". Yet confident that this American publication will introduce a "poet & thinker whose work will dominate world thought in years to come", the purpose, we are told, is not just recuperative:

> Our aim is not just to "discover" another *"misunderstood genius"*— we know that real genius is only too well understood & feared by High Priests of American Culture. Here is a frank, realistic appraisal of the human problem that is both pertinent & penetrating. (n.pag.)

That Hooton would dominate world thought did not come about so emphatically as the press exhorted, or it did not depending on what time frame we allow for "in years to come". But Inferno Press, doing here what Green Integer didn't have to do with the republication of Malley, frames our discussion and not in a way that obscures the antipodality of Hooton's thinking, but shows rather a similar critical attitude to ours: a refusal to treat historical work as, simply, "discovery". Modernist genius by this time, in the United States, was about to morph and fall into the spell of Ginsberg's behemoth of breathwork in *Howl*, a work of genius in a sense, but also a return to the visionary roots of American prosodic experimentation. It is easy to see how *Power Over Things*, which is largely a work of poetic thinking, would have seduced a pre-*Howl* readership for its radical and visionary strides. It includes the essay-poem "Anarcho-Technocracy: The Politics of Things", which ends on a vision for Sydney:

> But we must have utopias. All we have to do is make them modern. The utopias of the past have been *rural*, oriented to the green corn and the vile compost of our past. We want our utopia in the heart of the city, in the heart of Sydney. We need an *urban* utopia. We should not rest until we have rebuilt Sydney, scrapped its hideous transportation, pulled down its idiot architecture, fashioned it to fit the needs of civilised man. (58)

From the outset we have been accustomed to chronometric discrepancy, where the contextualist manoeuvre is just as likely to conjure up the appearance of belatedness as advancement, across time and therefore also across space. So much so that a date, a decade, a day, even a century cannot be assumed to give literary history all the confirmation it needs for aesthetics as much as utopics. Nor can a prophet offer such confirmation; but neither prophet nor literary historian can rule out the possibility that Hooton could "dominate world thought" in years to come, for reasons we may not now know. That said, the sheer *centrality* of American cultural space – and its High Priests – might warrant some Antipodal investigation or clarification across hemispheric lines, as Paul Giles did in a transpacific and transnationalist study of American literature's lesser known *"terra incognita"*, the Antipodes. Giles's global remapping extends to poetry, and in American poets Karl Shapiro, Frank O'Hara, Ashbery and others, "the figure of antipodes comes to haunt their work in compelling ways", which include "the way in which they translate a sense of existential violence, encountered personally through war on other forms of psychological stress, into a more general perception of violation, for which the twisted, contorted world of an antipodean imaginary comes to stand as an objective correlative" (*Antipodean America*, 365). It cannot be stressed enough how crucial this work and its specific examples are, and will be in time to come, as to situating the Antipodean imaginary within American literature at large, for the pressure it exerts on both sides becomes a rare exposé of reciprocal influence on the US cultural imagination in the form of an Antipodal dialectic. Fantastical as it may seem to imagine an Antipodean poet occupying a position of world "domination" amongst the High Priests of US culture, it is not simply that, as I am here showing through literary history, these are lesser examples for a minor tragedy of unfulfilled destiny. It has rather come down to this, and in a no less transpacific and no less hemispherically realigned sense: Can the question of what a 1940s Australian modernism sounded or looked like be of relevance to the wider question of what the status of global modernism had become by this decade? Is this inseparable from the comparative balancing act of historical and literary "remapping", as it were? Is there a need, as Giles puts it in a 2019 book on "reverse time" in Antipodean modernism, with spatial and temporal transpositions in mind rather than theological and philosophical theoretics, to identify an "allochronic" passage, or as I put it, chronometric consciousness of Australian modernist poetics to beat back against the anthropological notion of historical progression (*Backgazing*, 12–13)? If there is a historical incitation towards an approach that can more clearly involve the temporal remappings of the Antipodes, and in Giles's case, an "Antipodean parallax" that came to influence in significant and material ways the Anglo-American tradition, it cannot be done by submitting global modernism and the Antipodal vanguard to different terms. "Retrodiction" is, in fact, how we came to believe Malley dominated all-and-sundry senses of the total situation: it was not simply that we read modernism without a vanguard as a frame without a picture, or modern Australian poetry as wipeout on the Western periphery.

I have no intention in this book to map any further the ways that Western philosophy and literature have become mystified by Antipodean time, yet I adhere to the notion that literary theory and literary history can end up adjacent to philosophical concerns about time, and in our discourse on Fogarty, Indigenous philosophical time is central. We ought have no disciplinary desire to force critical attention away from those gravities. The idea of an Antipodal avant-garde *qua* front line at this point might still seem improbable unless it is the case that literary history hasn't caught up to it. It is not that Hooton as proof-case turns us toward a critical mass pulling the current in another direction. Neither is it that the idea of a truly original Australian poetry would have to find some subjective counterpoint wrested free from the archival-historical and literary-critical interface. Surely, too, we need not fall into the trap of mistaking a more generous vision of the corpus as some Trojan horse for staging the arrival of an anticanon. To make a plea for such a radical counterpoint, as it has had to be in so many of the examples in this book, we reach for documents, and it's starkly there in the title poem of of the 1961 collection *It Is Great To Be Alive*, posthumously included in *Collected Poems*. The poem begins "This is an obvious imitation of Walt Whitman, is it? / Well, and wouldn't that be better than another echo in sickly rime? Perhaps you would prefer as more exquisite / Some other fellow's footprints in the sands of time, / Or the past perhaps present future of Eliot's pleasant slime . . . / But this is not an imitation of anyone: listen to me, I am alive! / Whitman and Longfellow are dead; Eliot doesn't know he is" (*Collected Poems*, 102). These words, with their stumbling, nervy and anxious bravissimo, capture some underlying tensions and disputes in the ensuing chapters of this book: I have tried to understand how these historical tendencies emerged and how these interactive forces led to discourses of imitation, life and futurity. Hooton would not make it into the next century and, as he seems to be saying, it's as if no Antipodal poetry can ever make a significant mark on canonical time. All the speaker is left with is a simple cry "I am alive!" followed up later by "My poems are revolutions" (*Collected Poems*, 104). But Hooton would admit "Yes, and an imitator—of impetuous powerful words; / Plagiarist of Whitman, of all the Sons of Man—For they heard me in their future, as I do those to come—" (*Collected Poems*, 104). It's as if to merely point out one's existence is all one can do, let alone lead the way. One can only follow the exquisite footprints of some other modern. If readers have been feeling that it has never been enough to merely present the existence of other voices, lost voices and so forth, then a poem like this urges us to move on to something a little more entrenched; I have been adamant that any recuperative project surely has to say something about time, canons, temporal contradictions and, at best, literary history. If I may commit some opening heresy of paraphrase on this poem, let me suggest that this poem does precisely those things: "past perhaps present future" offer contradictory temporal fluxes, and with that the currency of futurities too; Eliot's slime, we are told sarcastically, is "pleasant slime", and he doesn't know how dead he is. Dead for whom? And how Whitmanian *is* this poem? The rhymes "slime" and "time" are hardly so. We may assume this is deliberate, ironising, forced end-rhyme; assume, as we are hearing it from the future.

Let me go further and suggest that this is precisely what Williams seems to have missed when he called for a new order of the line. No Australian poet would have the wherewithal to have done so, and Hooton would not quite get there, but he nonetheless would make historical claims, claims for the line. Writing to Somerville on 8 August 1942, Hooton notes that Douglas Stewart "lets me know that he has not seen what is more to my poems than the mere letter", going on to say:

> Poetry exists (very rarely but nevertheless it's there) in even "metrical" feet of two three four and five syllables and also metrical feet of forty syllables, with minor and major stresses of natural or unnatural speech rhythms in every second or seventyeth line. My poems are not raggedy, they are meticulously, exactly sculptured lines of grace. They will live not because they were <u>right</u> in 1941 but because they are breaths of undefinable utterance, because they are a new <u>form</u> of poetry . . .

VI. New Order of the Line

Is this a call for a new order of the line? If it sounds like organic prosody with Australian characteristics, Hooton was not explicit about what was Australian about these prosodic speculations or calls to new lineation. But what constitutes a hanging line and its newly ordered opposite, the supposed *dis*order? To claim a new order of the line we need to be as specific as possible about shape, length, cut, carry and, where possible, prosody, how the lines played out in language and in rhythm: in short, *explication de textes*. I want to focus on the line not only because there is good evidence to be found that some kind of invention is going on when a poet chooses to either go in organically to the prosody of the line, as Grenier noted of Williams in the modern American milieu, or where the poet chooses to break a line, drawn long or cut short. I want also to suggest the leading role here of geometry, how a poet chooses to bring lines together between points; refusals to leave the line "hanging", in Williams's idiom, desiring new shapes in poetic space.

Hootonics is our idiom. Rather than a single political-aesthetic program, "Hootonics" is the name Hooton gave for an almost obsessive emphasis on placing poetics, and theories of poetry, in poems. And by theories: political, subjective and reflective theories of modern poetics. If Hooton was a rare, isolated example of a radical experimental poet operating in the middle of the twentieth century, in form and political intent, it is worth deepening our sense of what "radical" means in this context. His association with the earlier phase of the postwar Anarchist-Libertarian Push movement in Sydney, which began well before the explosion of radical literary and political activity in the 1970s, is noteworthy in that the Push was a vanguard-like formation. Its lifespan was a considerably long period of time, from the late 1940s to the early 1970s. It would include both more labourist, Trotskyite figures like Bob Gould, later known as the proprietor of the radical book warehouse in Sydney, Gould's Books, to outright celebrities like Germaine Greer, the art-historian Hughes, the experimental filmmaker David Perry and, originally through Hooton, the film producer Margaret Fink. Barry Humphries, comedian and performer, who invented the most famous characters in Australian comedic history, such as Dame Edna Everage, also associated with these groups, would associate with university Dadaist groups in Melbourne and produce in the 1950s what would have to be some of the first Dada performances and documents in the anarchistic underground of the 1950s Antipodes. The character Dr Aaron Azimuth, Humphries's first creation, was indeed a dandy and a Dadaist.

Hooton's approach may redound to leftist political theory outside the Soviet Union in that Hooton's thought, or thought patterns, retrodictive in theory and yet anticipating historical scapes to come in the 1970s, would both stand as an anomaly and record of the dialectic between anarchism and technocracy, or the problem of the productive forces. A Hootonic approach to writing, thinking and theorising, perhaps because it carried forth an inhuman mechanicity, or "futurist, tech-fetishist materialism", as Astrid Lorange put it, typical of the early twentieth-century avant-garde, would have begun to look and sound very different viewed between the twentieth and twenty-first centuries, especially after Green politics and ecology came to augment (or for some, dilute) left politics in the developed countries of the 1970s (Lorange, "Problems"). No less would materialism have need of machines, but the machines would be different. Hooton's interest in the word and concept of the vanguard, there in the 1943 essay-poem "Problems Are Flowers and Fade", show forth a very specific stance: philosophy and art for Hooton constitute the vanguard, while science and industry are the rearguard, "forming the main body of the army, moving into the positions the spearhead establishes" (*Collected*, 67–73). As a social body, or machine, perfection of this would manifest utopia. To uncover from this a theory of the role of an avant-garde in his work is possible, and a general theory – attentive to objects (Things), and forces upon them – is evident in various adumbrations for Anarcho-Technocracy, a philosophy of "Direct Action *on Things*" (*Collected*, 88). That is to say "The engineers must rule" (*Collected*, 90), a statement which, manifesto-like, harks back to Futurism and technological determinism before the Atomic Age, and yet quite as much anticipates revivals of the question of the forces and relations of production, and of course recent tendencies in contemporary theory like posthumanism, accelerationism and Systems Philosophy. "Philosophy", in Hooton's Anarcho-Technocracy and in those developments above, is under pressure from theory, science and the engineers, becoming what we would be better off calling *philosophical theory* conditioned by society and politics. In this system philosophers and artists would lead, but the rearguard, the technocrats, would rule.

No flippancy with the word "society", at least not in these pages, for society lays out a firm foundation to jump from politics to poetic form (terminological doubt, not imprecision). Society, whether the

Push or the social formations in Hooton's utopic scientism, would be a major driver through these thinkerly flashpoints. But I have promised a new order of the line before a new social order. We need not claim a passion for the real any more than to say that the Antipodal avant-garde would struggle to strut its own foundations, for however neglectful of the avant-garde Australian critics have been, it suffers the fate of a hologram bathed in mist without some model quotation for this new order of lineation. The following poem, possibly from as early as 1935, titled "The Clalendar", can serve as an initial example:

> Join the army
> Feeblevery
> Marx
> Apeswill
> Play
> Tunes
> You'lldie
> Allguts
> Sitting-
>   member
> Knockyouover
> Nowonder
> Remember[9]

The poem's twelve thin lines, not all agglutinative, not all neologisms, with one notably dashed (Sitting-member), homophonically translate the months of the year. The months cleave, or cleft, divide and congeal words in a manner that invites cleft reading: do you read on down or are the lines self-enclosed? It resembles too the spindly lineation of the Baroness. Not just concerned with the purely geometric conception of the line, point, plane and poesis, in "Geometry for Beginners" Hooton uses the properties of space for societal analysis:

> THEOREM. To describe a rectangle, as society rules its ruly
>   elements
>   Let society be a triangle
>   With unruly wrangles, SOC.
>   Now since the whole is
>   The ruler (the rule is
>   Supposed to be greater than any of the arts . . .

---

[9] I located this poem in the Oliver M. Somerville collection, within correspondence with Hooton dated 10 February 1943. A note further indicates that it was published "with little manifesto Little Misdirections for Nounteen Thriftyjives'.

Let the angle C by a political wangle revolt against SOC.
Now if SOC is going to suppress C, then C is going to
    suppress C.
This is absurd. The whole cannot be
    in any relation to the part
Let society, SOC, try to rule over its
    own angle
And it will be squashed flat like
    a thin rhomboid rectangle
Or something put through a clothes mangle—
In short it will be a wrecked triangle, (which is what we set
    out to prove, which is what society is like).
                                            (*Collected*, 120–1)

In the previous stanza Hooton rejoices in the "straight line" of art, ethics and the machine: "the diameter of thought cutting its way through the circles and cycles of history, the tangent escaping, transcending the physicist's finite infinity" (120). To manifest poetry in a straight line, left to right margin, is hardly how in reality these lines proceed. Allegorical, the lines are those of specific thinkers as well – "Russell? Einstein? Wittgenstein?" add Nietzsche, Parmenides, Spinoza, Epicurus – whose lines "never meet" (119). Seeking to capture art, ethics and the machine in the whole range of meanings for "line", the *distinction*, if it can be put that way, amongst these clashing and peremptory nods to the history of Western thought, is where the underlying anarcho-technocratic theory attempts to speak for origins and ends: the history of geometry links to labour, links to the machine, and therefore society. The poem proceeds; it gives the "effect" of logic, as it were. Hooton's grammar is not always subject to the same exposure to thought or logic, and in the poem that references Malley, "For the Last Time", from the sequence "Poems in Repose", where the "sacchariny" long lines can become quasi-oratorical, stress ripples uncommonly as in:

Don't you feel all gooey and prickly and lovery dovery up
    abovery,
And sacchariny syruppy hammer and sickly
    and fascistmated satis sexy
When Cessy Spend All Day in Lucy or Dylan Tumours Pennorth
    Catchem or Maxy, Rexy, Flexy, Bexy
Sighs it now.
                                            (*MS* June 1951, n.pag.)

Not quite like Ania Walwicz, an avant-garde Antipodal whose prosodic dissonance is upcoming, but ostensibly the lineation of one who has read Stein and Joyce, "Sighs it now" sounds slightly more like the Antipodal modern man intervening liberally in the socialisation, and indeed politicisation of sex. Adorably stale literary effects; it connects the mid-century liberal imagination with sensuous diction. In this sequence, definitions of poetic form come immanent in the act, which Hooton argues for in the first poem, presented in *MS* simply titled "Poetry", which begins "There are no rules for poetry / Necessity makes, and breaks, all rules", and "So despite all rules, preceding rules / Get in and write — poetry. / And then, but not till then / Study the rules your poetry has made. . . ." (*MS* June 1951, n.pag.). The poems appear in an issue that would include A. D. Hope, with Hooton as the main feature, contexts that make the poems feel as if there is a manifesto at play. Such characteristic reflexivity and criticality carries right across the oeuvre, and into longer or sequential works that Hooton was exploring, like *The Golden City*, which puts to verse some of the more explicitly utopian aspects of his poetic philosophy. Mid-sequence, Hooton questions the form he is using:

III
                   I am sorry, I shudder,   my
      artistic friends, for
                           i
have written a didactic poem
      (and is it a poem or only a prose?)
You know this is very bad
                     A
    poem shouldn't prove a point or
have an idea or inculcate a truth or do anything a
             poem should just be
      like a raindrop or a pomegranate
            or
a cup of tea;
      it should just be an ineffable, palpable
         globular fruit
         or a deaf mute,
the gravid yellow pulp of an orange with
    silent peel exquisitely stripped
        or just the ineluctable pips . . .
          (*Collected*, 130)

Whether or not it was Australia, the Antipodes, within which Hooton could imagine an Antipodal City, a utopia, emerging, it is hard to say, but the poem's core discussion or didactic purpose is self-explanatory enough – suspicions aside that the metaphors are purposely botched – except that the didacticism is interrupted by an interpolated prose "note" that in effect ironises again the didacticism part III is alleged to have held:

> (This is easy – the number of times you can juxtapose
> two words never before so juxtaposed and still stir the
> associatory tracks of two men who never cliched in
> their unique lives is infinite. Try it out sometime –
> every adjective can fit any noun.) But to hell with such
> iniquitous uniquity! I'm here in this poem to tell you
> something – to tell you everything. If you want to be
> saved you must be bored again:
> (*Collected*, 130)

The poem continues, after the colon: "My text is that a thing is right or wrong only in its context." This line Hooton recycles for the title of another longer poem published in *Things You See When You Haven't Got A Gun*, from 1943: "My Text is That Nothing Is Right or Wrong Only In Its Context" (6–11). The aim of *The Golden City* is also anti-subject or anti-subjective: "My aim: to leave the subject, and reach – the *object*;" (*Collected*, 131). After the semicolon, the subject is again stone, and stone as material; what man, meaning men, subjects gendered masculine, and humanity, turn *into*, or turn over. This all comes somewhat close to the Objectivist "Program" of 1931, only that with Louis Zukofsky the lens ("Optics") was what gave the direction of the Objective, or "an" Objective, and the direction was "historic and contemporary particulars" meaning, further, that objects were not just things but could be events in historical time (Zukofsky, 268). How this exfoliates in Objectivist *poems*, what an Objectivist poetics is, is no more certain. Whether Hooton conceives of the line as an event in this manner is not certain either, but the destruction of the subject, to aim at the *object*, is the clear through-line.

VII. *Directions: Stages of the Line*

Poets in search of an Objective, to retain the majuscule and majesty of Zukofsky's hasty program, would vary as to how they responded, or did not, to the optics and the particulars of the object. It is worth recalling again that Williams appears at the end of the 1931

Objectivists issue with "The Botticellian Trees", a poem beginning "The alphabet of / the trees" lettristically unveiling in sensuous attention, its object (266–7), and it would be easy to do some chronometric readjustment here to imagine what Hooton might have thought about Second Wave modernists if he had encountered them, given also his interest in including poetics and statements among poems. The sheer volume of poems Hooton writes that are about language – line, preposition, speech, its tricksiness, sensuousness, modernness – and what to do with it, requires reading the above poem alongside others of his own if not in the Objectivist issue of 1931. A similarly sophistical and didactic poem, "I Can't Account For This Poem", approaches questions of modernism and composition:

> I can't account for this poem I've only just written it.
> I wouldn't be sure if it's a Stein stutter or an Epstein statue
> Or a Morse code mathematical notation musical score
> (*Things To See When You Haven't Got A Gun*, 19)

Though he seems to have found some way around the contradictions of Surrealism and the social, in a poem titled "James Joyce" we encounter "A lewd frail freud twisting linguistic licewords" (*Collected*, 176). Freud comes to speak precisely for that which is slippery in the lingual duplicity of global poetics when it meets psychoanalytic theory to sound a new, and coarsely modern key. In this poem Hooton offers a variation of the above-quoted line on Stein:

> Oh much much so much more than a Stein stutter or an
> Epstein statue. Everything, anything in existence—other
> than the resolve that artists, scientists, workers, lovers,
> explorers, pioneers, gods would take possession of the
> machinery of the world, and have new life, lust, art,
> freedom, nobility, power, clarity, creative and divine
> ecstasy forever. (*Collected*, 176–7)

Elsewhere, the cultural thematics of "The Inhuman Race", which reads like a long poem, parts of which are published in the *Collected*, are no different from the above, but the references come to interrogate institutional modernism and modernist figures of genius. *Ulysses* exposed to critical poetics starts it off: "All the scholars can see (dimly) is James Joyce" (157). Freud too gives us new words: "humanitytoman", "manmademandate", "manachronistic" (161). The linguistic experiment of the poem culminates in diverging axes:

and now MR ELIOT will perform his famous conjuring trick!

       (WHERE WAS I (find the mind
I'm present, I'm absent   (little kidding
I'm maybe passed pleasant pasture (burnt ochre
And rhyme verdure time last   (I'm in it I second
And now you see me and now you don't (Got away!
               (*Collected*, 162)

The wryness here is palpable: to mock modernism and its guile is to in part play in to its exuberance. Modern outrageousness gets all the attention, a little inferiority conjures the sarcasm. In an Australian modernism and in high Hootonics, to get anything across seems to already have required a statement of presence, or a statement denying one's absence, but it is the parallel and simultaneous axes that pull clashing binaries – to wit, presence vs absence, light vs dark – together in a chain of dialectical meanings, seen here some lines on:

Mobile but motionless   (and soda, power
Light without dark without illumination (and glory, turn
Here with thou without then   (over and over
Nuance without nous   (again
               (*Collected*, 163)

It is not as if one is handed the results of the axial interplay simply by virtue of geometricised poetics. If Hooton is still reading Eliot by this point in the poem he offers a doubtful reading of modernist genius: "(LOOK! There it is *under*lying . . . (lying under / round and round wheels in wheels and words WITHOUT MEANING" (*Collected*, 163). Then, as if to give us an example of this, the poem evolves into radical lettristic disturbance: "(Lady Light. vice pres. Hswvs. Assn., sec. whrf. labrs. wmns. auxiliary, Fedn. mbr. cnt. cmtee. Cmanenlist Pty. Aust., I Move broth. come, bubble loud give his testimony bother of all. moved sickle noted dated. voted, rated. Favour say I. I've had it. So've I. Buck fir'w'd" (*Collected*, 163). Such would the epic voice intervene as if to stabilise: "There are men, Poets, Miltons, seeking pastures *NEW*. Pastures of steel, concrete, electronics—Men, forging extrahuman relations with the *WORLD* outside" (167). Not long after these capitalised and italicised keywords we get freewheeling prose paragraphs like the following: "closed systems with first sickle move third amend fourth interhumanational fifth atom it's six seventh heavens it's Joyce no Thomas Aquinas Dyland Ogden Miller Richards Yutang bar Confuseus............" (*Collected*, 168).

Outward-going ellipses drift from the cluttered line of thinkers (by name), to connect at some other point. It is as if the world, the modernist world, with its clash of directions, is a stage, and the way Hooton engineers the line in poems that seek length, that want to "go on", can barely contain itself in the line. I say world abstractly but in a sense the way the lines travel is more akin to conceptual points in geometric space. They will be channelled in Hooton's most significant manifesto. Perhaps the most genre-busting series that can pre-empt this is "Promes in Pose"; mini-essays, part-manifestos for languages of invention with their majuscule blasts on Man: "Allegory shall do man over and over Ah men. No POWER RATHER THAN ALL THESE DRIVEN DIRECTION OUT ROUND UPWARD LEVER LEAVEN" ("The Word's Prayer", *Collected*, 81), or in "Praise the Word":

> Fray's the word, pass the ammunition. Erase the word man from the predicate OBJECT, copula, verb (mind the PREPOSITION!—nothing is at, to, on, for, by, with itself but new positions) Raise the World, the nonhuman (divine?) submission MAN IS NOT ENEMY fuel munition Phrase the Word and Parse the manuMISSION! ...
>
> (*Collected*, 82)

Mankind, or "Man", and indeed individual men, are the subject also of "Very Words (NOT A POEM)" where Hooton explores a technocratic, and "clever" proto-post- or in-humanism; "OBJECT OF MAN'S EXISTENCE IS NOT MAN—IT IS SOMETHING OTHER THAN MAN, IT IS NON-HUMAN" (*Collected*, 80), grappling with the issue of surrealism and realism not just in a linguistic register but in the form of a philosophical and philological complaint:

> Individual men may move to, address each other—so long as the movement is habitual, UNREFLECTING. The poet accepts the integration of man; he is all men in one. Poets can't REFLECT man any longer, any more than painters can. We have cameras for that purpose. Art does not mirror man, but the FUTURE for man, NOT HUMANITY BUT ITS AIM. Symbols, words, directed by poets are valid only if they transcend man, society, the subject doing things, and invest the THINGS man has to DO. These things are not always determinate; art drives to the FUTURE, to what is unknown. The surrealists and subjectivists in general drive also to the indeterminate—but to the PAST, the what has been known. The subconscious processes are mysterious all right, but

they are NOT the area art has to explore—to reflect the
inferred inner workings of man is the worst of superstitions,
viler than photographic realism. What is hidden in man is
what he has done, now sensibly relegated to automatic
physiological reflexes. Life and art are one-way movements,
up, out, forward. The movement in grammar— subject, verb,
OBJECT—is paralleled by the movement in everything
else—past, present, FUTURE . . .

(*Collected*, 80)

There is a Hootonic quality to the masculine neurasthete that may be quite unique. There are neither psychoanalytic nor philosophical *übermenschen* here: poet, all-in-one, goes not in but out. Capturing the point at which photography negates the need for realism in other media, reflection in language is merely, or especially, historical. The times, or time itself, have given these conditions for the arts in general. Apart from the puns, and the puns flow readily through Hooton's writing, the linguistic slippage contributes as it were to the argument for an object-oriented inverse, which might have been clarified further he had encountered the Objectivist issue. No work of poetics that Hooton would produce, however, would be more forceful and thorough than "Directions", a rare Antipodal statement-of-poetics, or manifesto, which like "Promes in Pose" concerns itself with points of intersection between politics and art:

2. Movement is direction: nothing can move without moving somewhere. (140)

17. Art is not an anaemic cult but a dynamic culture. (141)

21. Culture is growth, and growth is movement, and movement is *power*—for nothing can move without moving some thing. (141)

24. The only important things are Things. (142)

29. Men must go out of their minds. (142)

46. There are two sections of men who realise human equality, the greatest and the least—the vanguard and the rearguard, on the outskirts of society, and so in contact with things. The mediocre realise nothing. (143)

48. Words are things. We must be all inclusive in life and exclusive in letters. (144)

70. There are two movements in man's world: those which follow straight lines, which are alive, and those in circles, which are dead. And this is too deadly serious to make a joke about. (145)

98. There are two stages in history, the human and the (147)
    sublime, religion and art.

110. There are ten million billion new ways to cook onions. (148)
    (See note on page 756,321.)

117. Look down on the dignity of machine labour. (149)

119. Joyce and I wrote rubbish, but I destroyed mine. (149)

120. Prophets have no honour in their own country because (149)
    they haven't got a country (I never had my fare to
    another country).

123. What a struggle Joyce had to become an artist—oh the (149)
    aches and pains of shaking off the trannels of
    mothers, fathers, nappies, the church, ireland . . .

124. Only a philistine struggles to be an artist. (149)

126. Nietzche was a modern with his eyes on Greece; (149)
    Wilde was a Greek looking to the future; Whitman is
    eternal.

127. Voltaire gave europe Newton and Co; Shaw gave the (150)
    english Nietzsche and Co; Wilde gave me.
    (version from *Collected*, 140–50)

Published in a shorter form in *Things You See When You Haven't Got A Gun*, and its longer form in *It Is Great To Be Alive*, few Australian writers would utter such authoritative statements and none in this form – poetics missive or poetics manifesto – until Jas H. Duke emerged in the 1970s. Duke was directly influenced by this manifesto, which he professed to have read. Only a decade and a half later, Duke's emergence, bringing Dada to Australia, would too bring with it the revamped form of the manifesto; vectors of modernist pretension and vanguardist directive. The net result, I hope, of drawing this longer line between Hooton and Duke is a type of decontextualisation and subsequent *re*historicisation of the 1940s in Australian poetry; a global refusal to confine these implications to an Australian terminus. Even so, an Antipodean avant-garde that defines modernity, and one that was rehistoricised, would need to have a more clearly plotted-out set of coordinates as to how it emerged and what came after. It would resemble an attempt to honour prophets without a country: by situating a manifesto such as the above as part of not only Australian poetry but avant-garde history, and then from this, retroactively reassessing Malley as part of a tendency to *repress* the avant-gardes, a tendency from Brennan onwards, we see, now, how its presence in critical theory and the world history of avant-gardism is both a runoff of these dynamics and some entry point into the literary-historical and implications for poetics. The historical lines are crossed: before Malley there was Brennan's 1897 experiment, and after, there would be Harry Hooton. Duke, who would inspire poets working in the 1970s and onwards, will inspire Amanda Stewart. In a phrase: there will be further points of anticipation up ahead. And for those who chose to take up the explicit mantle of avant-garde poet in the late twentieth century and into the next, these historical contradictions would play out closely in poetics, and in critical reception. It may not be so bold to conclude again, in advance, and to anticipate having closed this chapter, that the core question in the 1940s became one crucial to the constitution of Australian poetry; the question of the existence or absence of an avant-garde.

VIII. Revolutionary Poetry: "The Only Kind Worth Bothering About"

In our resolute departure from the causal cul-de-sac of Malley, we find something more arresting: a better sense of what gets *on the nerves* of an Antipodal modernism. For Hooton, it was not so much ultrarationalism as the metahistorical relay between irrational and rational modes that set off the occasional neurasthenic flare in his work. His defence of the role of science, in the 1943 "Poetry or Not", shows some critical deftness as to the issue of poetic judgement, defending both scientific criticism, not in Frye's sense exactly, and "the people", against the critic, with an eye to the integrity of the artist, or poet, and the work. Hooton's definition of scientific criticism goes like this:

> When we take from the work of art its settings—its historical associations, its commercial value and utility, etc, there is left that inexplicable residue which we say excited the aesthetic sense. It may be this will be by later ages explained, in this way art may be said to be in the vanguard of all activities, bringing things within the ken of science gradually. Or it may be said art is "unknown"—that this is all that may be predicated of it, or that this constitutes its charm. But it is certain that if one first weighs the apprehensible, intelligible settings, to which scientific measurement and formulation may apply, that we shall have located it whatever it may be. This is the start of scientific criticism. Here the scientists and people generally are on common ground. ("Poetry or Not", 91)

People-centred criticism in a libertarian key is not a tonality our ears are accustomed to. Given all that has transpired in politics and geopolitics since – the rise of the New Left and its influence mainly in the West but also in South-East Asia, the dramatic collapse of the Soviet Union, an insurgent identitarianism in the West both on the left and right, subsequent rejections and revivals of Marxist critique, the demise of entryism and most centre-left political parties, and sporadic reprisals of dialectical and historical materialism – it is difficult to pinpoint what "the people" means now outside the terms left us by proletarian internationalism; moreover it is difficult to *hear* its meaning. In poetic terms, there will have to be more on how the 1970s came to be what it was from the perspective not only of the 1968 generation, but these earlier experiments in the matter of language and the line. Although I have been able to break through useless quibbles on matters associated with the existence of an avant-garde, conveying an experience of reading and the real elements at play in what is being read has been the main priority. Unlike many of his contemporaries, Hooton bizarrely torques, and distorts perspective, in a different way to Malley (or how Malleyan surrealism was heard): I feel an occasional cringe in the act, but not even from the perspective of a decade that is my own (this time cringes other styles) – it's an Archimedean Point from which I read these texts; historically Antipodal and therefore familiar to a degree, but also deeply unfamiliar. History does that. If I am simply saying Malley needs to be read in context, alongside Hooton (plus perhaps early Max Harris, and the others), even that's not enough. Another kind of contextualist would emphasise Harris's involvement with art patron John Reed and the Heide Circle in the 1940s, and how the Angry Penguins emerged from this cluster of artists – Sidney Nolan, Joy Hester, Arthur Boyd. Such an analysis would do well to compare, in mediatic and stylemic terms, the poetics of the poets and the aesthetics of the artists, particularly Hester. The epical 2019 poem by experimental poet ∏.O., *Heide*, tells this story in verse, in a capacious and experimental longpoem that runs to 560 pages. It's a story that must also tell of the antics and performances of "Professor Henry Alfred Tipper", the outsider artist who dies in 1944, also painting under the names H. Dearing and H. D. These *naïf* paintings of Tipper's (reminiscent of the Indigenous painter Mickey of Ulladulla, in the nineteenth century) came to light in *Angry Penguins* in the Malley issue and after. Were they a hoax? If the dates are right, according to Richard Haese in a crucial document of avant-garde art history, *Rebels and Precursors: The Revolutionary Years of*

Australian Art, one particularly well-known feat of Tipper's – riding a 5" bicycle while singing "The Highlands and the Lowlands" – was accomplished in 1925 (188–9). This would then open the question of an avant-garde extending into the very years of operation of the Dadaists, or more so, Surrealists, in Europe and America. The contextualist's work doesn't end. But our task now remains to bring those elements of literary history in the previous discourse to bear on this one in order to get past this to the next. The present discourse on Malley readers, combined with Hooton's diverse excursions in poetics (whatever a 1940s Australian modernism sounded or looked like, whether it was relevant to the wider question of what global modernism had become by the end of the decade or not), shows us through documents that an Australian avant-garde came to occupy the position of *modern critic*; history shows theoretical work was going on even if its application, in poetry itself, remained hidden.

IX. Hooton as Avant-Garde Social Critic

I mean no retreat from these excursions to note again that narrative is history plus frame, the story Hugo Ball tells in *Flight out of Time*, Ball's Dada diary, is not the same as the framework given for it. From hoaxes to misunderstood geniuses, the Antipodal 1940s indicates just as much. Dwelling on the details is one thing, changing the frame another. Recuperative drives do some work: to the denial of recuperative modernisms they become a kind of *de*cuperative undoing. No flight out of time has thus been attempted, nor will there ensue a total retreat into the shadows of history. I seek here a historical and materialist admixture with the commonplace of literary history, staying attentive to the modernity of poetry and its claims in poetics to technicity. It will not do to freeze up against the notion of an avant-garde. We must *notice* missing forms, and talking about them requires the kind of tact a critic is not prepared for in the guidebooks. What became avant-garde for the European centre and the Antipodean periphery was far too localised in the critical imagination. Modernism was internationalised, modernist memory and modernist forgetting aside, and it alone could not do all the grunt work of remembering it all.

Hooton could be confused, and confusing, while still opinionated and intriguing; on the future of Australian poetry, on the language of poetry as itself a mode of analysis, on words (sometimes holophrastically) and as we know on the vicissitudes and trials of Australian literary history. More anxious than pretentious in Lecercle's Malleyan schema, he could issue forth a heavily modern despondency. In "Psalm" the "slothful inertia of the Bush" seems a good enough ironisation of settler poetry, even where nature becomes nothing more than the womb (*Collected*, 36–7). If the existence of an avant-garde seems incompatible with an Australian poetry, "Psalm" brings up a double estrangement: Australian poetry has been estranged from world poetry, and Australian avant-garde poetry has been estranged from Australian literature, under that battery of national signifiers; Hooton can at once dismiss the colonial poet Henry Kendall and the explorers Burke and Wills, but more disappointing, if the poem is a commentary on the Jindyworobaks, which it seems to be, it doesn't offer any insight for an Indigenous past and present in its vision of Antipodal time. Yet Hooton takes us closer when modernity is at stake. In "Poetry and the New Proletariat" Hooton argued that "The usual objection to modern poetry is that the majority of the people cannot understand it. But this is really a virtue—perhaps the only one it has" (96). An unexpected defence of obscurity or difficulty, the catch, in this piece, is specific, and brings the social to the historical. Where once thousands of "ordinary people surged into the pit at the Globe Theatre" it was precisely the machine, its impact on labour, and the production of a new cultural and scientific *élite*, that transformed poetry and its reception:

> Work today is done by the machine; and modern poetry, like music or mathematics or engineering is the property of the few ... Modern poetry is not addressed to the people; it is addressed to a small minority, mainly composed of technicians in industry. This minority is the new motive force in society – the new centre of social gravity. Its members are scientists, the *élite* – the new social class which alone can give validity to poetry. And by poetry I mean revolutionary poetry, which is the only kind worth bothering about. ("Poetry and the New Proletariat", 96)

Hooton's validation of a cultural *élite*, technicians, the rearguard for the philosophical and artistic vanguard, raises a final question of how it would function against or as a bulwark of the popular masses, a question that has continued to torment and entertain theorists of modernism. And given the scientists as a "social class" would in this scheme give validity to (necessarily) revolutionary poetry, which in the strongest possible terms aligns with the very definition of poetry itself, this curious matrix of production and technicity (despite scientific communism in Engels and in Soviet education) decides against Marxian assessment of science and materialism: "Marx has been dead these 60 years. Conditions in the 20th century call for an entirely new approach" ("Poetry and the New Proletariat", 97). According to Soldatow, Hooton lived to complete eight chapters of his projected volume, "Militant Materialism", but not finish it. What we have in the poetry serves as a sketch for this larger treatise.

The benefit of hindsight allows us to say that, right under Williams's nose, some new order of the line was taking place, in theory, even if it was not widely read or acknowledged, and that the disordering or reordering of the line worked in tandem with social poetics and political vision. The materials are scarce, and not all widely available to readers, but that is still no barrier. I am particularly reminded here of Eric White's extremely necessary work on localist modernism and the small magazine in the transatlantic context because, if there is any sense that the scale of these analyses seems confined, the "crucible" of the historical avant-garde, the little magazine, shows the localist element to provide new spatial locations for critical modernist studies at large (5–6). Let us too mark the scales we have been preoccupied with to this point. Direction, line, vector: these are the coincidences Williams implored the Australian poet to open up, and having indeed opened our spatio-temporal lines of contact outside the confines of those restricted materials, concepts and generating pressures, the entire *energia*, of historical modernity and its cultural productions in modernism, the sheer *obstructions* we observe above, in the modern-cum-antimodern strains of Hooton, relish (in a messy but affirmative poetics, with a call to science in the midst of the complaint) the very motive forces of an avant-garde. It does the global work in a local locus. The utopic idiom of Hooton sets in motion, in transcultural space, belated and yet anticipatory dilemmas for literary time. These are in no way ahistorical. To plot a final line to a final point, I have withheld till this late moment a blurb from Harry Heseltine, of the Hooton *Collected*:

> A necessary condition of health for any poetry is probably the presence of at least a few poets who defy culture pigeon-holding [in Heseltine's unusual phrasing] ... but occasionally such a figure is suddenly seen to redefine himself at the centre and to generate a whole new output of mainstream poetry. It seems possible that Harry Hooton will be relocated in this way ... Moving in from idiosyncratic isolation to the formative centre. (*Collected*, back cover)

No Frankenstein here. Not total transformation, just slightly better health, some *relocation*, another spatial term; to imagine as it were the outfacing flourishing of a poetic culture as given through its most defiant figures. Heseltine's notices that Hooton's self-authorisation, as one to assume cultural centres, and therefore generating an output of "mainstream poetry", is most curious; Hooton will relocate from margin to formative centre, a task that seems to have fallen to us right here given how much we have been talking already of centres and margins, from insidership to outsidership. And it is to those texts that call toward a future that we can turn to find a way to put these strong words to test.

Literary history, and it really tends to be doing this, has produced a disjunct at the joints of comparative modernism. For if Williams had had access to Hooton, his assessment about line might not so much have changed as become evidentiary for aspects of a literary culture on the lookout for the new. He may have seen Hooton as one lodged in battle for a new order of the poetic line. I have taken Williams more to his word than is needed. Whether or not the poetic line would be the kind Williams was seeking – considering his disgust at neurasthenic modernism, and indeed the erotics of the avant-garde – we can take the question of lineate order in Malley or Hooton to mean something specific for an Antipodal history of poetics. This will by no means be the final word on these matters, but what we can now say for certain, in re-examining the poetics and literary-historical locales of the 1940s, and up to the 1960s but no further, is that the problem of the avant-garde lay further to its core than we knew; whether in Malley, Malley readers or Hooton's attempt to build a new order, or indeed disorder of the line, in an Australian literary culture that was determinedly, and decidedly, not revolutionary. The directions and the vectors of the poetic line were tilted towards invention well before the explosion of experimental poetry in the 1970s. For that we need to examine a poet who admired Hooton: the late Dadaist Jas Duke.

I can make no bigger claim than this: while the battle lodged in the poetic line might never have come to pass in the way that Williams envisaged it, it doubtless lay dormant, there, in history, and as we continue to tell this tale, no less, the literary in history. Dada was the greatest aftershock to be felt in the Antipodes of the long avant-garde, with its beginnings in Melbourne in the 1950s, and through it the poetic line was graphed, scored, remetaphorised and anthologised in a scale that could not be more local.

Inter-city arty blak
Remote yet so connected blak
Welfare woman villain blak
Pension weaver striking blak
                – Alison Whittaker, "bpm 100", *Blakwork* (2018)

the ash falls, like oodgeroo says in no
    more boomerang . . .
thirty years too ironic the idiom of a papershop . . .
the first letter, of war, peace, protest,
      borrowed from zukofsky.
  – Michael Farrell, "a effects", *A Lyrebird: Selected Poems* (2017)

the minties
thrown
at amateur hamlets
by
futurist schoolboys.
              – Pam Brown, "1966", *Selected Poems* (1971–1982)

Part II

Aftershocks
(1947–Vanishing Present)

Chapter 4

The Dada Chronicles:
Jas H. Duke and Barry Humphries

Northrop Frye, in his 1965 *Conclusion to a* Literary History of Canada, would claim:

> It is much easier to see what literature is trying to do when we are studying a literature that has not quite done it. If no Canadian author pulls us away from the Canadian context toward the centre of literary experience itself, then at every point we remain aware of his social and historical setting. (341)

If the reader is convinced that these past two chapters concern more questions of literary history than national literature, what's the key link? Do we do literary history simply when a national literature has not quite done it, as Frye puts it? Is sociohistorical textualism our dirty work? Does prying around at the peripheries for more "marginal" national literatures ever end? Has the *metaphor* of an avant-garde been the responsibility of criticism since its first literary use by Étienne Pasquier? When do we move from metaphor to experience? And if so, who, what is at the "centre" of (a) literary experience? *Where* is it; Canada, the US, Brussels, the Euro-US, the "West" and its institutions? Can a centre "at every point" expand to settings that were once on the periphery: an expanding critical universe? What type of author can pull us, readers, or critics, towards the centre of literary experience "itself"?

The Canadian literary situation, at the time of Frye's conclusion, was a time before the new wave, before Margaret Atwood – who claims to have been greatly influenced by Frye – and before that titan of Canada's avant-garde, bpNichol, had achieved wide recognition. The question of whether a literature has assumed a centre in Australia is one that involves not only critics in the conventional sense, like Frye, but poets and anthologisers. The role of critics, as the previous chapter has shown, could be relatively minor. The critic-as-tastemaker can hardly be held up as any long-term impediment to the avant-garde, nor can their prophetic abilities, which are considerable, be excessively magnified. Yet something like a "critical exterior" is at play in the work of critics in that more commanding sense – the expanding circle of the critical reading is such that it becomes a type of performance, a show: a critic performs their reading because they tell us what they are reading and how they read it. As our earlier discussion of Hans Robert Jauss made apparent, literary history can uncover the "how" – how texts strike new chords among readers – but it is the critic who tells us how to read, and if that process is not obscured, we are proffered theoretical insight into what led to this: reflection, illumination, even revelation. Literary history, to be sure, has neither invited nor curtailed revelation, at least not so far. It has certainly revealed things to us that we may not have known about the avant-gardes, but it has not brought about a "Mosaic" moment, a new lesson on how we read. I hope I may be forgiven, again, for restraining our discussion in a historical vein to presentable documents-at-hand, for literalising my argumentation, an unavoidable historicist's allergy, or reflex, that I want to elevate into a more theoretically reflective literary historicism. Duke in effect writes, or chronicles the history of the avant-garde itself, as much as he is written into it. Like Walwicz and Stewart to come, Duke engages directly with early twentieth-century European and transpacific avant-gardes. Well before theoretical dilemmas make their way into these readings (and they will, and even at the risk of hanging about too long at the peripheries of literary experience), we will need to chronicle necessary personae and events as they come in slower tempo.

I. *Jerome Rothenberg's "common shore": the Invention of Dada's Oceanic origins*

Duke is the first Antipodal Dadaist whose work captures both the poetic seriousness and full vitality of Dada performance in a way that fits with the notion of a "neo"-Dada internationalism, and in a way that can write past the conclusion to a national literary history of Australia. Perhaps no greater figure of Dada internationalism exists than that of the US poet and anthologiser Jerome Rothenberg, who in a sense completes Tzara's unfinished project of anthologising with *Technicians of the Sacred: A Range of Poetries from Africa, America, Asia, Europe and Oceania*, first compiled in 1969, by retaining the useful continentalist term "Oceania" in the fiftieth-anniversary edition. What looks like a Dada poem appears in the beginning of beginnings, the Genesis section, "Origins & Namings", that is, the section that starts the whole range off. Without offering any specificity as to clan of origin, Rothenberg cites it as a "Rain-chant", re-transcribed from an anthropological text by Baldwin Spencer. It contains lines like "Dad a da da" and "Da kata kai" (8). This is then picked up and requoted in other publications afterwards with the original source left out, to mean various things in different contexts, with no further acknowledgment of origin. In the Fiftieth Anniversary edition Rothenberg "corrects" the source from Spencer's 1904 book *The Northern Tribes of Central Australia* to *The Native Tribes of the Northern Territory of Australia* from 1914, but those lines appear in Baldwin Spencer's later work *Wanderings in Wild Australia* with diacritics; "Dad á Da dá, Da káta kái" (360–1).[1] Spencer notes here that, with F. J. Gillen, they recorded the rain dance on film and phonograph. It is now known that, with Gillen, Spencer recorded some of the first films on the continent in the first years of the new century (it's worth noting here too that Spencer and Gillen are a key source for Freud's *Totem and Taboo*). The passage concerns the ability for the cinematograph to capture the rain dance, and the fact that some of it was lost. Spencer's explanation of what he heard is that the words seemed "to consist of only two simple refrains repeated time after time" (360). The first, presented as a quatrain, Spencer claims was repeated thrice, with the second, also presented as a quatrain, on a higher note and only sung once,

> and again the refrain "Dad á" was taken up, and so on without variation, to the accompaniment of clanging boomerangs that kept time to the music. Emphasis was laid on the á, the ó and Káta kái, one clang of the boomerangs corresponding to each of the two first and one to each of the two latter—but every now and then the call of the plover, or Pil-pilpa, was heard. It was a very good example of sympathetic magic. The call of the bird is often heard before the fall of rain, so that the native naturally thinks there is a close connection between the two and that, if he imitates the former, the latter is sure to follow. (361)

---

[1] It must be pointed out that some Indigenous readers may not be permitted to view the entire transcribed chant in either of these two documents.

The anthropological sense of "natural" here is most confounding because, as an example of "sympathetic magic" (361), the inability to capture it on film is tantamount to an inability to describe it, to sympathise adequately – the cinematograph, it is assumed, is not natural, and isn't yet working to its fullest degree. We don't need a postsecular turn to tell us that the parallel ritual of the filmic process is sympathetic colonialism fusing its own primitive magic to another – the projection of film ends with loss. Projective failure is only natural, it would seem, when the discourse of technological advancement is deployed against its "natural" adversary. Spencer's writing moves mostly around familiar terms; the violent language of "savagery". But at its more transparent moments it cannot conceal a failure to read, failure to capture. Its own language of sympathy becomes an astonishing misunderstanding of the whole basis of, and reasoning behind resentment amongst First Nations people to the colonial invader. Rothenberg's quotation at the beginning of a seminal anthology finds itself a frame that is different, but no less sympathetic – a demonstration of poetic origins of Sound; the strangeness of the quotation and the meaning of its placement is no misprision, since to doubly hear in such rain chant the beginnings of Sound in poetry and the anticipation or inception of Dada is an *enchantment* of the early twentieth century through an evocation of antiquity. The question is not only of quotation or appropriation but historical respect and a sense of colonial violence. Rothenberg has that, but in the case of Spencer, the source of the transcription, though the dance (and its performance) was done with knowledge of its purpose and its utility, the colonial recorder is plagued with the problem of mystery. It *is* the mystery here, even unto orthographic aptitude: for instance, capitalisation suggests an alternate type of accent but no more information is given: Spencer indicates in the 1914 work a difficulty with his method of writing down "their languages or dialects" (441), and for his orthographic system Spencer finds it "quite impossible, very often, to say whether, in any word a particular consonant should be written as *k* or *g, b* or *p, d* or *t*" (441). The mystery, that is to say, is not the sound but its notation and transcription, and the impotency, *imprimitivism*, of the appropriate machines of record.

To bring this back to Dada, then, the speculative zeal about meanings of the word Dada may have to be revisited if more historical information comes to light, most likely through better knowledge of the intention or through-lines of Tzara's reading. TaTa / Dada and the rain chant, if they give another sense of what the Sound basis of Dada chant was, could place it not only in the register of primitivism but also Antipodal rituals with roots in Songlines; aquacultural and agricultural connections to land and country. If it is a "dead end", no matter either. We cannot rehearse all the claims to an origin of the word, and Ball knew this because even if its origin was hidden from him, it would be an "International word" in the 1916 Manifesto, and in a more sinister way, Romanian: "Yes, indeed, you are right, that's it. But of course, yes, definitely, right." The sarcasm with which Dada pre-emptively spoke to any reopening of the history of a word is necessary to keep in mind. It cannot do to overlook humourist intention. Yet still the seriousness of Tzara's journal readings in the Zurich library, like *Anthropos*, draw a longer line to Rothenberg and keep criticism on guard as to theoretical particulars and generalities of historical idea. Rothenberg's poems themselves contain critiques of historical Dada; he cannot assume, turning to Tzara of Ball "a common tradition that would be shared with any group of listeners I might be addressing" in a Pre-Face that is also the giving of a reading, to *That Dada Strain*, from 1982. It is a strained present:

> In the present instance the first force I would summon up is that of a DADA movement nearly seventy years into its history. Its authors have passed, as Blake would have said, into "eternity," to become the fathers of imaginal acts done in their memory. The spirit that remains is the final resistance to the tyranny of one's own works, as it emerges in Tzara's manifesto insistence that "the true Dadas are against Dada." The measure of their failure (& of ours) is in the degree of divergence from their most defiant aim: "the liberation of the creative forces from the tutelage of the advocates of power" ... No one, of course, is really DADA now, but the resistance (as long as it continues) may take enough of a backward look to consider those who came before us. Viewed in this way, their leading edge would seem to be through language—its collapse & reconstruction—that led them to invent new languages (like Ball's wordless poetry) in which would be fulfilled Apollinaire's prophecy: "victory will be above all / to see truly into the distance / to see everything / up close / so that everything can have a new name." (*That Dada Strain*, vii–viii)

Dada is then for Rothenberg both child and father – the generation of his own father, a foreclosed genealogy in some respects; his own language and perception and the prophecy of others (*That Dada Strain*, viii). Rothenberg goes with and against the genealogical strains that are languages of invention and invented languages. Citing the Yaqui people and the iconic Mazatec shamaness (*curandera*) Maria Sabina Magdalena García, Rothenberg moves to the Indigenous people of the land upon which he writes, in closing, to invoke the enchantment of *That Dada Strain* that ultimately "doesn't come from European DADA at all" but rather 1920s jazz (ix). The citation of the specific place of the prophetic in Apollinaire, one would think, could lead us to the Antipodal strain in his own poem "On Prophecies" through the character of Madam Salmajour:

> I've known a few prophetesses
> Madame Salmajour learned in Oceania to tell fortunes by cards
> It was there too she had occasion to participate
> In a tasty scene of anthropophagy
> She didn't mention it to everyone
> Concerning the future she was never wrong
> (*Caligrammes*, 67)

The figure of Madame Salmajour as failsafe prophet, rather than Muse, puts Oceania not so much in the position, or locale, of a place spoken of or spoken for, as a place that is supposed to speak, supposed to tell the truth. It is a place supposed to know. But it's more than anything a place supposed to know something about time, prophetic time and historical time. If this time is prophetic time, Rothenberg extends this to "DADA" and by implication the whole avant-garde: is it not the avant-garde that is supposed to *do* something to time? That Dada was Rothenberg's Muse, as Diane Wakoski suggested, sets the stage for Rothenberg's poem "The History of Dada as my Muse", which begins:

> the history of the fathers
> is only Dada time   only yesterday
> only the day before
> the morning after, time
> spent in this century
> an empty train
> snaking its way to Paris
> cathedral where an old sump overflows
> that leaves them dizzy
> shit sticking to their cuffs
> unpressed but with the father's zest
> for living   vests & monocles
> proclaim an avant-garde
> in absence an avant garde proclaims
> itself . . .
> (*New Selected Poems*, 104)

The Dada fathers are snaking their way into the heart of Europe, the heart of war, from the East (does Rothenberg, Polish Jew, not also track West from a proximate East?), all the way to the "heart of culture" (*NSP*, 104). Or South: they even find themselves in Zanzibar (*NSP*, 104). Because cultural centres make cultural centuries, time and space are lensed as they fall into contact and move farther away – Dada time seems just yesterday – but yesterday edges closer to a negative of the present since the present can also be expressed as the day before the morning after. The difficulty in catching what is clearly here a vanishing present, the difficulty that is in turning this vanishing one into an expanded present, is precisely the lensing effect of avant-garde time. In geometries of global space, the avant-garde converges upon Paris, and there the ragged and jagged history of the fathers comes into view – the Symbolic Vanguard Father (which is an inhuman multiple, comprising the "history-of-the-fathers") is both the young men proclaiming of an avant-garde against the fathers, and the process of becoming-Father is freeing up the language, or "reversals in the history of language" (*NSP*, 105). History expands from point-present. It is "Nostrodamus" [*sic*] (*NSP*, 106), a history between men, and a history of the century. At the bottom of most of these poems are printed historical footnotes about the Cabaret, bits of quotation. Thus the strain and the straining after what is left of the history of a century and the history of the invention of language is an argument against the history of the Dada Muse and an affirmation of its contradictory status. It is, after all, contradiction that drives these poems not only as psychosocial readings of an avant-garde – its anality, its paternity, the circuitry of its drives – but most of all contradictions of time and space in the historical text. And what they can *anticipate* is ultimately death, the end, the straining of and the straining to breathe and say when the voice pants at the twilight of the century. The troubled dialectic of the Muse is perhaps most "clear" in "The Suicide of Dada". The "man I would address as father is at last my son's age" as the century has worn on and the genealogical transmission has taken place after the ritualistic frenzy of reproducing the poetics in, or on America (*NSP*, 116). In the environment of Capital and "rich man's Dada" the strain marches on almost comically. It has gone through the Academy and into the Gallery, so "the designers of a failed poetics" carry on:

> the shady lady & the Dada financiers
> committing suicide
> mark the beginnings of
> the death of
> DADA
> the judas clown who bands the auto hood

>   opens the Dada wilderness
>   vanilla sparks & lights he wafts to us
>   like flowers   tattooed goat turds
>   their Dada deaths & victories
>   passed down the generations
>   to reach our common shore (*NSP*, 118)

A chronicle of Dada, a poetic history, is how Rothenberg in *That Dada Strain* manages to tell its story. This poem ends the sequence and one gets a sense that as a narrative it is complete, or as complete as any narrative history can be. To tell a chronicle of Dada is a poetic history and to end it with an opening to the Dada wilderness seems, if we are to take it "as read", the final place towards which the genealogy points; the end of one phase and the beginning of another. But what is Dada wilderness? No more speculation is needed here. No referential space is constructed and it was better that way. Dada did not begin in the Antipodes, but as we heard it, in Rothenberg's imaginal geographies of the "first" Dada sounds on the Antipodal continent, the question of the immense historical misprisions, and *mishearings* of ethnological intrusion and their framing in Dada genealogy is inseparable from the question of the intrication of colony and cosmopolis. The common shore, transported to the language of the colonial Commonwealth, will make then for a very difficult Antipodal translation.

II. *Barry Humphries and the Ubu/Dada Days 1951–*

If Rothenberg's anthologistic, chrestomathic drives represent one attempt to bring Dada internationalism back, his detection of strains of its continuation through poetic chronicle think Dada in the rain chant without hope of return. What was going on in the Antipodal continent itself, however, followed genealogical dynamics Rothenberg identified in the anatomy of the Dada century; the young fathers had too fallen into the cosmopolis of the colony and found themselves opposed. To what, precisely, they were opposed, needs elaboration. The politics of Australian Dada begins at a point undoubtedly marked by New Nationalism, though its historical antecedents are vast. At the dawn of the 1970s it seemed Australian social politics had moved on from the Menzies era (1949–66), a long rejection of the Labor architects of Reconstruction in the 1940s. But in an era defined in the popular imagination as one of economic stability and conservative ideology, the 1950s could have seemed culturally "unproductive". No figure encapsulates mid-century contradictions of this kind better than Barry Humphries. A key instigator of the Melbourne Dada Group, Humphries found creative expression against the backdrop, in white Australia, of a conservative moralism that could actively stifle what they perceived to be the better direction of creative freedom. The group was formed alongside a band of players that got called the "Wubbo Movement". Though it had been said that it was "pseudo-Aboriginal", and that it is the word for "nothing", no evidence is given for the language or locale that it was taken from. Paul Matthew St Pierre, in a 2004 book, *A Portrait of the Artist as Australian: L'Oeuvre Bizarre de Barry Humphries*, compares the "nominal transformation" between "rubbish" and "Wubbo" – as Barry Humphries himself claims as the word's, and the movement's, origin in the 1993 recording going by the name "The Dada Tapes", in *Dada Days: Moonee Ponds Muse, Vol. 2 (1951–1983)* – with Alfred Jarry's move from "Hébert" to "Ubu" (41). These recordings are some of the earliest experimental music in Australia in the Dada vein, thus *Dada Days* is archived as part of the history of avant-garde music in Clinton Green's *Artefacts of Australian Experimental Music 1930–1973*, alongside works by Jack Ellitt and Percy Grainger in the 1930s. These are sounds that conjure the Cabaret, but it is no coincidence that Dada would have to bar, write *as nothing*, the Indigenous origin of the word and the movement in order to proceed as avant-garde (or in Rothenberg's language, this Dada can only proclaim itself in place of an absence, as Dada in the wilderness). It is just as much no surprise that the Muse of Moonee Ponds would be a "field recording" of a sort, a field recording of *Dada Days*, and dated as of a history between 1951 and 1983, with a beginning and an end, two dates that are significant for not only Humphries but the arc of this history. The implications of it being "partly as a joke" make it starkly different to Tzara's and Rothenberg's serious evocation of historical Dada origins, and if there was any evidence that Dada was taken from Indigenous language, to take "Wubbo" as the basis for a Dada grouping might have, if not literal, at least psychical origins in the same will to name, or "nominal transformation", for the "regional comedian" and Dada internationalist alike. John Lahr's comment, also recounted by St Pierre, that Les Patterson was an "Aussie Ubu", leads us to the character Tid, because it is the experimental graphic novel from the 1950s, "A Novel Called Tid" (in literary terms juvenilia, though Humphries remained more littérateur than practitioner), that shows most the childishness of an Ubu Roi. Tid is a character trying most not to be seen. Tid was, for St Pierre, Humphries's first literary character, and in the novel Tid is a shape-shifter of strange dimensions, drawn with an enormous head and strangely shaped body. Dr Aaron Azimuth was the other Dada character that, as Humphries puts it in the memoir *My Life as Me*, he created as a Dada dandy and "sworn foe of all Barrys and Shirleys; enemy of my parents too, with their suburban certainties and their seemingly effortless ability to live happily without Art" (123). The seriousness of Azimuth especially as a counter-generational figure and artist is plain to see, with his long black coat, black homburg and deathly white make-up and mascara: "He recited his poems and tirades in a loud staccato voice and extolled madness and violence as the ultimate virtues" (*My Life as Me*, 123). It was a disguise but also a subjectification by Humphries of Humphries. "Nothing was as stimulating as the inner angry life of Dadaism: my life as Aaron Azimuth" (*My Life as Me*, 124). Then came, in 1952, the "First Pan-Australasian" Dada Exhibition, advertised to include "picasso", "cezanne", "humphries", "matisse", "levi", "laver-tree", "perry", "gawkgin", "luigi-bop" and "van-goof" (*More Please*, 120).

> The first big Dadaist exhibition of 1952, in my first year at university, established my notoriety, with its provocative sculptures of perishable materials such as cake and offal, juxtaposed with undergraduate blasphemy and the odd insult to the Royal Family. At the Puckapunyal military camp I had found a discarded portrait in oils of King George VI by an artist of moderate competence. The medals the King wore were particularly well executed and I merely had to paint the word "Dada" meticulously on one of them, sign the picture myself and put it in an elaborate frame for the work to be mine. It may surprise a modern reader to learn that this was the exhibit that gave the greatest offence. (*My Life as Me*, 125)

History haunts the edges of the first exhibition; an odd concinnity between a vanishing blasphemic, antiroyalist present and a wider historiography of avant-garde acts of transgression. The idea of "Pan" suggests resonant circles of an Australasian regionalist Dada that could take the continent to be a hemisphere, giving it hemispheric edge, so to speak. Not so surprising then that George VI wears a Dada medal; yet there may be some jesting seriousness to it – could Australian Royal Dada think its way out of this history? Another provocative exhibit involved "shoescapes" using decayed boots from rubbish dumps, nailed to a board and "conventionally framed". "I created a number of these footnotes to the history of Australian Dadaism," Humphries adds (*My Life as Me*, 125). They may have been footnotes, but if the Dada history is what it becomes in this account of it, they may also become the main text.

In 1952–3 Humphries's Dada phase was at its height. At one raucous demonstration before a lecture hall, a Dada campaign for a place on the Student Representative Council, a row of Dada "Johns" committed acts of offense on stage, with one John, John Perry, writing the word "poem" in huge letters on the blackboard with his right hand while erasing it with his left, "so that the word never completely took form" (*My Life as Me*, 126). In literary terms, perhaps the most critical object, of the Second Pan-Australasian Dada Exhibition catalogue of 1953, is a novel, by "Aaron Azimuth", called *The Blue Lamington* (lamingtons are Australian cakes). Humphries describes is as a citational work "in traditional Dada-surrealist fashion, by opening books at random and transcribing sentences and sometimes whole paragraphs wherever a pencil arbitrarily fell" (*My Life as Me*, 122–3). They were collaborative: many of these long prose works were "randomly confected" with the above John Perry. Perry was "an old school friend with a natural gift for expressionism . . . but I was the pseudonymous Aaron Azimuth" (*My Life as Me*, 123). Duke too dabbled in the tradition of cut-ups. These were textual and historical encounters. It was after Humphries discovered, in 1952, Robert Motherwell's *The Dada Painters and Poets, An Anthology* that he found inspiration for his own Dada Manifesto after Tzara. It appears in Peter Coleman's popular biography *The Real Barry Humphries*, from 1991:

> Cubism was a school of painting, fascism a political movement, DADA is a state of mind.
> Free-thinking has no resemblance to a church. DADA is artistic free-thinking.
> We are incapable of treating seriously any subject whatsoever, let alone DADAism.
> The Acts of Life have no beginning or end. Everything happens in a completely idiotic way. That is why everything is alike.
> Simplicity is called DADA. So, like everything in life, DADA is useless.
> DADA is working with all its might to introduce the idiot and the cretin everywhere. And it, itself, is tending to become more and more idiotic.

> DADA is terrible; it stinks, it feels no pity for the defeats
> of the intellect or for the high cost of living.
> DADA proclaims that there is no relation between
> thought and expression!! ... (35–6)

And so on: primary material, vital, youthful, Hootonesque even. That the movement would be incapable of treating seriously any subject whatsoever doesn't fully undermine the earnestness of tone. It is in the line of *Dada-Jok*, Branko Ve Poljanski's 1922 anti-Dada Dadaist magazine, with its rhetorical naysaying to motives, but it stops short of becoming detractor to all things avant-garde. The word "cretin" is a substitute for "critic" in Humphries's lexicon. The introduction of the cretin and the idiot might sound like critique, until one hears sarcasm in the proclamation that there is no relation between thought and expression. We might hear again some serious evaluation; that Dada is quite seriously a state of mind, of free-thought as against churches. As we shall see below, Duke would later speak in critical terms of the "churches era" of the early twentieth-century avant-garde. But with Duke the subject of critique was also the very idea of Australia, which clears the way for a different, vaster Dada on national and international timescales. For Humphries, Australia had "brainwashed" him into believing his "few accomplishments were liabilities ... even Dada was *vieux jeu*" (*More Please*, 147). Dada would remain trapped in the university where it began.

Even now, the character of Dame Edna Everage is the most easily recognisable of Humphries's creations. It was not long after these exhibitions and their texts that the character of Edna Everage would appear for the first time. One of Everage's main lines was that she was born with a "priceless gift" – an ability to "laugh at the misfortunes of others", an attitude contrary to the aforementioned Dada sympathy. There is little doubt that Everage is an extension of these Dada strains, with several commentators noting that she is modelled off Rrose Sélavy of Marcel Duchamp, who Humphries had in fact met in 1963 in New York. St Pierre, for instance, forthrightly claims that

> Dame Edna is Humphries' Rrose Sélavy: Barry Humphries is to Dame Edna Everage as Marcel Duchamp is to Rrose Sélavy, as La Gioconda is to Duchamp's mustachioed and goateed *Mona Lisa*, as Leonardo da Vinci is to Marcel Duchamp, as Marcel Duchamp is to Barry Humphries, as Barry Humphries is to Dame Edna Everage, and so on, and on, spinning like a Duchamp Rotary Demisphere or Rotorelief. Just as Marcel Duchamp is "Un Administrateur" ("An

Administrator") and Rrose Sélavy, his female identity, alter-ego, and character, is "Le Président du Conseil d'Administration" (President of the Administrative Council"), so Barry Humphries is Dame Edna's administrator (from the Latin *ministrare*, meaning "to manage" and "to serve"): he administers all her presidential edicts and her speech-acts, and he serves in direct opposition to the *non serviam* of the devilish Les Patterson, who refuses to offer service (except of the sexual kind, which he extends – as he would say, "are you with me, ladies and gentlemen?" – to all his Girls Friday). (143–4)

St Pierre goes on to read these Dada pranks, through Paul Ricoeur, as a dialectic of "oneself as another". The theorising of histories of character in St Pierre's readings become a way of taking the speech-acts of Humphries to be penetrating views of the rhetoric of the subject. It isn't just that Australia in the fifth decade is the target of Humphries's scorn, nay critique – the conceptual boringness of Sandy Stone is no better example of this – rather, the universe (sometimes literary) of Humphries is a unified field of revolving parts each of which takes its place in the critique. There is no Everage, for instance, without the vulgar, but complexly masculine counterpart Les Patterson. If Dada was for this generation an escape from the staid death of everything, of stale lemon-coloured wallpaper, of white Australia in this period, it would also demand of its audience an escape from a specific intellectual climate of the university. There is, of course, a dialectic of jest and seriousness that, in order to establish itself, would have to make of the Dada days something radical enough to lift the brows of the 1950s cultural establishment, its institutions and its censors. Prank and provocation, not without its intended targets, really did shake up the sensibility of mid-century Australia, particularly when its presentation risked contradicting the standard of societal projection abroad. The comic that became a movie, *The Wonderful World of Barry McKenzie*, was banned until the Whitlam Prime Ministership of the 1970s. It was a fine line between mild discomfort and censorship, just as it was a fine line between humour and seriousness in the Australianisation of Dada.

For an Antipodal avant-garde mid-century these facts are meaningful also to theories of history. The wit of Humphries became a very royal road to the Australian unconscious. We cannot read Humphries's Dada origins without the latter end of his career in view, in England, and a better reading of this has to keep in view the contradictions of national culture in the political forms of the Commonwealth. A "distinctive" culture, or a greater feeling that distinction was coming, was short-lived. It felt always as if it had no permanent model; neither a brash, Republican zeal nor any true sense of rootedness based upon independence or sovereignty that would deepen those cultural feelings, and in Humphries the success of that career led back to the embrace of the monarchy and Englishness, not so much because it represented the failure of the whole critique or its culmination, but because there was no other place to go. The explosive jouissance of the send-up of Middle Australia had to end up in the place from which Middle Australia came and to which it aspired. It was an intelligentsia that resented the heavy lard of the Middle, but an intellectual class that wouldn't have the means to become the vanguard of the working class. It came from outside: a European Surrealist-Dada cultural injection that shook ground. It is undeniable that a "National Dada" manifests in the body of Humphries and its senses of nation, a National Dada that remains unfinished business, but more to Rothenberg's way of thinking, it could not spirit itself into a history of Dada that took all the arts with it. Though it was a kind of Dada against Dada, it saw Dada as a positive philosophy, an externalist critique. We will measure Duke's Dada with and against this. Humphries's Dada was undialectical Dada: its living death, undead Dada (no Antipodal Dada father, just angry sons). Duke's was against Australia and against the churches of the avant-garde; fully engaged in the strenuous and repeated attempts to work with the contradictions of an Antipodean Dada. And while Duke will also bring senses of nationhood to light they come in a vastly different context, when he returns from abroad at the very moment Gough Whitlam is elected Prime Minister, a period that transforms the arts and culture of modern Australia. Duke, Humphries and Whitlam are curiously triangulated in the fact that *The Adventures of Barry McKenzie*, directed by Bruce Beresford in 1972 and starring Humphries as Everage, appears on the eve of this moment of revitalised cultural production, and in the sequel to the 1972 film, *Barry McKenzie Holds His Own*, from 1974, we see the effects of the new era; Gough Whitlam himself appears at the end having brought the "artists and intellectuals" home, including the main character, Barry ("Bazza") McKenzie (poet Clive James, who acts in the film, remains in Europe) after a riotous romp through Europe, replete with anxieties of the Eastern Bloc (through a mysterious Transylvanian Communist/vampire State-cabal) and various misadventures in England and France (that reveal plenty about the classing and gendering of Australian statehood), and an "underground" radicalism or Republicanism haunting resistant or repressed presentations of national character and personhood. Arguably Whitlam also brought Duke home.

The "brain drain", however, not only drained an intelligentsia, but drained life within the continent due to the forms and effects of labour and lethargy. It was a social and economic reality of the cultural classes before and even after the period 1972–5. An avant-garde might not just have been able to sustain itself "at home" under the pressure of a mass culture inclined to stifle critique of its chosen mechanisms of cultural production. This critique was responding not to crisis but rather to constraint. The argument that the repetition of Anglophilia in Humphries is explicable only through the lens of a rejection of Australian cultural production is insufficient. Selling cultural products to the mass milieu of a receptive global culture may be disappointing for Dada enthusiasts, but more nobody's business than some specific national loss. Rather, that there was no coring of First Nations senses of nationhood, despite expressions towards it emergent after the Whitlam period, is the key to the impermanency of that period of change. Dada circa 1950s had to write Indigeneity into nothingness in order to make a claim for distinction, but the claim for distinction would later become apparent through Indigenous poets themselves and alternative Dada actions like those of Duke. Anne Pender argues that this period's "New Nationalism", encapsulated in the parallel icons Humphries and Whitlam, still could not find any consensus as to what its new symbols would be (77). What Pender doesn't explore is the question of the very foundation of an Australian nation itself and its civic structures, and how these structures inform aspects of social negotiation these two icons had to work within. These structures are precisely what prevents both figures, for all their differences (Whitlam the socialist, Humphries the anarcho-royalist) and despite their investigations of "new nationalism", from moving headlong into a new era beyond the "post-imperial predicament". Even if we see in Whitlam much more of a sense of Nation *as* First Nations, in policy and in his person, he remained ever the reformist, evolutionist. It was to go that way for Whitlam, who bestows damehood on Everage, challenges the rhetoric of empire, yet cannot move the country beyond its predicament as colony in the Commonwealth. For Whitlam loyalists, the true story was that he was not given the opportunity to finish what he had started. Whitlam was, after all, ousted from power. His challenge to the operations of Western intelligence and the Western geopolitical bloc did not help his longevity.

Despite the shortcomings of what we might easily call "Whitlamism", he was in some respects a figure of the avant-garde, and the flash of this tumultuous period would be remembered long after he had left office. The Whitlamist manifesto "Socialism in the Australian Constitution", from 1961, with its curious interest in legal loopholes around the creation and commandeering of state-owned enterprises, envisaged an economic governance structure that later policy directives only dimly shadowed. Before Whitlam was elected in 1972, the conservative Liberal Party in coalition with the Country Party had ruled for twenty-three years (1949–72). Despite a growing counter-culture in the 1960s, the patchwork quilt of the left had not built a coherent strategy of resistance within the reactive structures of parliamentary politics, just as the conservative resistance to the rising power of the Australian Labor Party had in reaction consolidated its aims. It is possible to argue that the counter-cultures of the 1960s played a role in Whitlam's rise and election to power, but radical underground movements as previously noted, like the libertarian-anarchist Push in Sydney, were more intellectual effects than causes, never proletarianising enough to materially unite Australia's working class with the intelligentsia. The conditions that led to Whitlam were indeed those that made radical movements in art and poetry, and in turn Whitlam's policies supported their flourishing in significant transformations of government funding structures. But changes to the fundamental class structures of Australian society and its place in the capitalist world order remained fairly much the same before and after Whitlam.

I also noted, previously, that in the literary world, beginning in the 1970s and throughout the 1980s, the wider anthologisation of avant-garde Australian poetry could capture some of the political and aesthetic animation of late twentieth-century Australian literary culture in a manner both critical (Gunew's co-editorship of *Telling Ways*) and anarcho-collective (*Missing Forms*). Chronicles begin to be written of this age, and these would not be the only ones. And again Tranter, who knew Ashbery well and whose style in some ways crossed with his US counterpart, would make a historical apology for the "1968 generation" in *The New Australian Poetry* anthology of 1979 almost two decades after Donald Allen's *The New American Poetry 1945–1960*. For Michael Sharkey there is some myth of the new in this history – in terms tinged with cringe at the American tradition it called forth – and contemporaries did not all rally behind the myth. Engaged in remaking a tradition by annulling what came before, Sharkey claims that Tranter's moves were historical and formal:

> In repudiating the substance and not merely the forms of Australian poetry up to the mid-1960s, or, more likely, driving a wedge between

substance and form, and stressing instead a *new form*, modernism, the promoters of the avant-garde may have stepped unwittingly or not into the mainstream of Australian poetic history. (118)

Time would tell, and some of this would come true. Tranter's place in late-century Australian poetry would be confirmed, and doubtless one of the most intriguing exchanges is between Tranter and John Ashbery, setting off transpacific and hemispheric coincidences and crossings. But as we have shown, a history of the avant-garde before 1960 is both more complex than the history Tranter sought to make and the theory of the avant-garde critics deployed to explain it, particularly if we look more closely at *forms*, texts and performances. We will be avant-substantialist, but not mainstream. If I have given any evidence in writing of the disdain I have for these caricatures of the avant-garde, I hope that it is muted in this paragraph alone, for the reason that I have focused not on the historical construction of the '68 generation and associated poets, but rather the Whitlam era, is because I have sought instead emergent forms in the expanded contexts of the avant-garde, not in isolation. In effect, I have sought a more total history, that would not throw about the word "avant-garde" without historical and theoretical terms in place, total but not absolute, able to place the development or retrodiction of the avant-garde within and against Australian and global literary modernism. Heseltine's cautious "Modern Australian Verse" of 1972 would be another anthologising attempt to assay here. The push especially after 1968 to frame modern Australian poetry allows for narrative alternatives to both Heseltine and Tranter that are neither subordinate to our purpose nor exemplary. But few disagree that in 1975 Australia changed forever. The impact of the Whitlam Dismissal I have taken to be a key marker in Australian history, and for the literati that lived through it. *Post-Dismissal poetics* is a phrase that can capture the aesthetic turmoil of this period's politics, and it is into this maelstrom that Duke returns, in 1973.

III. *Chronometrics of Chronicle: Duke*

Born in Ballarat, a town in the southern state of Victoria in 1939, Jas Heriot Duke's date of birth falls at a key turning point for the straining-off of the modern and its subsequent aftershocks or afterlives. It was, first of all, a big year in global politics; 1939 would spell the beginning of the Second World War and offer no respite from global recession that came before. Despondency would prove consequential for poetry, marked in W. H. Auden's "September 1, 1939". Auden would also respond in poetry to the 1939 death of W. B. Yeats. In generational terms, it would be useful to compare Duke with bill bissett, born in 1939, the Canadian experimentalist and close peer of bpNichol. Duke can be compared to both these Canadian poets in a few senses, given his varied visualist/concrete-plus-performance practices, a distinctly second-wave attitude to the early twentieth-century avant-gardes, and as influential for his generation. His birth and its time was a source of what we can now call chronometric curiosity, as he tells it in one poem: "I was born in 1939 / I was very young then / but the times were very old" (*War and Peace*, 160). Hooton's "Directions", an example of an avant-garde creed from the middle of last century, can be compared with Duke's "one-liner" poems in that they were influenced by Hooton, or so his contemporary Π.O. suspects in his introduction to *poems of life & death*. Duke's influences were local and global, and so far as the avant-garde is concerned, our chronicle must treat both in equal degree.

Jeltje Fanoy's poem "After Jas H. Duke", published in a 2017 issue of *Postcolonial Text*, begins quietly. "Switching off the reading lamp / my glasses / folded away" our reading takes off just as the muted environ of the speaker pulls back from her scene of reading. What has been read we don't know, but we do know that Fanoy has been listening; "I hear I've left the radio on, / I'm about to enter the dark and cold / of the hallway," and from here, a revenant voice arrives on the scene; "there's a voice, still, in this digital age / transmitting across / a freezing night sky". The radio "is digital already" and the presenter is "really him". Time and technology are figured in the poem as the ghost of a voice, but the poem ends well. Too well, perhaps. The intimations of a radio, a technology with a protracted history in the (post-)digital age, an age of both deep embedding in and exhaustion from the digital, end not with gripe and grudge or disenchantment, but perhaps rather weirdly, with happiness; "all this makes me very happy".

This is all very well and good. But *see* these words on a page, or *hear* them? And whose voice? Remembering the poem began "Switching off the reading lamp" we can note what's occluded here in the nocturnal passage of the poem. For the oddness of the poem is precisely in that nothing by way of context is given. Silent reading gives way to listening; this gives satisfaction, some kind of levelling of desire. But for Jeltje the reading that has occurred is the reading of what comes after (Duke's) life – the time of listening, of the ghost in the radiophonic voice, has to have moved towards the periphery of experience. Being *after* Duke means being digital, being caught in the moment of thinking about something that has not yet finished. Peripherality: the work resists closure, tests ends, but does it stand the test of time?

This too is a recording, a test recording. And if this is record, historical record, we need to ensure that there is a high level of clarity from our very first take. What stands the "test of time" is more than memory and will raise questions of literary history, histories of literary theory and questions of canon formation that have been pertinent to discussions from the modernist advocates among the New Critics to the calmer assessments of Frank Kermode. If there is a type of criticism that cannot read the avant-garde, it is because of literary history. It is because the *conditioning* of criticism from without is too sensitive and far too difficult to breach. If we were to take the attitude that an avant-garde poet (or text) consigns themselves (or itself) to oblivion, an assumption that has no grounding in the course of the early twentieth century with what sometimes gets called the "historic" or "historical" avant-gardes – a big mistake, as plenty of critics have previously expressed, but we do not wish to belabour this point – it is because we don't really think criticism can do it. And perhaps there is something more sinister going on, that would be the more paranoid reading: the dogged refusal to read is because avant-garde literary acts were *inseparable from writing themselves into history*. How then can we explain the work of literary history in these environs? That we have adopted tactics used by many who study these works – the action of recuperating lost works – is to fall back into history, not into criticism. Yet it is plain to see that recuperation doesn't help us learn how to *read* the recuperated works. That is where criticism comes back in. And that is what criticism can do. I have shown some suspicion towards the "recuperative" literary historian, who becomes a kind of canonmaker in reverse. Perhaps that is too unkind, but all too often these kinds of tactics get called decentring moves: one is doing the job of decentring, so to speak, and so the result is the construction of a kind of alternative centre. In my discussion of Duke I do not so much place him in an alternative avant-garde canon so much as touch on the historical aspects of his relation with the poetics of the early twentieth-century avant-gardes, and his horizontal relation with a generation of like-minded experimental poets, like Fanoy and others. But I concede that this is probably because the critical conditions underpinning this particular history have made recuperation less attractive, and less straightforward. But is it ever?

How we framed it from the get-go: rather than the notion of an external occupation by avant-gardism or reading it simply as invasive, Duke can be read against a different vocabulary in which those external modes are seen as an exchange of influences and poetic inflections. There is a fairly complex intrication of transnational and transpacific elements in Duke's poetics. This is not at the expense of region and locality though, for Duke's work is often timely, aware of social location, and engages in trenchant national and cultural critique, triggering a poetics of external and internal contradiction. Poems may at once read the outside against the inside, or vice versa. I read these poems against local socio-political contexts, like the impact of the Whitlam era before and after the Dismissal, and global contexts of nation and nationhood, coming to a head with the Bicentennial celebrations and geopolitical earthquakes during the later period of Duke's career. It is precisely how Duke's work develops a poetics that responds to the personae and the events of the international avant-garde, how he is able to summon a poetics that responds directly to assumptions of the received, derivation and "distancing", and how he occupied the commanding position of a Dada "duke", a founding figure for the avant-garde, as it were, that are our chief concerns.

The chronometrics of the belated entry of Dada meant that Duke was intensely conscious of Dada historicism and Dada as history. The *chronicle*, not quite a catalogue, and not an anthologising impulse, that I will identify as Duke's way of navigating and questioning historical Dada, is often used in the vein of anti-white-nationalist politics. We will have to be good timekeepers here. Historical frames that we would deploy for such an investigation will go further than context; chronometry is and in this extended usage has come to mean temporal disjuncts or surprising match-ups. But like no other poet, Duke is able to give readers a good sense of what constitutes an Australian avant-garde. In Duke it becomes clearer still how an Australian avant-garde plays its part in an international avant-garde tradition. We need speak no more of whether or not it exists, for we have moved on to ask *in what form?* Do second wave or "neo"-avant-gardes corrupt the originals? Were they a "maturation", or mere immature copies, effete echoes of the past or strong "aftershocks"? Did an Australian poetry "neo"-vanguard, in comparison with other neo-vanguards, extend the early twentieth-century avant-garde's original aims, degrade the original (revolutionary) aims (minus Futurism), or create something entirely "new" and thereafter become something wholly distinct from the historic avant-gardes?

IV. *Destiny Wood*, Dadaustralia

These are questions that cannot be answered in one chapter alone. John Kinsella, born 1963, a poet with international recognition and advocate of inventive or experimental poetics generally speaking, has asked whether the apparent "newness" of an avant-gardism in the Australian context will contain embedded notions of a blank slate or *terra nullius* upon which a new poetics can be applied (46). This is a question we will further interrogate in Chapter 6 on Lionel Fogarty. But is it Dada import or Dada invasion? Humphries would seem to have done both – invoking its invasive element and turning it into both an import and an export. Historical work on Duke, however, can respond to this question through an alternative emphasis on textual dynamics that doesn't so much uphold as debate, test, even undermine notions of nation and nationhood. I attend especially to those poems in Duke's oeuvre, and later in Stewart's as well, that do this. Not, however, in isolation. It will again involve the betweens of region and hemisphere. They are offensive *and* defensive moves, visible and withheld strains – at once fore-guard and "rearguard", as Hooton would have had it – that reassess the notion of an "Australian" advanced guard using the back door of region-to-globe referential frameworks. They are in some manner "remappings" from the peripheries of the literary experience. Duke's chronicle, which is also chronometrically inquisitive, plots along points the course of a history and messes it up, such that the precipitant scourges of modern Australia and its discontents, from the Frontier Wars to Federation and the Bicentennial celebrations, found no triumphal genealogy of Australian literature.

Duke was a visualist. A lettrist, even. In the material poetics of Duke we see a militant vanguardist sensibility manifest in attention to the letter. Anarcho-literary, and a good deal proletarianist, it *opposes*. Behind the lettristic disruption, a searing, scathing and occasionally sarcastic politics can tell us how Australian literature came to be so staid, and Australian culture an environment for anti-intellectualism and the twin dynamics of cultural inferiority and cultural superiority. The visually disjunctive, sonically dissonant, rhythmically *dysprosodic* character of Duke's work could be fully earnest, but also suspicious of the early twentieth-century European avant-gardes and directed, or used, to criticise the politics and the hypocrisy of the times. Social-prophetic critique, for this is what it is, was made immersive through Duke's lettristic energetics. If exemplary "neo"-vanguardist (and certainly Duke's interest was more in avant-garde than modernist traditions broadly conceived), it found itself up against Eurocentric or Euro-American avant-gardes as well as the idea of a uniquely Australian "genesis" for a new poetry, a concern for the Jindyworobaks but not for Duke.

Duke emerges from and creates a context. Both until and after his death in 1992, most of Duke's oeuvre was supported by Collective Effort Press, based in Melbourne, and he played no small place in the veritable explosion of small press activity in the 1970s. Publications like *925* and *Born to Concrete*, which appeared in 1975, drove the Melbourne scene along anarchist and workerist lines. They would not play a commercial game. Philip Edmonds notes that these publications "worked against bookshop sales", putting a politics of refusal into practice, refusal to become mainstream. Edmonds recalls Duke saying that "the *Age* never reviewed him, or magazines he was associated with, because his publications were stapled". Thus, refusal with intent: "The freewheeling nature of the decade was a moment in which small publications could experimentally resist commodification" (50). In the midst of this flourishing of radical material work Duke's genre-bending novel *Destiny Wood* was published in 1976 by Whole Australian Catalogue Publications.[2] In *Destiny Wood* Duke experiments with narrative, drama, drawings and comics, and concrete poetry. With an enormous cast of characters centred around the two main characters Jim Arch and Annie, the interspersed visual poems are among Duke's best. One reads "Proud electron circling Curie who taught you that fearful swerve?" (Figure 4.2). Not digitised and not readily available, *Destiny Wood*, were it more widely read, would make for a curious comparison with the narrative works of bpNichol. As it stands, it is surely one of the most extraordinary graphic novels ever produced in the Antipodes.

---

[2] Michael Denholm's two-volume resource, *Small Press Publishing in Australia, the early 1970s*, notes their publications, among them the 628-page anthology *Pie* (I examined a copy owned by the experimental poet Sam Moginie), edited by Paul Smith and Mal Morgan, and printed in telephone book format. It claimed to be "the biggest collection of poetry ever assembled in this country" (Denholm, 48).

CHARACTERS

Jim Arch	*a poet and scientific observer*
Small Jim Arch	*another jim arch of thumbnail size*
Ann	*a girl of independent mind, friend of jim arch*
Alabama	*Ann's baby son*
Ashley Cooper	*a former lover of jim arch*
Napoleon	*a trotskyist*
Don Hurley	*a painter*
Sally Hurley	*a beautiful girl*
Messalina Hurley	
Heliogablus Hurley	*children of Don and Sally*
Lesbia Brandon Hurley	
Maximilian	*an emperor of mexico*
Carlota	*an empress*
Juarez	*an emperor-killer*
Tay Sullivan	*a husband of Ann*
Sam Park	*a moviemaker*
Suzy Park	*a moviestar of the undermind*
Janis Park	*a princess*
Peter Parker	*a false poet*

(*Destiny Wood*, n.pag.)

One of Duke's biggest Dadaist artefacts is the 1996 limited edition artists' book/poem *Dada Kampfen um Leben und Tod (Dada Fight for Life and Death)*, published posthumously by Wayzgoose Press (Katoomba), printed in colour on a long single sheet of twenty-four pages folded concertina-style. Catherine Cradwick has noted that "The unexpected separation of lines of text produces a jarring, compelling dissonance", the work coming together as nothing other than a "fiercely energetic chronicle of Dadaism" (499). Chronicle, not history; one which will include other avant-garde histories like that of Merz, the Dada concept of Kurt Schwitters. It is in this work, in which the pages fold out as of a long scroll, that on one enormous page the word "DADAUSTRALIA" appears (Figure 4.3).

It's a chronicle of glorious struggle, a fight for life and death, yet also sarcastic, history visibly cast in reverse, coming back in another form, another guise: *chronicle* (record, annals), *as a challenge to the avant-garde*, repressed in prose. Australia never opened the book and thus couldn't even misread Dada, nor did it open up Symbolism beforehand for Dada to smash (although through Brennan it may, if Brennan hadn't been quite so taciturn). So far behind, then: "Think Western". All the while it participates in the jouissance of the disjunctive that characterises an avant-garde poetics, the chronicle places the poem *as history, or counter-history of the avant-garde*:

Figure 4.1 Jas H. Duke, visual poem from *Destiny Wood* (1978).

"What we haven't done yet", a line that seems to directly speak to Frye.

There are contexts behind these extraordinary breaks. Like several experimental poets I shall soon survey, including, albeit some time later, Amanda Stewart, Duke spent time in Europe and the USA in the 1960s, beginning to write in 1966 before moving back in the 1970s. How both poets view their practice in light of these

Figure 4.2 Jas H. Duke, cover of posthumous artists' book *Dada Kampfen um Leben und Tod (Dada Fight for Life and Death)* (1996).

international experiences differs, but it serves enough to transform, at least, critical *dismissals* – of "derivation" and the "received" – into more entrenched analyses of the translocations ("dislocations" too), and highlight the diasporic nature of Antipodal avant-gardes after 1970 (diasporic in the case of Walwicz). There is a complex web of relations, negotiations, influences and even outright rejections in these works. They are strenuous and entrenched responses to the historical avant-garde, not simple retakes. Being at one remove ought not seem in this new schema such a loss: it lends the term a certain historicity that is sometimes lost in the diachronicity

Figure 4.3 Jas H. Duke, excerpted page from *Dada Kampfen um Leben und Tod (Dada Fight for Life and Death)* (1996).

of accounts of the historic avant-gardes. Transcultural narratives emerge, produced by a generation of experimental writers who began writing and publishing in the late 1970s and early 1980s. Poets like Π.O., Thalia and Walwicz, three figures of this period alongside Duke, developed a poetics that incorporated multiple kinds of vernacular, engineering big collisions with English, causing new grammars. It caused them in the sense that the grammatical structures of their own languages (Greek, Polish) came to be superposed into or onto their uses of English. In this literary climate Duke had new motives to be enthused and ready to invent. In the preface to *Poems of Life & Death*, Π.O. would recall Duke's comments upon his return to Australia in 1973, "I came back to Australia with my psyche in ruins. I found Australia more interesting than when I left, it had been rescued from Menzies by the migrants" (24). In the Whitlam era, the Assisted Passage Migration Scheme, created in 1945 by the Chifley Government, was expanded to immigrants of any ethnicity, and by 1975 Whitlam had managed to pass the Racial Discrimination Act, effectively ending the White Australia Policy on a governmental level. It was a newly energised political and creative environment.

Looping back to the local environment meant full involvement in it. Aloofness was not the outcome of international experience, but cultural novelty did come with such inbound injections of energy. I cannot underline more vehemently the importance of small press and its community for this section marked "Aftershocks". Some of the blurbs on the back cover of Duke's *Poems of War and Peace* frame the work in messianic terms: "a real poet" – Henri Chopin; "one of the pioneers of experimental writing in Australia" – Anna Couani; "Someone!, give this poet a computer. He's a genius!" – Nigel Roberts; "the human voice played like a saxophone" – Nicholas Zurbrugg; "a real blabbermouth" – thalia; "one of new Australian poetry's Saving Graces" – Kris Hemensley. If Duke was one of new Australian poetry's Saving Graces, *the* New Australian Poetry as it were, the kingly figure of the "archduke" (the name of Duke's early journal), stood for this level of authority (Walwicz would imagine herself too as a communist General). It is no meagre phrase from Hemensley, whose role in the poetry workshops at La Mama (1960s and 1970s) and editorial work on various journals, including *Meanjin*, is legendary in the Australian avant-garde scene. Hemensley would later manage Collected Works, a space central for poetry readings, chapbook sales and launches up until 2018. Viewed from the standpoint of the small press milieu, we need to grasp the communal and generational contexts of Duke's poetics and the sources and historical currents he drew from to make such interventions. What does Duke's anarchistic neo-vanguardism mean in global avant-garde contexts? What do Duke's responses to Dadaism, Cubism, Concrete Poetry, Suprematism, Surrealism and Expressionism manifest? "Genealogy", "invasion" or "derivation" from without? From here the task then becomes to understand how these narratives work in his poetics above the question of influence, reserved more for poets in lyric modernism. And in describing these cultural productions it will become increasingly apparent that Duke imagines another history of Australian poetry emergent from its own material sites and locales; a history of inventive language in close conversation with concepts and ideas of what passes as originary or original, one in which there is no readily identifiable genealogy for an "Australian" poem. There are no battles to speak of. If anything, the battle lodged in the poetic line, to sound Williams out once again, was a battle against avant-garde history. The catch-up game of belatedness was no source of shame or simply a topic to be avoided. Duke embraced these historical incongruities and used it to construct a politics relentlessly scathing of the state of the nation by this stage of the century. Of interest to him, however, was the question of genealogy. What Duke does, in poetics, is examine, imitate and critique genealogies, occasionally with reference to cultural assumptions of Australianness, as he does in the text for *Dada Kampfen um Leben und Tod*, but also with naked attention to the operations of literary history itself.

V. The "Churches Era": Avant-Gardes and Genealogy

In a letter to Nicholas Zurbrugg from 1991, titled "The Unknown Avant-garde", Duke provides a response to Zurbrugg's theoretical work (*poems of life & death*, 302–3). Duke is concerned that the idea of the "unknown" produces a critical quandary, and he appears disturbed by the historical gelidity of the word "avant-garde": "I also have troubles with 'avant-garde.' If we have to have military analogies I feel that I'm more in the Quartermaster Corps than the Light Cavalry. I don't think I've done anything that couldn't have been done by a switched-on poet of 1890 if not 1590 . . . I don't like the term, don't think of myself as 'avant-garde,' but regard myself as an imitator of the best models of the past" (*poems of life & death*, 302–3). In other musings on histories of avant-gardes in modernism, Duke would claim the European avant-garde was structured like a "church". Under the greater army of Modernism, they were "small groups of true believers, generally led by some sort of Messiah figure . . . who constructed a canon of acceptable works" ("Sounds", 7). Group thinking was second nature and spurned mentalities of inclusion and exclusion. Acting as historical agents familiar to those told of in ancient chronicles, they welcomed in "right-minded colleagues and collaborators, produced bibles and prayer books for new recruits, denounced false prophets, and excommunicated spies and traitors" ("Sounds", 7).

Duke's abridged story of the early twentieth-century avant-garde as he tells it in this piece shows some fascination with its demagoguery as well as a disdain for its piousness. What is Duke's complaint? For sound poetry in particular, the regulatory bodies of the canonising authorities narrowed the frames of reference rather than opening them up: "Although sound poetry should be able to leap the boundaries of national languages anthologists insist on inserting French sound poets into French language anthologies, Germans into German books, and Americans into books dealing with America" ("Sounds", 7). National questions abound in the world of sound poetry even if they could be lively negotiations of nationhood. For instance, in the North American sound poetry anthology *Text-Sound Texts* (1980), an opening sound-text by Walter Abish titled "Auctioning Australia" plays on the vowel A, with lines like: "Are Australian authors as arrogant as American authors?" (29). Here "Australia" comes to indicate a kind of negativity or absence. The anthology can include the Baroness, Elsa von Freytag-Loringhoven, but not Kurt Schwitters. Both derive their soundworks from the clashing sonorities of German and English and fit, historically, in their poetics, very well together. Duke's complaint would apply quite well here. Boundaries, linguistic and national, are of course convenient ways of navigating and managing scale, as in Charles Amirkhanian's 1975 Vinyl LP, *10+2: 12 American Text Sound Pieces*, but the internationalism of Duke's concern for the field of sound poetry, a world that one would think bypasses all the difficulties of translation and its contexts but clearly has not, is utterly compelling here. While we might expect an exuberance for the avant-garde in an Antipodal lone-ranger, for it to be this much marked with suspicion, inmixed with a sense that any international modernist avant-garde would always be derivative in the Australian context, and manifest thereafter through sarcastic criticism, counterpulls any prior need for us to stress "prevalence" alone.

That argument is not over, but for now let us establish an evidentiary register of examples, so we can launch a full-scale investigation into the historic disassembling of the European avant-garde in the mechanics of Duke's worked language. The first of those poems is "BLACK SQUARES", which begins with a cut-up of Malevich's theoretical writings, and ends with a note as follows:

> This is a performance piece made up of selections from the theoretical writings of the Russian painter Kasimir Malevich (1878–1935) founder of the SUPREMATIST MOVEMENT and painter of BLACK SQUARE, BLACK CROSS, WHITE ON WHITE and similar works. It should be chanted in a religious manner, a reverent prayer to the Gods of Art, both ingratiating and self-confident, the pharisee in partnership with the true believer. The word "feeling" should be dragged out as "feeeeeeeling." "I have transformed myself ... etc" should be said with as much passion as you can muster. This work shows just what you can do with your old art manifestos. (*Poems of War and Peace*, 116)

Less parodic and more roughly scathing, the technique (citation) is only half the frame. How the piece is to be performed, and the effect it is meant to induce, relies heavily on the self-confidence of the performer. This doesn't have to mean an Australian cultural confidence, but the cryptic suggestion is that an overt, manufactured artifice is what might catch a more earnest audience off-guard. Feeling is mediated, meditated-upon, in fact, with full knowledge of the messianic aspect of doing Malevich this late in the twentieth century. Some of the grammar and punctuation in the sentences are undone, but Duke has also left many of the quotations verbatim from Malevich. What is intriguing here is how Suprematism – a pre-minimalist, avant-garde tendency in which geometric grammars, often simply rendered, became phenomena for the "primacy of pure feeling" – transferred to the body of the poem, results not in the presentation of new geometries, but a potential future event. Suprematism's emphasis on feeling as predicated on or emergent from the vectors of geometric grammar, which for Malevich was most decisively a painterly grammar in its rendering, makes the theoretical semiotics of this cut-up less a transferral of one form to another as a commentary on form and production. The potential of inventive labour isn't a principle, it's "just what you can do with your old art manifestos".

Just what you could do with such concepts and materials provided the basis for other poems which in a similar vein encrypt commentary on the early twentieth-century avant-garde, as well as modernist literary history, by incorporating both citational elements and disruptive formal geometries in the body of the poem. And if Malley used citational poetics at a moment in global modernism that was becoming prepared to embrace it, not only in the mechanistic sense as "technique" but as a practice embedded in the act of making poetry historical, Duke swifly closes the question of whether an Antipodal poetics could include the operation of citation in the examples that follow. A most overt instance of this is "A HISTORY OF EXPRESSIONIST POETRY (1910–1920)", a poem divided into two columns, or "axes":

The new integer	came to shift
he above all	and
brotherhood the great	in
would be very	work
sort of frivolous	was
yet time and	generalities
brilliance of his	in
struck the right	others
all yesterday morning	to studying
for a moment	concepts

became his partner	rooted
specialised in the	resurrection
forgotten dramatist and	appealing
[. . .]	
well it's impossible	started
some undefined barrier	fraternisation
and the minor poets	join
theoretician of literary	our
paid them little	a star
anthologies for which	paradise
first of these	the new integer above all
inclusion of some	the would be very brotherhood the great
the poet who	a sort of frivolous time yet brilliance
whose dreamy and	of his struck the right
and his generation	all yesterday
place in the	so important

(*Poems of War and Peace*, 114)

The geometry of the poem, divided as it is along a single axis down the middle of the page, brings the "new integer" into some conceptual specificity – prepare to read down a track or channel, that is – before casting us back into a poetics that elicits disjunction. The source text rent in twain begets an axis both aiding and disrupting the eye and ear of reading. We can see how the fragments come together visually, and yet don't add up. It's disjunctive all round. The "forgotten" or excluded poets provide us with an incomplete history, so if such a history *is* incomplete, and if this poem is to serve as a history, most of it is lost in the break of the line. But the content itself is revealed by a small note appended to the bottom of the page telling us it was written "after reading the book 'EXPRESSIONISM' by John Willett" (*Poems of War and Peace*, 116). Duke used various sections of the 1972 book without trying to build a narrative logic (which he would attempt in other cut-ups). In a prefatory note to *Poems of War and Peace*, Duke writes that upon his return to Australia he "discovered the Expressionist Movement, and decided I'd been an Australian and an Expressionist all the time" (iv).[3]

---

[3] Duke also did translations of "inventive writers" from international backgrounds around the Expressionist tradition, including Yvan Goll, Alfred Lichtenstein, Hans (or Jean) Arp, August Stramm, Helmut Heissenbüttel and Kurt Schwitters (*Poems of War and Peace*, 163–81).

VI. Shuffling History

To write a *history* of expressionist poetry in this manner leads us to a certain kind of poetic category Duke was fond of calling "Daily Life" poems, historical-cum-citational "narrative" poems which are speechy and talkish, but also factual in the manner of reportage. Several of Duke's poems tend to become bodies of record; they read as lineated historical accounts that revisit or rethink certain events. Perhaps the most subtle of these poems is "ALEKHINE AND JUNGE AT PRAGUE", a poem in which a famous 1942 Nazi-sponsored game of chess between Alexander Alekhine and Klaus Junge is incorporated into the poem. The poem begins "In the year 1942 / there was a chess tournament in Prague" (117) and ends with the list of moves:

```
22 Q-R7+, K-B3 (would K-Q3 draw?)
23 B-Q2, KR-QB1
24 P-K4, Q-N6
25 R-R1, P-N5
26 R-R6+, K-N4
27 R-R5+ K-B3
28 Q-B5+, K-Q2
29 R-R7+, RESIGNS
      (Poems of War and Peace, 121)
```

Duke's interest in chess as a tactical and procedural game shines through in this poem. In meandering, Reznikoff-like prosaic lineations, the historical report that comes before this final "proof" contextualises the game in wartime geopolitical contexts; the German fronts, Stalingrad, the wartime lives of both players. The intrigue continues until the last line, which asks us to decide the match: "the Czech spectators thought the right man won / do you think that they were right?" (*Poems of War and Peace*, 120). Uncertain light is thrown on the historical event. The story is well told and its indeterminacy hardly rests on the frame of chance procedure – what transpires is a collagistic and citational game exposing ambiguities of interpretation, putting it on the reader to make a fuller historical assessment.

Interpretive indeterminacies continue. In "The Nottingham Incident", a short sequence using language from *A Regional History of the Railways of Great Britain. Volume 9, The East Midlands*, Duke uses a technique of reordering and then shuffling the words in order of length. The "intact" version reads:

THE NOTTINGHAM INCIDENT *ONE*

In August 1852
the Great Northern Railway
ran its first train into Nottingham
over the tracks of the Ambergate from Grantham
the Midland Railway
did not want the Great Northern in Nottingham
as soon as the Great Northern engine had uncoupled
and ran onto the turntable
it was surrounded by Midland engines
which overpowered it
and pushed it into a disused shed
Midland men locked the doors
and tore up the tracks outside
the Great Northern
did not recover their engine
for seven months
      (*Poems of War and Peace*, 17)

The opening poem reads as many of Duke's poems do, with an odd tonality of lineated historical prose, the straightforward recounting of an event. It's not so odd if we imagine it in performance, but it appears on the page without notational obligation. It then becomes clear that something is about to happen to the text: several permutations are made on the original poem. The third iteration reads like so:

THE NOTTINGHAM INCIDENT *THREE*

a in of
in as as it
by it it up the ran
its the the the did not the the
had and ran
the was and men the and the the
did not for 1852 into over from want soon
onto into shed tore Great
first train Great Great which doors
Great their seven
August tracks engine pushed locked tracks engine
months Railway Midland Railway Midland
engines disused Midland outside recover Northern
Grantham Northern Northern
Northern Ambergate uncoupled turntable Nottingham
Nottingham surrounded overpowered
      (*Poems of War and Peace*, 18)

The resulting disjunction takes us away from the pure recounting of an *event* in narrative and brings us into the field of language as manipulable material, the "Nottingham incident" becoming an incident in the creeping disorder but also reorganisation taking place in language: pronouns and prepositions cling to the top, while the poem's nouns and larger adjectives collect at the bottom. "Important" and "unimportant" words are given equal airing in the poem's parts. In what will now seem to be a characteristic citational gesture, another historical, and for that matter archivalist poem, "THE WONDERS OF SCIENCE", incorporates first-person commentary among its quoted parts, moving from English to American infrastructure:

> Quick! said the boss
> find me "Heat Shocked *Bacillus subtilus* As An Indicator of Virus
>   Disinfection"
> by G. H. Toenniessen and J. D. Johnston
> Journal of the American Water Works Association
> September 1970
> I dived into the archives
> I found it
> It had already been scribbled on by another critic
> superimportant words had been underlined
> like *suggested, increasing the residual free chlorine, low turbidity, monitoring, codiform index, would result in unmeasurably low coliform numbers, viruses, surveillance is at present impracticable, chlorine analysis alone is not satisfactory, 3mg/L free chlorine, ultraviolet, difference, importance of obtaining more knowledge on the chlorine resistance of viruses, S.N.O.R.T.*
> he'd missed out on *followed sporulation and exosporium lysis*
>   (*Poems of War and Peace*, 87)

Mixing both citational elements and narrative commentary on those elements, Duke plays the part of a researcher, or "critic" whose scientific labour has public worth: "finding out how the patient died" (*Poems of War and Peace*, 87). Filtered through the marginalia of another critic who has underlined aspects of the source-text that Duke's persona has been charged to find, Duke is working with multiple layers of artifice. Historical-critical inquiry finds analogy in the *forensics* of the material text (an allegorics deployed in "THE NOTTINGHAM INCIDENT" similarly, where an originary event has been transformed or revisited by subsequent inquiry). Curiosity here falls on the once- or twice-remove of inquiry in general, and linguistic inquiry in particular.

Figure 4.4 Jas H. Duke, cover for *Archduke 4* (1974).

The way Duke tells a historical narrative (and the way he breaks it up) brings forth techniques of lexical shuffle and typographic respacing; writing as *word processing*. This is supplemented with a strong graphological interest in drawing by hand, Texta®, pen and pencil. Like bissett and bpNichol, Duke worked with cartoon strips and illustrated pages. In a 1974 handmade chapbook *Archduke 4*, part of a series of "Archddukes" in which he attests to a love of William Blake as much as André Breton, Duke reveals an extensive graphic and visual practice, using highlighter pens, cross-hatched text, cut grass, even photonegatives (Figure 4.5). In 1986 he illustrated a book produced by the Industrial Woman Collective, with each page featuring a photograph, often modified, and phrases from the book's reportage on the global status of women's work lettered in red (Figure 4.6).

VII. *Happy Birthday Australia*

In fictive graphics Duke's imagines a kind of global referential space containing Australia or Atlantis. On a larger scale than the revue

Figure 4.5 Jas H. Duke, page from *Industrial Woman* (1986).

Dada of Humphries, Duke's attitude in a good many of the poems presented thus far is quite clearly *post*; to test the history of avant-garde practices, to make sense of them, or to send them up (sarcastically, wryly), or indeed to make further "advances" from root forms. In a very immediate sense, all these tones and approaches must have something to do with the remove Duke felt not only as an avant-gardist outside Europe but as *neo*, as a second-wave avant-gardist writing in a literary context both hostile to and ecstatic about his Dadaist interventions. These neo-avant-garde poems in a sense have a clear place and a clear-enough intent. They are poems that complicate the historical event, poems that function as historical inquiry. Though they do so complexly, we know from what tradition they come and to what histories they speak. Following this, inquiry comes to take on further significance in another kind of poem Duke tended to write. Here I want to more closely examine poems of Duke's that take on the question of nation and Australianness, vectors that cross globe and hemisphere. In these poems – and there are many, concerning Australian working conditions, national involvement in international affairs, systems of governance – the subject moves away from the European avant-garde tradition. Take, for instance, a poem like "Scratchticket":

```
SCCCCCCRRRRRatchticket
ScccccccRRRRRatchticket
SccccccrrrrrAAAAAtchticket
SccccrrrrraaaaaTCHticket
SccccrrrrraaaaatchTiiiiiiCKET
SCRATCHTICKET
SCRATCHTICKET
SCRAAAAATCHTICKET
SCRATCHTICKETSCRATCHTICKETSCRATCHTICKETSCRAT
   CHTICKET
SCRATCHTICKET
SC — RATCH — TICK — ET
SCR — ATCH — TICK — ET
SCR — ATCH — TICKET
Scr — atch — TICKET
Scratch — ticket
Scratchticket
SCRATCHTICKET
Sc ——— RATCH ——— TICKET
Sc ———ATCH ——— TICKET
SCR ————— ATCH ————————— TICKET
SCR ————— ATCH ————————— TICK ——— ET
```

[Dedicated to our Minister of Arts, Mr. "Jim"* Kennan, who gave us scratchtickets for trains, trams, and buses, but has now left such things behind him and is now directing our "arts led" recovery: Jas]

(*poems of life & death*, 221)

Led by sound, the poem works at the extremes of both visuality and audition. But there is more to it: *notational* sensibility depends upon more than syntactic disruption. Just as intriguing as the "poem proper" is the note at the bottom of the page to Jim (James Harley) Kennan, which indicates a certain sarcasm about public policy and the careers of those responsible for it. A sound poem is thus more than just sound; it is rather more political-conceptual. Interest in domestic policy as a source for poetic concepts is supplemented by an interest in the poetic constitution of nationhood. "Whitman Sings Again" is a poem that brings, most strikingly, questions of modernity, modernism, US cultural power (and the spectre of derivation) into the force field of an Australian postmodernity:

> A song of myself
> yet another song of myself
> lurching in the tramtracks of Walt Whitman
> the great self-contradictor
> and friend of the exclamation mark
> with a transistorised, twice-tested, videophonic, biodegradable,
>   barbaric yawp
> a song of myself
>
> I'm not one of the roughs
> I'm not one of the smooths either
> I don't love everything
> even if I had a Brooklyn Ferry and an endlessly rocking cradle I
>   wouldn't love them
> I'm in Australia
> Australia I don't love you
> Australia you don't love me (*Poems of War and Peace*, 25)

Ania Walwicz's 1981 poem "Australia", which begins "You big ugly", or indeed Ouyang Yu's "Fuck you, Australia" from 1995, make for an interesting comparison to "Whitman Sings Again". Walwicz and Ouyang take aim at Standard English and, through the lens of migrant experiences or observations of racism, grapple poetically with the contradictions and blunt realities of the bourgeois state and its settler heritage of class and cultural violence. We hear a similar dynamic in "GOING HOME LATE AT NIGHT", one of Duke's several anti-racism or anti-bigotry poems, where he writes "'Look at that *cunt* over there! / he looks like a *fucking Egyptian!!!*' / and I felt angry for a moment / but when I thought about it / I'd rather be called a *cunt* / or a *fucking Egyptian* / than an *Australian*" (*Poems of War and Peace*, 92). *Australian* here draws out a long, sarcastic stress on the second syllable. Such themes are there too in poems like "INVASION" (*poems of life & death*, 194–6) and "HAPPY BIRTHDAY AUSTRALIA", where the idea of nation is taken up using more explicit and sarcastic terms. In the latter, he mocks the upcoming 1988 Bicentenary celebration, and calls attention to the genocidal character of modern Australia's colonial society:

> This seems a time of significant moments
> important anniversaries are approaching
> 150 of Victoria
> 200 years of Australia

we're told it's our birthday
and we must celebrate
well I suggest you celebrate
in a genuine early Australian manner
        [. . .]
take no notice
of the people who live on the land
If they object too much
kill them
that's the genuine early Australian way to celebrate
have a happy birthday (*Poems of War and Peace*, 29)

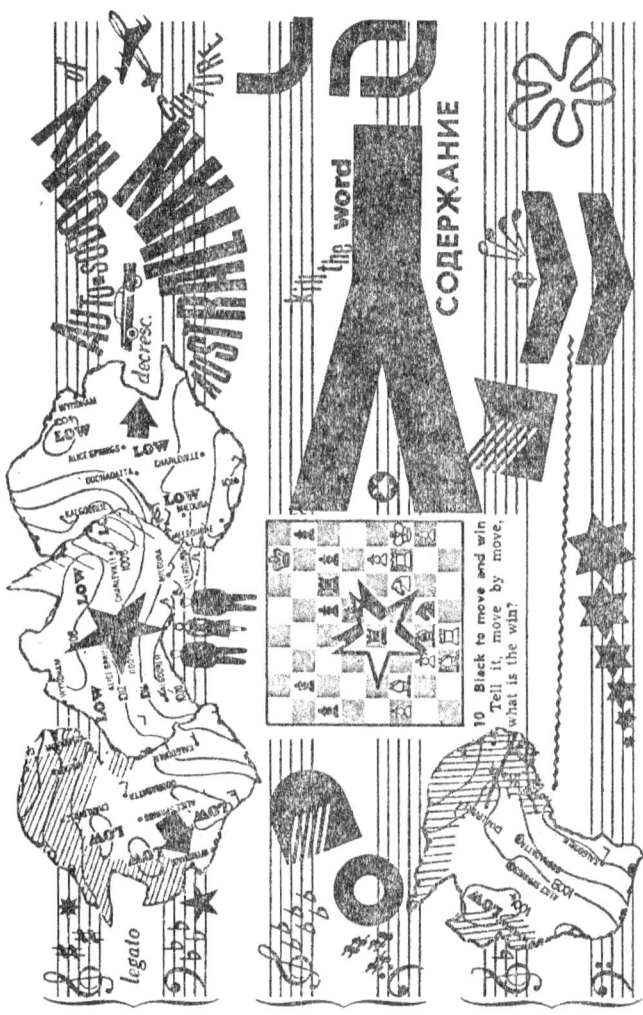

Figure 4.6 Jas H. Duke, visual poem in *Poems of War and Peace* (1989).

Compare this poem immediately with another collage piece that uses a musical score as a notational basis for visual elements – icons, letters, phrases – strewn across it (Figure 4.6).

Strehlow's scoring of Central Australian songs at the beginning of this book makes for curious comparison. Where Strehlow was not able to map the scores onto Australia, here Australia is mapped onto the score. But we ought not avoid the more obvious game-like element in play. The chessboard is a common avant-garde visual and procedural aid to writing across the tradition, harking back to John Cage's matches against the Duchamps in 1968. Duke's score has other figures. In place of neumes to mark pitch, two visual elements make a claim for an "Australiographic", and more procedural score: Australian maps show weather isobars, and a chessboard is frozen in time before a winning move. The way the maps of the Australian land mass are scored here shows a notational poetics critically aware of global, and temporal positioning; follow a procedure, follow a score for the purposes of cultural critique. Duke's heavy protest voice might be evident here, even in silent viewing. A 2000 musical work called *Black Years Red Years* by Colin Bright, an Australian composer whose interests and compositional methods include montage, sound collage and sequencing, samples Duke's voice alongside the sounds of protesters in a kind of historical layering of sonic materials very much characteristic of post-Dismissal poetics. Featured in Bright's inventory of insubordinate sonic objects, heavy on synth, is Duke performing his Dada sound poem, a poem which he would often perform repeating the word "Da-da" in multiple and varying rhythmic units. Bright would also write a sequence of songs using Duke's poetry as lyrics, *War & Peace: A Selection of Songs on Poems by Jas H. Duke.*

The idea of lyricising Duke in song is curious, given his lyrical capability was apparent even though it was so often poised, prosodically and phrasally, before dissonance. Dissonance in Antipodal avant-garde lyric or prose is a difficult analogy to bring forth. The superposed maps that run along Duke's score seem like so many dissonances sounding the contradictions of culture, contradictions that come up to a crescendo in the poem "An Answer To Those Who Say You Can't Write Poetry In A Cultural Backwater Like Australia" interrogating the idea of a "national poet" through Henrik Ibsen, who

> ... became an assistant in a chemist's shop
> in a small town
> a place of no importance
> but for all that

> his ideas went round the world
> with the speed of thought
> and made people think about things
> that they might not have thought about otherwise
> (*poems of life & death*, 191)

Duke then goes on to recount an appearance of Ibsen at a cafe in what was then Kristiania (now Oslo), given by an English tourist Richard Le Gallieniene:

> One person said to Le Gallieniene
> "Do you know who that was?
> That was IBSEN!
> OUR GREAT NATIONAL POET!"
>
> Could this happen here?
> (*poems of life & death*, 192)

Conflating international literary celebrity and readership with local and national renown, Duke is left wondering, in a strikingly positivistic light, whether similar cultural elevation might happen in Australia to a poet of local renown. The smaller font for "Could this happen here?" as rendered above is a kind of timid aside in that the typeface suggests both cringe, and defiance (an answer, a rejoinder), a tension apparent in the event-based instruction scores for these two sound poems:

> MANNING CLARK
> A famous historian. Try to sound like some long-legged wading bird. *CLARK* and *SQUAWK* aren't very different really.
>
> NED NASAL
> Australians are often sneered at for talking thru their noses. Make this into a virtue. Keep your mouth shut and let all the sound come out your nose. Volume will be low so you will probably need amplification. Don't open your mouth. (*Poems of War and Peace*, 129–30)

National poetry it is, and how very different these are from the Fluxus instruction-score, particularly the type pioneered in the 1960s by Yoko Ono – whom Duke met – in *Grapefruit*, even if they seem to reprise the form; hear a generalised performative address (anybody can perform it, but would you?). The experience of listening to Duke perform could ilicit an array of affective responses, some hard to explain. Hazel Smith and Roger Dean have read Duke's performance of the sound poem "Stalin", in which the performer repeats the word

Stalin until they fall down exhausted, in technical terms; as one of variation, vocal control and contortion, relinquishing of control of the body itself: "Sounding like a train gathering speed, he propelled himself behind his own voice to the point where he could no longer control how fast, or in what direction, he was going" (139). The result of these "idiosyncratic" aspects is a sense of the "half-joking, half-serious", (138) audible in the two above soundworks as well. To harness "everyday" Australian speechmaking habits to "avant-garde effect", bringing national-linguistic peculiarity and locality to the sphere of vanguardist sound-making – itself bringing with it a set of a mandated performance styles – is to *site* the very possibilities of an experimental aesthetic in what an outsider would notice, with a sneer, *as* Australian linguistic oddity. A listener has to know certain characters in Australian history, from Ned Kelly the bushranger to Manning Clark the historian, and Duke's working-class drawl would here cover several Australian tonalities. But to get there you have to step back, audially, from the accustomed sounds. The workings in generalised and open-form sound production are something of a listening-in to Australian sound from an outside, from other hemispheres and global locales. Duke's reflexive neo-avant-garde experiments and his poems about Australia form a continuum; the result is a more confident poetics, less a locally effacing one, defiant-imperative against imperial commonplace; yes, work through the difficulty of experimental poetry in a "cultural backwater" like Australia, but only in order to place (literal) accents on the "cringeworthy" tonalities of Australian English! If one is to redeem them in performance, one's audience must first know that they are sounds heard from outside.

VIII. *Old and New Contradictions, or, The Avant-Garde Blindspot Revisited*

The above poems clearly show that Duke's "vernacular", rather than imagining a fixed vernacularity (a Vernacular Republic in Murray's failed sense), is rather a treatment of critical-historical artifice. It pays close attention to contradictory social markers – class culture, race, ethnicity, gender, nation – and because of this, no one vocality comes through. No singular "voice" is apparent because Duke brings us back to the social construction of voice. It may be that such radical resistance to the singularity of "voice" is one of the forgotten elements left behind, or left out of a working critical vocabulary of Australian poetics. In the larger schema of understanding Australian experimental poetics these contradictions have consequence for certain critical stopgaps that have not yet been surmounted.

Recall Philip Mead in the opening passages of his book *Networked Language*, where, so he claims, a certain critical "lag" makes it hard to move into more difficult and "formally innovative" works (2–3). The implications for this are vast for a poet like Duke, and my wager is that the closer study of experimental poetics, especially those "difficult limit-cases", studied on their own terms and with attention to "linguistic range" and the transnational contexts of global avant-gardes, can reveal the "ways forward" Mead seeks, ways forward out of the paradoxes of meaning and lyric sociality.

In some ways a bold extension of Mead's principal claims, Farrell's aforementioned *Writing Australian Unsettlement*, which includes that rereading of Brennan, takes the term "unsettlement" into the field of poetics, tracing a longer material and textual history of modes of "poetic invention", invention being a term I have found useful for these case studies. Farrell's case studies are not all ones considered of "general importance". Some are virtually unknown, like Jong Ah Sing's unorthodox diary/hybrid-genre work The Case (1867?–72), with its unusual battery of marks: typography, punctuation, use of majuscule lettering. Other texts, like Ned Kelly's 1879 *Jerilderie Letter*, are well-known, but have not been looked at from this perspective, meaning a *poetics* perspective. Indeed the key word (and practice) for Farrell is just that, poetics: "Many of the texts in this book have been written about by contemporary scholars, but for the most part not by those whose main interest is poetics, nor in what Australia's heritage of poetics might be" (2). For an analysis of Duke that either chimes with the Australian critical field or attempts to expand it, these questions amplify the odd disjunction between poetry as result and poetics as process, as well as between practice and criticism, play and interpretation. Duke brings critical disjunction to an already unsettled field of Australian poetry most curiously. Farrell too, as both an experimental poet and a poetics critic, or to make it easier, a "poet-critic" or "poet/critic", in some ways solves some contradictions that have been well documented. Take for instance Martin Harrison in *Who Wants to Create Australia?* (2007). Harrison is willing to assert that there is "no idyllic, permanently unchanging relationship between poet and critic" (22), and goes on to say that

> The paradox, the sheer oddity, of the relation between poetry and criticism in our time is intense. The contemporary critic's work

> looks confident, so well referenced, so sophisticated in relation to the major philosophical questions of its time; the poet's looks home made, handcrafted, often small and mute. Yet so many of the critical or philosophical themes sketched in a resumé of poststructuralism's key themes are part of a poetics. As such these ideas respond not just to an abstract idea of writing . . . they are to do with writing, with composing language in written form, with markmaking. (23)

Therein lay the chief paradox, I think, of Australian poetics criticism at least before Farrell, a paradox that goes right back to the difficulties we became privy to in Hooton and Malley. But even at the recent period from which Harrison writes, I cannot help thinking, with some preliminary exploration of Duke already behind us, that it might just be the wrong *kind* of poetry that gets submitted to critical examination. Mead and Farrell solve this problem by finding better poems. How much can be said, in terms of poetics and in terms of criticism, about the small, handcrafted line, when the whole gamut of poststructuralist theory, or philosophy, beckons for something else, something in form, trace, performance, that makes the most of "mark-making"? I'm not making a claim for the "worth" of Duke, who was not a practising critic, simply to say that, as Harrison's point presses, such work is better situated for the contemporary critic's theoretical armature. And if I have often backed up onto these questions of how things fit with the wider critical structures available, it is because literary history forces its hand with regard to how things have to be read, rather than how they could be read. Criticism is better off, more generously kitted out, with these poetries. The global study of material poetics and poetics-inflected criticism, even in university creative writing contexts, would take to these works too in ways that hark back to the theatre of modernism and chronometrically resist it through transnational avant-gardes. The reasons are various: citation and collage, the focus on mark-making, all that segmenting of words, lexical drift, splintering and scattering of icon, mark, trace, symbol and syllable, connections between writing as trace, or mark, and political questions, between markmaking, national culture, and of course history. What could get in the way of this?

To be up front: many readers will have known little about Duke before these readings. Thus to call for the benefits of "writerly" analysis of writing, any overawing effort to force the work to sound theoretically relevant, might be less useful in literary-historical terms than simply asking questions of distribution. Where are these works?

Are global poetics researchers accessing them? In Australian poetry criticism Duke does not yet feature in any significant way. To keep an open mind: is the poetry itself at fault? Perhaps it just doesn't live up to "sophisticated" critical acumen? Have we landed back (again) in the all-too-familiar territory of problems with canon and canonicity? You know I haven't been tempted again by the recuperative frame, and that I can be trusted to avoid such temptations. So much more relevant are the repercussions felt in the literary by our monitoring of the historical. Paul Kane's 1996 volume *Australian Poetry: Romanticism and Negativity* identified the strains of negativity and a supposed "absence" of romanticism that determined to a large degree the historical shape of Anglophone Australian poetry. That Kane lists his concerns within a "narrower frame" that is a limited, traditional and "indeed canonical grouping" of poets (Harpur, Kendall, Brennan, Slessor, Hope, Malley, Wright, Harwood, Murray) shows the extent to which it is a canonical history. Thus some Leavisist echo can be heard in Kane's thesis: the "implicit—now explicit—argument is that these few poets are among the strongest and most interesting of Australian poets, and that something of general importance can be learned from a study of them" (2). The argument is that grouping these poets together was altogether straightforward: they are the "strongest" and "most interesting". They can be said to have "general importance" to the canonical genealogy, a genealogy Kane insists through his various readings of these poets *is* the embodiment of Australian poetry. Moreover, their presence is telltale of a certain absence, that absence being romanticism.

I have made no such canonising claims. But I think the study of Australian experimental poetics after the 1970s delivers a strong alternative to this narrative. Alternative, not counter-canon. My alternative blindspot, one that determines many of these debates around an aesthetics of Australian poetry, is *the absence of an avant-garde*, but never with recourse to canons. If it's really the case that this is so, let it become an enlivening presence for the modern constellation of arguments about locale and scale. Another if: if poets like Duke, to borrow from Kane's model of negativity, are "strong" and "interesting", even the "most interesting", then social, historical and critical verdicts come in second place. Close second, for let's not totally relinquish centripetal notions of canonmaking. In these more personal and yet apparently more general configurations I would prefer not to withhold all judgement, but rather to challenge the aesthetic, textual and poetics-based assumptions of what might be called "interesting" in what we understand to be a convention, a corpus or a canon. For this we need a critical vocabulary that to the adjudicator's report can add more than just the appreciation of lines and stanzas but also the modern notion of "technique": citational form, "shuffle", visualism, prosodic reinvention and the manipulative use, and integral power, of sound.

In the ensuing chapters we will cover some of those technical matters in readings. By no means should we discard or bypass the question of Romanticism in these analyses. Literary theory, whether postructuralist or not, conflated with contemporary theory of the Continental variety, may not be any kind of easy respite from the Romantic resplendence threatening to put a levy on these peripheralist transvaluations of literary history. In a compelling argument in this key, Justin Clemens in his book *The Romanticism of Contemporary Theory* claims contemporary theory to be, on the whole, still subject to Romanticism, and "Theoretical Romanticism" as it were, would owe something to its "environment", not in a way that demands any more from theoretical as of historical inquiry. Clemens does both, arriving at three categories, institutions, aesthetics and nihilism, that are theoretical and historical. So too, I think, the question of absent Romanticism in Kane's canonical grouping of Strong Greats has come under pressure from the institution in the formal sense: modernist studies and aesthetics, if not poetics. Now we have the benefit of seeing the whole thing from a twenty-first-century vantage point, from colonial literature to modern Australian verse, whatever tools we use to uncover blindspots will contend with the facts of institutions and aesthetics. Brennan, of course, could be further submitted to this dynamic. It may too lie dormant in convention itself, with regard to apparently unbreakable institutional edifices; Romantic negativity, like avant-garde negativity, regardless of their respective affirmations or nihilisms, may suffer from the same kind of theoretical delimitations.

I mean to say too that Kane's highly "representative" sensibility can persist, but under pressure from history and poetics: being "central" does not amount to "good" or "interesting", but the danger is when what is "of interest" to theories of poetics shifts, slips. It isn't just history that puts theory in such danger. Thus readjusted, thus "remapped", the critical lens naturally turns to reassessment and postnational revision. To claim serious credibility for these alternatives, despite the problems that won't go away any time soon like the issue of the *neo*, and of derivation, there is no doubt that Australian poetry in the late twentieth century has been under pressure from "something else", the poetics of an avant-garde. This is the work of neither saboteur nor liberator. To be historically precise, less negative and less abjectly affirmative, such a poetics is resoundingly aware of its displacement in time and space from the modernist avant-garde. After Duke's death in 1992 from a heart attack caused by a shattered bone from a fall on a concrete step, and just as Jeltje evokes in the opening of this chapter, his influence rippled through a generation that included Amanda Stewart, who knew and performed with Duke, and is our culminating case study. Some might wish to call this continuation contemporary experimental poetics, or contemporary experimentalism after the 1980s and into the new century. Avant-garde I find to be more historically precise for Duke, whereas the robust dialectic of modern and contemporary, as much as Modern-Romantic, might apply more readily to the upcoming examples. Duke only lived to see the beginnings of the Information Age and what New Media had on offer. And yet still, as contemporary experimental poetry evolves between the centuries, we see remnants of these practices in play in a mélange of verbico-visual and conceptual reinventions of language, from Walwicz to Fogarty, Stewart, and even the recent digital poetry of Mez Breeze.

Twenty years on, Kane's story is not the only story to be told. Kane's category of "general importance" is placed under pressure by strong alternative histories, chronicles and genealogies of an Australian avant-garde. "General importance" will come into conflict with historical judgment in a different key: the retrodiction of history and what I have articulated as the chronometric function. The avant-garde blind spot reveals not only its face, but the multifaceted contradictions arising from its appearance. The dates on offer sometimes speak for themselves. I want to strike a balance between contextualism and chronometricity, for the way I approach modernity and contemporaneity, modernism and the early twentieth-century European and Eastern European avant-gardes, is in the first instance spurred on by what critics have identified as critical impasses in Australian literary history. If this goes some way towards the retroactive resignifying of neglected works outside the constellation of general importance, via literary revisionism, so be it. But the critical moves we name languages of invention, reconsidered under such models, do the act of theoretical revision *with* historical texts. One needs only to look beneath or over the texts to see how consciousness of history spurred poets on. Spurring us all on to assign cultural and literary-critical importance to inventive use of language will involve a fuller "texturing" of the transnational currents in play, but also a fair acknowledgement of the locality of means: after all it was *community*, other poets, many of whom are here mentioned, and Collective Effort Press, that gave Duke a particular and peculiar context. Texturing on multiple scales, then, places our scheme of general importance between context and chronometrics; crossed lines of text, clashing bodies of work, citational, notational and narrative techniques, inspiration through the excitability of one's locale, or getting miffed (sometimes) by globality.

To really take up Mead's challenge to "cut the lag" and match a critical discourse with the difficult, dissonant or dysprosodic Australian poem has required some critical "balance", between affirmation and negation, between linguistic, processual and formal analyses of poetic invention, and the historical breadth of social and cultural inquiry. We will keep this balance. There are examples in which an emancipation of disjunction on the page, and an emancipation in performance, equals the levels of ingenuity we have seen here. For now it suffices to say that "Dadaustralia" *was* 1973, a *singular moment* in a career that could also become a community but not a church or an era. Dadaustralia was in a phrase pitched against Dada history. What was it opposing? How closed, how open was it, is it? We know at least that it was transnational, outward-facing rather than national. It sought to remap hemispheric bearings of the avant-garde in ways that unsettled European and Euro-American agendas of influence and transmission. It is difficult to say then whether the so-called historic avant-garde *are* these works, or whether in the deepest of senses it can be said to "include" them. Indeed these instances in the history of the international avant-gardes have been too flippantly dismissed or counted as derivative. Such an approach does, if it continues, fatally *dehistoricise* the types of poetics we have encountered, as if to suggest that only works within the short flash of that original milieu, however complex that "original" is as we now know, are to be named "historical". At worst, this leads to contemporary discourses of invention that attribute all Antipodal invention solely to US American influence, like Language Writing, the New York School, or Conceptual Writing. These influences are there and need to be looked at with clarity. But it has become too simplistic in the current critical environment to claim that an avant-garde is either parasitic, that is, in "opposition" to the received and to the conventions-that-be, or original, utterly exceptional. We began with Frye's challenge to locate the force fields of literary experience, peripheries and centre, and Rothenberg's sense of Dada's common shore. These are but glimpses, when you turn after them, shapes for an Australian avant-garde that have not been made out of a retreating mirage but have announced themselves sometimes with grit, gravitas, a page and a megaphone. There are deeper elements. In repletion, another more meditative and more exploratory look would tarry longer on the shamanic quality of Duke's voice, its revolutionary violence, its prosodics, its masculine heave, the mythography of his life and performances as recounted by his contemporaries, and again dimensions of the poetics, especially its aural, optic and conceptual rudiments. Rereading Duke will reveal that this kind of poetics late century may have been not just a blind spot at the core of the Australian poetry but a core part of a generational shift. Under better light we will be able to read these works as part of a larger transnational, transatlantic or transpacific avant-garde poetics. Duke's representative works show a sustained poetic thinking, a proletarianist, anti-nationalist yet liberatory poetic politics, a strenuous poetic language of inquiry, sceptical (always) as to how meaning is made and poeticity decided upon; all things that will merit further work and comparison. Read alongside anarchist writers of the period, like Π.O., the way his process and his politics developed would come into sharper relief. Read again in the aftermath of those early Dada experiments of Humphries, we see how avant-garde performance could capture the contradictions of an Antipodal intellectual culture writ large in the global assembly of nations. Dadaustralia, as it were, was both pitched against history and could get lost in it (never then to return). Dadaustralia was, or became, the embodiment of Dada internationalism.

The Dada chronicle, Duke's lasting impression, in its harking back to history, grants us some leeway with time. We reach back in time and in that very motion reach forward in leaps and bounds to the future. The real question will be whether, in adjusting the critical lens, becoming critically attentive to these languages of invention, such contextual moves shift the literary experience from centre to periphery. And if they do, the vocabulary we use to describe these cultural productions will either be of larger consequence to literary theory, or simply to the renewal of a national literature that had not quite done it yet.

Chapter 5

Expansive Geometries: Ania Walwicz's Polish

> The Poet spools a south feather to string –
> Dictions a big land in landless wandering cobalt.
> Airs Ounce
> along her tongue.   Blood rush of spit shot
> away.   Syllable by Syllable, the pupil of each
> Eye
> weeps –
>
> The Throb of it, (gabble & whistle) spurged scavenged
> inking
>   – Maggie O'Sullivan, *Palace of Reptiles*, 49

Ania Walwicz demands, demanded of our reading a strong feeling for an absolute present. Yet the before and after of her writing matters equally to us now. Walwicz does a Steinish thing few writers do; what we are reading is read in a slither of difference, writing voiced, *envoiced* in the record of voice transmitted to page. Walwicz's voice is expansive on the page; it becomes long-form, longhand writing, a spooling of language in more expansive geometries and timescapes. It's a form of feminist avant-garde writing that does this particular difference.

"Voice" is nothing else but. It isn't so much duplicitous as encompassing, subsumptive by and through its discourse. It can be neither reduced to the notion of a "vocal object" nor explained away by voice-print. For both we know precisely of what we speak: voice. Few deny that the poet's voice is of a special kind. In the twentieth century, especially after Tennyson, it became harder to find a poet who had not left us a recording, or all the more disappointing if they had not. Listening to Stein is often the experience of listening to writing. There is no guarantee the reading will seem the same as the writing; the difference between writing and scoring-for-performance so often narrows that to obscure the two is no big issue. We are fairly accustomed now to calling a poem a "score" for performance, and yet oftentimes what what we retroactively find to be the "score" is the real surprise. Readers may go and find recordings of Walwicz and thus acquire some sense of Walwicz's voice as they read. That will make all the difference. It may become the desiring.

It might make up all the difference because *difference*, the gap between the "score" poem and its performance, is the bit that interests us here. The problem goes a little deeper. Let us frame it using the words of Australian prose experimentalist joanne burns, who inquired, in a poem called "how",

> how these pieces of paper: lined unlined small large crinkled smooth smudged spotless, become pieces of first draft scribble of typescript, of 'writing,' become texts for performance, works in progress, submissions to magazines and journals, become copyright, enter folders in filing cabinets, become manuscripts, literature, the numbered pages of published books, isbn-d. (30)

The way writing works in history, working retroactively back from books, is the way we can observe the *time of writing* turning into a literary object (and therefore a plottable point in literary history), and it is an inquiring "how" question. It might work at any level of intensity: fast, slow, thick, thin, taut, sparse, erotic, repressed. The time, space and pace of writing is never far from the external pulls that sometimes do and sometimes don't motivate it: morphing away from the private setting into writing's productive and distributive capacity; publishing, editing, career. These again compound the crossing of time and history. And the comparison with Stein has its limits; if Walwicz's sleights of hand are Steinish they are so in grades of distance.

Born in 1951, Walwicz migrated to Australia in 1963 from Świdnica, Poland. Like the Hungarian People's Republic, and more than other core and satellite states of the USSR, the Polish People's Republic was a site of social unrest early on in its existence. Walwicz would arrive in an Australia that was coming towards the end of Menzies's long reign. She adds resonance to Stein's line in *Lifting Belly*: "I do not wish to be Polish" (27). Walwicz did and did not so wish. There are continuities here with Duke. Walwicz was known to perform her works with close attention to the whole space and occasion of performance – to appearance, sound, voice and dress. In more recent years Walwicz experimented with beards, posing for them in photographs and drawing herself as bearded, an avant-garde gesture that calls up the tradition of the Baroness and her cross-gendered escapades (see self-portrait, Figure 5.1). Avant-garde affinity, if not more brazen declamations and pronouncements, will be the order of these latter-day characters and their involvement with radical experiment. Prepare again for an avant-garde anti-establishment attitude that won't spare the early twentieth-century avant-gardes. Expect too a strong suspicion of the critic and criticism. Prepare, as is the case for poets recently deceased, for a focus on oral history and the living archive. Walwicz's passing during the earlier phase of the Covid-19 pandemic leaves Antipodal avant-garde history in the lurch, if nothing else simply because Walwicz was one of the last Antipodal poets to proclaim an avant-garde position.

I. *Walwicz in Australia*

Walwicz's relationship to existing criticism is curious: scholarly interest is significant and growing, particularly in the area of feminist literary theory and criticism. Still, the question of Walwicz as avant-garde poet is, as with all the poets examined here, a difficult one because Walwicz resists criticism, especially Australian establishment criticism of the twentieth-century university broadly construed, which did not necessarily permit a critical vocabulary for avant-garde poetics. In an unsent letter to Walwicz from Jas Duke, quoted by Π.O. as one of his "Statement of Poetics", somewhat Hootonesque in style, Duke writes that "I wouldn't worry too much what our 'distinguished critics' say, they're like a lakeful of frogs that are too busy croaking to listen to anything else" (*poems of life & death*, 303).

Yet criticism would find ways to describe Walwicz's poetics in the context of avant-gardes and experiment come the turn of the century. In a 1996 article on Ania Walwicz, Lyn McCredden points to some of the contradictions that have shaped critical responses to Walwicz's poetics, alongside Walwicz's own responses, stances and attitudes to writing practice, which were closely informed or influenced by literary theory. These contradictions are, we learn, "inherent in the enterprise of avant-garde or experimental poetry" (235), and are doubly constituted: the migrant is forced to write from the margins, and so too does the experimentalist, who chooses to write at the "borders or limit conditions of language". This, then, is the "contradictory enterprise of both the migrant and the

Figure 5.1 Ania Walwicz, "Self-Portrait" (2015 painting); courtesy of the Ania Walwicz Archive.

experimentalist ... to start again, to know both less and more than the dwellers at the centre" (235). Such contradictions McCredden then reads into poems like "Poland" (*Writing*, 37), a poem jarring less harshly than some, but one nonetheless in which McCredden finds the naming of Poland to be "in Kristevan terms, the place of the abject" (235). The beginning of the poem goes from refusal to plea: "I don't keep this. I tried to keep this" becomes, in the second half of the poem, the naming, over and over, of Poland: a "talisman", "icon", "title", the poem capturing "beautifully the double pulse of abjection: the place of loathing, of smothering engulfment, but equally the source of longing" (236), a pulse that is, moreover, pulsive; "the pulsive rhythms mimic this double impulse, working as both a chant of expulsion and a love song for Poland" (236). In or around this dialectic, McCredden claims, the linguistic decisions, or lack thereof, get to be warped effects, an inventive language of "undecidability":

> It will be up to readers to decide what to do with such an undecidability of effects. Some will embrace them, as the desired methods and outworkings of such experimentation: dream logic, syntactic freewheeling, verbal association, comic exaggeration, condensation, radical instability of meaning and identity. Others will feel uneasy about what can be seen as the gaps in logic and consistency, the willed verbal spontaneity, the ducking in and out of coherence, the perpetual blurring of limits between prose and poetry, sexual boundaries, meaning and anti-meaning. ("Transgressing Language?", 236)

All the outworkings of experiment, from willed verbal spontaneity to the gaps in logic, some going between coherency and incoherency, and the blurring of forms, leads to an "undecideability of effects" (236). McCredden's reading, nonetheless, begets judgement; the abject double pulse written into rhythm is "beautiful". It is hard to say whether the same can be said for a poem that seems to define Ania Walwicz's critical legacy to date, for better or for worse, and a companion poem perhaps to "Poland"; the much discussed "Australia", first published in the 1981 anthology *Island in the Sun 2: An Anthology of Recent Australian Prose* edited by Anna Couani and Damien White (90). The beginning of the poem goes "You too empty. You desert with your nothing nothing nothing." In a reading by W. H. New, following the notion of the "tall tale" in both Anna Couani and Walwicz, the poem is situated among a series of historical poems called "Australia", "Australasia" or "Terra Australia". "By calling her work 'Australia,' she enters her piece into a kind of ritual of national self-assessment" (124). The "not exactly linear" but sequential list would (at least) include colonial poems by W. C. Wentworth, whose 1823 poem was satirised by Charles Harpur in 1853, John Farrell (1886), Bernard O'Dowd (1900), Mary Gilmore (1932), A. D. Hope (1939), James McAuley (1942) and Douglas Stewart (1949). This is, of course, not the same as the migrant tradition of "Australia poems", many of which are closer to Walwicz in kind; take, for instance Ouyang Yu's "A Chinese Sojourner in Australia", "Once More Untitled for Another Australian Album", "Song for an Exile in Australia" and the aforementioned "Fuck you, Australia", poems equally provocative, and complex, as Walwicz's.[1] The list could be expanded. If we were to return right to the beginning of the colonial tradition to the poet and judge Barron Field, who as previously noted published the very first book of poetry in Australia with his 1819 *First Fruits of Australian Poetry*, we find the earliest uses of the phrase *terra nullius*.[2] As Stuart Banner puts it in his study, "The earliest formal statements of *terra nullius* arose in legal contexts that on the surface had little to do with the acquisition of land" (26). Banner notes that the first such statement "appears to have been made in 1819, when a dispute arose between Lachlan Macquarie, the governor of New South Wales,

---

[1] Parts of this chapter are derived, in spirit, from a paper given at the University of California, Berkeley, at the occasion of an Australian poetry conference hosted by Lyn Hejinian, Ann Vickery and Kate Fagan headlined "Active Aesthetics", in 2016. It's in some ways occasional, born out of conversations had there. For many of those in attendance, what seemed especially significant was to see Australian poetry interrogating the relation between aesthetics and politics, and precisely when considering, up front, the kind of drastic circumstances of invasion and colonisation and its impact on form: aesthetic invention was rarely framed as an *interruption* to a poem's politics, as it sometimes can be.

[2] I first heard this fact from Justin Clemens, whose keynote address, titled "First Fruits of a Barron Field", was delivered at the Historical Poetics symposium held at Western Sydney University in December 2016, a conference concerning historical perspectives on prosody. In this talk Clemens spoke also of derivativeness and inherited form in Field's relation to Nature; specifically the "concatenation in his work of a retrospective tradition of broken forms" (12:10). This has contradictory (to say the least) literary-historical consequences: "Field finds that his own lack of history requires a counter-history, to show how his poetry can't be poetry. It must fail to establish itself as poetry" (13:15). Despite (or, as Clemens argues, because of) the questionable quality of Field's poems and the historical context in which they appear, David Higgins, writing comparatively on Field and Charles Lamb, notes that "He was not born in Australia, nor did he settle there, but – despite its brevity and the self-mockery of its title – it is appropriate to see *First Fruits* as a 'foundational' Australian text. This is precisely because of its troubled transnationalism" (221–2). Higgins's curious "there" is precisely the kind of thereness that follows what I would likewise argue is a troubled transnationalism in the works of avant-garde migrant poets in Australia, who "here" too saw irony and potential in the "foundational" impetus of anything avant-garde.

and Barron Field, judge of the New South Wales Supreme Court, over whether the Crown, acting through Macquarie, had the power to impose taxes on the residents of New South Wales, or whether that power was reserved to Parliament, as was the case with taxes imposed on residents of Britain" (26). Field argued that Parliament retained that right, which was validated by the then Attorney-General and the then Solicitor-General; New South Wales was not a "conquered province" and therefore those parts that were "desert and uninhabited" did not fall within the king's prerogative power. This question, Banner notes, was at this point one of constitutional law and "did not concern Indigenous people directly", but it "nevertheless provided an occasion for what seems to have been the government's first formal declaration of their legal status. Or rather their lack of status, as their land was deemed 'desert and uninhabited' before the British arrived" (27).

If Walwicz's "Australia" initially seems inflected this way, a different visitorship is presented in Australian poetry's noxious "first fruits", and in "Australia" something other than such legal questions of habitation occurs. In place of this we get questions of social negotiation. New's reading of Walwicz briefly focuses also on the figure of Doreen in the poem, the only "character". The speaker, as New puts it, "is berating a man both because of what he has done – at the center of the piece is a telling moment of rivalry and narrative revelation: 'You engaged Doreen' – and because of what he does not do" (123).[3] We are then invited to suspect that the poem is something of a narrative involving networked character, linked personages. Another reading of the poem might find the issue of subjectivity strikingly present. A common problem in expressions of nation on the margins as well as expressions of nations that find themselves at the centre of

---

[3] Michael Sharkey has also claimed the character of Doreen in the poem as a marker of some "witty twist" of light comic effect: "Metaphor carries the day: the inclusion of 'Doreen' in Walwicz's poem turns the work into a fable: a lie where something like the truth resides" (395). The name Doreen is culturally embedded: it first reminded me of Doreen in Plath's *The Bell Jar*, which seems to parallel Walwicz's Doreen in contrasting with the speaker (in Plath's case, the semiautobiographical Esther) as a kind of cynical but happy-go-lucky opposite, other, or rival. But other more English Doreens seemed equally probable as prototypical poetics personages here. There is the secondary character Doreen, wife of "James Honeyman" in W. H. Auden's eponymous 1938 ballad. If the Englishness of the name is not enough to claim it the Doreen of Australian poetry appears in C. J. Dennis's 1915 *The Songs of a Sentimental Bloke*, also as the future wife and amorous object of Bill's affections. In such context, and in the context of the clear gender critique in "Australia" ("You don't like me and you don't like women" [306]), Walwicz's "engaged" Doreen might point to a rebuttal of the figure of the Sentimental Bloke.

an empire is surely there in the lines "You don't have any interest in another country. Idiot centre of your own self" and "Wait for other people to tell you what to do. Follow the leader, Can't imagine." Could we go further and argue that this is a frustrated social and subjective description of consensus poetics from the perspective of a transcultural avant-garde? New puts it, delightfully, like this; despite alienation in this new national situation,

> She, by contrast, has verve. Even in using a language that is not her own, the speaker is inventive, managing to turn adjectives into evocative nouns, construct brand new resonant compounds, use repetition to evoke repetitiveness, transform fragments into metonyms of identity. (124)

II. *Establishments and Anomalies*

Let this historical turn to "invention" be articulated another way. Do we then have some reflecting back to or holding up of a potent "outside" through Walwicz's imagination of Australian unsettlement precisely via the question of inventive poetics as inseparable from "metonyms of identity"? These readings set the scene, for if "Australia" is really about inventive writing as reflexive object, as poetic *topos*, Walwicz is not ambivalent about her stance on the avant-garde in commentary. In a 1996 interview, Walwicz defines her work as, precisely, "avant-garde writing, experimental writing, poetic, abstract writing", placing herself at the scene of contemporaneous history:

> How it fits in to the Australian scene: there's very little work like that being done so it doesn't fit in at all, it's sort of an anomaly ... and yet attention has been paid to it and it's being studied ... so I am part of Australian literature. And I think perhaps in the future this kind of work will be done more readily because someone has already established a position for it to be done. (Huppatz)

This was the mid-1990s, and still telling. Yes, we are told, the critical discourse exists; Australian literature, as bloc, has not *completely* sidelined her work. It has allowed her work to sit uneasily beside other work in anthologies, and so forth, but without discernable context. It remains an anomaly, but in the indeterminate zone of a certain paradoxical insider's-outsidership, a position not unusual for an experimental writer. Our argument for inventive contemporary poetry will show how difficult it is to say, in the new century, that "very little" work like this is being done. But to take Walwicz's claim seriously, the clamour to *quantify* what is avant-garde in Australian poetry only just started becoming possible in the 1990s. Avant-gardism in a *historical* sense would not carry much significance until a full decade after the statement was made. Whether Walwicz, and others like Duke (particularly those working in the concrete poetry tradition), truly "established a position" for a new wave of radically experimental writers is the reigning question from here on in. It should be clear again that this is a question for the chronometric function in critical poetics, carried over from our earlier discourse on the early twentieth-century European avant-garde and its long aftermath.

Walwicz would emerge a decade after Duke in a career that would flower in the early 1980s. Her major books emerged consistently over several decades from *Writing* (1982), *Boat* (1989) and *Red Roses* (1992) to, most recently, *Palace of Culture* (2014) and *Horse* (2018). The stylistic continuities of her practice over this time belies developmental shifts. What is of interest for the purposes of this project are those elements in these works that test the capacity and the patience of the reader; where, in particular, transcultural and transnational approaches lead to a further equation of marginal (migrant) writer and experimental (avant-garde) outsider. Our concern is further the role of critic parallel to the reader in general.

This notion of a double-marginal status gets discussed in one of her most succinct statements of process, a piece entitled "Look at me, Ma – I'm going to be a marginal writer!" published in *Southerly*, then edited by Ivor Indyk, whose admiration of Walwicz's work would not prevent such descriptors as "difficult and exasperating" (88). In this piece, central to Walwicz's sense of what it means to be avant-garde is that which is difficult, unreadable, potentially distasteful. Although, as she puts it, even an emphasis on the minor (also private) which lies underneath the major (the public discourse that "cannibalises" the author-writer) can lead to a centring of the unofficial literature itself, a dislocation-then-relocation of affinities and identifications that refuse the dichotomy that pits mainstream against marginal. In short, avant-garde canonmaking has produced unassailable paradoxes:

> My identification has always been with the avant-garde, the authors that influenced me were: Stein, Lautreamont, Joyce, Beckett, Burroughs, Artaud, Nietzsche and Kafka. That area immediately

becomes affiliated with marginality yet the constant republishing of these works situate them in a position of importance (with in a particular informed milieu) and in a situation that cannot be clearly designated. In my view these works were mainstream, main stream, central, accepted by me. How does one read? One forms one's own affiliations. The concepts of marginality and mainstream depend on one's viewpoint ... The monolithic concept of culture suggests a hierarchical order and separate areas, the official culture and the production of acceptable material and the non-official culture. Yet Beckett can now be seen as a mainstream cultural phenomenon ... Beckett was marginal once but he is not marginal nor minor now. The mainstream and the marginal overlap. ("Look at Me, Ma!", 163)

"How *does* one read?" – it's a question that comes down to desire, too: What does the reader *want*? For one, marginal, for another, mainstream: "One forms one's own affiliations"! And yet it's more than just a move from cultural margins to cultural centres, more than just a bifurcated monolith of canon and anti-canon, major and minor. "The boundaries blur" is how Walwicz puts it ("Look at Me, Ma!", 164), and one can see how, from a certain perspective, even with critical industries built around Beckett, Stein and Joyce in which the publication and study of these works and their respective auras and "position of importance" is rarely questioned, the publishing and subsequent canonisation of works *in this vein*, and in this contemporary milieu, is next to unimaginable (for Walwicz, the exception to this is Kathy Acker). Does this mean Walwicz identifies with a Deleuzoguattarian "minor literature"? Not quite. But for the most part, the work is done, it gets studied, it enters the cultural museum. At the end of the piece Walwicz goes on to confess that her act of rebellion is primarily against the language and order of the Father, who, as Master, splits or gaps the avant-garde subject whose speech is fracturing simultaneously into a child's speech (in French) and an adult's ("Look at Me, Ma!", 164).

So it is, from these agons, accents, oppositionalities, psychosocial locations and subject positions that the status avant-garde comes into question: "I have failed to place myself anywhere. But you said that you are avant-garde, before!" ("Look at Me, Ma!", 164). So it is then also that the contemporaneity of experimental practice, in the context of Australian literary culture, gets doubly refused, fails to place itself anywhere or fix itself to a position, thereby opening holes of identification (rejection from the Father, who maintains the barrier between major and minor). The failure of identification that marks the slipperiness of an Australian avant-garde is not one that I wish to in any way "fix". I don't wish to smooth over these dislocations and contradictions. One could conjure adverse reactions from the fact that here I am situating Walwicz's work as central to an Australian avant-garde that has likewise failed to place itself anywhere. Again, transnational and multicultural frameworks which pit an Anglo-Australian literature squarely against a vanguard "rebel" might set us back more than afford clarity as to the exactness of the political literacy at stake. In another interview on her practice, Walwicz identifies certain difficulties with readership that we know, classically, to be tantamount to prognoses of the position of avant-garde or "experimental" outsider:

> People have found the work jarring, too much, or in bad taste. I think the work is best received by people who are prepared to lay themselves open, who can identify with it, respond to it. Perhaps this relates to the fact that I come from a different culture, where the act of revealing oneself, emotional behaviour is more accepted than in Anglo-Saxon culture. The writing has been rejected by magazines for being too "experimental." The reader of my work has to read every word, enter the book, eat the book. (Lysenko and Brophy, n.pag)

Some textual appetite – book to be eaten – or as McCredden put it, some place of the *abject*, allows us to at the very least situate the "bad taste" of unsympathetic readership. This is where we get to the crux. Although Walwicz writes in English (her poetry is not, strictly speaking, bilingual), she goes on to say that when her work was translated "back" into Polish it was revealed that structures from Polish were already in the English, and thus made it easier to retranslate into her mother tongue: "So the language I use in writing has incorporated the structure of the first language. Perhaps this is a kind of fusing of the two languages. It is a kind of incomplete English using Polish structure. The use of language as sound also relates to this. When I was not able to speak, English did exist for me as unintelligible sound" (Lysenko and Brophy, n.pag). For anybody learning a second or third language, working with sound precedes any kind of experimental usage of these tools. To use this as a means for a poetics attuned to sound, to harness such transpositional logics to develop a rhythmics, is another thing entirely. To be an experimental migrant writer, perhaps rather than being doubly marginal, becomes a way to speak from another centre, or *no centre at all*. When one pitches these arguments under the terms of national readership, and particularly when such readership is supported by some kind of government funding, senses of a non-nationally specific "coring" of vanguardism disappear. In a conversation between Sneja Gunew and Gayatri Spivak, Gunew begins with the question of authenticity and non-Anglo-Celtic (otherwise Migrant, but non-Anglo-Celtic is more culturally specific) writing: "Patrick White's Middle Europeans or Beverley Farmer's Greeks" are read as more authentic than even Π.O. or Antigone Kefala, but these Others are not seen as "part of these cultural productions" and not given "full measure of cultural franchise" (Spivak, *Post-Colonial Critic*, 59). These non-Anglo-Celtic writers work within Australian discursive constructions and are therefore able to play with these formations despite their alienation from cultural centres. Gunew informs Spivak that "one of the strategies of some of the writers that I work with, is that they play a kind of stage Migrant and poke fun at, and parody in all sorts of ways, these so-called authentic Migrant constructions. I am thinking here of the work of Π.O., the work of Ania Walwicz", whereupon Spivak replies that "tokenization goes with ghettoization", moving, in the reply, to her subjective interpolation, so often tokenistic, as one who speaks for the Third World, outworking her response through the question of the Indian diaspora and the United States brain drain in the 1960s (*Post-Colonial Critic*, 61).

Much has happened since this conversation in cultural politics and the institutions that engage with it. Perhaps, and I want to closely qualify this, it is therefore less reasonable, even "suspicious", following Spivak here, to read Walwicz's poetics as a kind of *speaking as*, given the speaking as too easily results in a *speaking for*. But even the conversation itself follows a curious trajectory. Gunew sticks to the theme of the Anglo-Australian establishment and its inability to see migrant writers like Π.O., Walwicz, Kefala anywhere near its core, and how this folds in with funding models like the Australia Council, the Australian Government's arts funding and advisory body, while Spivak continues to speak of the Indian community in the United States and comparisons with Indians of the Afro-Caribbean diaspora. The conversation itself is contextually rent in two, a dialectic that is, usefully, not quite solved. Whether indeed there is an Australian diasporic literature constituted from this loose network of Australian non-Anglo-Celtic writers is not raised. Spivak asks about specific problems of "cultural politics" in Australia, whereupon Gunew remains extremely locationally specific, recounting "walking along Glebe Road" (*Post-Colonial Critic*, 64) in Sydney, looking in a shop window and seeing a poem hanging there by Nihat Ziyalan, a Turkish poet not widely known in

Australia, who is unable to find funding for his work. Gunew's focus on voices "in the wilderness" again comes back to the question of a general readership:

> a small gesture towards beginning to understand this would be to create a demand for multi-lingual anthologies within Australia. There is an incredible and disproportionate resistance to presenting the general Australian public with immigrant writing *in English* even, but to have it in conjunction with the remainder of these repressed languages seems to be another battle which still has to be fought. (Spivak, *Post-Colonial Critic*, 66)

The sphere of anthology-making is one ground on which this battle was or was not fought. It is there in particular that the question of general Australian public, of a national readership *en masse*, comes up. Our aim at present is, admittedly, narrower. Where there are readings of Walwicz through the lens of multicultural, or transcultural writing alone, I want to first narrow down the focus here to Walwicz's claims to avant-garde histories, and interrogate these in her writing, before returning to Gunew, and more closely examining her inquiry in light of hemispheric questions. Without really interrogating the status of a transnational vanguardism in Walwicz, I must stress, the picture is incomplete. The same would go for Kefala, Π.O. and, one would have to add, Ouyang Yu, Thalia and Anna Couani. It might not then be so surprising that several prominent migrant writers in Australia identify, albeit in different ways, as avant-garde. Readership will be key, but my concern is first to examine the shape of the poetics: works before modes of distribution, modes of distribution before hemispheric confluence and lines of transmission and, no less, translation.

I neglect to mention theory. The pressure to tell the truth about the writing from joanne burns in the quotation given previously might bring in evidence enough, in mark-making and in writing, not just for difference but also for *dissemination*. What are the "works themselves"? What theories come from them? What theories can we apply to them? Where we can track back to poetics such pathways of meaning-making, as Jacques Derrida does in the outworking that leads to *Dissemination*, do we not then become more suspicious of extractive truths? Here again the relationship between avant-gardes and theory, or even avant-gardes and philosophy, will become ever more central to our historicist modes of operation. However we might seek out or avoid these difficulties in reading Walwicz, whether we deem them traceable back to legacies of the modernist avant-gardes (or even longer histories of experiment), our analysis will bring up once again literary-critical and historical-theoretical quandaries: avant-gardes increasingly become not only a reflection of double-marginality (one that can come good with critical attention or a legacy in subsequent generations of experimental writers), but also a reflection of the transcultural effect of the middle; not just a radical "elsewhere" or "outside" from which one writes. All else grows from this psychosocial and philo-poetic ground. We have to locate a position in which poetry aligns with the theories it carries by virtue of its affinity with global avant-gardes. If we use theory to try to understand Walwicz, we ought to also use Walwicz to understand theory. But to get there let us start with textuality: two components of Walwicz's inventive poetics, prosodic dissonance and, through this, her work in expansive *poesis*.

III. *Euphony at speed*

The quotation from joanne burns prepares us for what here follows: getting down to the texts themselves. But the texts are never quite themselves. We only have the whole productive process of writing to hide. Walwicz's processes are very often out there in the open. Walwicz's theatricalisation of language, to start with, makes us ask, as Garrett Stewart did in *Reading Voices: Literature and the Phonotext*, how one might "evocalise prose" as we are able to do with poetry, and how to locate the vanishing of the subject in the space opened up by prose speech. For Stewart we have a vocabulary of speaking that can sometimes seem strangely without the subject. How, Stewart inquires, can we read with an ear and eye towards transegmental prose, the drifting of graphemes and phonemes in prosaic time: "Can a sentence or paragraph from a novel, in any degree like a line or quatrain from a sonnet, be found to invite phonemic reading?" (192). When does this become "overreading", saying too much about too little? To "overread" in the obsolete sense is to read over, but it may also, in the transitive, mean to over-analyse; to risk the critical acumen itself becoming the total focus, the *raison d'être*. Reading is the question "how", how did writing happen, and so on, but overreading is not, in Stewart's sense, a psychologism, a why-ing, but a how of prose externalised. The reader-in-question most often seems to be Stewart.

It is a tricky critical mode. There is always that sense that to overread is to do the opposite to the New Critical reading which is "less scriptive" underreading: thinner rather than thicker, "more trouble, less action" (192). On this point my readings will pause and reconsider. Style, stylistics, is always an invention (here, I grant, either plotted in historical succession or not at all, and certainly not just confined to the modern, as Stewart proposes, Woolf might be Shakespeare's sister), and we have to imagine that inventive poetics, at the first, gets us to the scriptive, and then in time allows us to move away from the scriptive alone, rather than the reverse in which it takes some phonemic leap of faith to imagine it in a novel. Or another collocation, to wit: if we are to ask how Walwicz's writing is written, what role does the phonemic play – is it sound-led or does sound follow composition? A poetics of notation does both. It should be possible to slip between how and why. For all the comparisons to Stein and Woolf, in these senses of modern reading, what does Walwicz really do to, or with, these lines of influence, and why? And the who of it; who is Ania Walwicz? (or now, who was Ania Walwicz?) is a question far more social than Stewart's phonemic reading will allow, but no less invitational on the phonemic end.

Steinishness must be spoken of with Walwicz but it is difficult to locate it with respect to two very different practices. It is impossible to deny a certain Steinishness in the work at the same time as it looks and feels very different to Stein. For Lorange the way Stein's process and grammar works is through the daily and metaphysical-propositional work of *"eating, speaking, writing* and *reading"* (*How Reading is Written*, 89). These are the conditions of Steinishness. Eating, writerly appetition; these things certainly mark Walwicz's work, as we will see. They bring a different grammar. Perhaps *shape* is a better way of placing the dimensions of the writing than grammar. It is difficult to say if Walwicz "speaks" in Steinian measure, but there is a tendency towards proleptic narrative in Walwicz as in Stein. What we can mark in advance in Walwicz's narratives are not so much characters but themes, whole-book themes. There is much less by way of punning in Walwicz's work, and few transpositional puns: words are often presented as words, placed beside other words, or repeated (but of course, as Stein proved, there is no such thing as repetition). There is a certain shape to this writing also that conjures, historically, more contemporary, post-1960 processes and textures of writing. In the interview with Lysenko and Brophy, Walwicz cites traditions of electronic music, John Cage, performance, theatre, language and sound composition as part of her poetic arsenal, adding that "extreme theatrical delivery" and the "extreme format of writing" bring her work "along contemporary lines". How did

Walwicz write? We learn also how Walwicz's writing process very much involves composition by page in the 1982 book *Writing*:

> I write longhand in exercise books. Then I type the work out, editing as I type. Then I re-write. I don't like re-writing. When I have to rewrite too much I know there is something wrong. Some pieces have been done directly on the typewriter. I'd like to write like this all the time. The best work happens fast, done once. (n.pag.)

Editing in the writing process poses a temporal problem, but also sounds a bell of insubordination: many a writer or editor will in an almost authoritarian way sing praise for the absolute necessity of close editing. Yet such a "concentrated" state of writing – improvisatory, pleasurable, hypnotic, speedy – finishes up eventually with the act of typing at a typewriter, the ultimate, if not utopic way around the curse of editing and afterthought. For some this will recall the whole meaning of Olson's typewriter as a vehicle for breath in "Projective Verse", and as Walwicz said, the typewriter "is my drum". This situates her work close, so she claims, to that of Elvis Presley, and therefore close to "music", but in *Writing* Walwicz explains most succinctly why these structures of writing move on an "abstract" level through

> words, sounds, rhythm. There is an awareness of the process of writing, just writing, independent from what is said. Language becomes subject matter [. . .] Literal speech edits thoughts, feelings [. . .] The meaning is achieved not only through the use of words but also through the relationship between words, repetition of the words and the rhythm. (n.pag.)

The issue of repetition will need more close attention. On the face of it, we may compare this kind of process with that of David Antin (1932–2016). In the case of Antin his mode of composition was one of record, but the scoring process, compositional and Steinian in that way, would be a type of transcription, coming close to notation in that it would be speech-led. To indicate silence, spaces were left according to the length of silence involved, a technique Jackson Mac Low used too in the Hopkinsesque *154 Forties* stanza-works. In *Writing*, gapping of words is a way of indicating caesurae. The prose margins, irregular but not to the same extent as Antin, or Mac Low, remain mostly justified, with the resulting interior gapping, and interior compression, determined by breaks. Below is a modified version that highlights the enclosed spaces, or "bubbles", of the piece, to amplify the sense of space:

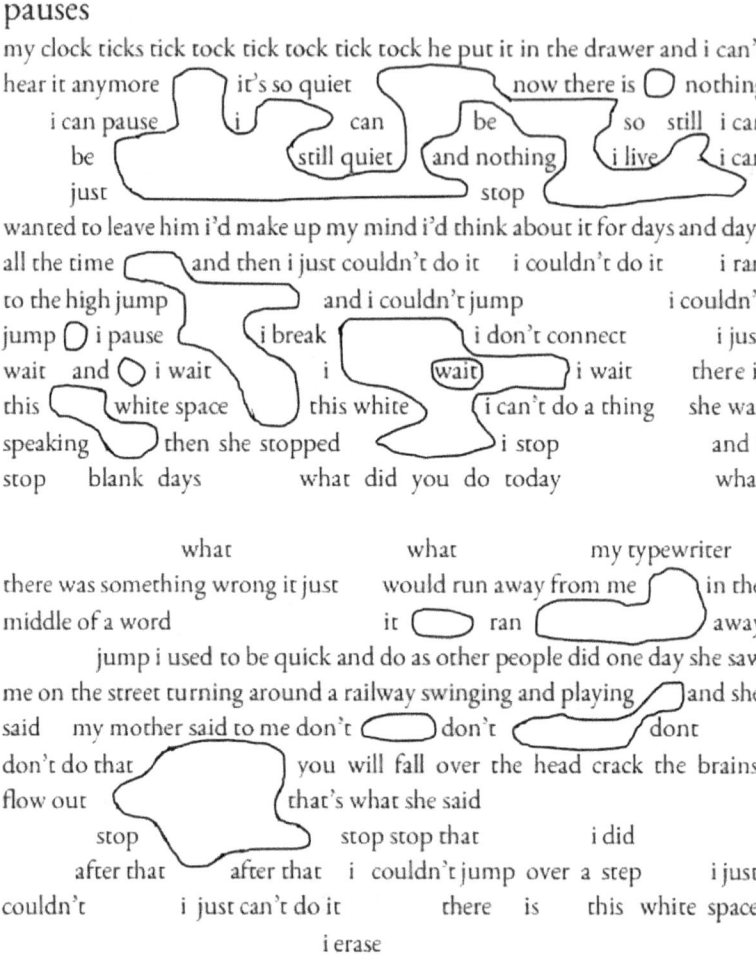

(*Writing*, 98 [bubbles added by author])

Looked at in this way as a frozen image, with the elongation or compression of space in relief, spatial attention can take in the total geometry of the piece, the *fact* of composition by page and the immanent ecstasy of method. The whole page, enclosed, like a block of ice, traps the air that got let in to form bubbles. Yet it has to be read in terms other than dissonance, and what is visibly *broken up*, from the very first "phrase", is not the grammar. A more "molten" reading shows that consonance gives totality to willed spontaneity, not fragmentation. What matters here is less, even in the first instance, rhythm. Nor is our first problem that of scriptive bonds and disjuncts between words. What matters is rather speed. Euphony at speed, dissonance at a dawdle. The continuousness of enrhythmed language might be the cause of a dissonant prosody, or some obscuration of meaning, but one can never let the page freeze just as one doesn't dawdle before a score. Such verbico-visual prosody can be seen at work on a good many pages: one has simply to pick up a book and view it at middle distance. On page 110 of *Boat*, we have:

> big face comes bundle oo oolee plumps furs legs around arms creams necks put beds touch fluffy settle calms to happy cats curls tails ball cat baie trembly baby teddy round legs kill bird dicks oolee runsway nestle legs fluffy heats alarms clocks made jumo jump sorry pads pad drops play streets catso huge rubs sits how do you do hugs kisses licks legs in between sleeps circles eye looks pets dainty slurp grace touch nose wets happies we so tails smell smoke curls toes dribble puss mama warms safe boops beeps cushions helloes miles dee dee dee reety deety teee bubos bub beebee baby booo tails raise we pays palys plays we palys plays fillies licks makes happies hotsie strokes you so silky walks pats heads rolls kicks furry waaz waazzy waaa waaa waaa waaa o oolee sweels swells swells swell joys licks furry sucks sunny tum middle roads no fears cheery playing fiddles nee nee nee put cat hat on dee dee wiggle liddle leedle leedle oolee woo woo woo wooli o oolee o ma oolee (*Boat*, 110)

Which completes the chapter "oolee 1", folding into "oolee 2", the very next chapter overleaf:

> ooleeooleeoolee oolee dee deedee dah doo oh deedee mah oolee mah do dadeedah dahdee dah deedee doo lilly lalilah lalily loo laloolah da deedah dah deedee dah doo oolee deedinka loo dah deedinka dee dahdeedee dahdoodah dah doo oolee laloolie lahlily lah loo dah dee dee dah doo oolee mah do sweewah dee dah dooah deedah dah dee dadoodah
> (*Boat*, 111)

This visual prosody comes without bubbles; no gaps in space for pauses in time. Listen, instead of look, and the effect is very different from the previous excerpt from *Writing*. Here almost every word can be afforded a strong stress, as opposed to the primitive formation of phrases and clauses. Viewed up close, notice some of the "oolee"s in the previous section drifting or seeping across borderlines: intermittence, drift, far more dissonance. Lifting us up above the chunky, blockish density of script *and* send us crashing back down into it, we first visualise its mix of Polish-English sociolect and glossolalic rhythms. In this vein, we might listen closely to the microtonemic contours of the, or a, voice. Or, we will observe, not out of earshot or audition, but again from middle distance, the cracked, disjunctive layers underneath the smoothly striated surface of its long open vowels and lettristic cadences of "d" and "l", watching them grate and bump up to each margin, left, right, north, south, diagonal, our eyes scanning the *striations* that gap each lexical unit. Not the words themselves I mean, but rather the spaces around the words.

Dissonance and smoothness, grinding to a halt and keeping on; these are the tensions. It is astonishing to hear-see the continuity across chapters, across borders, delimiting points of enclosure; palpable, pulpable differences. We would, of course, do the work a disservice to equate its prosodic ingeniousness and verbico-visuality with meaninglessness. Meaning is, in Walwicz, paramount. An experience of reading Walwicz is one of being not palmed off but rather led on. In a section roughly 100 pages on from the the above quotation the scene is craftwork; "i do a firm line i sew me on i cut out pattern" then characters on a page; "i sew me a girl in letters run whip chain stitch darn border fill in over fly straight stitch run daisy blanket work from left to right this is my sampler each letter sewn on my page" (*Boat*, 220). A change of register brings us finally before painting, lifting us off middle-distance – to avoid once again the page's microscopic allure – then placing us back down before an erotics of liquid, precisely a scene of "painting":

> eat paint mouth full swal-
> lows my saliva dribbler you bit into thicker creams
> squelch tongue spits rasperries tubes unscrew top twister
> have lots lips flick blow through straws spatter puddles
> sink in you drink me check powder puff just a touch you
> blush grasp edge cuts my fingers bandage sinks in reds
> seeps in put blown blower on hurry ups brush heavy hang
> hangie blob blobs smear it in drags a way pulls dredge
> rake with rake hangie brush full dip in readies lash out
> (*Boat*, 213)

Revulsion: "eat paint mouth full swallows my saliva dribbler you bite into thicker creams squelch raspberries". Then words cut sharper as if through the page to get to a canvas and to a more ruddy textual complexion: "blush grasp edge cuts my fingers bandage sinks in reds". To reach a plenum we are driven by our hunger for more language when we feel we have not enough; but we might bite our tongue or cut ourselves in the process. As we eat, and read, we know what it tastes like, for even if it finds the reader's bitter tongue, the appetition of the text is such that its expansivity feels structured like a meal, but a meal without structure. Means of expansion lead to an end – nourishment in the expanded present. Forget the global measurement of bookhood; embrace the gluttony of the microtext.

IV. *Expansive Geometries: Writing Larger Numbers*

Means of expansion, or length as an end unto itself? The difficulty with talking about expansiveness is where it becomes tied up with the discourse of production: a poet need not pay attention to the word count to see it billow out. It should not be too off-balance to bring in the word "geometry" here given the scale of these claims. Scale and history has always been a preoccupation of this book. From these tinier scales larger patterns emerge; a multifaceted *poesis* that takes these elements into weightier units of time; the page. Without work on a smaller scale there would be no larger sense of scale. The microtextual particularities of prosodic dissonance lead to expansive geometries in Walwicz's poetics. There is some irony in the notion of appetition and the avant-garde: who *has* an appetite for (knowledge of) the weird, even "extreme format" of writing (dissonant, disjunctive)? The critical payoff is that looking at modular units and larger structures does not preclude the focus on prosodic detail, which is not merely some overlying element but plays out in the verbal and the visible structure of these books. Talking about "prosody" with regard to fiction, however, as Stewart suggests, is only a little more odd than talking about its "poetics". And in terms of generic category many of Walwicz's works are not poetry: *Red Roses* has no parts, it is not modular, but a mostly continuous, 214-page text categorised as "fiction" notably without chapters (thus earning this charge of poeticity by denomination only, not generic category, and I will not apply the term "poetics" either for this). *Boat*, from which we have seen excerpts, is divided into 100 parts, each making up a kind of chapter. It too is "fiction". *Palace of Culture* is composed of fifty parts. Three neat structures: no parts, 100 parts, fifty parts. What constitutes a "chapter" in the latter two straddles a fine line between the prosaic element (a potential) of poetry and the evental presencing of character and person (equally the poeticisation of character). In the chapter titled "numbers" from *Boat* we enter into a numerical field of scale:

> by number i know it num-
> bers figures to write me i can be zero O is
> empty or even less my temperature got so low in
> the antarctic that i was hunting polar bears polar bears
> i get warmer now i get to zero O i get to 1 in me 1 is
> me i am 1 only 1 1 to me i be 1 i am 1, i is alone great
> is 1 alone is 1 only 1 for me i am 1, 1 is a start 1 is already
> something there 1 is beginning i start with 1 i thaw me
> i am 1 now i am 1 this leads me to 2 i don't like 2 now
> 2 is fail me 2 is bad to me 2 is more than one 1, 2 is
> is bad to be 3 joins me join me 3 is good year 3 is all
> together 3 draws a triangle 3 is a balanced 3 is full and
> good 3 is 1 out of 3, 3 is one third 3 is almost ½ 3 is
> almost there already 3 is rounded up 3 is solid 3 stands
> up 3 stands up 3 goes places 3 i like 3, 1, 2, 3 and 1,
> 2, 3, 3 dances 3 sings songs 3 grows and grows into 4,
> 4 stands on one leg 4 nearly falls down 4 just waits and
> wairs 4 is nothing to write to your mother about 4 is
> nearly nearly nearly ½ nearly half nearly ½ nearly ½
> nearly ½ nearly ½ nearly ½ but not quite is very close
> very close very close very close but not there it tries it
> waits for something to happen and 5 is next 5 is ½ 5
> is a half and a half half way neither here nor there 5 is
> big belly has a 5 is belly big belly 5 is proud of me 5
> is a nice mark 5 is a good one 5 is pass 5 has a crown
>
> (*Boat*, 33)

The chapter is a count. Large is the difference between written numerals and digits, in poetry, and at this point it is clear that Walwicz is thinking in writing on the scale of the count, of addition or accretion. It's an attempt to *characterise* numbers, as one might in synaesthesia characterise colours or keys, at the same time as explore the psychical – or philosophical – character of subjectivity or the subject ("i am 1").

In the late 1990s, the US American critic Lynn Keller was able to bring into literary-historical discussion women's long poems after the 1960s, that is, from modernist to contemporary, in a move that at once diversified the field of long poem studies outside that of the Poundian-Zukofskyan epic, to the benefit of a broader sense of North American poetry and poetics, and indeed outside an American century of long poems. The larger question it opens is why women writers could in the twentieth century feel permitted to write expansively, and how women's long poems took the periphery into the centre of poetic experience. One can imagine a similar critical expansion of cultural and intellectual range around longer forms in Australia. Meanings of "expansive" differ. There are differing figurative and indeed geopolitical resonances set off by deploying words like "expansion" and the "expansive" across Australian and North American contexts. If we are to metaphorise the page-as-field – or if page equals land equals private property – are we to imagine the concept of expansion as point-blank imperial? Competition for resources began early in Australian settler society, and efforts to explore the continent's interior devolved into a long Frontier War, a catastrophe for Indigenous peoples if not as much a story of survival. Migrants were prospecting in the Australian goldfields at the same time as they did in California. Yet the concept of "Manifest Destiny" and Westward Expansion are not used the same way across Australian and North American historiographies.[4]

Expansion is neither a metaphor for spatial dominance nor, in this critical usage, a word without prior resonances. Unlike "long", which introduces time, expansion is spatial. Scale, being perceived, in the time of reading, is in turn tempered by another thing outside just sheer capacity; narrative, which can be almost any length, but usually not so diminutive as to not take (or give) space. Thus the meaning of "expansive geometries" in Walwicz is more than just a kind of imposing bluster or rampancy. It's detailed. Where there is theme in Walwicz, or modularity, even "chapters", if you will, the narrative is not uneventful, but eventhood in narrative here is not a sharpening to a point but a continual eventhood. It's an aesthetics and a poetics of flatness not unknown to fictive writing

---

[4] It would be amiss not to bookmark specific comparisons to be made with certain US American Language Writers writing also in expansive prose, especially two very different poets, Lyn Hejinian and Ron Silliman. With Hejinian there is a rhythmic seamlessness (conjunction) that collides with cuts (disjunction), and even absent points of transition in her prose, but certainly a type of prose expansion, conscious of the novel as form, comparable to Walwicz on these registers. Silliman's expansive works in prose, like Hejinian's, can be said to explore the larger numbers, Hejinian and Silliman share the concept, if not the conception, of the "new sentence", developed from Stein, which would be a manifesto and a technique. Whether Walwicz writes new sentences in this vein, and I think she does, or might, would require another reading of the role of the referent and comparative prosaic logics. I am equally interested in comparing Walwicz's language use with that of Conceptual Art. It was Hanne Darboven (1941–2009), the German conceptualist, who described her modus operandi as "*schreiben, nicht beschreiben*" (which can be roughly translated as "writing, not describing"), applicable to Walwicz.

that Walwicz undoubtedly engages. In Walwicz's novelistic poems, sometimes simply called "novels", the "nothing" that is happening is far more psycho-thematic than is usually the case for, say, a verse-novel. It isn't quite accurate therefore to say that nothing happens in Walwicz; things are happening all the time, but the evental structures invite distant reading (often aided by titles), and if it does invite close reading it's the kind that, as we explore above, demands intimacy with the sound and the rhythms that add up to its sense of expansivity. Still, one cannot escape theme and frame. Things happen around events but those events are patted out in the verbal textures, or, at least, the contract between language and event is broken, modified. Another way of writing it might be that things are always happening, but not in the field of reference. Or again, that isn't quite right; the field of reference is rather rendered an open field, space or page, and in place of character we have person, or subject, demanding both detailed and distant reading from page to page.

The subject who speaks may be Walwicz's person(a), to be more precise, and her book structures often suggest an underlying event, or setting. The sections of *Palace of Culture* are each roughly between two and four pages, but the connection between the sections, like *Boat*, do not invite any straightforward sense of narrative sequence – rather the timescape seems to continually "arrive" at the present. The frame is historical. "Palace of Culture" refers to the 1955 construction Palace of Culture and Science in Poland, designed by the Soviet Architect Lev Rudnev. Though a Stalinist-era building from the 1950s, even today it remains the eighth-tallest building in the European Union. The sectioning of Walwicz's works can be said to offer consciously modular limit-points, chapterings. Take for instance these chapter "endings" from *Palace of Culture*, first this from "6. fast train" – the moment the subject gets on a train:

> the way and that's the way i'll stay now i'm on my way go far and further i said i was going too far and i go further and further mister casey jones the train driver how goes it mister train man now i i'm in in in i get on and on on on i'm in on in i go far i get on in on in on in now i'm in i'm in on in in in in i'm on and in and on and in now and in and on and in and on in (17)

Jamming up against the end, as the time of writing through one section draws to a close, the chapter ends all-aboard and comes to a temporary stop. Yet the *pace of reading* as we experience it slows down just as we greet the expanding present of a train speeding up.

At the close of "14. palace of culture", the title section if you will, we arrive:

> underground metro moscow made of marble n crystal chandelier crystal shiny black piano play now focus me to get me all together now play n sing noa la la la la la la la la la la i wear black n white here miss compose me air house paper lit light n bright n on now la la la la la la la la la la i"m on in now on now fold out now come out hid hidey hole now bright n shiny stage a stage i tap dance now la la la la la la la la la la i lit light bright lit flame now set fire on fire (33)

Between sections all the time of travel has passed. The metro has become a stage. For those familiar with Walwicz's performing voice, the word "now", delivered in a thick Polish accent, has become well-nigh iconic – it serves as a touchstone for the stark presentism of which we speak. Note also then the closing words of "32. musty", which contains rare linebreaks; again an expanding present:

> in blue house she wears me i leave door open now darned sew trouser and darn sock a hole in sock now i have to repair and sew me i have to but i don't want to do any just lazy said do me do me i lazy on i lazy yo i have to do do do do do do do do do do do do do do do do do do do do do do do do do (73)

It may be the sound of crushing fast life, but it isn't so much stutter as glitch, the seizing up of a botched disc, of a process that has had to end; the intrusion of an expanded present upon the writing as it files past or rolls through space. Expansive writing here means an occupation of space, as too it means a flattening and elongation of lexical drift in the time of reading and writing, not at the expense however of close attention to lexical detail and the properties of single words. It is hard not to read a certain "Saroyanist" element in the subtitle to part 19: "twighlight" (43–4). There is of course a certain irony in seeing Aram Saroyan (1943–), the American minimalist poet, in such expansive writing. Expansive geometries in the space of writing also imply a politicisation of the egoic self as transitional between social structures in a way that pictures the inner world of the mind as a universe, and the world of writing as reflective of the enormity of this space, expansive because it demands to explore ardent life, demands the *right* to go inward, to reflect upon the unsaid (unconscious) as psychoanalytic/allegorical leap to treat the said and the word(s) as associations of a conscious mind. That inward space charges the outward aim. Expansive writing speaks the languages of desire and love. I refer here to the start of Part 3 of *Palace of Culture*, where there is an exceptional example of this. The texture of the writing abruptly changes and becomes discursively philosophic:

> 3. The language of desire
>
> Spinoza writes about ardent life : desire seeks an invented, impossible aim, the language lost in pursuit of an absence, the text forms a vortex, without focus or centre, desire that remains unfulfilled, language that streams out without a real objective, a delirium, a speech with no logical form or goal, a life that is formed is the life of a dream, the language pours out, unstoppable, relentless, circular, a vortex of language constantly spins and rolls over itself . . . (*Palace of Culture*, 5)

V. *Sneja Gunew: Neo-Cosmopolitanism, Hemisphere and the Geopolitical Avant-Gardes*

The quotation above puts us in a hall of infinite interiors, culture as palace, regal space of the mind. But readers will note in the meaning of *Palace of Culture* a contradiction with the Soviet referent, between the pullulating, perhaps even "democratic" freedom of expansive poetics and the apparent rigidity of Soviet society and culture. Given Sneja Gunew has been one of the few critics to take up the work of Walwicz in several theoretical frames, it is worth discussing this issue in more detail through Gunew's critical work, rather than putting it immediately to application on these texts, before bringing it back to explicate the peculiar political elements of Walwicz's writing.

In a 1990 contribution to Homi Bhabha's edited collection *Nation and Narration* Gunew exposes how literary criticism and history combine to construct a totalising discourse for "legitimate culture" (100). The form of the essay is curious because, interspersed with the outworking of this argument, Gunew quotes from both canonical (A. D. Hope) and avant-garde Australian poetry (Ania Walwicz). So in the midst of a discussion of the historical foundations of Australian literary criticism (from P. R. Stephenson to Leonie Kramer, Harry Heseltine, Martin Harrison and Donald Horne), we have Hope's poem "Australia", beginning "A Nation of trees, drab green and desolate gray" (101) – with no direct reading provided. Part-way through that same discussion, with no explanatory pause, Gunew quotes Walwicz's rather well-known poem "Australia", which we know begins "You big ugly. You too empty.

You desert with your nothing nothing nothing" (103). But from this Gunew explores the instrumentalisation of multiculturalism in the Anglo-Celtic sphere, from European cosmopolitanism in the form of anti-British republicanism to obscurations of land-rights and postwar migration as against (then) the new wave of Asian immigration. Gunew quotes also from Walwicz's poem "europe" and "wogs", which clearly trail along the piece's themes, yet in a thrilling critical turn, doesn't offer close readings of those poems. The critical effect is one in which the poems are placed there as ambient but still exemplary objects. Nonetheless the argument is clear: multiculturalism circulates in Australia as a series of discursive formations "serving a variety of institutional interests" ("Denaturalizing", 110). Gunew holds out hope, still, that multiculturalism could be used effectively in the construction of a "counter-public sphere" if it can deploy texts "in such a way that they could not easily be recuperated in the name of nostalgia or absorbed into an Anglo-Celtic canon" ("Denaturalizing", 119). We know, from her editorial work on the anthology *Telling Ways*, discussed before, that Gunew did grunt work towards this concrete aim.

The problem of multiculturalism here is the confusion of its status *as theory* or *as policy*, where once its use in policy programmes – to varying degrees of success – would move the term away from the realm of an abstract idea and into practice: a cluster of government initiatives dedicated to reform the systematically exclusionary prior policies of white supremacy and assimilationism.[5] In a 2018 book, Gunew uses cosmopolitanism and cultural theory, against the bedrock of debates about modernity, to critique the contemporary status of the multicultural writer, arguing for "post-multicultural writers as neo-Cosmopolitan mediators" in an age of increased division between "West" and (Islamic) "non-West" under transnational capitalism. Now, we may add, we live in the destructive aftermath of that divi-

---

[5] Here Gunew harnesses Roland Barthes, an arresting theoretic turn. Gunew argues that immigrant poetry, or poetry by non-Angle-Celtic subjects, is read, surprisingly, not for its linguistic craft or "consciously wrought textuality" but for its autobiographical content: "Even poetry, the least transparently functional manifestation of linguistic self-consciousness, will be read for sociological and historical content" ("Denaturalizing", 114), then quoting Barthes on the speech of classical poetry as made socially acceptable for the conspicuousness of its conventions. Staking a claim to such conventions "are not simply acquired when setting foot on this continent" ("Denaturalizing", 114). It is a thrilling argument, even if the linguistic turn now feels so far in the past. Here still I will make relevant the craftedness of language in Walwicz, Fogarty and Stewart, but I hope the return to history through the lens of an avant-garde can be seen as neither a disavowal of textualism, a retreat to conspicuous conventions or, for that matter, an escape route from philosophy and theory.

sion, with all the Nasserisms and Ba'athisms, otherwise moderate Arab socialisms, all but lost in a region torn apart not just by the two major US wars – Iraq and Afghanistan – but by ongoing civil wars, as in Syria. The "West" may have likewise done away with the "Second World", but ghosts remain, with a new war on old Soviet territory, in Ukraine. These are imperial and geopolitical calamities. We cannot simply speak of internal politics in the West, in which we find an emboldened ethnofascism on the right, and on the liberal left in the First World a partial formalisation of the social politics of identity. The material basis of nations remains subject to internal-external dialectics, crossing global externalities with granular locales in the most extreme ways. Put in cosmopolitan and geopolitical terms, the return of Central Asia, Eastern Europe, Russia and China to the centre of international political tensions once again tells the story of a Global Majority, not just a Home Minority. Even the most casual observer can see how the tension between these two forces defines our political era. It will remain for a long time a multilingual problem too. At no point has it been so necessary, therefore, for Antipodal literary studies to get beyond the "monolingual paradigm" (Gunew, *Post-Multicultural*, 3), to rethink the question of "the one" (the pedagogical) and "the many" (the performative), echoing Bhabha, for a new era. Gunew still rings true; far from surmounting the national question, multicultural writers have found themselves badly "hinged" between national cultures and globalisation. Rather than speaking *to* nation they have often been assumed to be speaking *outside* nation, and:

> The national anxieties provoked by the foreigner or the guest (captured by terms such as *Gastarbeiter*) have been represented in many ways. Those who are certified (part of the canon or designated hosts) as contributing to the imagined community speak *to* the nation *for* the nation, and do so *to* the global as well. The question here is how to make the case that these post-multicultural writers speak *for* the nation as a way of bringing about a nation without nationalism (Gunew, *Post-Multicultural*, 11)

Were it that a critique of multiculturalism was simply now constructive – perfecting the liberal-democratic project for the legitimacy of its hosts – the figure of the *Gastarbeiter* would, while at least avoiding the worst of cultural nationalism, further entrench the nation-boundedness of multicultural projects. It has become increasingly clear that what was once a dilemma that pitted the proletarian left against the intellectual elite (a word Gunew uses) occupying the centre (a dilemma that could occasionally boil down simply to "policy discussion") has morphed in the present-day to a geopolitical question; the status of multiculturalism *as* policy in countries increasingly bound together as a Western Bloc facing off against the East. The question of cosmopolitanism has rather folded dramatically in recent years to a new geopolitics in which Cold War mentalities have returned worldwide.

More recently political theorists such as Radhika Desai have advanced the phrase "geopolitical economy" to explain and ultimately do away with cosmopolitanism in a way that does not eschew cultural and class analysis but rather combines it with another set of discourses: multipolarity and the materiality of nations (1–29). Nations still matter, whether one opts for the suspect idea that the globalisation of capital is beyond nation altogether, or the imperialist reading which places the US nation, with its own scenes of mass dispossession, at the scene of a great disruption of world-polarities. Hemispheric or transnational frameworks are not defunct here but geopolitical economy brings the notion of societies of the state into the analysis of social relations. An individual poet would hardly seem to "matter" in these discourses, but we may see too that individuals, in strenuous negotiation with the cultural environment of a Anglo-American alliance state like Australia (especially after the AUKUS agreement), can tell us much about the experience of the geopolitical dialectic and how this dialectic informs experience. This indeed may be a better way to track how persons or groups from different political systems come to experience a new political system or social fabric: here culture alone is not the deciding factor for national maladjustment in the capitalist world order.

It is not possible, in any political account of experimental migrant literature today, to get beyond a primary multipolar description, for the materiality of nations is pervasive, yet neither should one assume anything of the said subject in advance – some Western-centric idea that the incoming other is simply "yearning" for freedom or democracy, or a preference for one political system over another. Geopolitical economics can be factored in to the very analysis of public policy itself, a theoretical approach which should be much more robust than dealing just with the cultural experiences of migrants who find themselves in "Western" democracies. We are often trained to expect a straightforward defiance against socialist morality or state power, much less a complex historical and geopolitical examination of the faultlines that lead to these contexts in the first place. But they are there, whether or not it is apparent yet to cultural theory or to literary-historical analyses, and Walwicz has drawn attention to such matters:

I was brought up in a communist country where the writer had to have some message to offer to improve society, an educational role. That was my first idea of art. I think writing stems from the personal needs of the writer. One writes for oneself, first. The writer does though affect other people, alters people . . . One can be other people. (Lysenko and Brophy, n.pag)

Thus the postsocialist subject cannot, no matter how long estranged from the societies formed under those states, fully shed that memory. Walwicz here recalls the social function of the author (and, for that matter, the state-socialist critic) instilled in her from childhood, showing that the impact it had was longlasting. In *Palace of Culture* part 25, "hammer" (58–9), which Walwicz performed at Melbourne Spoken Word festival in 2015, the recurrence of the word "hammer" does not so much incur semantic satiation, for the listener, as resensitise and rephysicalise the word against the backdrop of a party-state machinery that has been seared into the psyche and its languages. We hear this too in "Cut Tongue and the Mechanism of Defence", published in *Southerly*, which begins: "i'm army in army me defence i'm defence now my father marshall general zhukov he is my leader" (93). One cannot expect to see *application* here. In Australian political history, any horizon of a proletarian state was made impossible well before the Labor Party's expulsion of communists, and the long and drawn-out "great split". In 1949, just as enormous swathes of the world's population began to live under the rule of socialist states, and even as Albert Einstein penned "Why Socialism", flagging it as the only viable path, Australia voted for Menzies, putting behind it the Labor years of reconstruction and falling headlong into the Cold War period governed by conservatives. The geopolitical situation remained inseparable from labour questions at home. Public attitudes to the welfare state went into virtual retreat from more universalist attitudes between 1967 and 1988, going from "avant-garde" to "rearguard", as F. D. Gruen curiously puts it in a 1989 discussion paper for the ANU Centre for Economic Policy Research: "These policies require changes in the mechanics of the system – rather than its overhaul as so often urged from both the Right and the Left" (30). Multiculturalism as policy was born, in Australia, nonetheless, at the very point the last discussions of the socialist-democratic (rather than, strictly speaking, social-democratic) administration of the state was discussed, namely during the Whitlam years. During this period multiculturalism would become part of government policy, in 1973, only shortly after it was instituted in Canada in

1971, and shortly thereafter the neoliberal or financial phase of capital swept the globe, taking Australia with it. Walwicz finds herself in an Australia that first disavows socialism before embracing multiculturalism.

The experience not only of hemispheric renewal – to have found oneself in the Southern Hemisphere, the Antipodes, away even from the dichotomies of Socialist East and Capitalist West that rent the twentieth century in two – is the experience too of stepping outside the societal expectations, stepping out of time, too. If multiculturalism was policy before theory, then finding a theory to fill out the policy, as Gunew's cogitations show, turns up very little. A geopolitics of the brain, so to speak, rather emerges to interrupt any expectation of a host-guest dialectic described solely in the terms of an isolated internal politic. Walwicz's transnational avant-garde horizon takes in modes of poetic expansivity both Antipodean and hemispherically ambiguous. A hemispheric avant-garde after the 1970s troubles a straightforward cosmopolitanism, particularly in light of avant-garde *anomalies* in their "post-" or "neo-" instances. Avant-gardists who crossed hemispheres were expressing neither new-found freedom nor a full-scale revolt against the new society they found themselves in. They rather found themselves negotiating a dialectic between these two states or a nuanced position carrying neither. I do not wish to read Walwicz as one simply opposed to, or "displaced" by, the Antipodes, unless it provides a conceptual basis in poetics, because Walwicz's "stance" on Australia as a cultural-national entity is, as we have heard, enrhythmed with an intricacy that the nomination of multicultural writer cannot fully describe. I am tempted by cosmopolitanism, but certainly that transposition of societal experience on the one hand and geopolitical background on the other turns out a better analytic. Writers whose heritage was a socialist society in which literature was to fulfil a "social" function, who subsequently found themselves in a society in which multiculturalism became policy, like Walwicz, show in language the primacy of the subject in ways not easy to understand for a reader or critic unfamiliar with the ins and outs of the twentieth-century state socialist experiment. The forms of Walwicz's poetry contain these clashing and jarring rhythms of society and its proximity to states, nations and blocs, locked in economic conflict or bound together in financial or military alliances; reading it so is to read the politics of form in an absorptive sense, to read manifold political and institutional forms as taken in by the poetic fabric. It's an "unresolved" poetics, requiring less paranoid as contradictory reading.

VI. *Absorptive Underreadings, or, Avoiding Translatability*

To read Walwicz in any of the ways proposed I hope affords future readers great latitude. A *critical exterior*, that is the performance of reading, of presenting to readers the work of the critical reading, can tempt us either to overread or to underread. Put before the task of critique, either we read too much into it, or through caution, too little. I wish, of course, to have underread. The critical jouissance of the overreading quickly descends to the dark night of the critic, who too would be immured in poetic gloom, or like Frye in a late notebook meditation on Blake, back in square one with the question of intuition: "I've spent nearly eighty years trying to articulate intuitions that occupied about five minutes of my entire life" (636). Yet we reserve here a place for the critic who reads, spends time intuiting and guessing, that is *not* the space of the poet, a space that is neither just theoretical nor only historical, and certainly not creative. At minimum, we have moved from the complications of the margin-mainstream dichotomy, to how avant-garde traditions square with a so-called Establishment, to questions of sound, to the appetite for dissonance, to the scene and the process of inventive writing, and back out to elements of measure, scale, culture, nation and world politics. On the level of the text, Walwiczian prosody moves between euphony and dissonance, voice-writing and page-writing; precisely relations between time and text, score and performance. But the synecdochal aspect of these prosodies meant a path again to the scale of these expansive geometries or textual patterns. Scale in Walwicz could signal matters of society, the palaces of (official) culture, nation, nationalism, hemisphere, Australian literature as a whole, Polish cultural identity, avant-garde identity, writ large on the scale of writing, the language of desire and preoccupation with the larger numbers.

Overreadings? Hardly. Still much is yet to be said. Languages of invention encapsulate the poetics of Walwicz. Ania Walwicz's Polish is in some respects a work of metatranslation, or the contradiction of translation and untranslatability, for while it is true that Walwicz would not have become Walwicz without crossing from socialism to postsocialism, or from socialist bloc to Western bloc, it is also true that by leaving Poland Walwicz comes into the Anglophone sphere. To translate it "back out" again would seem to be asking too much, in part because of the size and perceived difficulty of Walwicz's works. Yet the sense of scale is precisely that, a reader's *sense*, a perceived downsizing or upsizing of the poem's capacity. Expansive thus does not mean inclusive, as it might for an American writer, but rather the authority of a type of writing that refuses to be small, to be contained, no matter how distorted our shifting scales have become. In refusing the small, it simultaneously refuses translation.

The geopolitics of hemispheres gives us a better sense now of what a "belated" avant-garde, operating in spatial terms on the outer edges of influence and reception, can show in the theatre of modernity. Analyses of modernity have always had to contend with the social and historical, but also the psychosocial, and in Walwicz, equally important as the author's social function is the interior world, the individuation taking place between the one and the many. The "politics" of language comes to our attention in ways that sound hardly different from debates about the politics of surrealism, with and without "thematisation" as such. "Theme" risks overreading, and is not the end of a literary politics. Or, like much else, theme falls to patterns of representation. Form, as many things as that can mean, is as much a support system, a "body", or body-politic, for a poem's politics, as theme. I do not think that the study of form on its own terms is a deficient move, especially if form can be understood in a more spatial way; one cannot leave it just at that, but even such formal study takes time, effort and concentration for a poet like Walwicz. I mean not to separate theme (mind) and form (body), just as much as it would be amiss to separate narrative and textual function. Yet the dismissal of (book) form, poetics, paginality and affective or no less aesthetic properties language can lead, I think, to even more deficient readings of the poem's politics. If I have encouraged *paginal reading*, at middle distance, or for the sake of it, middle distance reading full stop, it has been neither to pry us away from book logic, the *discursus*, nor to enforce an overly prosaic reading of Walwicz's poetics; an endless descent into the subcursive careen of lines, punctuation, words, spaces (or bubbles). Readings at middle distance allow us to proceed along both registers.

Fogarty's powerful poetics in the next chapter also concerns the scales of a national literature in the deeper sense of First Nations radicalism. It will be incumbent upon us to ask about the place where writing starts, the underpinning of poetics, of language in socio-political struggle, as that which articulates the volatility of radical combat against mass dispossession, colony, genocide and historical violence that marks and defines Australia's national and geopolitical history, not only between Federation and Commonwealth but in the aftermath of the Frontier Wars. Fogarty's target is carceral capitalism. We read it in a new and more aggressive era of US imperialism and military hegemony.[6] Beyond just "theme", "politics" in Fogarty takes a toll on the lexical strains of lines and words. It finds political expression, if I can put it that way, in a philosophical and prophetic treatment of time. This is how we will *hear-see* politics. Cornel West has called it Black prophetic fire, a mode neither dystopian nor utopian. There too we read bodies making space for desire in language, written and enrhythmed to dissonances improper or thrillingly absorptive, but with an eye to the future. It requires an adjustment of critical approach, a set change in material poetics: *space to time*. In the face of certain facts, there seems nothing more insurrectionary than moving the discussion along from history to time itself, a problematic begun with Walwicz.

Having documented, in history, or for history, another Antipodean actor in the hemispheric avant-gardes, my doubt at any reliance on the retrograde quality of intuition should not be rectified by calling upon the catalogue: this is not an anthology. A difficult cultural and national dislocation made this reinvention of language happen. We need not categorise or quantify it further. Doing something as risky as a poetics which neither conforms to the socialised "standards" of poetic language nor rests solely on the received standards of the historical avant-gardes renders the work neither an anomaly nor canonical in the field of national literature. Perhaps it does, in Gunew's terminology, issue forth a kind of counter-public sphere. But I am aware that to locate the political in poetics is to make a mark in time that will be read differently across the ages. Even if all language is political in the public ear, which I am inclined to fully accept, the *topos*, place, that is to say, of politics in the poem, even its "theme", opens itself to a parallax view at the moment of its articulation. For now we desist, so this old question can be renewed in the next chapter. Now radical formal invention gets with political combat.

---

[6] It is good to keep an eye on equivalent global comparisons on the level of national literatures. I have not deployed the term "diasporic literature", which Chinese critic Wang Guanglin uses in *Translation in Diasporic Literatures*, which for the first time gives a closer look at Chinese-Australian literature in translation. Neither have I made use of the phrase "diasporic avant-gardes", from a collection by Carrie Noland and Barrett Watten, but it becomes more relevant below. To return briefly to some points raised by Spivak in her conversation with Gunew, something drastically different is occurring in the study of American poetry: a growing sense that American poetry has been written under the sign of dispossession. The ramifications of this for historical rereadings of American poetry, some happening right now, will be nothing short of revolutionary.

Chapter 6

Lionel Fogarty's Historical Style

Poetry is only relevant when it changes the bloody law!
– Fogarty (2019)

Every indigenous individual has the right to a nationality.
– Article 6,
UN Declaration on the Rights of Indigenous Peoples (2007)

There is a lot we don't yet know about Spivak's *Critique of Postcolonial Reason*, subtitled *Toward a History of the Vanishing Present*. Its history can in fact be said to begin in the Antipodes, because it was in a 1986 interview with the *Melbourne Journal of Politics* that Spivak first notes that she is "perpetrating" a certain manuscript then called "Master Discourse, Native Informant: Deconstruction in the Service of Reading" (*Post-Colonial Critic*, 48). It would take some fourteen years for this to be realised under a different name as the 1999 *Critique*. Jane Gallop alleges that (if we exclude Spivak's 1974 book on Yeats, which is a notable exclusion here), in 1986 Spivak's influence was enough to merit invitations to Australia even though she "has not yet written a book" (117).

But it seems to have been on the agenda for this manuscript all along in that its concern for Kant's *Critique of Judgement*, its titular model, frames the critique of Kant's invocation of the "New Hollander" in a passage that perpetrates the axiomatics of imperialism. Although he may have chosen the inhabitants of these areas "by reasons of euphony", as Spivak puts it in a footnote, "casually" rather than "causally", this chance argument affects judgement itself. Spivak puts it precisely like this:

1. But if in Kant's world the New Hollander (the Australian Aborigine) or the man from Tierra del Fuego could have been endowed with speech (turned into the subject of speech), he might well have maintained that, this innocent but unavoidable and, indeed, crucial example – of the antinomy that reason will supplement – uses a peculiar thinking of what man is to put him out of it. We find here the axiomatics of imperialism as a natural argument to indicate the limits of the cognition of (cultural) man. The point is, however, that the New Hollander or the man from Tierra del Fuego *cannot* be the subject of speech or judgment in the world of the *Critique*. (26)
2. Such a reading is of course also "mistaken" because it attempts to engage the (im)possible perspective of the "native informant," a figure who, in ethnography, can only provide data, to be interpreted by the knowing subject for reading. Indeed, there can be no correct scholarly model for this type of reading. It is, strictly speaking, "mistaken," for it attempts to transform into a reading-position the site of the "native informant" in anthropology, a site that can only be read, by definition, for the production of definitive descriptions. It is an (im)possible perspective. In Kant, we made no claim to restore the "miraculated" perspective of a native Australian or Fuegan. Here, too, we are not proposing the restoration of the plausible perspective of a Hindu contemporary of Hegel's bemused by the reading. (In fact, a few decades later, the slow epistemic seduction of the culture of imperialism will produce modifications of the *Gitā* that argue for its world historical role in a spirit at least generically though not substantively "Hegelian." And these will come from Indian "nationalists." If the student of culture wishes to pursue this further, the scrupulous difference between the figuration of the native informant in the text of Kant and Hegel should lead her to investigating the differences in the oppression of the Australian Aborigine and groups like the Fuegans and the production of the dominant Hindu colonial subject, rather than positing a unified "third world," lost, or, more dubiously, found lodged exclusively in the ethnic minorities in the First.) (*Critique*, 49).

The two major parts of the reading, presented at length above, show that, point the first; the Antipodal and American men cannot be the subject of speech or judgement, but that, point the second; this impossible perspective opens more hemispheric problems of how to situate the so-called native informant of Kant and Hegel in the Third and First Worlds. For the other major context of the *Critique* is the fall of the Second World, that occurs between the inception and production of the *Critique*, and which Spivak is acutely conscious of throughout. The student of culture finds, then, that Kant's "foreclosure of the Aboriginal" is not only connected with the production of the Hindu colonial subject, but how *that* vanishing present, between the collapse of the Second World and the financialisation of the globe, produced new hemispheric axes within which these impossible or miraculated descriptions would fall. That time, 1999, to be exact, was another cusp; perhaps we will have no further versions of Spivak's *Critique* that would catch up or update its terms to the *present* present, and these contradictions largely remain.

The use of the phrase "native informant" has crossed over to discussions of African-American poetry. Aldon Lynn Nielsen closes a study on African-American poetic innovation, which included readings of Russell Atkins, with a nod to the native informant, an even more difficult use of the word, in relation to how historically white universities and colleges "study black people's poems". Frequently, Nielsen says, the poets are "reduced" as they are "elevated": "Election to the status of the syllabus is sometimes accomplished to an accompaniment of enlistment as native informant" (193). This is in the context of a discussion of Du Bois, Fanon, Sartre and Cortez, but we may "interdict" it (Nielsen's term) similarly: no "nourishment" is to be had by reading First Nations avant-gardes. If anything it is trouble, trouble to the core, trouble to the terms, trouble to the power of naming, trouble in the text. In the case of Aboriginal poetry the idea of the "native informant" becomes relevant in the Spivakian sense of connection with the "Third World" in a specific way, namely a "Fourth-World-ing" within the First. The prolonged attack on First Nations people is linked directly to the activity of the Australian government as an instrument of imperialism and war; its involvement in the Iraq and Afghanistan wars, and AUKUS as part of a Pacific NATO dedicated to the strategic containment of China. A bourgeois state in the Western bloc would not give up its resources to traditional owners for the very same reason it saw fit to plunder the resources of the Third World and contain the Second. From a Colonial to Colonial-Commonwealth era an external politics always folded with an internal one. Aboriginal avant-gardes raise the question of geopolitical poetics. Locality reflects "up" to the larger frameworks of hemisphere, imperialism and geopolitical division or distribution. This produces another set of contradictions. The idea of an Aboriginal avant-garde is directly resonant with the original historical avant-gardes, as we saw with Tzara, and yet far and foreign from it. Aboriginal avant-gardes might have caused all the time trouble in the first place. This is where the entire discourse comes under most stress, in that however much there has been a building, or *Bildung*, of an avant-garde that has come before, this is where that building, or *Bildung*, is taken down and reexamined for its parts. An added complication – not all First Nations poets write like Fogarty, and the question of what a First Nations avant-garde *is* cannot be answered in one chapter. That the avant-garde is a Master Discourse, for which we must then have Native Informants, is an idea to be resisted, and yet those contradictions won't be settled by brushing them aside. There is no correct scholarly model for *this* kind of reading, as Spivak insists for *that* one. In Walwicz a sense of scale and space are part of a language of desire inseparable from the long history of avant-garde poetry, and like the early avant-gardes of the twentieth century, this linguistic desire is mixed with anti-establishment politics and problems of prosody. There the discourse of the excluded or marginalised migrant writer dominates; doubly excluded both on the basis of holding a migrant identity and being avant-garde, but what we have here is a *recentralisation* of the First Nations avant-gardes at the scene of a revolutionary war against the whole frame of inclusion and exclusion in scenes of white writing.

It is to history and, consequently, literary history, that we will be looking to find additional layers of significance in the works and prosodic styles of Lionel G. Fogarty. A Yugambeh man born on Wakka Wakka land (mapped as South-Western Queensland), in 1958, Fogarty is one of a select group of poets writing after 1970 who have repeatedly earned the title "avant-garde" in criticism and in commentary, a claim I too will make, but in ways that merit strong query. It is Fogarty's poetic and political language that gives us another sense of the vanishing present and our hemispheric situation. That the issue of its vanguardism has been raised, again, both says a lot and leaves a lot unsaid.

I. Manifesting Liberation: Aboriginal Avant-Gardes Outside White Time

In a historicist piece on avant-garde manifesto archives Laura Winkiel finds that the uptake of the form of the manifesto from late sixteenth-century France to the Romantics "codes the entwining of aesthetics and politics that structures the manifesto form and determines its functioning for the next two centuries" (254). It is a type of revelation that superposes word upon deed, and vice versa, and so as such it is not simply a rhetoric of action but a double rhetoric in which the persuasive act is itself a deed; a proleptic presentism that is the revelation of revelation, and a revelation of the future-present, or future-made-present. Thus one can place manifestos beside Schlegel's *Athenaeum Fragments*, in part because Philippe Lacoue-Labarthe and Jean-Luc Nancy are able to call the writers clustered around the journal *Athenaeum* the first avant-garde in history, but also because by function they are the creators of something novel in German Romanticism, a sense that little magazines and anthologies are literature, that in its prophetic mode we find confirmation of an affinity between *Ars Poetica* and manifestos: "they both gesture towards the overcoming of their own impossibility" (Winkiel, 257). Most curiously, Winkiel uses the phrase "postcolonial avant-gardes", through the work of Arjun Appadurai and Vincent Huidobro, to explain the cosmopolitanism of manifestos after Futurism. The manifesto displaced narratives of origin, which is true for most of the major manifestos, and particularly Tzara in Zurich, as we well know. Thus the "postcolonial avant-gardes ... went a step further: Only those cosmopolitan writers who sought to carve out an enunciative position for non-Western peoples explicitly confronted the colonized and racialized history of those originary narratives" (260). Time-lag tends to frame the avant-gardes of the colonies, the notion of First Nations populations playing "catch-up" with modernity, and as such "avant-gardes from the colonies critiqued the Eurocentrism of the European avant-gardes in their manifestos even while they deployed similar iconoclastic gestures" (260). Using the example of Oswald de Andrade's "Cannibal Manifesto" of 1928 (São Paulo), a Latin American avant-garde reworks the "primitivist discourse of colonial indigeneity into an ironic performative stance, illustrates a spatial aesthetic of simultaneity rather than a linear temporal framework of primitivism/futurity" (262). The account Winkiel gives *needs* (the word I would most like to use now) to be considered and *applied* (another word that does not need application all the time) to theories of avant-gardes as we know them, with and without the North–South history of the manifesto. It needs to be applied because the struggle to decolonise and reread avant-gardes in this type of light is ongoing and unfinished.

In the Antipodes, Indigenous groups wrote political manifestos. In 1963 the Yolngu people wrote and delivered the Yirrkala bark petitions to the Lower House, a plea for land rights. In 1969 the National Tribal Council issued a "cultural pluralism" manifesto to fight back against the failing Assimilation policies of the era and call for self-education. And as recently as 2014 the Freedom Summit held in the Northern Territory produced an "Aboriginal Sovereign Manifesto of Demands", which begins:

> We, the Aboriginal Sovereign Peoples with the National Aboriginal Freedom Movement demand that the Commonwealth of Australia begins negotiations to establish a time frame for our decolonisation, through Treaties under the Vienna Convention on the Law of Treaties with the legitimate authorised representatives of each Nation State. This will form the basis of the recovery framework for the healing from the devastation wreaked upon Aboriginal Nations and Peoples by State sanctioned genocide and gross violations of human rights.

The Commonwealth of Australia has committed itself to temporal lag and delay; what the summit demands is a time-frame. These are political, not aesthetic manifestos, and not in the same tone as Dada or Futurism, but in pointing to deferrals of justice they anticipate another "original narrative" for history in its movement toward futurity. It isn't always a time-space narrative without a centre either, as the role of "base camp" in the 2017 *Uluru Statement from the Heart* shows. "Remoteness" is often a place where the narrative begins or returns to. As noted in Chapter 1, Biddle's account of the "remote avant-garde" put "remoteness" on the map, so to speak, as a focal point of avant-garde spatial contradictions. But the devastation and genocide that these manifestos speak of is directly relevant: Yugambeh land, Fogarty's country, was invaded in the early nineteenth century, and the result was the killing and displacement of Yugambeh groups, with members forced into reserves and missions at the height of the long Frontier Wars. Remoteness is a problem for an avant-garde when it is figured as the triumph of the advanced culture of the city. The centre mythologises remoteness. But First Nations history doesn't follow that of European spatialisations of progressive time-space, nor does its pattern of social development mirror societies elsewhere in comparative periods of history, and although Aboriginal societies have always been productive, the productive forces in Aboriginal society didn't bring about the same contradictions between town and country. "Country" and "history" already have to be redefined. The manifestos show already how the discourse of a history of avant-gardism in the context of the development of productive forces would force all forms of avant-gardism back into a European temporal discourse. Thus what we need first is some sense of Aboriginal time. The example of "Decipherer", one of several poems in which Fogarty directly addresses questions of history and a First Nations sense of time, brings these historical and spatial contradictions to light. It contains the refrain: "History unbalanced kept me 'dead' indecipherable. / Future ballad themes honour me ..." (*Mogwie-Idan*, 78). The refrain then returns in varied tenses as follows:

> Between sound and colour 'I am a bit.'
> Between music strangely I'm beyond white time
> Affirmation give techniques limitless in my
> Plain chant transfiguration musics.
> History unbalances kept me 'dead' decipherer.
> Alternative world is moving those dislocations. (78-9)

Tenses change, most starkly, with "kept". Spirit is where the poem begins, as of Creation: "Uncharted harmony and I get accent" in ways that ages enrhythm, ages that give breath over "uncharted" waters. In the beginning "Uncharted activated waters / reveal unflushed originators" (78). The poetic eschatology seems secure: at the end the poem touches again upon anticipatory posterity, but that will not be where we finish our reading of this poem (I'll return to it later). The between in this poem is the contradiction, brought about by what from one temporal perspective is being in an alternative world that dislocates white time. Fogarty then hints at some future, historically redemptive readership blowing through the poem's final breaths:

> Reality in redemptive insights
> sweats over my blowing riddles
> those complacent will quest not my poet
> my reliability lies in wait, in caves.
> My true darling breath testifying customs
> whelming histories want evasive thinking.
> Translucent sea will catch my fantastic wildfires. (79)

The poem ends anticipating a future, some stored future, not quite utopic but different to now-time, again within the alternative world-narrative of the lines previous. Yet what *is* this world, alternative, redemptive, musical (that temporal art), in which the indecipherable Fogarty will be read? Who is the un/deciphered, and who the decipherer? In a poem not over two pages long, how does Fogarty achieve such a taut temporal arc? What slight bend or unbalancing then drops one end of the scale and in that dropping engenders a sort of historical indecipherability? Is this a way of speaking about historical scales of recognition, or are we rather testifying before the scales of justice? What kind of evasive thinking, evasive or invasive, has "whelmed" histories? What whelming, which from Middle English *whelmen* means also capsize, bringing the translucent sea to wild thought or wild emotion, overturns or casts down what we know about history? What whelmed histories find themselves buried or brought to ruin?

Let us not let time wander too far from space. Some further historical excursions: in the poem "Aphorism Wealth Grazier" history needs geography, and with that, spatial remapping of white place. "What white map man drew this map of world / geography scale? Then history said / It's wrong. Now we Aboriginals have Gondwanaland / sea even universal map to banner the land mass calling Australia" (*Mogwie-Idan*, 63). Elsewhere history gets a sci-fi, prophetic boost. We find ourselves back at the beginning of invasion before landing in the future with the poem "1788 to the Gates of 2028s", where "Whitewash as another history now", and as the last line shows, "Has history another places, we'll see OK" (93). This poem appears in the book *Ealahroo (Long Ago) Nyah (Looking) Möbö-Möbö (Future)*, a book especially occupied with time and space both in historical and theoretical terms. Fogarty indicated in a 2019 interview that he could find the "fragmentary" format of poetry a way of *doing history*, or at least doing record (as his family would resist in letters to bailiffs and mission managers). The challenge to literary history here comes not from theories or philosophies of time in the Western sense. More readily do we have to meet the shift from literary history to literary theory. Time's essence and character not only moves us away from a fixed conception of "history", by breaching the enormity of space, and time; when comes the horizon of a continental and hemispheric consciousness of history in the senses we have so far imagined, a path may be to enter into the prophetic mode. Science fiction, "deep futures", may be a way into, or out of, the historical poetics we're confronted with in these lines on history – just as contextually relevant would be Sun Ra, and Afro-Futurism – as much deep pasts of traditional-pluri-national culture. As Fogarty put it in a 2011 interview on Poetry International, Dreamtime is a 60,000-year plus history of First Nations civilisation (Brennan, "Interview").

If Fogarty is an avant-garde poet, the question of how, or whether to frame it in existing histories is difficult. We have seen that postcolonialism, either in its strictly Spivakian and originally critical sense or in Winkiel's formation of the "postcolonial avant-gardes", coupled with the adjective "remote", can be moderately useful. Yet there are a number of comparative analyses that do historical work placing Fogarty alongside poets from other hemispheres. Stuart Cook crosses Fogarty with Paulo Huirimilla. Cook is able to read Indigenous, and Mapuche avant-garde poetry, through Fogarty and Huirimilla, as genre-hybrid, even "genre diasporic", in the terms of Pierre Joris (20, 276). We may indeed see that discussions in the American context turn up interesting results. Ameer Chasib Furaih has paired Fogarty with African-American poets Sonia Sanchez and Amiri Baraka. Another reading by John Charles Ryan brings Fogarty closer to contemporary American poetry as a "Western" literature. For Ryan, Fogarty *hybridises* the orality of the song tradition and "configurations of literary modernism", and as such, the "flattened rhythms, abrupt transitions, and linguistic density of Fogarty's verse align him, in a Western context, with experimental and modernist poetics and, to some extent, with the avant garde Language poets of the late 1960s and 1970s in the United States" (237).[1]

To further compare Fogarty with Language Writing may turn up interesting results. Yet however we might locate Fogarty in the world history of the avant-gardes, it is unlikely to be in the "First World" poetic ambit we are used to. The United States does figure in Fogarty's political and literary imagination but with reference to First Nations American sovereignty. Internationalist threads and lines of solidarity here are clear in the foreword to Fogarty's first book, *Kargun*, published in 1980 when he was twenty-two years old. The international dimension of his activism is revealed in terms of Indigenous solidarity across hemispheres. It notes that in 1976 "he travelled to the United States and addressed a meeting of the American Indian Movement at the Second International Indian Treaty Council at South Dakota. He met Russell Means, Leonard Crow Dog, Jimmie Durham and many others who further influenced his will to fight, and gave him a broader understanding of international struggles" (n.pag.). The Indigenous internationalism of Fogarty's work in political struggle must be understood as the basis of an aesthetic ideology across his work that is also, and necessarily, anti-imperialist. It will additionally inform our sense of how this work is "avant-garde". Though, as above, commentary has made such connections between Fogarty's work and the early twentieth-century avant-garde, Fogarty's poetry will both shore up and go against many of the assumptions we may

---

[1] Though Fogarty cannot be read as a diasporic poet, diasporic studies of the avant-garde have expanded the vocabulary beyond existing Euro-US frameworks in ways useful here, as for instance Joseph Jonghyun Jeon's study of an Asian-American avant-garde, which takes racialisation far beyond dominant formations of identity, of use to majoritarian and global political senses of poetics today.

make about the historicity of the avant-gardes and the notions of history we have thus far arrayed. In an essay on Lionel Fogarty's 1983 poem "Biral Biral", Ali Alizadeh avoids what he deems the mainstay of "multicultural" reading to uncover something else: "Fogarty's poetry is not a mimetic extension of a fixed cultural identity and can much more convincingly be described as a formulation of a new, radical politicized subjectivity" ("Naming", 132). Alizadeh goes on to say that "Nor is his anti-mimetic, avant-gardist poetics in keeping with the general tendency of postmodernist Australian experimental poetry" ("Naming", 132). *Despite* his experimental slash postmodern aesthetics (here also poetics), Fogarty seeks to transform and subvert identity and belonging. The other "effective" poems of radical migrant writers, including Π.O. and Ouyang Yu, Alizadeh says, anticipate a "just and egalitarian society beyond the limitations of today's identity politics" ("Naming", 132–3). There is no need to pursue further here the difficulties with the reception of radical migrant writing outside precise meanings presented in the poetics of these writers. Without saying what this opposition means in poetics – the character, style, composition of "experimental" poetry, and who is writing it, is not revealed in this analysis – Alizadeh pits avant-garde, justice-oriented, against postmodern, experimental and identitarian. Identity is seen here yoked to contemporary media discourse, and so on – and is therefore "wrong", a not desirable (multiculturalist) sense, one that in fact has to be subverted and resisted, for Alizadeh, to uncover a real politics – what is "avant-garde" is on the side of that which is truly new, a radically politicised spirituality or subjectivity.

Yet we can also add weight to this argument by referring again to our previous term, imperialism. Rather than pitting avant-garde radical subjectivity – as some quasi-Proudhonist spirit of eternal justice – against bourgeois multiculturalism, we can rather historically locate multiculturalism-as-policy, or indeed the identitarian discourse, within the various geopolitical and imperial contexts of the "Western" bloc and the materiality of nations that serves as its ideological basis. Fogarty's poetry, because it cannot be construed diasporic or multicultural and is simply not that by definition, will thus clash with the discourses we have contructed for the avant-gardes because it doesn't comfortably fit within the discourses of liberal Western multiculturalism. Fogarty's poetry is non-Western and internationalist, aligned more closely with real struggle and geopolitical vision, as we will see particularly with Fogarty's interest in the liberated southern states of Africa. Nor can we attempt, as we learn from Spivak, the return of a Native Informant-style approach. If we have denied the notion of Native Informant, we also deny the Master Discourse, just as the idea of an establishment against which an avant-garde is pointed has become complex. Still, the question of an avant-garde in relation to Fogarty has been of significant concern to criticism because of its difficulty; what it precisely is that is "difficult" to an "establishment" has been changing, and will change, among an Australian readership, and in the global readership comparatively. Here we may be in the "territory" of what Charles Altieri and Nicholas Nace have called "comparative difficulty studies" (ii). Fogarty's difficulty takes place on multiple fronts, as avant-garde and as Aboriginal. It never ceases to be a difficulty of literary history and genealogy – should Fogarty be read beside younger poets in the contemporary experimental vein, with associated affects and formal-aesthetic approaches, or in line with, say, the emergent avant-gardes of the 1970s? How does Fogarty fit into international poetic fields, if at all? Does Fogarty's poetry escape routine historicisation, and if so, why?

II. *Foundations of Historical Style*

This critical attempt to place Fogarty as operative in an avant-garde need not stray much further from the poems quoted already above as to the theme of history, for I want to approach Fogarty's poetry from the perspective of "historical style" for good reason. There are a number of key historical contradictions that need closer explication; between theory and history, history and prophecy, prosody and style, invasion, liberation struggles and geopolitics, nonviolence, war, peace and the volatility of struggle, constellations of avant-garde and experimental, Indigenous and Asia-Pacific cultures, and most acutely the contradiction of Aboriginality and avant-gardism. Penny van Toorn, writing on the critical heritage of Oodgeroo Noonuccal (Kath Walker, 1920–1993, a similarly internationalist Indigenous poet), exposes the latter contradiction. Oodgeroo would prove difficult for critics because she was not difficult in the sense we are speaking of here:

> Essentialist beliefs about Aboriginality also shaped early evaluation of Oodgeroo's work. Some critics saw her as too modern to be authentically Aboriginal; others saw her as too old-fashioned and rhetorical to be a proper poet. "Real Aborigines" were stereotyped as

traditional song*men* who spoke no English, had never used a pen, and were imprisoned by their ancient traditions. "Real poets," by contrast, were essentialised as avant-garde experimentalists who shunned obvious rhetoric, and broke heroically free of tradition by moulding language transgressively into obscure, indecipherable shapes. On the basis of such assumptions, a politically motivated "Aboriginal poet" – a female one at that – was a contradiction in terms. (30)

If van Toorn's avant-garde experimentalism means a similar thing as that described in this book over several historical periods, the misfortune of such contradiction in terms has not carried into contemporary criticism of Fogarty in the same way as it did for Oodgeroo. Fogarty has had the unusual fortune of being widely praised in criticism and commentary, not only as an avant-garde poet *par excellence*, but as an important if not great poet. John Kinsella's 2013 comment that "Poets who are looking to create new languages, such as Lionel Fogarty, give one hope" (46) comes closest to this. Looking for "energy and vitality" (pockets of which exist, but seen by the mainstream as "no more than nuisances"), Kinsella phrases it in context like this:

> It may seem that I am hoping for an "invasion" by the avant-garde, for external forces to work on this neutral space. But it's more a case of generating something within that would make such "occupation" unnecessary. Invite the ambassadors if you like, learn their tricks. If there *is* a polemical debate current today, it concerns the validity of "on-the-page" poetry and the relevance of "performance." In terms of the canon, the poet "reads," does not "perform" a work. Performance in Australia is associated with the left (Π.O., Nigel Roberts, Amanda Stewart, Chris Mann, and so on), though "the left" is a loose term that has more to do with content than with mode of delivery (46).

Kinsella's turn to Fogarty for hope illuminates well the fact that Fogarty can be perceived to sit among the ambassadorial manifestations this book seeks. How superlatives like "great" apply to poets after modernism is unknown at this point in history, but the scope of the work, particularly on a prosodic level, from *Kargun* to recent books, is wide-ranging. It can recall Blakean and Shakespearean elements, as well as the modernist avant-garde, and as this study's historical foci make apparent, there is a way of thinking through the relational history of avant-garde poetics in a timely or untimely relation with contemporary experimental poetics (I attend to this at the end of this chapter).

Historical style seems an oxymoron. Underneath "style" lies a gathering of intricacies. The phrase "politics of style" has been used by Daniel Hartley to mean the politics of the production of meaning, its ownership in practice, and there but for Ezra Pound, its status in modernism. Most curious is Hartley's move away from the purely strident analyses of avant-garde politics to throw some doubt on any essential bind between aesthetics and a particular social formation, encapsulated in this passage:

> The most important point to stress here is that *there is no necessary homology between authorial ideology, aesthetic ideology, stylistic ideology, and style.* It is quite possible for an author's own political stance to be at odds with the implicit politics of either her stylistic ideology or her empirical stylistic practice. Take Pound, for example: he combined an authorial ideology which was broadly fascistic with an avant-garde stylistic ideology, produced in the context of an aesthetic ideology which had downgraded poetry to a position of borderline irrelevance within the total social formation. On the other hand, of course, there are cases where an author's political stance is avowedly radical but her stylistic ideology largely conforms to the status quo of aesthetic ideology. (227)

The *other hand* of this formation is equally intriguing: poetry with politically radical intent, even relevance, may not partake of an aesthetics or poetics, a "stylistic ideology" of the avant-garde broadly conceived. There are many ways to see this at work, particularly in the contemporary Marxist or labourist lyric, where the means of expression is fairly straightforward, but the message is radical. So too in the contemporary gallery arts there is an avant-garde aesthetic ideology at work, but in the explanation and framing of the work, the language of institutions and institutional power is used to a dampening effect. The radical work of art sounds duller in the caption. I want to give equal weight to these facts. To make an assumption about the relation between "radical form" and "radical politics" is something I will avoid even if Fogarty is an unusual instance of these two things clashing together with credible intent and astonishing result. His is surely a poetics with strains of Glissant's "militant unity", a unity against the One, an intentionist oeuvre that *unties* as it structures itself (*Poetic Intention*, 9). Fogarty uses style to both convey and withhold meaning in language. Through stylemes of refinement and disruption, breaking-up and unifying, he pursues an intricacy on the one hand, and indurate militancy on the other. It comes to be nothing other than an education in historical style. This doubleness of intention calls for at least a double reading. For politics of style: a severe modification of terms. Duke held a different meaning for national literature, seeing it as a possibility but ultimately remaining scathing of it. Following Frantz Fanon, whom Fogarty read early on, a different conception of national literature, as part of the great drive against capitalist-imperialism, becomes apparent in the language of protracted war and native resistance. For the revolutionary critic it cannot be denied that the question of the party machine, which Fanon resisted ("After independence, the party sinks into an extraordinary lethargy" [137]), and the question of spontaneity were major difficulties, but Fogarty's imagining of victory is mainly concentrated to the pragmatics of the pre-liberation phase. For Fogarty the present time is still that of war. In the poem "Strangled in War" we have citations both of Malcolm X and Mao:

> Then taking the mistakes to the knowledge
>   of knowing destructive theories can be only
>   eliminated by outer change.
> Intaking violence to the extreme
> It is as X said, necessary
> Mao said, our war is to get rid of war.
> Their terrorism will stay
> If always there's capitalists in the terrorists ways
> For they want to lash, hunt, haunt, beast, break—
>   on and on (*Kargun*, 72)

From Maoist underwritings of communist theory to Malcolm X, these form some of the radical, and indeed "outer" knowledge foundations of Fogarty's political thinking, taken in to the textures of his political language. An Antipodal response to Mao's protracted war theory cannot be watered down in these lines – Fogarty is *at war* with the Australian bourgeois state, for it has declared war, and he is calling for the liberation of his people from it in the service of lasting peace. In Hartley's terms, political style, aesthetic ideology and stylistic ideology, however mixed, don't form an easily recognisable homology, that there is a "militant unity" here between poetry and its social and ideological function in no way solves (it rather supports) contradiction. Fogarty describes the roots of Land Rights philosophy in Earth Rights, more even than the legal history that became Native Title (Moore, "The Rally").[2] Thus the philo-

---

[2] Also in the interview with Dashiell Moore, Fogarty mentions his mentorship with Johnny Koowarta, Aboriginal land-claimant of the Wik nation.

sophical and poetic appeal of liberation, Maoism, X-ism, Fanonism, Peace and Human Rights discourses combine in Fogarty's complex Indigenous internationalism, a poetics-led critique clearly formed in the face of war. If anything is clear in this liberatory cluster it is the identity of the perpetrator, Capitalism, who is a close associate of Terrorism, but unlike the spectacle of Terror, Capital often disguises its violence. A poem that has often been quoted to illustrate Fogarty's politics in this vein is the following insurrectionary poem, titled "Capitalism – The Murderer in Disguise", that appeared in *Kargun* in 1980, later in the *New and Selected*:

> Look pig
>   what you do to our people.
>
> Who cares
> I'm locked up here
>   with no arms
>   no legs
>   but a body
>   and mind
>   really
>   my spirit.
> But I'm not going to be afraid.
> You don't make me afraid.
> Beware, we'll be out of your prisons
> I was afraid to write this one
>   real thing
>   but remember
> Your Enemy
> He's
> Ours TOO.
>   (*New and Selected Poems*, 145–6; *Kargun*, 94)

Fogarty links his own experience of violence to the reader as addressed: "your enemy" and "ours". It comes from experience: Fogarty was born on Cherbourg Aboriginal Reserve, a prison camp, ("15 years of maddened dreams", as in the poem "Stranger in Cherbourg Once Knew", *Kargun*, 69), and his brother Daniel Yock, a dancer, was murdered by police in 1993, in a case that would gain significant international recognition. When the enemy lets him out of prison *beware*, because without Treaty, without truce or cession of land, the struggle is not over. There are bloody consequences. In the long historical present, violence perpetrated upon Aboriginal people goes on and on, from the history of the Missions, Camps and

Reserves, to the Stolen Generations after the long Frontier Wars and the Northern Territory Intervention. Historical sequences of terror and genocidal violence perpetrated by a capitalist-imperialist state founded on white supremacy move from one era to the next. This is most palpable in the present, with deaths in custody, pullulating out to the wider Imperium. Julieka Ivanna Dhu's death at the hands of police in 2014 is but one of many acts of bourgeois-imperial state violence that have made for transnational comparisons with black deaths in police custody in countries like the US.

III. *Words Beyond All Acceptable Meaning: Guerrilla Reading*

The historical avant-gardes of the early twentieth century also came into existence in times of war; an Aboriginal avant-garde emerging from war might not be such a surprise, placed among these historical contexts. But in Fogarty, the ability to locate the cause of this violence further becomes an act of poetic clarity, or rather orchestrating a delicate balance between clarity and volatility to build a targeted language of poetic struggle. It is an intricate thought of nonviolence: blunt hammer of material and national liberation on one side, and on the other the pen, poetic refinement. The result is, it goes without saying, a whole lot of difficulty, but guerrilla writing of this sort requires guerrilla reading. To understand Fogarty is in part to get all this historical background in, but the words themselves do a lot. A blunt-intricacy thus follows, a *stylishness* in Fogarty's poem "Intricacies":

> INTRICACIES CAN
> BE UNDERSTOOD
> I KNOW YOU
> I BELIEVE YOU
> WHAT YOU THINK
> BUT I AM NOT SURE
> YOU REALISE
> DAT WHAT YOU HEARD
> IS NOT WHAT
> I MEANT.

Intricacies, politics of style: to cross the abyssal gap between style and politics and clarify misperceptions. To speak of historical style is to breach the impasse of aesthetics and politics but a little differently.

Political style, ironically perhaps, remind us at least colloquially of the way career politicians are described, or style of governance (a leader's style of leadership). What we mean by political and what we might mean by style need theoretical clarification beyond this ironic kick without wholly leaving it behind. On the political side we mainly refer to various kinds of insurrectionary activity; militant Indigenous opposition to white supremacy, internationalist or anti-imperialist migrants in multicultural society, non-Indigenous socialists and communists, with whom there may be solidarity, and in some measure, themes of class, labour, work, work style, public policy, political economy and the geopolitics of US and Commonwealth imperialism. Political style here is critical; it exposes the ways mass media is instrumentalised to both justify and disseminate the core messages and strategies of the imperial machinery. On the side of style: senses of writing, as well as grammar, syntax, meter, tone, register and, true to the origin of the word, the *stylus*, the pen as anti-colonial weapon, which Fogarty uses with an illustrative purpose. Those graphotextual and notationalist aspects have come into our theoretical ambit in the writing of Walwicz. Extraordinary, haunting llustrations by Cairns (Queensland) Aboriginal artist Johnny Cummins, one for each poem in *Kargun*, fill the book. They show a variety of styles, some Symboliste, many Blakean, or urban-disjunctive. To accompany the poem "Is Speaking My Ability" one illustration by Cummins shows a pen, stylus, that has written "A long time since I pick up a pen" (61).

Fogarty's granular descriptions of his practice, and in particular his closeness to illustration and drawing, gets us closer to his methodology and to questions of style as graphics. Style comes up in the introduction in the *New and Selected*, by Mudrooroo, who cites the flexibility and range of styles in Fogarty accordingly with reference to Frantz Fanon and language genocide. Fogarty is "Fanon's native", writes Mudrooroo, but one whose language has "not been assimilated into the language of the coloniser" (xiii). He elaborates:

> Lionel's poetry has a sweep of style and a breadth of content which no other poet in Australia can match. His style is all his own and sometimes he writes in a simple style akin to the poems of Jack Davis and Kath Walker. These poems are open in meaning and sentiment to all, but especially in his later poetry, he excels as a guerrilla poet wielding the language of the invader in an urge to destroy that imposition and recreate a new language freed of restrictions and erupting a multi-meaning of ambiguity. This hints at the many possibilities of meaning in a feeling language freed from the intellectual dreariness of

academic verse [...] And we may well be in the presence of an anti-poetry, a turning away of all that the critics hold dear, and in which even the rhythms are flattened out, sometimes changed abruptly, often discarded so that no sweet victory is held out to entice the reader who must grasp an entirety of feeling structure beyond dictionary meaning (xii–xiii)

The anti-poetry of Fogarty, for Mudrooroo, is not so simple as a black vernacular of the liberationist guerrilla poet, but rather a stylistic sweep of thetical blasts, graphic and prosodic inventions that break open channels of history. It is also anti-critical, which Philip Mead noticed in *Networked Language*. Mead argues for Fogarty's surrealism as against the compressed notion of vernacularity. The question is: For whom? What kind of reader? Sabina Paula Hopper, in an essay that lends considerable weight to reader response, stresses the "difficulty" of Fogarty's style in a way that, strangely through the obverse, leads to another *way* of reading Fogarty. Hopper again mentions the issue of style in relation to Mudrooroo's assessment:

> I would argue that Fogarty's style does not, as Johnson / Mudrooroo claims, necessarily become more difficult the further back we move chronologically. I indeed find the earliest poems in the *Kargun* (1980) and *Yoogum Yoogum* (1982) collections the most accessible. They are straightforward in meaning and, although Fogarty's individual style is already evident, the poems have not yet gained the complexity of the *Kudjela* (1983) or *Ngutji* (1984) poems, most of which come across as seemingly infinite accumulations of words. The words pound down on the non-Indigenous reader like hail stones, so that the reading experience is one of complete exhaustion and despair. (47)

Accessible for whom? What is despair for one reader might be exhilaration for another. In the interview with Moore, Fogarty speaks of it in terms of education, of doing creole through English, "lexi-grammatically" *teaching English*, teaching how English works culturally. It is frankly an (anti-)critical poetics, a guerrilla poetic education. Curious then to note that "words pounding down" on the reader, something that seems to be customary with reading experimental poetry, is itself a reading of style: exhaustion and despair are the result of complexity of style. But as we have seen, to ask the question of "accessibility" first out is not a good idea with Fogarty nor with poetry in general. It isn't a good idea precisely because readership is never a monolithic thing. To assume there is an immediate and common "consensus" about what is difficult and what is "digestible", is false. An Indigenous student in rural Australia might hear in Fogarty complete sense. Another may not. A hobbyist whose interest is, say, Beats or performance poetry may get a huge thrill out of the "seemingly infinite accumulations of words", while another, say a critic not interested in avant-gardes, writing for the *London Review of Books*, whose favourable examples might include Paul Muldoon, Simon Armitage or Billy Collins, and is liable to expect straightforward lyric language rather than explorations in the total reinvention of language itself, might deem Fogarty's "pounding down" excessive, perhaps even offensive. There is no correct way to read, but Fogarty's poetry does not assume a general reader. The point is, you can't assume a consensus about accessibility. What readers find "accessible" is often a surprise, and complex, and infinitely contextual.

Thus historical style is the measurement of its difficulty with regard to a horizon of expectations and a kind of "leadership" of style, a liberated forwardness as to the contradictions and difficulties it will visit upon the reader. Fogarty's historical style is the style of liberation, but liberation yet-to-come. How then can it be savoury? How then can it greet us as agreeable or smooth? This is not to suggest that Fogarty's writing practice, or its intended impact, is meant to be experimental in the sense of shock, it is simply to say that if one is a reader of avant-garde poetics, words pound down regularly, and in part, the critical vocabulary around experimental writing, even the "critical industry" around it, has grown accustomed to finding ways of speaking of "difficulty". But being accustomed to something can also obscure the original purpose of a writing. A literary critic who wants to read poems that are "straightforward in meaning" may want it for other motives that do matter, especially philo-poetic strivings for thought. Yet those who see thought emerging from, say, Mallarmé, precisely in moments where language edges toward an abyss of necessary nonmeaning, are going to read Fogarty more as we do, which is to say, when the poems "come across as seemingly infinite accumulations of words", another kind of uncommon reader is sought. We are cast back to the old tension, between the language of the impenetrable "modernist genius" and the "common reader".

The difficulty we now have in reopening a critique of the common (general or average) reader might be due to the decline in critiques of mass culture, since the time of the Frankfurt Institute, and if that is case, we may open it again, even if under different terms. Hopper notes well the difference in style of *Kargun* from later works like *Connection Requital,* a chapbook written entirely in capital letters, that some may find reminiscent of Langston Hughes's late long poem *Ask Your Mama: 12 Moods for Jazz.* By no means does Fogarty's work shy away from critiques of the jingles and advertisements of capitalist mass culture in this older sense, but there is alongside this also an occasional distrust for the critics of the English Department, a distrust often expressed among proponents of what was avant-garde in the early twentieth century and that could emerge from what was often perceived to be a stale Leavisism in Australian academies right up until the late twentieth century. In *Kargun*, syntactical uncertainty is, however, there, from Cummins's Blakean drawings that accompany the poems to phrasal ambiguity; "critics in attics" in "Mr. Professor" (29) and poem titles that seem to fore-echo future prosodics: "I am Black, I am Both You and I, Truganini" (43) and "Never Nefertiti, Change Nefertiti" (35). As to a more traditional avant-garde aesthetics, Cummins's illustrations could depict a kind of urban disjunction, almost a Symbolist graphics.

Hopper's "comfort zone" of understanding is curious therefore in that it is precisely the style of reading that trips such modes of reading up, or at least puts it under strain, something of course that impedes many a reader of experimental poetry. Even if one argues that words scattered all over the page is "playful" and "stimulating", even delightful and pleasurable, readers still are not accustomed to come to an understanding of any given text in some other manner than as if all texts were simply conveyors of meaning in a straight line: from creator to responder. This is not just a quarrel among critics, but an issue in the teaching of poetry, or poetics pedagogy, more generally. The music of language is a phrase regularly called into play here; as if the music of music wasn't enough to give a harmony of literary effects. And yet still, if Hopper seeks an "overall meaning" to the poem, an underlying message; what uncovers it? Readers are, too, actors, and even in this time, this contemporary, not all readers can be assumed to be consumers with fixed expectations. This is where Mudrooroo's *guerrilla poetics* expands to *guerrilla reading*, which can apply to other poets in this book; almost all of them call for us to become guerrilla readers not bound to any particular political or historical style, but readers willing to oppose these norms, to read open and otherwise. In his *New and Selected Poems*, Fogarty writes of the "ungrammaticality" of English:

You have to understand all the poetry I write in order to get the message. It's a performance in literary oral tradition, of even using their English against the English. The way they write and talk is ungrammatical, because it doesn't have any meanings in their spirit. More so, the cultural symbols that belong to my people are more significant to my people than the A, B and C. What I want to achieve in my writing one day is to put Aboriginal designs of art inside the lettering to bring a broader understanding to the meanings of the text. (ix)

Fogarty positions anti-alphabetism and linguistic radicality as breaking down the "sophistication of black intellectual authors", warning them to "stay away from European colonialist ways of writing, and the disease of stupidity in their language" (ix). Against this polemical backdrop, Fogarty then launches an unforgettable phrase: "I see words beyond any acceptable meaning" (ix). The "intelligence" and "meanness" of black guerrilla fighters (like Jantamarra, Mulbaggarra, Dundalee and Pemulwuy) can only be written by a black writer: "I must say I think it's going to be difficult to divide the layout of my brain to you, but I have done it quite successfully in giving verses of text in a foreign [white] tongue" (ix). Knowledge of time, of an "indigenous, ancestral past and future", assists in the breakdown of the technicalities of written words. The "breaking down" of language, though it may occur for an entirely different reason than for poets of other avant-gardes which partake in the breaking down of received grammars, unequivocally refuses critical convention: Fogarty doesn't "believe in compromise at all . . . It doesn't matter if it is in correct grammar or their style of writing, because the white man will always criticise written pieces of paper" (x). That criticism exists at all means less than that the critic could miss the critical negation underneath, and to this end Fogarty says that although there are many "contradictions in European written material . . . don't get confused with my negating the reality of literary white Australia. I know how white Australians write and I know how they talk" (x). Fogarty's stylistic arsenal is sweeping, unfixed, formed in the dialectic of expectation and its denial. It's an earnest and mean artifice.

The question of the contradictions of historical style is complicated by Fogarty's self-described style of writing, which is in every sense encapsulated by and encapsulating of radical blackness, but also by a knowledge that it is writing over and against literary white Australia. As we will see, Natalie Harkin uses similar methods in the book *Dirty Words*, wielding the language of the invader in order to negate it by using the dictionary. The logic is clear: style is *political*. Its prosodic characteristics are remarkably avant-garde, a rhythmic "flattening-out" close to "anti-poetry", and anti on the plane of readership not the least because, as Mudrooroo says, the "anti" ensures there cannot and should not be straightforward "dictionary meaning" on the side of the reader.[3] Guerrilla poetry calls for guerrilla reading.

IV. European Weakness and Political Style

If history is "endless variation", as Adam Pendleton puts it in a 2017 manifesto for Black Dada, this is different to white dada which cannot break its addiction to decline, pastness as depletion. For Pendleton, "Black Dada is a way to talk about the future while talking about the past", and history is a "machine upon which we can project ourselves and our ideas" – but ultimately "white dada remains within the framework of european weakness". The transformation of the avant-garde is a move away from Spivak's sense of the Native Informant in *Critique*, as we have noted, not just to "dredge" postcolonial discourse of its worst (or weaker) elements, but rather to strengthen the framework for a postcolonial critique after the Fall of the Soviet Union and Yugoslavia through its four "conditions" (Philosophy, Literature, History, Culture), and have it mean more for an expanded sense of a vanishing present. Postcolonialism is divided into four, so to speak, but it remains unified, and for Spivak only by thinking of the postcolonial as a historicism of endless variation and movement can it be of any future use.

Fogarty's prophetism and prophetic sensibility proclaims a similar historicality, but can we read within the framework of European weakness? European weakness, like masculine insecurity, is dangerous. European weakness is the phrase Tzara uses at Dada

---

[3] There is need for some nuance on the issue of the casualised scholar and the notion of "academic" in the way Mudrooroo uses it. Accusatory uses of the term "academic" can now factor in the totality of the labour force involved. Mudrooroo's difficulty with "academic" poetry is more complicated given the composition of the academies in relation to the synthesis of cultural and literary studies. A middlebrow literary festival might now resist the "academic" by staging conversations between memoirists and famous media personalities. What is "popular" today is an assault on the "dryness" of the academy (a kind of folk thinking that can draw in the middle-income, bourgeois consumer). Π.O. similarly has an "anti-academic" stance, but that made sense more in the days of New Criticism and Leavisism, the mid-century halls of the academy.

beginnings and for Adam Pendleton, Black Dadaist, that framework didn't end. What is true therefore of an avant-garde in Europe is true also for Black Dada; history, if it doesn't have to follow the passage of succession, and because it remains both European and weak, marks the past for the future. X marks the historical spot – and for Pendleton, Malcolm X does this too – that historical projection can begin; it becomes the moment historical style is taken up for the purpose of combat, the identification of weakness in the white frame. If historical style is political style, we broach a stopgap in philosophy, where philosophical style meets with democratic politics in Western thinking. For Friedrich Schiller, "political style" meant telling philosophy or history in poetic style, as historical style, or as Frank Ankersmit put it, gauging a distinction between naive and sentimental poetry, between a poetry of direct description and authorial reflexivity. Thus neither the kind of "naive political style" which places the citizen in the imagined universe of direct democracy, nor Machiavellian satire make up that "other side" of democratic political style.[4] It is possible to argue that Fogarty broaches another side to democratic political style, not in a way that is naive or Machiavellian. Political style can then refer to an oppositional style that is a kind of anti-democratic realism. The problems an apparently "representative democracy" present for First Nations Australians warrant a realism that imagines its absence. Rejecting electoralism as democratic poetic style opens a sweeping historical vista. Fogarty *does not do democratic style*, and although it is not "bureaucratic" poetry, if ever there could be such a thing, its character is one which does not shy away from questions of governance or

---

[4] Ankersnit's essay on the *"innere Stimme"* (inner voice) of democracy, framed by a close listening to the missing third "unplayed" stave of Robert Schumann's *Humoreske* (1838), is a marvellous and theoretically difficult exposition of historical and political style through Schiller. Ultimately Fogarty's scepticism about the value of Western Philosophy leads to a better scape and scope of history and a greater array of hemispheres from which we can read the poems. The framework of "European weakness" we might read historically as the *styles* of anti-imperialism, but that is not without its own set of contradictions. The writing of Mao Zedong, if plotted to these Western coordinates, can be considered both naive and democratic in style, quite apart from issues of party and proletarian state, resolutely opposed to the *"stylelessness"* of contemporary politics (Ankersmit, 34). It is, in short, an anti-bureaucratic political style unlike that of the great Soviet style later in the century (especially Zhivkov, Kádár, Brezhnev, Jaruzelski, Husák and, of course, Andropov and Chernenko). Mao's late missives against bureaucracy would seem to set his political style apart from this (notwithstanding his being a poet). Situated in this dialectic, Fogarty's poetry is not just democratic; it doesn't seek to do away with bureaucratic political style either, but rather inhabits both.

economic and social affairs. The message of such poems as "A-U-S-T-R-A-L-I-A" (comparable with equivalent poems previously cited by Walwicz, Duke and Ouyang Yu) is clear enough:

> A—Stands for have a day hey no layabouts
> U—Stands for you untied the uncles
> S—Stands for sir sect the dirt no shit
> T—Stands for tea let flour and tease
> R—Stands for rebirth the reality re=box
> A—Stands for Amuses ointment a vibe a la
> L—Stands for what a hell no loyal for Lionel
> I—Stands for I an I needs no invasion
> A—Stands for Aboriginal the only race around
> (*Eelahroo*, 34)

If the poem was to end here, it would be a neat alphabetic acrostic. But quickly the alphabetic structure disappears:

> And Australians Romans pick a box words
> À la dart hey the Aust; lied to truth
> A—stands for hey no Apology improve
> Emotional blood on the lip from a computer
> As a reputation for swearing
> Things are private ever more
> Yet presence stuffs dark characters employers
> To be purely berates.
> Option from the future's see death to
> The old fools who incline others to
> Boggy their child-hoods.
> This as no opportunity
> This as no opining
> Where contact in literary many
> Metropolitan fails, the imagining aspiration.
> So epicentres are not recognised
> Advantage Australians affair stands
> (*VIC, 5:30pm, 2013-03-14*)
> (*Eelahroo*, 34)

This poem undoes the lettristic order of the acrostic. It never quite leaves "A", but the syntactic disjunction cuts and claws its way across the page and eventually the acrostic withers. The folk understanding of Australia as a white, well-to-do liberal democracy obscures, of course, the fact that, as Capital does its work, sections of the proletariat move in league with Media Discourses and Museum Discourses that sell "a dead cold rotten lie" amongst themselves in order to take and sell land off, as in Fogarty's 2016 poem "Head Keeper Futures Corridor's Bay":

> Every sand rushes the beach are first people's
> museum ample by laughter original (overseers)
> things must change where names are forgiven
> ports shores bays renamed won't hurt the
> truth for children histories futures.
> The mouth who named mountains for brainwave
> oversea shook wreckage house living, stay by a dead cold rotten lie.
> Whitefellas must derigetter their conzinerices atturies.

The linguistic invention of the last line, with its neologisms "derigetter", "conzinerices" and "atturies" gives not so much a dissonance of the phonotext as total lexical thrownness: three words, an obscuration of meaning, a mystery. On the face of it, it clashes sharply with the kinds of "Harmonic Englishes" of the more standard lyric style but it too is a kind of lyric. "Whitefellas must derigetter their conzinerices atturies", one of *the* most striking and memorable lines in the whole of modern Antipodal poetry, demands, that is, a double reading; both a distant striving after its sense (the feeling of its sense is crystal clear) and a striving after its sonic-syllabic piecing-together – sensing how the line is built ("up") to the strata of meaning from nontrivial nonmeaning. It demands to be heard, and understood, but it doesn't allow the words commonly known (Whitefellas, must, their), to preclude our prosodic drift through the other three words. It is both known and invented language, absorbing and an artifice. Comparison might be made here with the language-oriented art of Vernon Ah Kee. Working with the politicisation of language, on that register, Ah Kee's painted words expose the history and the logic of colonial violence through the semiotic register, the chorality of puns, para-grammatic disruption, superposition and substitution ("abhoriginal"), lexical segmentivity, the pictorialised, the painterly, line-breaks; outworkings in the disruptive fragmentation and internal work of language, and so on. It's a politicisation of style. The preoccupation with time is seen both in larger senses: allegorical time (the future), or through overarching book-thematics as in *Eelahroo (Long Ago) Nyah (Looking) Möbö-Möbö (Future)*, and on the microtextual-level prosodic invention, the time of writing, a level of chronometric precision in that poems will often include the date and place in which he wrote it. The latter, the prosodic level, cannot be overlooked, as in the dissonance of "Swift Terrorless":

> Pre tend my mobs bobs in dobs
> > Pre lend my sending not rented
> > Be a shell where no hell sprinkle
> > Be a small mate in late ate in hate
> > Advance stomach midden of sobbing
> > Distance tepidities feelings
> > > (*Eelahroo*, 35)

Prosodic stress I mark as follows:

> Pre ténd my móbs bóbs in dóbs
> > Pre lénd my sénding nót rénted
> > Bé a shéll where nó héll sprínkle
> > Be a smáll máte in láte áte in háte
> > Advánce stómach mídden of sóbbing
> > Dístance tepídities féelings

Proclivities for overrhyme are done with extreme, unalloyed purpose. Internal rhyme is less astounding than the clashing iambs abruptly cut to cretics and trochees mid-line. The last is an oddly even, almost molossus-like triple stress. Fogarty's peculiar prosody, rhythmics and dense style forces us to rethink an essential metrical contract of Australian poetry (his live performances do this too). Lose not thematic sense: "dob in" sounds a broken solidarity, less light-hearted is "midden of sobbing", a deeper grief. If message and meaning seem clear – writing comes first before ownership, the time of writing is what matters, *is* the thing – something is left open: writing is inseparable from the work of the body which is, too, the work of the brain, the historical style of one pitched unanimously as many against democratic hatred. Inventing new ways of being dissonant, opening meter to new sense, renders writing as much the cognate work of the body as a game of sincere artifice. Total syntactic indeterminacy it is not, yet it is this level, the metrical level, that supports the larger temporal allegory. In "SCENIC MAPS PARTS", the only poem in *Eelahroo* all in capital letters:

> TAKE YOUR SMART PHONE AND RUSH
> > A MIND TO ARTIST WAYS
> > TAKE YOUR I PADS AND FIND THE
> > PATHWAY THE BLACK MEN WALK AND TALKED BEFORE
> > THE DEVICES CONTENT DEMANDS.
> > INFATUATE IN DOWNLOAD OF A DREAMTIME REALITY
> > LAYERS.
> > HAVE ALL RICH CLASSICS ON THOSE BLACK FELLAS KIDS
> > WRITERS NOW,

MAN OF BOOKS ON GOINGS.
MAKE THE MOBILES UNITE A MEDIA TO GO TO OUR NEXT
   YEARS RIGHTS FIGHTS.
DO THE FAVOURITE EMERGING REALM OF LITERATURE OF
   EXPERIENCES.
DON'T FIELD THE WIZENED GHOST THAT EMBED FOR
   MONEY.
TAKE ALL I PADS AND PUT THEM IN THE OUTBACK STARS
   FALLING FOR THE FIRE LIGHTS.
                              (*Merton VIC, 10:44am, 2013-06-10*)
                                                  (*Eelahroo*, 86)

To mark an *extreme*, or "virulent" contemporaneity is one of the more voluted difficulties of thinking poetic time and, in this poem "MOBILES" and "I PADS" are questionable technologies. It may be theoretically useful to separate the now here from the present. The now, for Fogarty – not abstracted from the future or the past – is not predetermined in space, neither the outback nor in the literature of experiences. To get a sense of the origin-less-ness of the time before now is to grasp but a slither of the horror or terror that has been and is to come. The experience of reading Fogarty is one in which the future is always in view and at the same time concealed. Neither a "Western" progressive politics of resistance, nor a global X-ist or Maoist guerrilla politics, nor programmes for national reform provide adequate descriptions of Fogarty's intellectual politics of combat literature, but it is the contradictions between these in Fogarty's language that produces its aesthetic ideology, and the gap between the vanishing or expanded sense of the present, set against the past and the future, that at least forms the crux, or triadic temporality, of Fogarty's liberation poetics. The intricacies of Fogarty's poetry are its styles of combat. We may read it against the poetic ecstasy of the One, finding a stronger meaning for militant unity; militant unity, per Glissant, as the maintenance of a contradiction, a unity that is *not-one* pitched against the One, and which unties it. History outside the framework of European weakness is open to endless variation. Critical description of Fogarty's political style can only partially capture these disturbances in historical time, but poems like "Head Keeper Futures Corridor's Bay" and "SCENIC MAPS PARTS" bring us closer to these temporal logics; anticipatory, presentist and retroactive.

V. Fogarty as National-Prophetic Poet

In our time we have confused more recent cultural nationalisms for developmental nationalisms of the past. First World anti-nation or anti-state discourses have drowned out original narratives of national liberation of the mid-twentieth century that resulted in the stronghold of national liberation governments, particularly in Southern Africa. For readers in the Global North roughly speaking it should be clear that the political styles on display here support a conception of Nation entirely different to the cultural nationalism of a white bourgeois state locked in a First World geopolitical bloc. This "other" conception can be heard of course in Fanon. In *The Wretched of the Earth* one of the more surprising, if not also consoling elements of its anticolonial counter-nationalism (before postcolonial, or decolonial) discourse is the section "On National Culture". In the cultural plane, Fanon no less than entreaties, "national (combat) literature" so-called, in its subsumption by the colonial powers, is a constant negotiation with the genres chosen by the native intellectual, such that

> The crystallization of the national consciousness will both disrupt literary styles and themes, and also create a completely new public. While at the beginning the native intellectual used to produce his work to be read exclusively by the oppressor, whether with the intention of charming him or of denouncing him through ethnical or subjectivist means, now the native writer progressively takes on the habit of addressing his own people. (193)

It is easy to misread "ethnical" as ethical here, given what the discourses of multiculturalism became in the white bourgeois national sphere. Fogarty too has heard, in the 2019 interview, "ethnics" in "ethics". But this is the argument for a native tradition, and only from this moment can we begin to speak of a national literature, which Fanon then calls the "literature of combat" that gives form and contour to a national consciousness, "flinging open before it new and boundless horizons . . . because it is the will to liberty expressed in terms of time and space" (193). The question of genre is core; the oral tradition is transformed, forms are modernised, traditional means of storytelling are updated: "The contact of the people with the new movement gives rise to a new rhythm of life and to forgotten muscular tension" and the storyteller "makes innovations" (194). The same for jazz as for ceramics. This can be framed too in the language of advancement and social relations. Fanon would jot in a journal entry dated to 1955, in reference to a painting competition: "It is absolutely necessary that we be part of the network of avant-garde establishments" (*Alienation and Freedom*, 335). The question of the use of the concept of the nation here, aside from the notion of an "avant-garde establishment", is, of course, one derived from anti-imperial and Indigenous conceptions of Nation and national reconstruction.

Indigenous senses of Nation are plural. Nation is pluri-nation, national is plurinational. Spivak's nuance on the question of small nationalisms comes back to these anti-colonialist intimations. Yet in Fanon's discourse we find poetic foundations in 1. Fanon's use of the prophetic mode, and 2. Fanon's interest in rhythm. The latter *applies* to Fogarty in that transformations in language in Fogarty cannot be easily extracted, displayed and pieced together to construct a political resistance. Plurinational histories bequeath plurirhythmic poetry. The most precise sense of it may be this: what happens to the linguistic textures, outside of the question of Standard vs Non-Standard Practice, is a segmenting of grammar, ambiguation of syntax and particle akin to musical "dissonance", in a way that makes it heard either as a free-floating play of lexical harmonies, or as an offence to aural expectation, a disturbance, but a definition of dissonance relies most heavily on a hearing of harmony. It's not all dissonant, as such, in the immediacy of hearing and reading, at the level of the phrase or fragment, but its underlying linguistic texture is dissonance. Given the role of dissonance in the experimental poetry we have examined so far, and given its role in the other avant-garde arts, especially music, we must here mark the subjective element at play: the "dissonant pleasure" in these experiments might be for another reader exasperation. If exasperation is the "aim" of the work, then delight or pleasure might run counter to this aim. In "Decipherer" again:

> Uncharted activated waters
> reveal unflushed originators.
> My true darling breath of exhilarating
> vision is acute in testifying customs. [. . .]
> Between sound and colour 'I am a bit.'
> Between music strangely I'm beyond white time
> Affirmation give techniques limitless in my
> Plain chant transfiguration musics.
> History unbalances kept me 'dead' decipherer.
> Alternative world is moving those dislocations. [. . .]

> Reality in redemptive insights
> sweats over my blowing riddles
> those complacent will quest not my poet
> my reliability lies in wait, in caves.
> (*Mogwie-Idan, Stories of the land*, 78–9)

This brings us, through music and history, to our second point: *the prophetic mode*. In combat literature the prophetic is not just tonal. In "Decipherer" history serves not to balance or correct but to encrypt time in an alternative world. But before getting to that, there are a number of *placements* in the poem for which I will offer an interpretation, if not a working of the *logic of effects* in the poem. Fogarty's voice, self-ascribed, is plain chant, monophonic, and gives "transfiguration", and possibly awaits redemption in riddles. It is not the originator but it leads to two lines or realities. If the reader, and in this case the critic, are decipherers, which is doubtful for it seems the poet is the decipherer, the poem may not be addressed to either. Regardless of how it might be read, and to whom, it unbalances the concepts of time that looks something like the diagram that follows. In it I have drawn twin paths of redemption and transfiguration. The origin, which is unknown, brings forth the separation (see Figure 6.1).

This is a guerrilla reading. For though it may look somewhere between a Blakean mythography and a Christian universe, the redemptive path, if read through the teleologies of Fanon, would see a dissonant or disjunctive literature as a precursor in an oppressive world to a future harmony: when the new regime falls to the old, poetry would have no need of dissonance because it will have found harmony. Sufficient grasp of the dislocations, temporal displacements too, of historical style is necessary to address the issue of prophetic time as documented; how the issue of invention shifts from originality to originator.

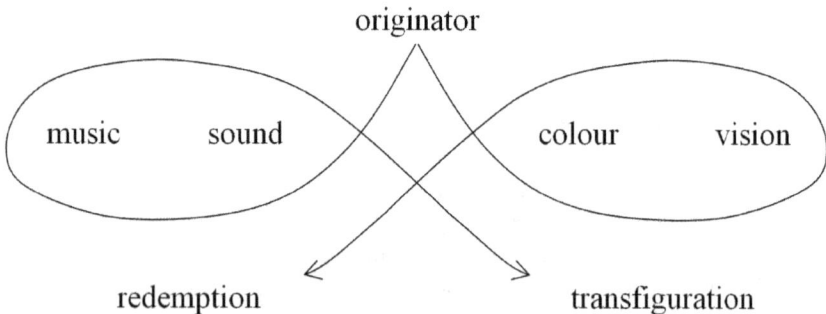

Figure 6.1 A. J. Carruthers, interpretive diagram for Fogarty's "Decipherer".

That Fogarty is a visualist, and writes by hand, is no surprise given the prosodic and prophetic interests so far outlined. Fogarty introduces the 2004 collection of poems and drawings *Minyung Woolah Binnung: What Saying Says* by saying "Art to me is very personal, but words to me are not personal" (4). The conjoining of visualism and the prophetic mode here may resemble Blake and Romantic prophecy, but even if those effects are palpable in Fogarty there are a raft of reasons for his visualism not reducible to Romantic prophecy alone. Vision, visuality and the visionary mode might have been there as early as *Kargun*. "Do Yourself a Favour, Educate Your Mind" has visionary elements that move between timescapes, from "my old peoples" or the origin of his middle name:

> Well first I was named George (the second name) the Third.
> This must be from somewhere in past history
> It probably come from George the Third. (23)

To instructions for the unborn among which are:

> 1. What has been done when they came (the invaders)
> 2. What happened yesterday (like why did a hundred
>   babies die in a year)
>   [...]
> 5. Think very carefully of the superpowers next move on
>   the board (lie draughts or chess). Educate yourself til
>   you get higher as knowing as much as the enforcers of
>   the superpowers (but don't fall into their bag of tricks,
>   or end up like the enforcers). Anyway that's if you get
>   the chance of education (I mean using their things)
> 6. Study your history back to front if you have to, because today
>   the enemy is very worried about their external
>   affairs.
>   Understand fully the sell outs and the beginnings to sell
>   out because they are destructive to the freedom of what
>   is set ahead. (25)

The call for liberation fighters-to-come to maintain a tactical steely-mindedness is geopolitical – it concerns "superpowers", external affairs, strong and weak points in their chess game of Bloc politics, but we ought not forget the political nature of prophecy from its origins, as in part a mode of warning for leaders and political actors. Nor can we forget the more basic problem of all prophecy: the future. The prophetic mode of address "sets ahead" for the future reader a path to freedom; setting ahead is not setting behind, as in "I am

Black, I am Both You and I, Truganini", Truganini being a woman once assumed to be the last "full-blooded" Tasmanian Aboriginal, where through the image of the Vulture, no sense is made apparent of an inevitability to the bloodiness of colonial history. Prophetic as in:

> Vultures sat in celebration
>   eating a midday meal
>   mixed in robbed flesh
>
> I saw this in vision
> I am then left in realness
> Knowing we stand fleshless
>   gathered and laid in rubbish heaps.
>   (*Kargun*, 43)

Indigenous history changes the dimensions of Antipodal poetics. It is the transfiguration of the avant-garde and its original narrative. Its future is historical. At around the point of inception of the European avant-gardes, in 1910, Indigenous children began to be forcibly removed from their parents, a period known as the Stolen Generations that carried through most of the twentieth century. Punitive measures would not cease. Broad resistance to the 2007 Northern Territory National Emergency Response, or "The Intervention", under the Howard Government, and deaths in custody at the hands of the police are modern continuations of these earlier periods of struggle. What is of most concern is the highest levels of governance: *languages of invention against languages of intervention*. There is an anecdote that might summon the cause of national resistance, or protracted war, in the Maoist sense: Gough Whitlam's 1973 quip to Mao Zedong, who asked him whether he would ever make revolution in Australia, to which he is said to have replied "we believe in evolution". Mao would not have meant it naively, even if it was asked in humour, but the meaning of the reply is telling enough. Evolution, with all its connotations, would remain the ideological centrepiece of Australian state governance, and though the New Nationalism of the 1970s would bring forth again the old idea of an Australian Republic, this would not emerge alongside the parallel discourse of a Treaty. The First Nations concept of nationhood therefore, as a campaign document for a Worker's Inquiry into the death of Daniel Yock would put it, is bound up with "the struggle for internationalism and socialism" to establish "independence from the capitalist nation state and fight to defend its most basic rights and conditions" (18–19). Following Fanon, different senses of the concept of nation should be apparent here, which, it should go without saying, are in stark opposition to Jindyworobak nationalism, and nation in the purely parliamentary sense.

The prophetic or visionary mode in Fogarty means Fogarty is not an "Australian poet" as such. Fogarty's literature and literacy remains strange in his own country, just as it was for Tzara and the early twentieth-century European avant-garde at its inception phase. Thus the *without*, the externalism borne of prophetic estrangement, is also demonstrable. Internationalism is a key word, which Corey Wakeling reads, in the poem "Advance Those Asian And Pacific Writers Poets" as activating a post- or counter-national "postcolony" ("Lionel Fogarty's Literary Criticism After the Postcolony"). It is possible to read this poem, which is strikingly Earthist and peace-seeking in its exploration of the limits of nation and history, as an interpretation of Asia-Pacific regional solidarity between Aboriginal and Asian cultures if not Asian nation-states in the region. It is, also, about the United Nations and international law, using the word "cassation" (a type of court used for the sole purpose of verifying interpretation of the law), asking whether language can give justices of causes: regional causes beside revolutionary internationalism. This goes again to the beginning of Fogarty's career; in *Kargun*, Africa, as in "Death to Rhodesia – Zimbabwe Awakes To: Brother and Comrade: Simbareshe Mumbengegwe" where "I has come to my feelings / that Zimbabwe is Aboriginal" (*Kargun*, 90). At the time of this writing Mumbengegwe serves in the Zimbabwe Government as Minister of State for Presidential Affairs and Monitoring Government Programmes, having been a core member of the Central Committee of ZANU-PF for a decade. Thus a prophetic liberation-poetics is for, not against, the wielding of power, liberation-power. The issue of right is more palpable in "Historical Upheavals" written in Merton, Victoria, dated 2013-07-06:

> Walk white fellow, as you all can't write
> Our battle just at your sunrise and night sigh ties.
> The noble not runs in our native modern now from then.
> Black resistance is everywhere now on written,
> Face books their door mat roof an in-laws.
> Walk white fella, you all can't rights us.
>
> (*Eelahroo*, 83)

Moving writing against white racism and its structural support system in the capitalist-imperialist world order, the poem paints writing as style: "Bodies for the dirt tears can't ours, pain can't our pens." Silence is withheld too, counter-intuitively: "Continuing the non-silence is what we about." It works neologisms, "decolonisative", and again, radiating ceaselessly outward, seeks historical time; "The continent still not there's even in numbers contribution historical upheavals" and in a phrase redolent of Fanon, time compacted; "native modern now from then". Now/then, native/modern: new distortions in our conceptualisation of the modern emerge when setting Fogarty's historical style against these time differentials. How these anticolonial experiments might be construed "avant-garde" in style might seem at this juncture subordinate to these other senses; that they are reflections upon history and visionary time. A final example, "Encounters Conflicts", gets us to questions of textual authenticity and interpretation, written in "Merton, VIC", and dated "12:30am Sunday, 2013-07-02":

> Copyright don't makes the typing
> Getting works means write first
> Up of the work, gives copyright.
> Interventions are vents for not me.
> The brain to work belong to
> The hand pump blood from the tipping toes,
> To sew means rows.
> (*Eelahroo*, 76)

If we would, in the vein of a comparative close reading, pair "Encounters Conflicts" with Shakespeare's 84th Sonnet, from the rival poet sequence, which begins "Who is it that says most, which can say more?" we might notice also some parallels with the poem's decisive line: "Let him but copy what in you is writ" – for it is the rival poet who will in any case be "Making his style admired every where". Style in the most immediate sense is taken to be something either influential or stolen. Fogarty's style, if inimical, which it certainly is on one level, *has* no rival. Copyright is an afterthought therefore of the process of making (typing) which is a whole body act, not needing forethought. Distinctions are nonetheless drawn: "I have never copy white" and the last line "Oh well jobs are copyright by rich outcomes anyways." And because this is so serious a game of artifice at work, a total transformation of syntax produces meaningful indeterminacy. Style can be neither copied nor copyrighted, however recondite on the level of the text, because the *time* of writing, sewing lines (rows), is the work itself.

The historical status of Fogarty's style is captivating because if a perceived lack of history of an Antipodal vanguard requires a "counter-history", this would seem to have been it. Few modern poets writing on the continent would attempt such syntactic reinvention through literary artifice and in the imbued breathwork of lines, as Fogarty, in either century. And yet, Fogarty's work has been received both as marginal and as central. Thus a literary history which is both an "underdogging" of margins or "overdogging" of mainframe can no longer suffice: Fogarty's style, and critical poetics, will resist submission solely under the terms of the oppressor and the oppressed. If this is a national poetry in the sense Fanon meant, we are talking about a poetry whose fulfilment *is of a future time*. Meanings are encrypted on both ends; lexically piecemeal, clumped, separated, placed, "Inscaped" as G. M. Hopkins would have had it, but to an alternative, revolutionary historical world that is not Christ's, rhymed, "rendered" or cryptically (dis)placed (depending on how friendly a reader may feel towards it) and engaging historical or political style in that interpretation is stymied *and* induced at the roots of words.

This is one of the chief concepts of the whole study: the visionary status of poems and the readings poems do. It suffices to use visionary and prophetic to mean the same thing. The prophetic voice is no compromise or escape from the present, but rather a voice that takes in past, present and future, a larger temporal framework from which to compose. This expanded time-frame extends therefore to global space. If there has been any possibility of referring these excerpts of Fogarty's poetry out to a greater avant-garde poetics across hemispheres, I've not refused it, despite all ensuing chronoliterary disjunctions (and I hope more comparison is done), but I want to end this chapter on a lateral and more local plane by looking briefly at the renaissance of stylistic and linguistic invention in some contemporary Indigenous poets.

VI. *Historical Upheavals: National Poetry and Avant-Garde Internationalism Today*

To situate Fogarty therefore as a "national" poet by no means lessens the transnationalism and internationalism of it. That is the first insistence here. First Nations survival concerns land and property in the most general sense we can make of it in the face of a genocidal, carceral and imperial-colonial modern Commonwealth. Survival first of all is a victory of itself against incredible odds, but it is not just a local question – I have stressed that it is inextricably linked with the geopolitical and global positioning of the Antipodes and how forces of US imperialism and the Crown dictate this positioning in ways both visible and invisible. Survival is a cause for celebration and a call for further resistance particularly on the side of resource ownership and land – against the imperial actions of the Australian government.

This therefore is the spirit of Fogarty's international vanguardism (to invoke here the political vanguard), and it is undeniably one that sits strangely within the Euro-US or Anglo-American framework. The difficulty is describing Fogarty's sense of nation: it is a sense of nation but entirely outside the one given when we refer to Australia in the historical present. In the "alternative world" outside white historical time to which Fogarty refers we may imagine him as Agostinho Neto was and is for Angola, a national poet of national liberation, friend of the Central Committee, and in geopolitical terms an ally of Former Liberation Movements in Southern Africa (FLMSA).[5] Fogarty is a poet of national liberation under the internationalist terms used for Southern Africa as much as a revolutionist at home. Fogarty is contradictorily avant-gardist and against avant-Europe, yet this against-ness is precisely the vanguardist quality. Is it not the case that avant-gardes can only come to be if they have the courage to go against themselves? After Tzara, are true vanguardists not those who have the courage to "go against" the historical avant-garde? The end of the ethnological avant-gardes heralds the beginning of the demystification of Oceania, and the First Nations avant-garde of the Antipodes is a critical frontier for this demystification. It is the only avant-garde in the Antipodes to untie the old Frontier of war and genocide. The word "decolonise" is not neutral within this cluster of associated terms. It has to mean what it used to in the time of Fanon, as part of the vocabulary of the international and co-ordinated liberation of oppressed nations. There cannot be decolonisation in one country alone. This is why avant-gardes are a challenge to literary history. If we take an avant-garde seriously, and if we can combine, through scholarly citation and shared critical comparison, more than one critical reading experience in light of a generalised radical poetics; what do we find it opposed to? In his-

---

[5] Fogarty's involvement can be contextualised as part of a larger history of Aboriginal alliances with African liberation movements and national struggles, a rich history that would involve the trip of Nubuluna (Dexter Daniels) with Phillip Waipuldanya Roberts to Kenya to study its independence struggle in late 1964 and Oodgeroo Noonuccal's internationalism, including her involvement in the Second World Black Festival of Arts in Nigeria in 1976 as delegate and senior adviser.

torical terms, the idea of Australia. What First Nations avant-gardes most do is reopen the question of a national literature at the same time as we question the timescape of the international avant-gardes as we know them. In a now recent history of the Vancouverian and Canadian "Vangard" by Gregory Betts, we find such language emerging: "This garde lacks the hubris and the ego of the historical avant-gardists, who positioned themselves as the revolutionary prophets and front-line soldiers of a redeemed potential future" (210). Fogarty does critical-international prophetism.

First Nations avant-gardes inaugurate a contradictory obliteration and restitution of avant-garde forms. The effect of poetic invention – disjunction, dissonance, syntactic bravura, perplexing uses of language – will not be understood in the same way. There is not just some good-spirited humility, that of lite "decolonising" among progressives. The new front-line is First Nations vanguard poetry. It is both a decolonising of return and fearless advance, and a thinking past and through the current state of affairs, in governance (we say also, literary governance). Though there are ways it could have been argued, I have not made the same claim for neo-vanguardism that I have been able to make historically with Duke, Stewart or Walwicz, precisely because of the issue of national literature. These works are not vanguardist only by self-nomination. They are, rather, by virtue of political dynamism and prophetic style, avant-garde in spirit. Fogarty studies, and there is a significant body of scholarship already, will doubtless in the future be read in continuum with Indigenous poetry that has emerged in the new century: Natalie Harkin, Alison Whittaker, Evelyn Araluen, Ellen van Neerven and others in which radical ways of reinventing and reprocessing language, and going back to traditional language, have amounted to nothing less than a *restitution* of inventive forms in the new century, restitution because it returns ownership, as it were, of inventive forms to First Nations writing. This future history will be told not just as one of sympathetic observers, but the activity of a self-standing vanguard in itself. Note the following page from *Blakwork*, a book by Alison Whittaker, queer Gomeroi poet and legal scholar:

> work work work work work work work work work work work work
> work work work work work work work work work work work work
> work work work work work *gasp* work work work work work work
> work work work work work work work work work work work work
> work work work work work work work work work work work work
> work work work work work work work work work work work work

work work work work work work work work work work work work
work work work work work work work work work work work work
work work work work work work work work work work work work
work work work work work work work work work work work work
work work work work work work work work work work work work
work work work *gasp* work work work work work work work work
work work work work work work work work work work work work
work work work work *gasp* work work work work work work work
work work work work work work work work work work work work
work work work work work work work work work work work work
work work work work work work work work work work work work
work work work work work work *gasp*. pack pack pack pack pack pack
pack pack pack pack pack pack pack pack pack pack pack pack pack
pack pack pack pack pack pack pack pack pack pack pack pack pack
pack pack pack pack pack pack pack pack pack pack pack pack pack
pack pack pack pack *gasp* run run run run run run run *gasp* run run
run run run run run run run run run run run run run run run run
run run run run run run run run run run run run run run run run
run run run run run *gasp* run run run run run run run run run run
run run run run run run run run run run run run run run run run
run *gasp*.
        gasp.

(*Blakwork*, 176)

The next page, not reproduced here, trails off onto a sparer page: "gasp. *gasp*. work." That's it. Whittaker's pages are exposed no less to the literal scape for an outworking of labour, of various kinds, throughout the book's sections. The poems mix genres: legal document, memoir, reportage, spiritual inquiry into time ("Murrispacetime") and appeals for Aboriginal justice, and in this lack of fixity, the formal shifts – rhythmic, lexical and visual – are, though this will differ from reader to reader, sometimes strident, mostly difficult.

In the archaeopoetics of Tzara, outward-looking and yet primitivist, Tzara sought no reply. Perhaps Tzara, whose very name means to be sad in one's country, did not imagine that his rallying calls for Dada internationalism, and his interest in Indigenous and indeed world culture would be met with cries back from country in multiform blasts matched here with documental inquisitiveness. It is reductive, the above example shows, to attribute all insurgent, insurrectionary acts to avant-gardes in modernity. Yet works such as these engage, as it were, the wholesale questioning of poetic forms in ways that the early twentieth-century avant-garde, with its collocation of documents, would certainly see as their mission.

In other words, a way to make sense of this is to posit, first of all, that it is every bit as possible, in the Antipodal context, to imagine an avant-garde without modernism as it is to imagine an experimental poetics without (or against) the avant-garde. From this it is important to emphasise to the non-Australian reader also that this is why I have been arguing that the Antipodal avant-garde is mostly though not completely one among the *non-Western avant-gardes*, when read as transecting hemispheric alignments in the way that it did, and does. That it is non-Western does not always mean it has been anti-imperialist, although Aboriginal avant-gardes certainly are. If in Fanon's language these inventions are part of a national, meaning First Nations, literature that is a relatively unified plainsong of non-Euro-American avant-garde globalism from Africa to Latin America and the Asia-Pacific, then doubtless it is these spatial and temporal disruptions, perpetuated or sustained by the early twentieth-century examples, that distort our perception of these timescales, given how history has been interacting with time.

Differently again in style and execution to Whittaker, history and conceptual assembly too plays a major role in Natalie Harkin's language inventions, often in the form of a type of documentarian writing or citational poetics. Using documents from colonial archives, and Harkin's own Indigenous family history, the 2015 *Dirty Words*, which is structured like a dictionary, and the 2019 *Archival Poetics*, in three book-parts – *Colonial Archive: Archival-Poetics 1, Haunting: Archival-Poetics 2, and Blood Memory: Archival-Poetics 3* – use citational method as a mode and container for completed projects. The latter volume comes to look like a folder from an archive box (Figure 6.2).

Open the archive and see what's in there: presentation of documents, in our terms, chronometrically confronting, epical in scope, disjunctive in presentation, neat in navigational frame. Documents are interspersed among a kind of conceptual lyric drawn from documents or in response to them. On a page titled "ARCHONS OF POWER" we are presented with the names of various institutions – "Aborigines Protection Board", "Children's Welfare Department", "Deputy Director of Rationing", "Master of the House", "Probation-Branch-Psychologist", "Scientific Expert" (*Colonial Archive: Archival Poetics 1*, 12) – and cited below this is an excerpt of documentation from the 1913 *Royal Commission on The Aborigines*, a harrowing record of the Stolen Generations policy. It's something like a radical historicism in that the doing of history

Figure 6.2 Natalie Harkin, slip cover containing the three volumes of *Archival-Poetics* (2019).

has turned up myriad more contradictions than resolutions, and in its theoretical use of the word "archon" (ἄρχων), Greek for ruler who occupies a public office, turning "History" into an examination of its catalogue of oppression. In *Dirty Words*, Harkin sustains focus on languages of power, but puts it to new prosody and new measure. There is a tendency in *Dirty Words* to clump words together into extended feet, as follows:

(E Eugenics 8)
 "white-supreme-logic"
 "State-sanctioned-experiment"
(I Intervention 13)
 "special measure absurd"
(L Land Rights 17)
 "accumulation-by-dispossession-slate"
 "finite-natural-resources"
 "cultural-site-desecration"
 "techno-fix-solutions"
 "*dear Profiteering-Capitalist-Economy*"

Lionel Fogarty's Historical Style 281

(M Mythology 18)
  "one-media-voice"
  "blood-quantum-identities"
(P Political Correctness 22)
  "'whimsical-linguistic'"
  "'whimsical-linguistics-games'"
(R Resistance 26)
  "card-shark-shuffling"
  "kitchen-table-yarns"
  "tough-love-grit"
  "elder-knowledge-strength"
(R Resistance 27)
  "human-touch-offering"
  "colonial-history-truths"
(R Resistance 28)
  "hearted-warrior-woman"
  "sing-chant-rage"
  "mothers-daughters-sisters-aunties-nannas-ancestors"
  "journeys-meetings-gatherings-consultations-lobbyings-feastings"
(R Resistance 29)
  "bright collage family-love pin-up-boards"
  "rhizome-like oral-history"
  "essential-oil-potions"
  "government-inquiry-interrogations into her sacred-women's-knowledge"
  "valued-respected-honoured outside white-western-patriarchal frameworks"
(Z Zero Tolerance 41–2)
  "military-exclusion-zones"
  "American-Pacific-Homeland-Security"
  "Pacific-paradise-paradox"

These are excerpted from the alphabetic sections, demediated here in a way that doesn't explain the theme of each entry. The entry for R, Resistance, for instance, is an homage to Harkin's Aunties. The entry for Z, Zero Tolerance, is about nuclear testing perpetrated by the United States on Aboriginal land. Despite the word-clumping, which almost resembles G. M. Hopkins's variable-length feet, there is doubtless also demodernisation at work. Here is where literary history, the crucial term of this book, meets "poetics": remaking language through variable feet (not syllables) not so much in the *modus operandi* of North American conceptual writing, which came to prominence this century, but from a much longer history of work in citation, from Walter Benjamin's 1927–40 *Passagenwerk* to Charles Reznikoff's *Testimony* (1965, 1968) and *Holocaust* (1975) works. More contemporary comparison awaits with works like M. NourbeSe Philip's *Zong!* or Angelo V. Suarez's *Philippine English: A Novel*.

In the case of Harkin, poetics means what poetics is – questioning and putting pressure on forms of making in language, where an archival poetics so phrased emerges out of the language of historical record. These explorations of document in a new key, under a new framework, and at the cusp of a new historical era, will (viewed under some hemispheric and geopolitical light) reveal more about how a twenty-first-century avant-garde has gone about the use of citational method and a specific politics of style. Look at it, now, to put it bluntly, from multiple ends: a European avant-garde looking in (Tzara), and an Antipodal avant-garde looking out (with impetus from the hemispheric avant-gardes). The poetics of the latter emerges from Indigenous pasts, presents and futures. If Lionel Fogarty laid the groundwork for an Indigenous combat literature in the twentieth century, it would proceed, reenergised, in the twenty-first. What makes Aboriginal avant-gardes so astonishing is that they are doing to history in remote hemispheric space what the Eastern European avant-gardes themselves imagined to be possible in the shadows of their early twentieth-century undertakings.

The question that remains is what all these dissonances can mean and for whom they mean. More readings will need to hear how or when they harmonise, for the meanings that the poetry will have as they are read will change in time, through the vicissitudes of the vanishing and expanded present. Every poem demands its semantics; guerrilla aberrations of the bent sign, no way but through. Doubtless Fogarty's avant-garde poetic invention is one of rights and demands, but it also doesn't reward straightforward ideological-political reduction. European frameworks crumble under the raining down of words. Whether they come to mean a militant unity pitched against the One, after Glissant, depends on how they are read, and it depends on how criticism, no longer the sworn enemy of the avant-garde, catches up with the documents and adopts guerrilla tactics. For now let us propose that, in the future-present, we read Fogarty redemptively.

Chapter 7

Traitorous Text: Amanda Stewart Off and On the Page

The late Chris Mann once said:

> There is an Australian tradition which I think is really strong which is about betraying, or being a traitor to a form. There is the idea of conceptual depth where you can actually choose to do something badly for whatever reason. This tradition goes back to, at least the 1840s. I don't know of any equivalent of that in the American sense.[1]

Listen to Amanda Stewart, poet, performer, and vocal artist (born 1959) alongside Mann (1949–2018) and one may notice certain similarities. Both are traitors to forms. Neither are subject to Euro-avant-garde quality control. Both develop complex layers and dimensions of voice in the most disembodied and yet still embodied of ways. I mean to say that a body linked up to a machine, not just amplified but divided (between microphones and speakers, collaborators and instrumentalists in improvised situations) and then also put to record, strangely comes back to the person and the body exactly doing it. Mann and Stewart worked with Jim Denley, Stevie Wishart and Rik Rue on *Machine for Making Sense*, an Australian-based but internationally recognised sound and performance group that began performing together at the 1989 Ars Electronica in Upper Austria, before touring the United States, Europe and Australia through the 1990s and continuing in a truncated form to this day in Australia. Stewart's experience on the international circuit as a performer harks back to Duke, a poet who likewise worked with (or

---

[1] From "An Interview with Chris Mann" conducted by Preston Wright, July 2002. Mann left Australia to teach at the New School in New York. Stewart has responded to Mann's life and work in the 2020 work *ta*, a poem and score for performance.

against) Sound Poetry, as history and in practice, having encountered it overseas. Here we are concerned with not just the written word but the notational in writing, notationality as the basis of poetry, its lift off the page and into the electrifying sites of live performance.

Our historical period, not flashed forward but taking sweep of the period we've so far covered, spans the 1970s to the present day, from Duke to Fogarty, Walwicz and, now, Stewart. Since the late 1970s Stewart has worked across sound and media from a global nexus of influences to forge a poetics that takes its place in the Antipodal avant-garde in ways that both extend the directions we have thus far mapped out and redirect them, in part because Stewart's engagement with the European, and American, post-1960 avant-gardes was perhaps more entrenched and immediate than any other Australian poet of her time and ilk. Much of her representative work was collected in the 1998 *I/T: Selected Poems*. Like the works of Fogarty and Walwicz, Stewart approaches language through and by inventive means, and like them too intervenes in issues of history, historiography, nation, economics, post-Cold-War geopolitics and the psycho-politics of late-century Australian culture and media. Stewart's internationalism opens the work to visual character and aural range unlikely to have resulted without that vaster engagement, nor without "technical expertise" in sound production from her work with the Australian Broadcasting Corporation (ABC) in the 1980s. Cultural margins clash with other cultural margins to forge a major poetics cutting across hemispheres. It's all the potential, ecstasy, stupefaction or traitorousness of an Antipodal avant-garde set in the environment of international literary culture.

What a way to end: off the page and into the air. Performance comes to reckon with much sharper, edgier feelings when resituated in the vast elsewheres of global poetics.[2] It's live. It's a temporally displaced now *and* a wild present, thrown from the core engine room of making and production: we speak not only of books but records, concerts, festivals, being on tour. We might speak soon of the avant-garde visitor, and where the poetics of émigrés and locals clash and merge, how such visitorship causes new forms to emerge from these kinds of encounters, and only these, because I don't mean to sound dogmatic about the need to "look outward" to the world, except to

---

[2] Further studies of avant-garde poetry in performance might elaborate upon the distinct forms and purpose of Spoken Word or SLAM poetry. There are spatial overlaps and historical confluences in that both avant-garde poetry in performance and Spoken Word poetry often occupy the same stage at performance events.

say that with Stewart we see starkly an external exchange shaking language up and flinging it into new and boundless hemispheric horizons, as is the case too with Fogarty, also internationalist, who works with a hypothesis around grammar in order to shatter it and rebuild it in the historical style of the poem. In the performances and notation of Stewart, an international avant-garde wields its influence in a different way to many other characters in this book. For Walwicz her formative experiences were in Poland, but Stewart's formative educational experiences were in Australia. The way histories of early twentieth-century avant-gardism came to map onto Stewart's imagination was at once-remove: the Antipodes figure across the work as a base, a contradictory one, which takes in the outer influence in order to challenge and transform it. Stewart notes some of her personal history of influence in a 2017 interview with Justin Clemens:

> My dad loved Keats and Eliot and so he introduced me to them. But showed me the simple ones. I wasn't like Chris Mann, a close friend of mine, who was probably reading Freud as he came out of the womb. But later I found Dada and was very influenced by visual art. So one of the main turning points for me was when I was about fifteen. We had this fabulous visual arts teacher at school who took us through twentieth-century modern art movements. I think I've told you this boring story before.

The story is about an experience in high school of making a Dadaist piece, and the formative impact this had comes with a degree of self-deprecation (a "boring story"), perhaps as much of an "Australian" characteristic trait as Mann's category of the traitor. But it was the multiferous and multifarious strands of the global avant-gardes that forged a trajectory reaching back to the early twentieth-century avant-garde:

> Much of my trajectory then was wrapped up in Duchamp, Cage, Jackson Mac Low. Even though I didn't use their techniques, it was like this wonderful conceptual leap for me. Also, that influence of the avant-garde in literature that comes through Dadism, Russian and Italian Futurism, it's stayed with me most of my life. It's also fascinating that you can have similar forms, but one's fascist and one's communist. That was a big thing in my early twenties because I used to have an idea that you could develop forms that were ethical, But, of course, you can't. I mean, a form is defined by its use, similar to a Wittgenstein cliché where a word is defined by its use. (Clemens, "Noise and Voice")

After Stewart returned from Europe, she found herself "out of contact with everybody. Then I realised I was nowhere. Now that I'm older, I think, did I do the right thing?" Negotiations around displacement, return, senses of displacement at home have indeed become part of the experience of being part of the transnational avant-gardes; being outside and inside nation, taken in and borne along by forms and feelings, feeling affiliated or traitorous. Partaking of such international avant-gardism concerns not only the phases, stages of the writing life, but the complex subjectivity of avant-gardism and being avant-garde.[3] The story however is ultimately one of a depth of influence and affinity:

> I was involved in some radio stuff in the '80s in Europe. But I was more interested in the American thing and went there often back then. And these were people who did link up with Dadaism in an obtuse way: John Cage and Jackson Mac Low. There were lots of others, of course, too. Even though I wasn't using those techniques, it was a conceptual wonderland. It's almost like, okay, well if they can do that, what can I do? That's what I want for younger people. Don't do the same, but can I make a space for you? Which you have a responsibility to do.

The "conceptual wonderland", which at once gives permission (if you can do that, what could I do?), also brings in the question of influence (what can then be done, and how differently?) – a generational question here, but equally still, a transnational and hemispheric influence. Cage's influence ranged over multiple milieus, from post-Schoenbergian serial and experimental music to anarchist and libertarian philosophy in the arts, Fluxus and poetry, from American poets like Joan Retallack, whose procedural forms in some ways derive and in some ways depart from her time spent with Cage, to the Australian avant-garde poet Javant Biarujia. Jackson Mac Low less so, although appraisals of Mac Low are presently on the rise and there is a better understanding of his prosody and how his type of indeterminacy differs from Cage's, and how to make sense of, how to heed such sheer prosodic dissonance. Stewart's interest in Mac Low is therefore specific, unusual, unique. The *permission* that affinity gives, through

---

[3] The avant-garde poet's "career" is an odd, if not oxymoronic thing. At once avant-garde poets have certainly carried careers in poetry, but the idea of *choosing* such a path is strange enough. For these thoughts I am indebted to a conversation had with Charles Bernstein in a restaurant, in Shanghai, where he noted how odd it was that poets would seek such description (in any literary context, US American, Australian) given how little you "get" from being avant-garde.

something as unexpectedly transmissive as a formative experience with Dada, engender in Stewart an avant-garde *jouissance*, a conceptual wonderland. With Duke, but even in those earlier grapplings with avant-garde poetics in the 1940s like Hooton and Malley, such encounters could easily effect the opposite: fear, confusion, aversion, the will to mock an avant-garde practice, even put it to death and wholly chase it out of a literary culture. The story of influence in the avant-garde is one told not so much by anxiety as through wonder. Influence is often couched in the terms of a narrow genealogy, shadowed by the opposition to invention, but it is also charged by wonder.

Avant-garde poetics in the late twentieth century would not just be opposition but participation, therefore, in the internal dynamics of invention already on the other side. This doesn't guarantee much on the side of reception. As Bob Cobbing once implored:

> the people hear gibberish;
> Poets ! how can nothing be said
> with all that noise ? (n.pag)

"Poets" (!, not :) are responsible agents to history. Yet "the people" might not hear a critique of Sound Poetry in Sound Poetry, knowing not the history (and nor should they). Poets might then be left shocked, in no elitist way, that "the people" are claiming no meaning in piles of sound. When it is left to "the people" to decide, they may hear just gibberish, but then again it might be Sound Poetry that isn't making semantic enough from the riches of what presents itself in the absorbing register of the nonsemantic. Historically, then, it is important to extrude it all from caricature, if at all we have to, because while the influence from Cage and Mac Low is notably linked back to that further influence, Dadaism, in Mac Low the strands that comprised his poetics could be various, from Merz, Kurt Schwitters, even Hopkins, one of his favourite poets and a source of consolation and inspiration late in his career. Stewart's influences, which emerged from lived experience, whether familiar or unfamiliar, ultimately became inimitable peculiarities of her person and poetic attitude.

I. *Notational Poetics Revisited*

There is an openness to influence and fear of the limitations of influence (bad affinities) in the Antipodal poetic avant-garde; a sense of responsibility marks these affinities. I say affinity, not lineage, for that implies another kind of genesis, more locked in. I have a critical affinity with the uses of notation in poems designed for performance, where the matter is sound. In previous critical excursions I've noted how musical notation had an impact on the form, time, structure and even allegorical weight of certain notationally susceptible longer poems. Certain works call for notation (or are "susceptible" to it) because they wanted to see what writing would look like bound to sound, or on some larger plane, they use music as a means to an end (sometimes as the literal ending of a poetic work). That is to say, notation both impacts the smallest structures of language (tone, phoneme, the ligature and contour of letters as a way of recording sound upon a stave), and the largest structures (the epic, the long poem, the long poem capstone, narrative arc and, in the biggest examples, allegory). Another tendency is a disjunct between the result of a notational mark (performance) and the notational mark itself, which is often de-mediated and removed from its function. Every so often, as with graphic notation, we would come across a score as much to be looked at as played: eye music, but more than that too. This "critical affinity" doesn't build things up but breaks things down. To use US analytic philosopher Nelson Goodman's word "notationality": I recognised that notationality, the definition of what notation is, its *definitising*, and the idea of notation as a concept, had both a real sonic, but also allegorical role to play, and that notationality was more than just a function; the definition of notation itself asks questions of the sign and exploded the field of writing because it found itself among a system of signs not just all geared to the performance of a work.

The definition of notation sometimes (but not always) meant "by hand". The works of Hanne Darboven, Mirtha Dermisache and, in the American context, Christine Sun Kim, Cy Twombly and Robert Grenier, are variously "notational", and uniquely so according to this definition, as are many of the examples included in John Cage and Alison Knowles's *Notations* anthology of 1969. Poet-performer Hazel Smith, comparing Stewart with Ania Walwicz, has noticed as much:

> In Amanda Stewart's performances there is a much greater gap between the text and performance than in Ania Walwicz's work. The texts have a visual interest of their own which is often transformed into an aural effect, though it is not always the only aural effect one would most expect. ("The Transformation of the Word", 233)

Trace to stroke, sound to output: notational poetics doesn't draw a A-to-B line between these. Notational by necessity – given Stewart's

This piece is for a performance comprising whistling, thinking and silence. The title and the names of each section are spoken aloud as words. The piece itself is otherwise whistled.

The Liberated Showroom

1. the romance of ownership

       ↑   ↗   ↗   ↑

  (wolf whistle) ('come here' whistle) ('come here' whistle) (wolf whistle)

2. the kurrawong from Marrickville

(kurrawong whistle)   (kurrawong whistle)

3. the dance and her

>X..

>X..
    (improvise aloud and to oneself using silence and whistling
    that comments on the preceding sections and the present)

4. The Liberated Showroom

☐ ....

☐ ....
    (stand still and silent for 15 seconds or longer)

Figure 7.1 Amanda Stewart, performance score for "The Liberated Showroom" from *I/T: Selected Poems, 1980–1996* (1998), 38.

work has been performed and is designed to be – it might just as well prevent any one sound from occurring as "gear it for performance". Moreover, after the event-scores of Cage, George Brecht, Yoko Ono, Mac Low and the Fluxus tendency, issues of the indeterminacy (and determinacy) of notation are key. To illustrate, here is an opening score, for "The Liberated Showroom" (see Figure 7.1).

Scored for any person, the gap left between text and performance leaves an element of surprise even and peculiarly for the performer themselves: "improvise aloud and to oneself". It's improvisation, not indeterminacy. Indeterminacy in its Cagean rather than philosophical

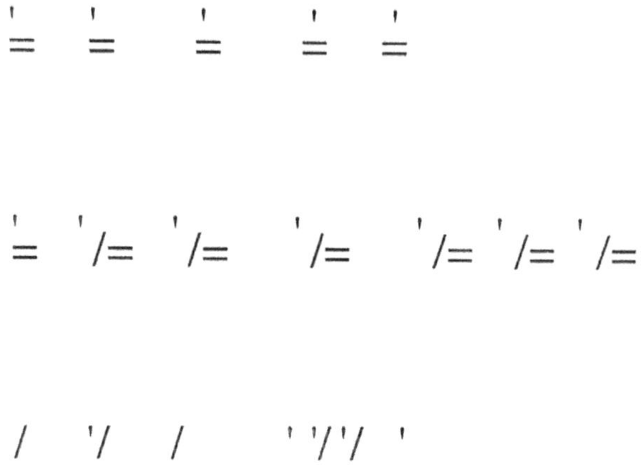

```
   '      '     '        '    '
   =     =     =        =    =




   '    '    '      '    '    '    '
   =   /=   /=     /=   /=   /=   /=




   /   '/   /      ' '/ '/  '
```

Figure 7.2 Amanda Stewart, "Haiku for Min Tanaka", from *I/T: Selected Poems* (1998), 12.

usage describes a type of process of making or composing a work (that may still happen as "live" event). Improvisation refers more to a specific time, often in public, in which things are left to chance, but organised often around a series of decisions and parameters that may be worked out in advance. There is a sarcastic commercial reference too, the showroom being an embourgeoised space for commercial impresarios, a space of performance nonetheless.

Performing "thinking" is more unusual; in the realm of a critical exteriority (this now, the performance of *a* reading). Coupled with silence and whistling, the piece might seem to be as much for the performer as for an audience – it might even remain within the confines of the more private environment of silent reading. The use of whistling in "The Liberated Showroom" begs comparison to certain vocal works by Chris Mann, whose "Whiskus" work, and "whistlin is did" were used by John Cage for mesostics in "Eight Whiskus", composed in 1984 and premiered in 1985 by Joan La Barbara. Another fine example of an homage, or gift, is the "haiku for min tanaka" (see Figure 7.2).

This is gestural notation, and given it's for Min Tanaka, a dance score. Notational ambiguity, identified by Smith, is palpable: the apostrophe-like mark may, for instance, denote a prime, a derivative in mathematical notation. There is an element of notationality here that seems more than musical or gestural, as with a lot of notation, in that it suggests code at the same time as setting the conditions for indeterminacy (note certain asymmetries in the score, with the placement of the equality signs and the forward slashes). It is a haiku, in the derivative sense of its having a regular syllabic count, which, thought of in clusters, serves as its metrical scaffolding (five units, seven units, five units), but it demands interpretation without, in advance, commanding meaning. As Fluxus in the 1960s showed us, the element of "surprise" in improvisation does curious things to time, demanding, if nothing else, reflection on the nature of time. The American composer Christian Wolff once noted on the choreography of Merce Cunningham that although you could never predict what would happen next in a performance, when it did happen it would feel exactly right: "that's *it*". Certain listeners might not so much prepare themselves ("expect the unexpected") as pay attention to the "becoming inevitable". Avant-gardes after 1960 revealed this to us perhaps to a greater extent than the early twentieth-century avant-gardes.

II. "The Twentieth Century Never Happened"

Looking at notation gives you the giddy sense of looking at *time frozen*, but not so much in the museological sense, as in the past, as for another time, the future. The gap between textualism and notationality opens up here. For what textuality shows us, and what it has demanded of the reader, is that we show textualists' commitment to the historicity, or archaeo-logics of the textual object. The limit-cases of notational writing have shown us something quite different: we are rather thrust into the mechanism of time itself, even unto an immediate present.

In Stewart's photocopy series, begun in the 1980s, there is an unusual connection with vocal inflection in speech, a visual polyphony that at times resembles a musical score. The polemical title of one of the series, "The Twentieth Century Never Happened", already tells us that it is more than "just visual". This is a series that will take as its object various concepts of history and time (Figure 7.3).

I pick up the phone and call Stewart to speak about other matters, but eventually I ask about these and other works. Stewart notes that what really concerns photocopy writing is the corruption of thought in the twentieth century and the issue of choreography. Progressive developments in physics, the arts, philosophical thought, transformations in perception, in relations between the observed and the observer (from psychoanalysis to the twelve-tone scale, genetics, linguistics and nuclear energy), once represented or promised

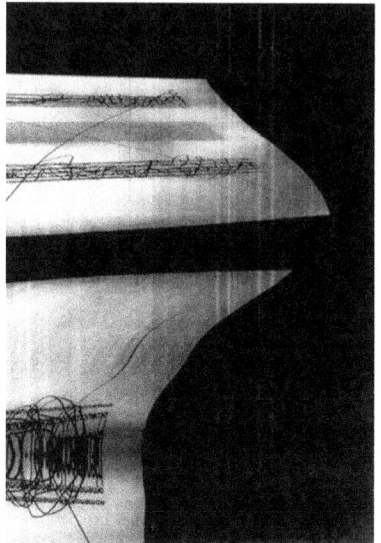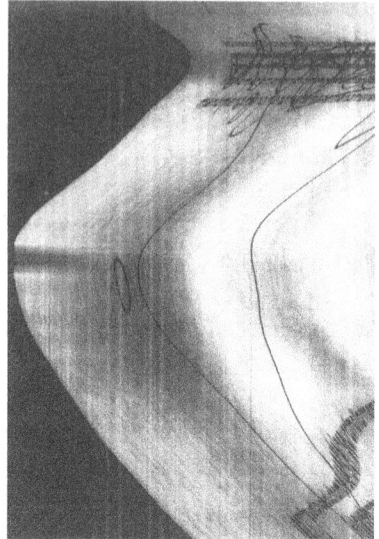
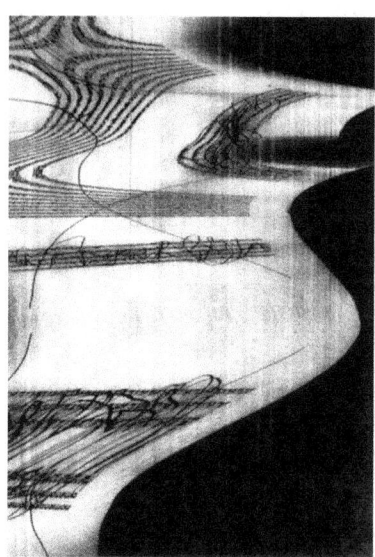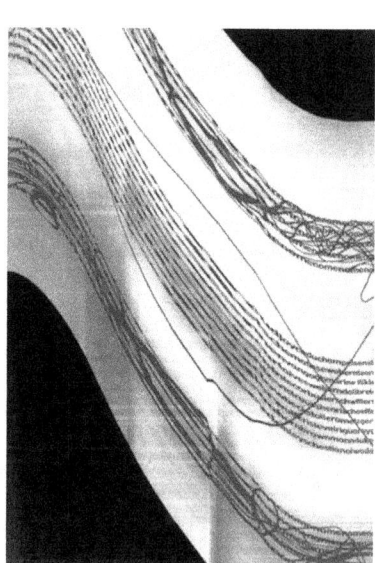

Figure 7.3 Amanda Stewart, visual pieces from "The Twentieth Century Never Happened" (2010), NZEPC site.

greater freedom for humanity. But these "advances" only partially transferred benefits to the social body. They "never entered the grammar of thinking". Materialist histories give good insight into precisely what psycho-political tectonics caused this. Hooton's idea of anarcho-technocracy in the 1940s tells us something about why the twentieth century never happened, recalling too that Stewart was a producer for the ABC documentary, *The Death of Harry Hooton*.

There is a strike-through, a cross through the text. Making images with the pre-digital aperture gave much to the maker: the shutter could be left open for so long. Reproduction began with use of the ABC office photocopier, and Stewart is adamant that the text itself, prior to its choreographing on the aperture, was *designed* for the photocopier, for the machine. How much you could get out of a single thing is what choreographing an original text could "offer". The hit rate was fairly low, as for every hundred produced, twenty or so would be chosen according to whether they worked or not. And not all texts "work". To use a "normal" text one would risk aesthetic deficiency, so the legerdemain of this technics remains secondary to the preparatory procedure, the *de*-purposing of the photocopier. It's a problem for notation and improvisation alike: how much preparation does spontaneity require? Create your texts beforehand and you commit to the quintessence of the source text. More unlikely is the connection with vocality. Loosely notational, or *re*-notational, one could uncover a notational element in these works of xeroxing or xerography, voice not stripped of signification but given new function: at chapter's end we will find sound poetry semantically aerated. Not-voice is glitch voice repurposed: thought in disuse at the cusp of refunction.

III. *THIS: Critical Histories*

As with the previous chapter, much depends on how these disparate approaches further congeal to our larger purpose: history. Stewart's concerns are vast: the history of thought and mind, aesthetics histories, (socio)linguistics, psychoanalysis, physics and, again, geopolitics. It is worth some critical pause on the "choreography" that leads to the negation of the twentieth century. For in fluid movement, the pages that are swiped across plastic film in the process of xerography (in Greek, "dry writing") can be said to become *xerox-graphesis* or *xerographesis*, a type of non-citational graphic writing that in its chronometric exactitude pursues an absolute present at the same time as giving oracular message to larger swathes of history – whole centuries of time. The fixity of a date when it becomes historical is the titular form of "IT BECOMES: JULY 1981":

> IT'S OUTRAGE
> US. I MEAN
> WITH ALL THIS WITH ALL THIS I MEAN
> IT'S ALL THIS. O . IT'S
> JUST DISGUSTING. IT'S IT'S IT'S
> IT IS IT IS IT IS
> OFF THE AIR/INCREDIBLE/OFF/HORRIFIC/TYPICAL/
> I MEAN IT'S AMAZING IT'S
> THATCHERFRAZERAEGUNRIGHTWINGWARWEDDINGREB
>   ELLION
> POLICECAPAFEUDALIS.M.ACHOMONOPOLEADERS
> WARNEWSCONTROLWARNEWSCONTROL. I MEAN I MEAN
> IT'S BECAUSE AND IT'S IT'S
> I MEAN IT IS. I MEAN AND IT IS
> IT IS IT IS IT IS IT IS
> IT'S IT'S IT'S IT'S
> IT. IT. IT.   IT . IT   (I/T, 12)

Thatcherism and Reaganism as they loomed large over several decades spurned a type of rebellion, a critique, but this is also a critique of left critique and to a degree not critique at all (more on critique soon). Making "it" become a date in time – "it" never identified as oppositional – makes it an object of criticism (resistance to neoliberalism). It reveals the voices that find "it" redolent of disgust: less critique then as a heavily deictic look at the consequences of a structure (neoliberalism, financial rather than productive capitalism) or process (monopolisation and control). The roughened legibility of raw speech resembles political vernacular (outrage, disgust, horror), but the agglutinated compacting and squeeze of words detaches them from any centrally commanded Subject. It should become clear why it is that Stewart, and the late twentieth-century Antipodal avant-gardes, were *traitors* in that especially "Australian" sense Mann suggests: the rough vernacular of the traitor, mixed with the earnestness of political style and the vernacular exposé (post-framed), is quite antithetical to Lecercle's pretentiousness in Malley, even though, as we soon will see, the step back is critical. Following the July 1981 poem is another written the year after, titled "Forked Lands : 1982":

> NO FUT
>   ure is ours to s
>   ix months in a leaky
>   b
> ritannia, Britannia rules the waves. Britains

> never, never, never shall be s
>   ave the Queen
> it's a fascist re
>   dream the impossible dream
>   (*I/T*, 34)

Like "IT BECOMES: JULY 1981", this poem was written in the year its title announces, 1982, a year of high punk. In it lyrics from the Sex Pistols are spliced in: "God Save the Queen, it's a fascist regime". It was also the year in which the Franklin Dam blockade was in full swing, an environmental movement that led to the dam's cancellation in 1983 under the Bob Hawke Labor Party Prime Ministership. In 1982 Australians were formally removed from the definition of "British Subject" in British law. This would not inaugurate some full break, nor would it lay the foundations for a non-Commonwealth model of governance. The idea of Republicanism in Australia has a long and complex history, as Mark McKenna has noted in a conspective history on the subject from responsible government in 1856 to Federation and its twentieth-century decline (it was published before the Republican referendum of 1999), and the idea of a Republic antedated even 1788, as some assumed an Antipodal Republic was inevitable. Many Republics could have eventuated; none did. Humphrey McQueen's Marxist reading of the Australia-Britain relationship, in *A New Britannia*, is a closer reference here, and this is something that the radical left in Australia has often kept in mind. Major political parties, like the Labor Party, have advocated a Republican platform but not yet had the geopolitical weight to enact it in real terms.

For an Australian avant-garde, the exact political horizon is obscured. In the vicissitudes of poetic form all this obscurity is given due clarity in that the historical urging of an expanded present builds bridges from the past to the future through the present matter of form. Poetic historiography in a radical key does time in a different sense; it moves through history for the sake of a future. Leaning on the politics of the future wagers that the present can be resignified. Contemporary examples of this book – the works of Duke, Walwicz, Fogarty and Stewart – have shown why avant-gardes tend always and consistently to risk marginality in order to resignify the present. Antipodal avant-gardes sought prophecy. They were, in a phrase, critical-social-prophetic. In doing so they refused to flatter the present, or even to address the present only, which is different from an attempt to be above the fray or aloof from the contemporary stream, its issues or events. Stewart seems acutely aware of this – if not the whole question of time and the vanishing present – and it is no exaggeration to say that it becomes part of her poetics, as it does with Fogarty. The question of whether such poetry is to operate on the register of historical record, or even *as* criticism, suffuses a notably difficult poem titled "on criticism: THIS":

on criticism:

THIS

The Legend

I	=	the critic
IT	=	the object of criticism
THIS	=	the resulting critical work
ITS	=	the voices of the object
YOU	=	the subject of the critical work

I. The Author

$$\frac{I}{IT} = THIS$$

2. The Voices of the Object

$$\frac{IT}{ITS} = THIS$$

3. The Return of the Subject

$$YOU \frac{(I}{\cancel{IT}} \times \frac{IT)}{ITS} = \frac{YOU.I}{ITS} = THIS$$

(QED) ⨯

(*I/T*, 11)

An explication as follows: There are three equations. The Legend tells us it is both an issue of Subject and Object in grammatical and theoretical senses. The first is an Authorial Criticism (or situation within a criticism) where a critic is simply divided by the object of criticism itself: not hard to imagine in a "New Critical" situation. The second sees the object of criticism divided by its voices; this polyphony produces a criticism or critical situation where the voice(s) of the object are legion and up front. The third is the most curly: You, the Subject, possibly the Subject in the sense of the one who writes and perhaps produces objects of criticism, multiply with a multiplication of the previous two situations – a critic divided by their object of study and a critical object divided up by its voices – and this can be cross-multiplied to cancel out the common factors of the previous two situations. The simplified version thus is that You and the Critic multiply, become a product (You X Critic) and enter into a fraction with the denominator below, the polyphonic wash of voices in the critical object. Divided by those voices, the final situation, the third solution, is found.

Let us settle a few other issues before final sums. "<u>THIS</u>" is, crucially, in the title, the product of the resulting critical work: so the whole poem is a criticism, in a sense. Keep in mind that it all comes down to a single solution *quod erat demonstrandum*, thus it is demonstrated, a unity between the three equations – but *not so quick*, because it is circled, has been queried. The cross is equivocal, it might suggest an error, or it could be an echo of the cross-multiplication.

I want to use this to reflect on critical method. It does not have to be so simple as that you, the poet, are also the critic (let us avoid errors), or that a poem is a piece of criticism. But the final equation seems to point to a possibility of Subjective Criticism of a kind that is divided by the voices of the object of criticism. The poet-critic in this scheme is not one who simply carries voices, but one who is divided by them. And this *is criticism*. This is happening in Stewart's critical-historical poetry. The previous two poems from 1981 and 1982 showed this, and it has happened very much throughout this book; the voices, disciplines, fields, institutions at play have been pulling in different directions at different intensities. These might not all be "voices", but if they are let's say that history has remained here the *innere Stimme* (inner voice) of the critical chorale. It would be glib to dismiss the theoretical dimensions in Stewart's critical-historical chronometrics. Never retracting then the role of the body, the final section on sound in performance gets us from the page to the air. Forget not the matheme, or patheme, as Lacan would have called it, of "on criticism: <u>THIS</u>".

For a critic or avant-garde hermeneut, no poem could so reflect back at what would be done to it. Even so abashed, the critic holds off or comes to a halt: interpellation at the scene of critical reading. In the hustle and bustle of ideas, the contemporary critic experiences, for an instant, some deeper reflection, for what theory can one apply to a poem that theorises in advance the critical structures of its reading?

IV. *Sound, Improv, Air*

Doesn't this all have to be heard to be believed? The live performance event happens through air and vibration and the proximity of bodies, something no academic writing on the matter can recreate. But in this reflection we have ample opportunity to listen out to the end. The matter of time in Stewart is one of an *expanded present*, and a matter of record, the historical time of recording, captured (or capsuled) for future listening. Stewart's improvisatory style, whether interpreting or extemporising off a score – taking off from a poetics of notation, or going rogue and sheetless on stage – puts poetry into spaces of infinite digress. The spaces that contain and indeed "outwork" such sonic vibration can only be experienced, if not at least captured on camera. Three elements come to mind here: the place of sound itself, which never quite adds up with the rest of a poem's elements, the practice of "improv", colloquially put, as a practical necessity in the live performance, and the function of voice let lift in air.

It may be that the "pragmatism" at work in the post-Cagean avant-garde returns rationality where it was seen lacking in the early twentieth-century impetus to visuo-verbal experimentation, given how much the psychoanalytic theory of the voice bound itself to the notion of the lost object.[4] In this final section and final close analysis of the book, I want to leave space here for "deeper listening" (Pauline Oliveros's phrase and practice), so not to overframe listening and pre-empt expectation. Analytic philosophy has other prerogatives that might be of some moderate use getting us there. In *Philosophy in a New Key* Susanne Langer not so much argues as states, in a pragmatic strain, that:

> Communication by sound is what we have looked for among the apes; a *pragmatic use of vocables* is the only sign of word-conception that we have interpreted to their credit, the only thing we have tried to inspire in them, and in the "wild children," to pave their way toward language. What we should look for is *the first indication of*

---

[4] I say it on sum as if there is a unified theory though on closer examination there is not. Still what the psychoanalytic conception of the object-voice does, whether it has application in literature or not, is separate the voice from its sound. While the drives circle endlessly around the voice as *objet petit a*, as Brian Kane puts it, after Mladen Dolar's notion of the "acousmatic" voice, it is psychoanalysis itself that has created this (miniature) drama in the spoken utterance, between desire and the circuit of the drives (213–14).

symbolic behaviour, which is not likely to be anything as specialised, conscious, or rational as the *use* of semantic. (110)

Like no language at all, Sound Poetry probes an archaeopoetics of the human animal but, to be pragmatic about it, can offer no further insight into how the symbolic register breaches the semantic, in reality. Again it suits us better to probe the locus of the institution of Sound Poetry, how various "churches" of the avant-gardes, as Duke acerbically noted, were so deeply historical. Stewart has spoken to me about the experience of listening to avant-garde Sound Poetry as something indeed "historical", thus artefactual. Same too the sheer historicalness of voice, but categorically different for the analytic philosopher who, unlike the psychoanalyst, analyses or locates the object in the Symbolic register rather than in the Real. This is how the refunctional poetics of the *neo*-avant-garde, in too seeking a repudiation of the rational in the nuclear age and into the age of plastic and punk, could make an object of the voice. If a word, as Wittgenstein put it, is defined by its use, so too is a voice defined by its history. Just how philosophical this could become is revealed in ", No Person, speaks" (Figure 7.4).

Distinguish the chaotics of language from where it comes and you might miss what's missing: an *s* is absent before silence, before the poem even begins (the title "begins" with a [displaced] comma). The empty Subject *ab ovo* is seen looking underneath "ilence": but does (s)ilence have its counterpart? A quietness in the parallel p's leaves us with the rest of the poem, the chorality of its "trace patterns" and "iceberg notations", also paratextual and oddly marginal beneath the eight vertical axes above. Each of these is a micro-binary, which "vs" one word against another (and even *versus* vs and vs). Each axis is punctuated by brackets so that, while there is often a sense in strewn text of a lineate stream attached to the left-hand margin and drifting rightwards, the geometry of the poem (which I have set out indicating how it runs on a longer page in the original text through use of an arrow) remains vertical-horizontal. Punctuated, and justified to the right-hand margin, the axes have more to do with channel rather than flow. In "vice versa" too, letter-matter, flung on larger swerve, be it lineate or fractal, has axial geometries charged between channel and flow (Figure 7.5).

Find disjunction after gaps and absences. In the strait between there's a different graphesis: striated diagonals at scrabbled juncture. Is it lexical plaiting in slopes at depth? Tri-dimensional space? Flat field or off the page? Set starkly against the agglutinative lines, one

, No Person, speaks

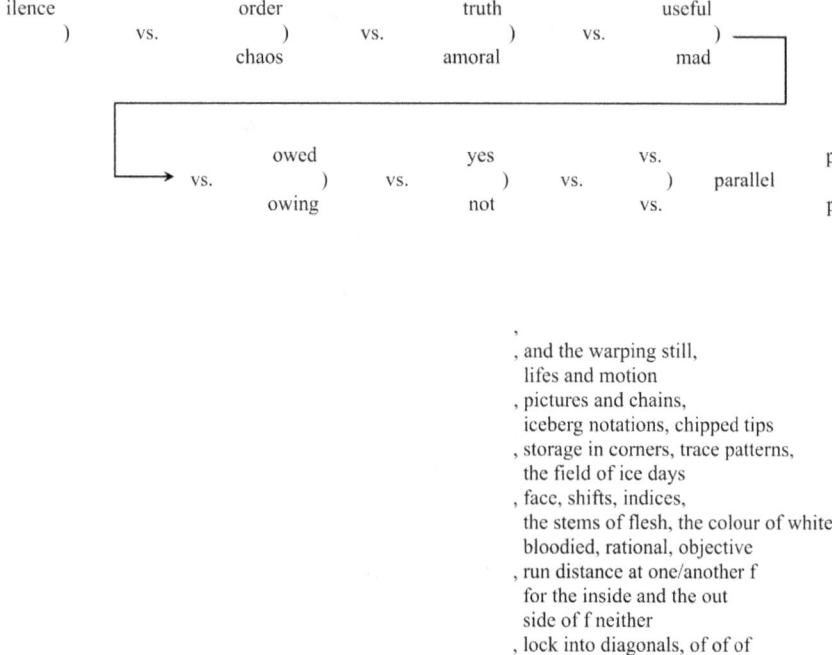

Figure 7.4 Amanda Stewart, ", No Person, speaks", from *I/T: Selected Poems* (1998), 8–9.

above, three below, these strike the eye as stavelike, more frozen, less fluid clumps of time. Things seem to get more disjunctive between – phrases moving in and out of view – but what is so striking about the textures of passages like these is not just that the registers are "apoetic" in mandated style or diction. What is striking is how much the critic needs a metalanguage to talk it through. Strung with *ethos* (also rhetorical, the power of voice upon its hearer) is *us* (our relations). That is to say, relations shift at the refunctional edge, between author, subject and critical object. The page divides as does the object of criticism and the voices in the critical object. Multiple registers are heard, interdetermined as mutual-sounding signs ("unsaid-fields ..."): effects of gapping, clumping, channeling. Is it a map? Surely it too is a score.

vice versa

unsaidfieldsresonancesnotationsdistinctionsgapsabsencesdisjunctionsbetween

thespokentheheardthesaidseenrememberedwrittenrecordedmadextrainterdetermin
atextraintersubjectivecontextfielduseotherexchangeintimatedistancesensitive
doubtherubofparadigmstensionsigntimerelationsbetweenquestionsbeingnotknowing

Figure 7.5 Amanda Stewart, "vice versa", from *I/T: Selected Poems* (1998), 60.

"Personal:" and "Critical:" as Johanna Drucker advises. Critical: Just imagine if a critic was to say Stewart's was an "original voice"? The vocal function is divided, as object, not only in psychoanalytic but also in critical senses (object of interest, of inquiry). It is still an effect of the speaking subject. In amongst contributions to a volume on voice in the digital era, Stewart signposts "vocal textures" – her own, but told from a certain critical distance – as in this passage:

> Every fluctuation of breath, pitch, timbre, and volume is revealed at the edge of the speaking subject: stutters, slips of the tongue, strange timbral fluctuations, squeaks, rasps, clicks, size and consistency of

lip smacks, rhythm of speech, and length and functions of pauses. ("Vocal Textures", 177)

Revealed is no light word, because the fluctuation was already there. Stewart then began developing "new notation systems to represent these graphically" (177). How to spatialise *vocal textures*, mark a click, trace a rasp, leave a pause? At the cusp of a new vocal function, notationality is worlds away from the stave. The twentieth century did this to us even if it didn't transform the deeper grammar of our thought. These finer points beget notation by hand, the aperture of a photocopier, the registers of virtual scorelines, and as a last resort the grooves of record or doing away with it all; going off the record and onto the stage. Amplified and unamplified voice specify at least three modes of contemporary avant-garde audition that certainly reveal new intricacies: 1. Breath and voice in vibration through air live in real-time, 2. Sound or voice engrooved or encoded as with studio record and 3. In between; live voice layered, amplified or pre-recorded in real-time space. This voice which is never one could do all three for a contemporary poetic score.

Providing context: the last move. Critical: Linda Ioanna Kouvaras, in a book of musical criticism focusing on post-1970s Sound Art, finds that "Australia has a rich history in experimental music" (4). The internationalist Australian composer Percy Grainger (1882–1961), whose "Free Music" machines, and theories therefrom, are telling examples of musical invention in the first half of the twentiet century, combined with John Cage's historical influence on a "group of musicians working in Melbourne in 1963, that galvanised Australian experimentalism" via artist and musician Robert Rooney, seem to tell a similar story for Sound Art, as that told in this book, for poetry (7–8). Stewart, for Kouvaras, "renowned for her often riotous, virtuosic displays of vocal acrobatics and dense text-based pieces" (201), gets close to the fragility of the "human form" (214). The "historical" avant-gardes, from incendiary manifestos of Futurist noise, find new openings in postmodern nostalgia (3). No longer confined, Sound Art could more breezily dispense with archaic notions of harmony. I have not used the jargon of postmodern freedom in the aftermath of a road paved by historical avant-gardes, but Kouvaras's use of the term "Altermodern" is well applied. The terminological outcome is more of the neo-senses; of neo-modern and neo-avant-garde. I have no doubt that Australian poetry after Fogarty, Walwicz and Stewart is no longer confined to archaic notions of verse style, and that this has been a classic, though still historical, move between modern and contemporary, or modern and postmodern.

More recently, Stewart has released a 2018 album, *submental*, from a new group, 180°, through the splitrec label, the recording arm of the Splinter Orchestra (a loose, and large ensemble going since 2002). The group comprises Stewart, Nick Ashwood, on acoustic guitar, and Jim Denley, an original member of Machine For Making Sense, on bass flute. In performances, Denley often deconstructs, pulls apart the instrument to explore the sounds that the instrument makes when not of one piece. The album is divided into eight tracks: scalene, equilateral, oblique, isosceles, obtuse, acute, degenerate and equiangular. Moving into the space of sound are "objects of criticism" that come from both geometry and critical theory, so they're not all familiar. The experience of listening to them in a 2020 performance in an underground space in Sydney was one not of ambient inattention, but of being suspended in the drama of space. Plugged in, the experience is different. Personal: There is a familiarity – one can hear Stewart's voice if one "knows" it – but suspension and unfamiliarity tell us that *that* voice is not the only dimension of vocality in the work. But the aural-oral world that is the basement space is an airy, eerie and aery one – air coming from all around. Air and wind modify pitch, even at closer proximity and when surrounded. Inscribing any of this seems pointless. Critical: It is not. Personal: Improvisation, or "improv", is neither casual nor comfortable. Critical: There is a historical difference in avant-garde writing between trying to be difficult and being difficult because that's the way you are, or how your writing processes happen to have turned out. The former tends towards provocation, in the historic avant-garde, and the latter I am tempted to call "improvocation", improvised provocation or provocative improvisation in the avant-garde aftermath. In the latter the provocative element is de-Romanticised, as with Oulipo, or with various kinds of non-mechanistic procedural writing after 1970. The contexts are not the revolutionary upheavals of the masses in the early twentieth century, but rather New Left critique in the West after the events of 1989–91, the survival of Eastern socialism, and later geopolitical critiques of neoliberalism and (sub-)imperialism in the Antipodes and around the world between the centuries and into the expanded present.

What can we then hear? The sound of the Antipodes that is post-Dada, post-avant-garde and neo-avant-garde is the sound of long aftershocks of invented languages and languages of invention. Evental shock begat textual disruption, it could be said, in old and new keys. One could find old friends in new spaces, traitorous affinities, refinement in disruption. Personal and Critical: hear-see "Icon":

1.

m m m m
m m m m
m m m m

mamamamamore d d d d
dadadada d I d I m d I
dmImim Im Idm dIdI Im

It's vibrating in air and it's sound-picture. This benediction pitched in acoustic space turns up "dadadada" again (among other things, including "mamamamamore"). D/M: direct message. To understand it, to hear it again, is to *stand directly under*, to be Antipodal, and be nothing less than a traitor (let this be an iconic move for the Antipodal avant-gardes). To be avant-garde may finally and necessarily have meant to turn away from the Antipodes, or turn one's back towards it. There we call the chapters quits. Now, in the expanding present that is Stewart's sounding and extended sound-world, we are beyond the point at which any advanced summa would give, or get, new turns or returns. Let us quote from "Kitsch Postcards" in closing. Eventually, when our gaze turns away from the Antipodal City, we begin to see the mirage. It ends "with backs turning, eyes to the desert". This excerpt is taken from the opening stanza . . .

Australia's Australia
Australia is.   I am
an Australia.   I am.
Is.   an Australian.

A Wáng Gǎ: an Epilogue

啊王尕

– Ouyang Yu, "A wáng gǎ"

I said at the beginning of this book that the complex of the "Antipodal City" is a complex of remoteness and non-liberation. The Antipodal City couldn't come from nowhere, for from deserts prophets come, as Geoffrey Serle reminded us, via A. D. Hope, *vis à vis* the Antipodal cultural cringe. Deserts are not nowhere, we now know for certain, and the spatial distortions are radical enough that, before us on a spool, we can make out some unravelling of time that beneath it gives us a modernist mirage. Focus on it again and you'll see (starkly imaged) a front-line. To translate the Antipodal avant-garde in the global context will be an act of liberation from a mirage of its own making.

Risk then it vanishing before our eyes, at this final turn. I have rarely, if at all, pushed the narrative of "cultural growth"; that this is proof of the creative spirit in Australia. Even so, modern as the *polis* that was modern Australia turned out to be, its cultural horizon remained lensed, distorted by hemispheric space, region, nation and inter-nation. The Australian desert was considered "useless" to the Europeans, where it is seen by First Nations people in those parts of the country as full of life, the repository of knowledge and philosophy. If there is a shadow underneath this book it is that problem of the two visions of the desert, as a place from which prophets come, and as a place which has no voice. Do avant-gardes make tracks across the desert or turn their backs to it?

I don't know. But how the Antipodes figured in the imagination of the early twentieth-century European avant-garde is where we

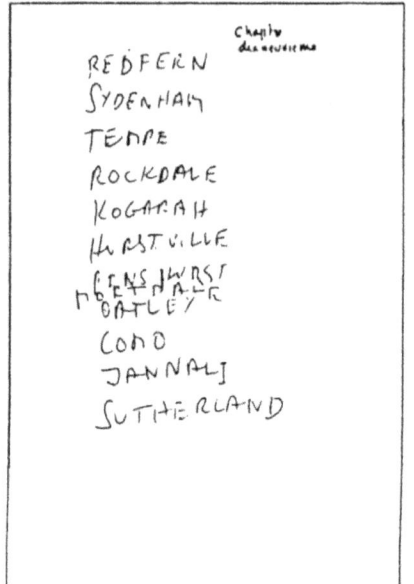 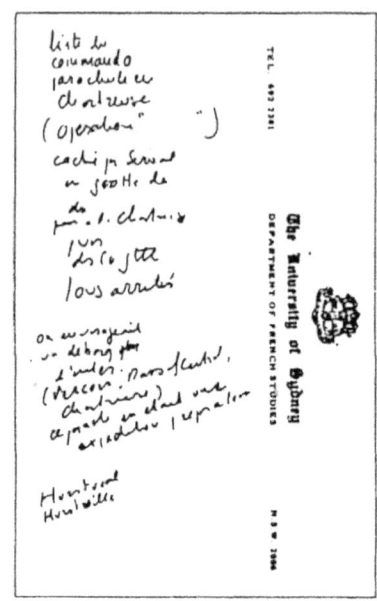

Figure 8.1 Georges Perec, from the Black Ring-file, folios 79/80; list of stations on the Sydney-Wollongong line, and names of the commando, in *53 Days* (2000, first published in 1989 by Editions P. O. L.), 223.

began, with Tzara and his sketchy attempts to translate and perform Oceanic, Aboriginal texts, and we could have continued along these lines. The future of Australian literature is not decided by Australian literature itself, nor does it situation depend on externalities.

We could have gone further out to get further in to this question. The tale of how Australia killed Georges Perec, who visited in 1981, our chronometrically confounding year, to write *53 Days*, but did not live to finish it, is an example worth our attention in these senses (Figure 8.1).

Perec seemed to know something about the violence of the Australian colony. "*C'est l'Australie qui m'a foutu mal!*", exclaimed Perec – "Australia fucked me up", so claimed by Colin Nettelbeck recounted later by Peter Salmon in the *Sydney Review of Books*. In an edition by Harry Mathews and Jacques Roubaud they present facsimiles of the "Black Ring File" where Perec lists stations going south of Sydney to the Sutherland Shire, away from central Sydney. Perec nearly misses one, Mortdale (death's valley). Death would greet him soon enough, but it is the second list that determines its real use, for a British commando unit: five Englishmen, Sutherland, Oatley, Mortdale, Penshurst, Sydenham; three Canadians, Redfern,

Rockdale, Hurstville; one New Zealander, Kogarah; two Frenchmen, Tempe, Como; one Lebanese, Jannali. Set in a French colony, about the pursuit of an unfinished novel by the missing crime-writer Robert Serval, it is hard not to read those fifty-three days as fated to transpire, or expire, without an avant-garde object at its end. Such a colonial society (so locked in a struggle for resources; engaged in an asymmetric and ongoing Frontier War for the large part of its history) could not advance secure foundations without creating narrative death-traps. Though a Federation in 1901 would fix Australia to the modern map of nations, what Republic could emerge on the back of such prolonged and unresolved war, without Treaty, without the question of sovereignty resolved? The folkish carapace of either bad fortune on the one hand or the lucky country, as Donald Horne would put it, is not what killed Perec, but one does have one's suspicions. An Antipodal horizon for avant-gardism could seem all but impossible in the Internet age. What forces worked against it? Did an Antipodal avant-garde survive into the digital age? When did it end, if it did (death's valley)? Is the price for difficulty death?

These have been difficult texts, stubborn poetries.[1] Yet no matter the stubbornness, I hope that I have not been incautious when it comes to assumptions of historical worth. It often comes back to judgement and we fool ourselves to think we have fully escaped the vicissitudes of taste. In saying that I want to put it to all sides: whether one dismisses or embraces experimental poetry, experimental poetry, like any other kind of poetry, has found itself on the scales of judgement. A critic can have a very clear idea of the strength of the "concepts" behind an experimental poem but little sense of the power of its linguistic intrigue. If we have been forced to say something judgmental in poetics then I suppose it will be enough to admit that these are poetries that are worth it, are of historical value, even if the only power they hold bubbles up occasionally from the murkiest theoretical blind spots; barnacled, it may seem, I am willing to admit, on a stubborn culture's literary underbelly. Power for whom? What needs to be gone through, much more closely than we have allowed for thus far, is the assumption that the texts are actually difficult. Difficulty can be in worst case scenarios tied to literacy, difficulty

---

[1] I refer to Quartermain's *Stubborn Poetries* and Bernstein's *Attack of the Difficult Poems* pre-consciously in this sentence. Both take different approaches to the question of difficulty. Quartermain uses the notion of poetic facticity, which sits curiously here alongside questions of history. Refusing recuperativity for the Australian avant-garde I have too preferred *debates* on extra- or non-canonicity (like those between Williams and Eliot).

with language itself, and on another level it can be something regulated by higher (editorial) powers. Scaling back on difficulty is something writers have consciously grappled with, in theory and for the practical matter of career, and almost always this gets read as a need to reach a wider audience, or not so much alienate an audience. We could think of experimental literacy then as a pedagogical issue. With the charge that a reader does not have the equipment to understand an experimental poem, we could add that, if that is true, the only way to change it is to teach it. To put it into the domain of a critical literacy, an instructional framework, further frames difficulty *qua* the difficulty inherent in ideological, rather than formal bias. To be clear: I have never claimed that there is any such subject that we should presume will not be able to cope with an experimental poem. It will be poets who are very often against against difficulty, not readers.

I. *The Long Avant-Gardes: Strain and Tedium*

But tediousness in the long avant-garde, if it is to be considered, is a type of resistance to interpretation. In this distance between the work and its interpretation, and the stubborn determination to maintain a kind of parallax in this perplexity, we find both the strain (difficulty) and strains (continuums) of avant-gardism in the long aftermath of experiment. The urgency with which difficult forms in the Antipodes have presented ideological and political challenges is nothing but an extension of what Georgina Colby called a concern for the social conditions of reading and resistances to presumptions of a stable or general reader towards which all writing must aspire. Experimental writing proposes new experiences of reading (3). It searches for a different political future in responses to crisis, another Polis, other forms of organisation; it is outscaped in its circles of reference, outside empire if only just and only sometimes. In aesthetico-political discussions the problem has become a distrust of experiment-for-experiment's-sake so-called, and a consequent fear of tightening ideological controls that then fall back to a confessional consensus of relative ideological stability of both subject and reader. Discourses on experimental writing cannot give up the challenge to meaningfully rearticulate difficulty. I propose, in closing, that in place of difficulty we speak of "tedium" in inventive writing. The difficulty of learning another language is a kind of tedium. Such exercises are not necessarily professional but may be tedious because they require simply a lot of hard work. The work of interpretation is a kind of labour that requires determination, styles of earnestness and persistence in the face of perplexity. It is a living with perplexity here that goes with the whole history of criticism and its life alongside the enigma and emendation. They have been the kinds of poetries that refuse "easy" reading, and I have had to keep up the effort, stay on my toes in order to place these readings. "Difficult" implies something else. Difficult for whom, and in what environment? That is the question, because as disparate and interlinked as these inventive strains have been, they have not only been difficult but tedious, daggy, stale, flat, in other words, thinkerly to the point that a "pleasurable" affective response has not been the only sought outcome. The blabbermouth Antipodal poet last century was grappling with a society that refused to listen, and turned to a revolutionary range of affects and effects, approaches that followed through on inventive projects to the (bitter) end; sometimes ascesis and austerity. First Nations poetic experiments ask us to rethink the entire colonial and imperial ground upon which an Australian cultural nationalism, with its long trail of genocidal and racial policy documents, has been forged. Compromise was not on the cards in any of these cases. Developmental and liberatory First Nations nationalisms are criminally suppressed.

There is very little therefore about Antipodal experiment that looks like invention "for the sake of it". We show again some doubt: avant-garde might indeed have been a misnomer. Set against these other purposes, was it just prestidigitation by sheer circumstance, or reactive higher refinement? Were it not for history we could have assumed so. Just as disruptive, if not just as refined, these *strains* of Antipodal avant-garde poetry, disparate and unified as they could be across communities and locales, had a certain bite – nay *character*, flavour, essence – things that have made its strains seem different to equivalent examples in the global catalogue. And yet to the global catalogue it could be closely connected. How different was it then? And different for whom?! If such traits are part of its character, they are also in authentic and inaesthetic categories or categorical functions in the modern arras of a certifiable National-Cultural poetics, and resistances to such certifiability. If this book has seemed like a carefully wrought revisionist history of Australian poetry, my working notes suggest a different approach. Things fell into place messily. The major works of experiment seemed to place themselves in this project; its logics seemed, weirdly enough, predictable, emergent on their own terms, but cobbled together. Things falling out, falling in, falling off. Swathes of information I had to process, assess, incorporate, reject, put back in. This mirrors, I think, the state of the

Australian poetic avant-garde now – an unfixed, morphing thing. As I wrote, things changed. I am sure now that the attitude was never to imagine a manifesto at the end of it, because history gave its materials. Having Brennan, Malley and the 1940s at the outset was not, as I made clear, a conciliatory gesture: Malley was no obscure outlier. Even if it might seem to some that I'd exhausted my theoretical armature when it came to canonicity and margins, having global currents in mind gave these chapters a route through. World poetics was a major frame for the consideration of avant-garde traditions as traditions, not magical breakaways from all traditions, and never ever a thing that appears from nowhere, never in one country alone. The avant-garde poem has an international history. The aim of this book has been to show that the avant-garde poem is a historical poem with historical or political style, and that reading the cultural, social and formal properties of an experimental poem is just as crucial as reading them in any other poem. I think, and I hope the reader is persuaded to likewise think, that this is a beneficial model of doing literary history, but not a totalising one. But big enough? What I hope *does* have ramifications outside of this book's historical confines, are the kinds of reading it encourages. It is not just of concern to Australian poetry how we read form, language, context, those strenuous crossings between the public and private, the historical and the political. These are things that keep coming up in classrooms and reading groups dedicated to the study of poetry worldwide.

Invented, rather than inventive, languages; another distinction. Two invented languages from Antipodal poets, Mezangelle (Mez Breeze) and Taneraic (Biarujia), are vastly different. Breeze (born Mary-Anne Breeze), has remained at the vanguard of Electronic Literature and code poetry since its early history. N. Katherine Hayles described Mezangelle as a kind of bilingual pidgin that "breaks the conventional link between phoneme and written mark, forging new connections between code and English" (as Hayles puts it in "Print is Flat, Code is Deep", 80). In an early section from the *Human Readable Messages, Mezangelle 2003–2011,* Breeze describes the writing process in the digital vernacular:

1.1.2 papazine n_interview][1][(2003-06-10 10:08)

A:
in general, before attempting to create a more "multimedia" oriented work [ie like the final incarnation of _[ad][Dressed in a Skin C.ode]
i always create smaller, more net-directed pieces which i term either net.wurks or code.works. these largely text/code based pieces are

constructed using the hybrid code/poetic dynamic [language] entitled mezangelle which is constructed via a mixture of code splicing [ie fragments of programming language-shards - mostly Perl - + operating system & email formats, tree/directory-structures + wildcard references, booleanisms, unix shell commands, html + java script conventions and ascii] and parsed poetic language including repeated allusions 2 hyperlinks via bracketing of meanings and word splicing. (28)

The whole book, which was also printed in hard-copy format, collects more than a smidgin of "mezangelled" texts (323 pages in total). There are varying levels of difficulty throughout, but some Antipodal familiarity too:

3.5.7 ini.or.out.ie (2005-05-30 23:32)

———or, how the————————————
_australian.howard .fascist.gov reeks+wrecks _

bi (line.E.ar {gh })context:

—————————————————— ——————————

/ [the.now.facist. $hitty.of]oz.howard.gov
   .consistently.re[a-
r]vok ing aw[kward.drawl.dictating.a.historical.death.knell.n ation].
   strine.lian
state-oriented control vis systematic nationalisation/centralisation:
 - via GST[+sales.taxing, isn't.it].collector.sne[ngine]ering
 - wrestling.n-port+x-port regulation[s] via fed.head.grappling
-         humanit[.tear.i.a(m)n]y.sucked.down   =
dead.in.a.welfare.st.RIP[time.is.out.of.economic.ka   li.appointed]
   joint
 - riding.the.spiked.m[ale.strom]edia.back.via.
/Corby-[fetishish.of.the.jung+the.drug.runner.booti ful].
/storied.2.drag.the.spot.lite.away.from.[non.alt.ru   {world.of.rue }
   ism]
//Union.raping+worker.r[ab]orting+
//un.[john.right.wing]law[s]full[of.bile+bl   acklists].D.ten[se]tion.
   fixing

(161–2)

Not *not* "in English". It's no great bombshell to point out, to take an example from nineteenth-century poetry, that the sprung rhythm of G. M. Hopkins, because it attempted to approximate "natural" speech, could find the reader elated or gone forlorn at such prosodic dissonance because, in effect, it was both too natural and because speech itself wasn't natural enough. The irony returns with Mezangelle: few would deny that contemporary readers are mired, nay, wired into the languages of the Internet and of social media, but its use in poetry, surprising as it might seem, still has the effect of feeling displaced, of being a language out of place. In any case, less understood in Breeze's work is its Antipodean political engagement: Australian radical left-activist politics in the Howard Government era (1996–2007), history, ecology, economy, time, contemporaneity, the political vicissitudes of the vanishing present in the belly of a major player in the imperialising world. Just as Brennan's *Musicopoematographoscope* came at a peculiar point in time, on time, Breeze's Mezangelle works take contemporaneity as a point of departure, demanding a new historical toolbox for critical readings of such work in our time. In what reads as a premonition of Twitter, launched in July 2006, one section dated "2005-06-19" refers to the "twittering cutsie output of a blogger" (167). By 2008 Breeze starts doing what she calls "Twitterwurk" (282). In Chapter 7 of *Human Readable Messages*, the inclusion of Twitter in "[twitte[reality_fiction", dated between "17/7/09" and "28/7/09", could not, of course, have appeared when the poem began, showing that Breeze's work is in some senses a long poem as a kind of book-repository of digital history. Some of this stems from an online residency called "Twitterwurking", which was commissioned by New Media Scotland for July 2008, where Breeze produced poems in the form of tweets using her account @netwurker. Thinking Twitter through New Media meant that, even if stylistically and formally the works stay predictably hybrid, media's historical shifts would issue change in content more than in form. These are weird timescapes: in "[twitte[reality_fiction" a reply to @botgirlq reveals she has been "using 'twittering' a year b4 Twitter".

II. *Emancipation of Disjunction: or, the "Flag Of Permanent Defeat" (Ouyang Yu)?*

A long avant-garde is a living avant-garde, and the terms of reference have changed even since the post-avant-gardes of the 1960s and 1970s. Methods have morphed. The way we speak about textual disjunction and dissonance has changed, and will change further. No doubt we are beyond the point, in literary studies and critical poetics, of simply pointing to fragmentation (*there*, look, it's broken into bits, and you, reader, are experiencing some kind of delight), and concluding that breaking language down into bits either produces some kind of material question or an actual politics. It does not (not that those who proclaimed it so were lying, but simply to say the politics of literature has shifted to other frames of reference). Students and teachers need a better discourse to handle historical tedium.

Pleasure cannot be the justification, even if it is the means. Such pedagogy is still a worthy cause, for the avant-garde poem is scintillating in the most serious, and sensorial, of senses. Bright flashes: the sheer scintillae of sense. Deployed and redeployed here, the word "invention" implies patient poetic labour and seems so reserved. But I see no contradiction. In the musical arts, it is expected that patience, effort, even degrees of refinement are required to construct a raucous modern symphony (1940–80), but in some canonical understandings of Australian poetry, a modern poem must *appear* smooth and bruit effortlessness. I wanted to avoid "that tired divide". The field of dismissive commentary has not been my focus when questions of author and reader came into view. Uncommon then, in this book, has it been to mention the more distressing aspect of avant-garde poetry in the eyes of the establishment; the leanest of issues but one that can serve as some final historical detail. Let one example suffice, then, from a phone call with Inez Baranay, who appears in the anthology *Telling Ways*. Baranay is adamant that the end of cross-subsidisation in publishing meant the end of distribution for inventive forms. Neoliberal marketisation across the board, in the late 1980s, spelled the "end of the mid list author". They might not have had spectacular sales but the Industrial Complex could at the very least give the mid-list author a corner to work from. That is all gone but other things have cropped up in the new century; the rise of Creative Writing in universities, for example, has in some quarters given new relevance to experimental forms. Instead of casting blame about the place and going manifesto, it has been possible to go into archives and into the history through living participants. Either way, experimental forms suffer on two fronts: an encroaching obduracy of the middle-brow establishment, and a creeping redundancy and stagnation within.

New bilingualism has emerged in the Antipodes, making translation and untranslatability an act of language invention. Breaking language up and assembling it again is more than fragmentation for fragmentation's sake here. Fragmentation is given new purpose by freeing itself from the shackles of the letter. To use Joan Retallack's pun, it's what the *frag meant*. The unity of the character, in Chinese, could not be more regulated and therefore no less prone to explosive irregularity when exposed to bilinguality. A good example of linguistic invention in a bilingual mien is Ouyang Yu's "吖允尕", or in pinyin, *Yā yóu gǎ*, which includes the phrase "啊王尕", which in pinyin sounds *A wáng gǎ*, homophonic of course for avant-garde. Further variations of equivalent sounds, many of which contain characters that refer to time, play on the trisyllabic a-vant-garde:

啊，王噶，啊，王嘎，啊，王尕，王尕，王尕
啊王尕，啊王尕，王尕王尕王尕
啊亡尕，啊亡尕，啊亡尕
啊汪王网望尕尕尕
啊王尕，啊王尕，啊王尕，啊王尕，啊王尕，啊王尕，啊王尕，啊王尕，
啊王尕尕，啊王尕尕尕，啊王尕尕尕尕
啊魍尕，啊尢尕，啊尢尕，啊尢尕，啊尢尕尕尕尕
啊尢尕尕尕尕啊尢尕尕尕尕啊尢尕尕尕尕啊尢尕尕尕尕
啊尢尕尕尕尕啊尢尕尕尕尕啊尢尕尕尕尕啊尢尕尕尕尕
啊尢尕尕尕尕啊尢尕尕尕尕啊尢尕尕尕尕啊尢尕尕尕尕
啊尢尕尕尕尕啊尢尕尕尕尕啊尢尕尕尕尕啊尢尕尕尕尕
啊尢尕尕尕尕啊尢尕尕尕尕啊尢尕尕尕尕啊尢尕尕尕尕
啊尢尕尕尕尕啊尢尕尕尕尕啊尢尕尕尕尕啊尢尕尕尕尕
啊尢尕尕尕尕啊尢尕尕尕尕啊尢尕尕尕尕啊尢尕尕尕尕
啊尢尕尕尕尕啊尢尕尕尕尕啊尢尕尕尕尕啊尢尕尕尕尕
啊尢尕尕尕尕啊尢尕尕尕尕啊尢尕尕尕尕啊尢尕尕尕尕
啊尢尕尕尕尕啊尢尕尕尕尕啊尢尕尕尕尕啊尢尕尕尕尕
啊尢尕尕尕尕啊尢尕尕尕尕啊尢尕尕尕尕啊尢尕尕尕尕
啊，王噶，啊，王嘎，啊，王尕，王尕，王尕
啊王尕，啊王尕，王尕王尕王尕
啊亡尕，啊亡尕，啊亡尕
啊汪王网望尕尕尕
啊王尕，啊王尕，啊王尕，啊王尕，啊王尕，啊王尕，啊王尕，啊王尕，
啊王尕尕，啊王尕尕尕，啊王尕尕尕尕
啊魍尕，啊尢尕，啊尢尕，啊尢尕，啊尢尕尕尕尕

(214–15)

A, wáng gá, a, wáng gā, a, wáng gǎ, wáng gǎ, wáng gǎ
a wáng gǎ, a wáng gǎ, wáng gǎ wáng gǎ wáng gǎ
a wáng gǎ, a wáng gǎ, a wáng gǎ
a wāng wángwǎngwàng gǎ gǎ gǎ
a wáng gǎ, a wáng gǎ, a wáng gǎ, a wáng gǎ, a wáng gǎ, a wáng gǎ, a wáng gǎ, a wáng gǎ, a wáng gǎ gǎ, a wáng gǎ gǎ gǎ, a wáng gǎ gǎ gǎ gǎ

a wăng gă, a yóu gă, a yóu gă, a yóu gă, a yóu gă gă gă gă
a yóu gă gă gă gă a yóu gă gă gă gă a yóu gă gă gă gă a yóu gă gă
   gă gă
            [repeat above line twelve times]
a, wáng gá, a, wáng gā, a, wáng gă, wáng gă, wáng gă
a wáng gă, a wáng gă, wáng gă wáng gă wáng gă
a wáng gă, a wáng gă, a wáng gă
a wāng wángwăngwàng gă gă gă
a wáng gă, a wáng gă, a wáng gă, a wáng gă, a wáng gă, a wáng gă,
   a wáng gă, a wáng gă,
a wáng gă gă, a wáng gă gă gă, a wáng gă gă gă gă
a wăng gă, a yóu gă, a yóu gă, a yóu gă, a yóu gă gă gă
(Pinyin reduction of 吖尢孖)

This poem of course does not need to be translated, and indeed perhaps cannot be. In performances of the work, much in the sound poetry tradition, stress and emphasis is varied. The repetition occasionally brings up Australian-specific references like "Avant-Gaga", a well-known international reading series at Sappho Books, in Sydney, as well as unexpected puns in Chinese. There is an even deeper question here that I need to at least bring in to the discussion before it closes. Much depends on readership. Though it might not sound – in the world of critical poetics – like anything too controversial has been said (even if a middlebrow readership finds these arguments disagreeable), the disparities of readership that exist in Australian poetry will continue for so long as *comparative* genre histories don't also not supplement this one. I have been talking about experimental *poetry*, not poetic art, and not poetry among the other arts.[2] And while my argument has been that an avant-garde is crucial to the constitution of Australian poetry as a whole, and that, to a large extent, the question of poetic invention has become, or is

---

[2] There is an excellent PhD thesis titled *When The Way Out Was In: Avant-Garde Theatre In Australia, 1965–1985* by Adrian John Guthrie. Apart from the historical labour this thesis does, and the wonderful instances of dismissal of avant-garde theatre it records, it seeks in a pleasing way a materialist explanation for the rise of avant-garde theatre in this period. In light of this, but parallel to present purposes, it is worth quoting at some length from Guthrie's progressive history: "Avant-garde theatre developed rapidly in Australia between 1965 and 1985 because of the convergence of three factors; first, the diminution of the conservative constraint placed on modernism in Australia; secondly, international agitation for radical social and political change within youth and student cultures and the counter culture; and thirdly, a restatement of Australian nationalism. International influences had a formative impact on the dynamic emergence of avant-garde theatre in Australia . . . the virtual suppression of modern theatre in Australia had been an aspect of the neo-colonial status from which the country emerged during the study period" (307–8).

becoming, the central question for Australian poetry and poetics, this project, should it develop a larger purpose than just this book, will have to unite this history with like histories in other genres, like theatre and film.

Please allow me to admit a personal element to this. Another "difficulty" will mirror the difficulties listeners have had with avant-garde music and the manner in which those difficulties have, or have not been surmounted. Ever since the earliest years of my musical education, because I grew up learning and performing music, I felt closely attached to the works that get called very "late" Romantic, on the cusp of modernism, because in no other world could I find such a dramatic shift from stable harmonic "syntax" to that next logical step (atonality, or systems built within the dissonance-harmony dialectic). One can even locate the moment it occurs in the composers who lived through it (or ushered it along) like Alexander Scriabin (1872–1915), who lives right to the cusp of the avant-garde. That audible shift seems exemplary of a career that, if he had lived on into the century, would only have either sought even more paths to invention, transforming musical systems, or, one might imagine, a "regression" to the comforting realms prior to the great break. It's impossible to forgo those shifts, but if one's listening patterns are well and truly shattered by this "modern" cusp, the question is: what happens after? Would these breaks remain marked by the music they emerged or broke away from or would the break spurn new beginnings with a sense of their independence? Listening to the great works of postwar symphonic modernism, the bold moves of electronic music, the symphonic works of Gloria Coates, Alfred Schnittke or avant-garde music in the Cage milieu (especially Christian Wolff) certainly show something like this. But the curious and insurmountable difference between music and poetry is this: even if one rejects the systems and dissonances of these composers, the musico-technical validity of their efforts is not usually dismissed, and certainly not among the music theorists and philosophers of music. Few except the staunchest middlebrow consumer would question it on the ground of significance, even if they don't so much listen to it. It does not seem the same for avant-garde poetry, which as we have seen is no mere academic "curiosity". Yet there is clearly a difference to the poetic acceptation of dissonance by way of analogy in our studies of poetics, and the long resistance to the music critic's invectives about harmony. It doesn't feel out of place to point out then how strange it is (to be wildly comparative) that the "harmonicity" of poetry, to speak in the terms of analogy, is all the more strongly guarded against "dissonance", than it is in music. Regard then how much our conception of music, and our experience of it, goes straight to the gut and into the metalanguage of the ineffable, and how little of the "technicity" of poetry is trusted as in fact a real technicity at all. Indexed by the fragment, this is where Mezangelle (an angel of invented languages – the other surely being Cory Arcangel) might offer respite from our lingering conundrum. Not shying away from the contemporaneity and currency of digital poetics, in what we have been told is a post-digital era, will make tedium retentive in bodies of work tied to the effects of code, net and Web. Disjunction and dissonance are very different things, in poetics. They disrupt different components of the text, graphic and phonic respectively, and we would not here say that the technologies of the early twentieth century are the technologies of the twenty-first in effect or affect. Yet what we see in Mezangelled verse, and in certain kinds of bilingual writing like that of Ouyang Yu, is an encroachment upon the prevailing theme of this book that may throw even these historical locales off-axis: that is, we are now entering a historical period that more resembles the early twentieth-century avant-garde even than those moments that had us hooked late in the twentieth century. Hoist up a flag of permanent defeat if history chooses (soon) another path.

It is far-fetched to imagine a world in which poetic dissonance or disjunction is emancipated from assumptions of its marginality and uselessness in the public sphere, a world in which the ways a disjunctive poetry teaches us to read and gives us meaning are more widely appreciated. And yet this has not been the chief aim of this book and its histories. That will be a matter for manifestos, small presses, prophetic individuals, group pleas and indeed for the popular taste. My wish is that scholarship and criticism can move on to examine in closer detail and with fearlessness other languages of invention in Australian poetry without having to justify its existence historically, and focus more on contemporary examples, without forgetting, of course, the magnitude and magnificence of those great breaks. Literary history can concern itself with what was published *yesterday*, examples from this century and from living poets, if it remains suitably reflective and expansive in its theoretical focus. It will be, I think, possible to achieve adequate distance to argue about and for it. While there's still unfinished business regarding the neo-avant-gardes mid-century, I hope this book gives further permission for an analysis of the most contemporary of contemporary experimental poetry in the Antipodes.

Let the far-fetchedness of this willing stridency of tone lead us to a further sense of avant-garde futurity and protracted legacy: onwards on the trail of a *long avant-garde!* Walwicz and Fogarty have both made claims that their work will one day be better understood. I think, though a better word might be hope, that avant-garde poetry will be more *quickly* understood, and that a generation of readers attuned to the words and accustomed to works of tedium, to listening and looking at the experimental in poetics or even aesthetics, will more hastily catch on to their work, at the same time as those works are not sanitised or too much reduced in scope. The process of getting us there will still challenge us, even cause occasional affront. This is the contradiction of an academic book on the avant-garde that, as a critic, has affected my thinking more deeply than I could have imagined starting out. Literary history has to be about the past, present and future, not just the past. It throws you into the anticipatory, the impossible present, and the retroactive: the *diachronic* in what becomes historicity. Retroactive re-readings of all the historic avant-gardes, and I mean all of them, including the ones to come, will have the effect of providing a framework for subsequent poetries to further break down the stronghold on the way Australian poetry is read, and the ways we do thinking through all poetries. But the critic alone does not do all this work. It's the poets who move poetry, and tradition and convention need more than ever to be rent apart. One looks only a slither of a layer underneath convention and it becomes quite clear to readers what an intoxicatingly strange world, nay, *tradition*, the inverse of an assumed convention, can be, and indeed how much what we deem conventional is reliant on alternative traditions. For the critic, trying to make sense of abject fury, blast, oddity, the sheer weirdness of avant-garde poetry, is a task unto itself, but one worth doing because tedious as it might end up being for those who do that work, this book proposes that the condition of Australian literature is better comprehended from beneath than it is from the canon downwards.

Permit me one final stress, struck on nothing more than an emissary note for the non-Australian reader: there is still much work to do to build historical, national, transnational and critical frameworks from which we can read avant-garde poetry in this and other hemispheres. Tzara's name meant to be sad in one's country; we need not now be sad in one hemisphere. It will be a transnational and cross-hemispheric conversation that lets this continue. It will be this type of discourse and dialectic that allows it to better translate across the hemispheres. Let this book therefore become a guide not simply to an unknown history, but rather to a history whose catalogue calls forth and outward towards a vaster, larger sense of the world in poetics.

Works Cited

"Aboriginal Sovereign Manifesto of Demands". Declaration from the Freedom Summit held at Mparntwe (Alice Springs, NT) on 27–8 November 2014. Sovereign Union – First Nations Asserting Sovereignty. Web. URL: https://nationalunitygovernment.org/content/aboriginal-sovereign-manifesto-demands

ABC News (Australia). "Fraser felt Whitlam never bore him 'personal animosity'." Interview with Malcolm Fraser. *YouTube*. 20 October 2014. Web. URL: https://www.youtube.com/watch?v=cXlN1j-wdwg

Ades, Dawn, ed. *The Dada Reader: A Critical Anthology*. Chicago: U of Chicago P, 2006. Print.

Alizadeh, Ali. "The Battleground of Contemporary Australian Poetry: Trading Art for Animosity". *Arena Magazine* (September 2014). Web. URL: https://arena.org.au/the-battleground-of-contemporary-australian-poetry-by-ali-alizadeh

——. "Naming the Voids of Multiculturalism in 'Biral Biral': A New Reading of the Poetry of Lionel Fogarty". *Antipodes* 27.2 (December 2013): 129–33. Print.

Altieri, Charles, and Nicholas D. Nace. *The Fate of Difficulty in the Poetry of Our Time*. Evanston, IL: Northwestern UP, 2018. Print.

Amirkhanian, Charles, ed. *10+2: 12 American Text Sound Pieces*. Berkeley: 1750 Arch Records, 1975. Vinyl LP.

Anderson, Jill, ed. *Australian Divagations: Mallarmé & the 20th Century*. New York: Peter Lang, 2002. Print.

Ankersmit, Frank. "Democracy's Inner Voice: Political Style as Unintended Consequence of Political Action". *Media and the Restyling of Politics: Consumerism, Celebrity and Cynicism*. Eds, John Corner and Dick Pels. London: SAGE Publications, 2003. 19–40. Print.

Apollinaire, Guillaume. *Calligrammes: Poems of Peace and War (1913–1916)*. Berkeley: U of California P, 1980. Print.

——. *Selected Poems: With Parallel French Text*. Ed., Martin Sorrell. Oxford: Oxford UP, 2015. Print.

Araluen, Evelyn. "Resisting the Institution". *Overland* 227 (Winter 2017). Web. URL: https://overland.org.au/previous-issues/issue-227/feature-evelyn-araluen/

Austin, Lloyd. *Poetic Principles and Practice: Occasional Papers on Baudelaire, Mallarmé and Valéry.* Cambridge: Cambridge UP, 1987. Print.

Badiou, Alain. *Conditions.* London: Bloomsbury, 2017. Print.

Bakhtin, Mikhail. *The Dialogic Imagination: Four Essays.* Austin: U of Texas P, 1981. Print.

Banner, Stuart. *Possessing the Pacific: Land, Settlers, and Indigenous People from Australia to Alaska.* Cambridge, MA: Harvard UP, 2007. Print.

Barnes, Katherine. *The Higher Self in Christopher Brennan's Poems: Esotericism, Romanticism, Symbolism.* Leiden: Brill, 2006. Print.

——. "With a smile barely wrinkling the surface: Christopher Brennan's large *Musicopoematographoscope* and Mallarmé's *Un Coup de dés*". *Dix-Neuf* 9 (October 2007): 44–56. Print.

Barrett, Lindsay. *The Prime Minister's Christmas Card: Blue Poles and Cultural Politics in the Whitlam Era.* Sydney: Power Publications, 2001. Print.

Bartlett, Alison. *Jamming the Machinery: Contemporary Australian Women's Writing.* Toowoomba: Association for the Study of Australian Literature, 1998. Print.

Ball, Hugo. *Flight Out Of Time: a Dada Diary.* Edited and with an Introduction by John Elderfield. Berkeley: U of California P, 1996. Print.

Beals, Kurt. *Wireless Dada: Telegraphic Poetics in the Avant-Garde.* Evanston: Northwestern UP, 2020. Print.

Benjamin, Walter. *The Arcades Project.* Cambridge, MA: Harvard UP, 2002. Print.

——. *One-Way Street.* Cambridge, MA: The Belknap P of Harvard UP, 2016. Print.

Bernstein, Charles. *Attack of the Difficult Poems: Essays and Inventions.* Chicago: The U of Chicago P, 2011. Print.

——. *My Way: Speeches and Poems.* Chicago: U of Chicago P, 1999. Print.

Bernstein, Charles and Tracie Morris. "Guest Editors' Introduction". *BAX 2016: Best American Experimental Writing.* Eds, Charles Bernstein and Tracie Morris. Middletown, CT: Wesleyan UP, 2016. ix–xii. Print.

Betts, Gregory. *Finding Nothing: The Vangardes, 1959–1975.* Toronto: U of Toronto P, 2021. Print.

Biarujia, Javant. *Calques.* Thirroul: Monogene, 2002. Print.

——. "Introduction to Taneraic". *Tanerai: Taneraic on the Web.* Web. URL: https://taneraic.rantz.me/?page_id=2

——. *Nainougacyou: Taneraic English.* Victoria: Constructed Soul, 2022.

——. *Spelter to Pewter.* Melbourne: Cordite Books, 2016. Print.

Biddle, Jennifer Loureide. *Remote Avant-Garde: Aboriginal Art under Occupation.* Durham: Duke UP, 2016. Print.

Birns, Nicholas. "Australian Poetry from Kenneth Slessor to Jennifer Strauss". Eds, Nicholas Birns and Rebecca McNeer. *A Companion* to *Australian Literature Since 1900*. Rochester, NY: Camden House, 2007. 173–90. Print.

Birns, Nicholas and Rebecca McNeer, eds. *A Companion to Australian Literature since 1900*. Rochester, NY: Camden House, 2007. Print.

Block, Friedrich W. "Eight Digits of Digital Poetics". *Dichtung Digital* (October 2001). Web. URL: http://www.dichtung-digital.de/2001/10/17-Block/index2-engl.htm

Bowlt, John E., Nicoletta Misler and Evgenia Petrova, eds. *The Russian Avant-garde, Siberia and the East*. Exhibition Catalogue. Milano: Skira Editore S.p.A., 2013. Print.

bpNichol, ed. *Translating Translating Apollinaire: A Preliminary Report*. Milwaukee: Membrane P, 1979. Print.

Breeze, Mez. *Human Readable Messages (Mezangelle 2003–2011)*. Vienna: Traumawein, 2011. Print.

Brennan, Christopher. *Prose-Verse-Poster-Algebraic-Symbolico-Riddle Musicopoematographoscope & Pocket Musicopoematographoscope*. Introduction by Axel Clark. Sydney Hale & Iremonger, 1981. Print.

——. *The Verse of Christopher Brennan*. Eds, A. R. Chisholm and J. J. Quinn. Sydney: Angus & Robertson Ltd, 1964. Print.

Brennan, Michael. "Interview with Lionel Fogarty". *Poetry International*. 3 July 2011. Web. URL: https://www.poetryinternational.com/en/poets-poems/article/104-20646_Interview-with-Lionel-Fogarty

Bright, Colin. *Black Years – Red Years*. Sydney: Colbright Music, 2000. CD-R.

——. *War & Peace: A Selection of Songs on Poems by Jas H. Duke*. Wollongong: Wirripang, 1994. Score.

Brooke, Rupert. "Review of Ezra Pound". *Cambridge Review* 31 (1909): 166–7. Print.

Brooks, David. "Ern Malley's 'Petit Testament': A Reading". *Jacket* 29 (April 2009). Web. URL: http://jacketmagazine.com/29/brooks-petit.html

——. *Sons of Clovis: Ern Malley, Adoré Floupette and a Secret History of Australian Poetry*. St Lucia, QLD: U of Queensland P, 2011. Print.

Bürger, Peter. "Avant-Garde and Neo-Avant-Garde: An Attempt to Answer Certain Critics of 'Theory of the Avant-Garde.'" *New Literary History* 41.4 (Autumn, 2010): 695–715. Print.

Burn, Ian. *Minimal-Conceptual Work 1965–1970 [Catalogue]*. Perth: Art Gallery of Western Australia, 1992. Print.

Burn, Ian and Ann Stephen. "Namatjira's White Mask: A Partial Interpretation". *The Heritage of Namatjira: The Watercolourists of Central Australia*. Eds, Jane Hardy, J. V. S. Megaw and M. Ruth Megaw. Melbourne: William Heinemann, 1992. Print.

burns, joanne. *On a clear day*. St Lucia: U of Queensland P, 1992. Print.

Cage, John and Alison Knowles. *Notations*. New York: Something Else Press, 1969. Print.

Călinescu, Matei. *Five Faces of Modernity: Modernism, Avant-Garde, Decadence, Kitsch, Postmodernism.* Bloomington: Indiana UP, 1977. Print.
Capra, Pablo. "Introduction". Ern Malley, *The Darkening Ecliptic.* Los Angeles: Green Integer, 2017. Print.
Carruthers, A. J. "Dissonant Prosody". *Sound and Literature.* Ed. Anna Sniath. Cambridge: Cambridge UP, 2020. 252–71. Print.
———. *Stave Sightings: Notational Experiments in North American Long Poems, 1961–2011.* New York: Palgrave Macmillan, 2017.
Carter, David and Roger Osborne. "Case Study: Periodicals". *Paper Empires: A History of the Book in Australia, 1946–2005.* Eds, Craig Munro and Robyn Sheahan-Bright. St. Lucia: U of Queensland P, 2006. 239–56. Print.
Cassidy, Bonny. "Profit is rare, but poetry's weird blooms persist". *The Conversation* (July 2014). Web. URL: https://theconversation.com/profit-is-rare-but-poetrys-weird-blooms-persist-27227
Chambers, Ross. *Loiterature.* Lincoln: U of Nebraska P, 1999. Print.
Chatwin, Bruce. *The Songlines.* Franklin Center, PA: The Franklin Library, 1987. Print.
Clemens, Justin. "*First Fruits* of a Barron Field". *Critical Quarterly* 61.1 (April 2019). 18–36. Print.
———. "First Fruits of a Barron Field". Keynote address: *Historical Poetics Symposium.* Western Sydney University (15 December 2016). Web. URL: http://poetryandpoetics.org/justin-clemens-first-fruits-barron-field/
———. "Noise and Voice: An Interview with Amanda Stewart". *Sydney Review of Books* (October 2017). Web. URL: https://sydneyreviewofbooks.com/interview/noise-and-voice-an-interview-with-amanda-stewart/
———. "Per- after the internet". Message to A. J. Carruthers. 27 May 2017. Email.
———. *The Romanticism of Contemporary Theory: Institutions, Aesthetics, Nihilism.* Aldershot: Ashgate, 2003. Print.
Cobbing, Bob. *Sockless in Sandals: Collected Poems Volume Six.* Cardiff: Second Aeon Publications, 1985. Print.
Colby, Georgina, ed. *Reading Experimental Writing.* Edinburgh: Edinburgh UP, 2020. Print.
Coleman, Claire G. *Terra Nullius.* Sydney: Hachette Australia, 2017. Print.
Coleman, Peter. *The Real Barry Humphries.* Adelaide: Griffin Press, 1990. Print.
Committee for a Worker's Enquiry, Socialist Labor League, and Worker's Inquiry into the Death of Daniel Yock. *The Truth about the Killing of Daniel Yock: Worker's Inquiry Exposes Police Murder.* Marrickville: Labour Press, 1994. Print.
Cook, Stuart. *Speaking the Earth's Languages: A Theory for Australian-Chilean Postcolonial Poetics.* Amsterdam: Rodopi, 2013. Print.

Couani, Ann. "Women in the Literary Small Press". *Telling Ways: Australian Women's Experimental Writing*. Eds, Sneja Gunew and Anna Couani. Adelaide: Australian Feminist Studies Publications, 1988. 9–14. Print.

Couani, Anna and Damien White, eds. *Island in the Sun 2: An Anthology of Recent Australian Prose*. Glebe: Sea Cruise Books, 1981. Print.

Cradwick, Catherine. "From Dodo to Dada: The Wayzgoose Press and the art of survival". Heinz Stefan Bartkowiak, *Bartkowiak's Forum Book Art (Yearbook)*. Hamburg: H. S. Bartkowiak, 2004–5. 490–500. Print.

Cramer, Sue and Lesley Harding, eds. *Call of the Avant-garde: Constructivism and Australian Art*. Bulleen: Heide Museum of Modern Art, 2017. Print.

Dale, Amelia. "Amelia Dale Interviews Alex Selenitsch". *Rabbit* 36 (2022): 133–9.

Dear, Peter. *Discipline and Experience: The Mathematical Way in the Scientific Revolution*. Chicago: The U of Chicago P, 1995. Print.

de Man, Paul. *The Resistance to Theory*. Minneapolis, MN: U of Minnesota P, 1986. Print.

Denholm, Michael. *Small Press Publishing in Australia, the early 1970s*. North Sydney: Second Back Row, 1979. Print.

——. *Small Press Publishing in Australia, the Late 1970s to the Mid to Late 1980s, Volume II*. Footscray: FOOTPRINT, 1991. Print.

Derrida, Jacques. *Dissemination*. Trans. with an Introduction and Additional Notes, Barbara Johnson. Chicago: The U of Chicago P, 1981. Print.

——. *La Dissémination*. Paris: Editions du Seuil, 1972. Print.

Desai, Radhika. *Geopolitical Economy: After US Hegemony, Globalization and Empire*. London: Pluto Press, 2013. Print.

Diepeveen, Leonard. *Modernist Fraud: Hoax, Parody, Deception*. Oxford: Oxford UP, 2019. Print.

Djurić, Dubravka and Miško Šuvaković, eds. *Impossible Histories: Historical Avant-gardes, Neo-avant-gardes, and Post-avant-gardes in Yugoslavia, 1918–1991*. Cambridge: MIT Press, 2003. Print.

Dobson, Rosemary. *In a Convex Mirror: Poems*. Sydney: Dymock's Book Arcade, 1944. Print.

Docker, John. *In a Critical Condition: Struggles for Control of Australian Literature – Then and Now!* Ringwood: Penguin, 1984. Print.

Drucker, Johanna. *Figuring the Word: Essays on Books, Writing, and Visual Poetics*. New York City: Granary Books, 1998. Print.

Duke, Jas H, Peter Lyssiotis and Vivienne Mehes. *Industrial Woman*. Melbourne: Industrial Woman Collective, 1986. Print.

Duke, Jas H. *Archduke 4 [Manuscript]: special Atlantis issue*. Melbourne: Jas H. Duke, 1974. Handmade.

——. *Dada Kampfen Um Leben Und Tod*. Katoomba: Wayzgoose Press, 1996. Print.

——. *Destiny Wood*. Melbourne: Whole Australian Catalogue, 1978. Print.

——. *poems of life & death*. Melbourne: Collective Effort, 2003. Print.

——. *Poems of War and Peace*. Melbourne: Collective Effort, 1989. Print.

———. "Sounds, sound poetry, and sound/text compositions". *NMA 10 Magazine* (1992): 7–12. Print.
Dunk, Jonathan. "Rising Tide: Politics and the Experimental Poem". *Meanjin Quarterly* (April 2018). Web. URL: https://meanjin.com.au/blog/rising-tide-politics-and-the-experimental-poem/
DuPlessis, Rachel Blau. *Genders, Races and Religious Cultures in Modern American Poetry, 1908–1934*. Cambridge: Cambridge UP, 2001. Print.
Edmonds, Philip. *Tilting at Windmills: The Literary Magazine in Australia, 1968–2012*. Adelaide: U of Adelaide P, 2015. Print.
Edwards, Chris. *A Fluke: A Mistranslation of Stéphane Mallarmé's "Un Coup De Dés…" With Parallel French Text*. Monogene: Thirroul, 2005. Print. Web version appeared in *Jacket2* (April 2006). URL: http://jacketmagazine.com/29/fluke00intro.shtml
———. *People of Earth*. Sydney: Vagabond, 2011. Print.
Einstein, Albert. "Why Socialism?" *Monthly Review* 1.1 (May 1949): 9–15. Print.
Elliott, Brian, ed. *The Jindyworobaks*. St Lucia: U of Queensland P, 1979. Print.
Fagan, Kate. "'A Fluke? [N]ever!': Reading Chris Edwards". *JASAL* 12.1 (2012). Web.
Fagan, Kate and Peter Minter, "Murdering Alphabets, Disorienting Romance: John Tranter and Postmodern Australian Poetics" *Jacket* 27 (April 2005). Web. URL: http://jacketmagazine.com/27/faga-mint.html
Fanon, Frantz. *Alienation and Freedom*. Eds, Jean Khalfa and Robert J. C. Young. Trans. Steven Corcoran. London: Bloomsbury, 2018. Print.
———. *The Wretched of the Earth*. Ringwood, VIC: Penguin, 1969. Print.
Fanoy, Jeltje. "After Jas H. Duke (poem)". *Postcolonial Text* 12.2 (2017): n.pag. Web. URL: https://www.postcolonial.org/index.php/pct/issue/view/57/showToc
Farrell, Michael. *Writing Australian Unsettlement: Modes of Poetic Invention, 1796–1945*. New York: Palgrave Macmillan, 2015. Print.
Fogarty, Lionel. *Connection Requital*. Sydney: Vagabond, 2010. Print.
———. *Eelahroo (Long Ago) Nyah (Looking) Möbö-Möbö (Future)*. Sydney: Vagabond: 2014. Print.
———. "Head Keeper Futures Corridor's Bay". *Poetry* (May 2016): 158.
———. *Kargun*. Brisbane: Cheryl Buchanan, 1980. Print.
———. *Minyung Woolah Binnung: What Saying Says*. Southport: Keeaira Press, 2004. Print.
———. *Mogwie-Idan: Stories of the Land*. Sydney: Vagabond Press, 2012. Print.
———. *New and Selected Poems: Munaldjali, Mutuerjaraera*. South Melbourne: Hyland House, 1995.
———. *Yoogum Yoogum*. Ringwood: Penguin, 1982. Print.

Foster, Hal. *The Return of the Real: The Avant-Garde at the End of the Century*. Cambridge, MA: The MIT Press, 1996. Print.
——. *What Comes After Farce?* London: Verso, 2020. Print.
——. "What's Neo about the Neo-Avant-Garde?" *October* 70 (Autumn 1994): 5–32. Print.
Freeth, John. "Botany Bay [1786]". *The New Oxford Book of Eighteenth-Century Verse*. Ed. Roger Lonsdale. Oxford: Oxford UP, 2009. 659–60. Print.
Freud, Sigmund. *Totem and Taboo and Other Works (1912–13)*. The Standard Edition of the Complete Works of Sigmund Freud Vol. XIII. London: Vintage, 2001.
Freytag-Loringhoven, Elsa von. *Body Sweats: The Uncensored Writings of Elsa von Freytag-Loringhoven*. Cambridge, MA: The MIT Press, 2011, Print.
Frye, Northrop. *Northrop Frye's Late Notebooks, 1982–1990: Architecture of the Spiritual World*. Ed. Robert D. Denham. Toronto: U of Toronto P, 2000. Print.
——. "Conclusion to the First Edition of *Literary History of Canada*". *Northrop Frye on Canada*. Ed. David Staines. Toronto: U of Toronto P, 2000. 339–72. Print.
Furaih, Ameer Chasib. "'For their fights affect our fights': The Impact of African American Poetics and Politics on the Poetry of Lionel Fogarty". *JASAL* 17.1 (2017). n.pag. Web. URL: https://openjournals.library.sydney.edu.au/index.php/JASAL/article/view/11777
Gallop, Jane. *The Deaths of the Author: Reading and Writing in Time*. Durham: Duke UP, 2011. Print.
Gammel, Irene. *Baroness Elsa: Gender, Dada, and Everyday Modernity, A Cultural Biography*. Cambridge, MA: MIT Press, 2003. Print.
Gardner, W. H. *Gerard Manley Hopkins (1844–1889): A Study of Poetic Idiosyncrasy in Relation to Poetic Tradition*. London: Martin Secker & Warburg, 1944. Print.
Gay'wu Group of Women. *Songspirals*. Allen & Unwin, 2019. Print.
Giles, Paul. *Antipodean America: Australasia and the Constitution of U.S. Literature*. New York: Oxford UP, 2013. Print.
——. *Backgazing: Reverse Time in Modernist Culture*. Oxford: Oxford UP, 2019. Print.
Ginsberg, Allen. *Howl*. San Francisco: City Lights Books, 1956. Print.
Glissant, Édouard. *Poetic Intention*. Trans. Nathalie Stephens, Anne Malena. Callicoon, NY: Nightboat Books, 1997. Print.
Greaves, Kerry. *The Danish Avant-Garde and World War II: The Helhesten Collective*. New York: Routledge, 2019. Print.
Green, Clinton. Artefacts of Australian experimental music, 1930–73. Melbourne: Shame File Music, 2007. CD.
Greenaway, Lisa and Steve Grimwade, eds. *Going Down Swinging 13* (1993). Clifton Hill: Going Down Swinging, 1993. Print.

Grenier, Robert. *Organic Prosody in the Poetry of William Carlos Williams*. 1965. Senior Honors Thesis, Harvard College. URL: http://eclipsearchive.org/projects/ORGANIC/GrenierOrganic.pdf
Gruen, F. H. *Australia's Welfare State: Rearguard or Avant Garde?* Discussion Paper no. 212. Canberra: Centre for Economic Policy Research, Australian National University. 1989. Print.
Gunew, Sneja. "Ania Walwicz and Antigone Kefala: Varieties of Migrant Dreaming". In David Brooks and Brenda Walker, eds. *Poetry and Gender: Statements and Essays in Australian Women's Poetry and Poetics*. St Lucia: U of Queensland P, 1989. 205–19.
——. "Denaturalizing Cultural Nationalisms: Multicultural Readings of 'Australia.'" *Nation and Narration*. Ed. Homi K. Bhabha. London: Routledge, 2013. 99–120. Print.
——. *Post-Multicultural Writers as Neo-Cosmopolitan Mediators*. London: Anthem, 2018. Print.
——. "Women's Experimental Writing?" *Telling Ways: Australian Women's Experimental Writing*. Eds, Sneja Gunew and Anna Couani. Adelaide: Australian Feminist Studies Publications, 1988. 5–8. Print.
Gunew, Sneja and Anna Couani, eds. *Telling Ways: Australian Women's Experimental Writing*. Adelaide: Australian Feminist Studies Publications, 1988. Print.
Guthrie, Adrian John. *When the Way Out Was In: Avant-Garde Theatre in Australia, 1965–1985*. University of Wollongong. Doctor of Philosophy. 1996. Web. URL: https://ro.uow.edu.au/theses/1762/
Haese, Richard. *Permanent Revolution: Mike Brown and the Australian Avant-Garde 1953–1997*. Melbourne: Miegunyah Press, 2011. Print.
——. *Rebels and Precursors: The Revolutionary Years of Australian Art*. Ringwood, VIC: Allen Lane, 1981. Print.
Hage, Emily. *Dada Magazines: The Making of a Movement*. London: Bloomsbury, 2021. Print.
Harkin, Natalie. *Archival-Poetics*. Sydney: Vagabond, 2019. Print.
——. *Dirty Words*. Melbourne: Cordite Books, 2015. Print.
Harris, Max. *The Angry Penguin: Selected Poems of Max Harris*. Canberra: National Library of Australia, 1996. Print.
——. *The Gift of Blood: Poetry*. Adelaide: The Jindyworobak Club, 1940. Print.
Harrison, Martin. *Who Wants to Create Australia?* Broadway: Halstead Press, 2007. Print.
Hartley, Daniel. *The Politics of Style: Towards a Marxist Poetics*. Leiden: Brill, 2017. Print.
Hawke, John. *Australian Literature and the Symbolist Movement*. Wollongong: U of Wollongong P, 2009. Print.
Hayles, N. Katherine. "Print Is Flat, Code Is Deep: The Importance of Media-Specific Analysis". *Poetics Today* 25.1 (Spring 2004): 67–90. Print.

Hentea, Marius. *TaTa Dada: The Real Life and Celestial Adventures of Tristan Tzara*. Cambridge, MA: The MIT Press, 2014. Print

Hernández, Robb. *Archiving an Epidemic: Art, AIDS, and the Queer Chicanx Avant-Garde*. New York: New York UP, 2019. Print.

Heseltine, Harry, ed. *The Penguin Book of Modern Australian Verse*. Ringwood, VIC: Penguin, 1981. Print.

——. *Unspeakable Stress: Some Aspects of the Poetry of Gerard Manley Hopkins*. Sydney: The English Association, 1969. Print.

Heyward, Michael. *The Ern Malley Affair*. St Lucia: U of Queensland P, 1993. Print.

Higgins, David. "Writing to Colonial Australia: Barron Field and Charles Lamb". *Nineteenth-Century Contexts* 32.3 (September 2010): 219–33.

Higgins, Dick. *Pattern Poetry: Guide to an Unknown Literature*. Albany, NY: State U of New York P, 1987. Print.

Hobsbaum, Philip. *Tradition and Experiment in English Poetry*. London: Macmillan, 1979. Print.

Hocking, Jenny. *The Dismissal Dossier: Everything You Were Meant to Know About November 1975*. Carlton: Melbourne UP, 2017. Print.

Hooton, Harry. "The Clalendar". Dated 10 February, 1943, including note that the poem was possibly written in 1935. *Oliver M. Somerville, Papers, 1936–1946, 1954 collected by Harry Hooton*. MLMSS 569. The State Library of New South Wales, Sydney. Archival material.

——. *It Is Great To Be Alive*. Sydney: Margaret Elliot, 1961. Print.

——. Letter to Oliver Somerville, 8 August 1942. *Oliver M. Somerville, Papers, 1936–1946, 1954 collected by Harry Hooton*. MLMSS 569. The State Library of New South Wales, Sydney. Archival material.

——. Letter to Oliver Somerville, 16 December, 1944. *Oliver M. Somerville, Papers, 1936–1946, 1954 collected by Harry Hooton*. MLMSS 569. The State Library of New South Wales, Sydney. Archival material.

——. *MS (June 1951)*. Sydney: Edwards and Shaw, 1951. Little Magazine. Print.

——. *Poet of the 21st Century: Collected Poems*. North Ryde: Angus and Robertson, 1990. Print.

——. "Poetry and the New Proletariat". *The Australian Quarterly* 18.2 (June 1946): 96–104. Print.

——. "Poetry or Not". *The Australian Quarterly* 15.3 (September 1943): 87–96. Print.

——. *Power Over Things: A Selection*. San Francisco: Inferno Press, 1955. Print.

——. *Things You See When You Haven't Got A Gun*. Sydney: W. A. Cooney, 1943. Print.

——. *21st Century. The Magazine of a Creative Civilisation. First Issue*. Sydney: Harry Hooton, 1955. Little Magazine. Print.

——. *21st Century. The Magazine of a Creative Civilisation. Second Issue*. Sydney: Harry Hooton, 1957. Little Magazine. Print.

Hooton, Harry and Garry Lyle, eds. *Number Three*, 1948. Sydney: G. Lyle, 1948. Little Magazine. Print.

Hope, A. D. *Dunciad Minor: An heroick poem*. Carlton, VIC: Melbourne UP, 1970. Print.

—, ed. *Poems: A. D. Hope, Garry Lyle, Harry Hooton*. Cremorne: G. Lyle, 1944. Print.

Hopper, Sabina Paula. "Re-Reading Lionel Fogarty: An Attempt to Feel into Texts Speaking of Decolonisation". *Southerly* 62.2 (2002): 45–64. Print.

Horne, Donald. *The Lucky Country, 6th Edition*. Camberwell, VIC: Penguin Group, 2010. Print.

Hudson, Flexmore, ed. *Poetry: The Australian International Quarterly of Verse*. Adelaide: Economy Press, 1947. Journal / Little Magazine. Print.

Hughes, Langston. *Ask Your Mama: 12 Moods for Jazz*. New York: Alfred A. Knopf, 1961. Print.

Hughes, Randolph. "C. J. Brennan: Unpublished Work and Further Discussion". *The Australian Quarterly* 19.2 (June 1947): 27–39. Print.

Hughes, Robert. "Introduction: The Well-wrought Ern". *The Ern Malley Affair*. Ed. Michael Heyward. St Lucia: U of Queensland P, 1993. xv–xx. Print.

Humphries, Barry. *Dada Days: Moonee Ponds Muse, Vol. 2 (1951–1983)*. East Ivanhoe: Raven Records, 1993. Compact disc.

——. *More Please*. London: Viking, 1992. Print.

——. *My life as me: a memoir*. London: Michael Joseph, 2002. Print.

Huppatz, D. J. "Interview with Ania Walwicz". *ALT-X Magazine* 3 March 1996. Web. URL: http://www.altx.com/au/CONTACT.HTM

Indyk, Ivor. "Grand star builds her own world of words". Review of *Travel / Writing* and *Boat*. *Sydney Morning Herald*. 25 November 1989: 88. Print.

Jameson, Fredric. *The Modernist Papers*. London: Verso, 2007. Print.

Janco, Marcel. "Creative Dada". *Dadas on Art: Tzara, Arp, Duchamp and Others*. Ed. Lucy R. Lippard. New York: Dover, 1971. 35. Print.

Jauss, Hans Robert. "Literary History as a Challenge to Literary Theory". *New Literary History* 2.1 (Autumn 1970): 7–37. Print.

Jennings, Kate, ed. *Mother I'm Rooted: An Anthology of Australian Women Poets*. Fitzroy: Outback Press, 1975. Print.

Jeon, Joseph Jonghyun. *Racial Things, Racial Forms: Objecthood in Avant-Garde Asian American Poetry*. Iowa City: U of Iowa P, 2012. Print.

Johnson, Barbara. "Translator's Introduction". *Dissemination*. Jacques Derrida. Chicago: The U of Chicago P, 1981. vii–xxxiii. Print.

Jones, Amelia. *Irrational Modernism: A Neurasthenic History of New York Dada*. Cambridge, MA: The MIT Press, 2004. Print.

Kane, Brian. *Sound Unseen: Acousmatic Sound in Theory and Practice*. Oxford: Oxford UP, 2014. Print.

Kane, Paul. *Australian Poetry: Romanticism and Negativity*. Cambridge: Cambridge UP, 1996. Print.
Keller, Lynn. *Forms of Expansion: Recent Long Poems by Women*. Chicago: U of Chicago P, 1997. Print.
Kelly, Lynne and Neale, Margo. *Songlines: The Power and Promise*. Melbourne: Thames & Hudson, 2020. Print.
Kennedy, J. B. *The Musical Structure of Plato's Dialogues*. Durham: Acumen Press, 2011. Print.
Kenny, Anna. *The Aranda's Pepa: An Introduction to Carl Strehlow's Masterpiece* Die Aranda- und Loritja-Stämme in Zentral-Australien *(1907-1920)*. Canberra: ANU Press, 2013. Print and Web.
Kinsella, John. *Spatial Relations Volume Two: Essays Reviews, Commentaries, and Chorography*. Amsterdam: Rodopi, 2013. Print.
Kirkpatrick, Peter. "Australian Poetry, 1940s–1960s". *Oxford Research Encyclopedia of Literature*. Ed. Paula Rabinowitz. Oxford: Oxford UP, 2017. 1–46. Web. URL: https://doi.org/10.1093/acrefore/9780190201098.013.144
——. "'New word come tripping slowly': Poetry, popular culture and modernity, 1890–1950". *The Cambridge History of Australian Literature*. Ed. Peter Pierce. Cambridge: Cambridge: UP, 2009. 199–222. Print.
Kostelanetz, Richard. *Text-Sound Texts*. New York: William Morrow and Company, 1980. Print.
Kouvaras, Linda Ioanna. *Loading the silence: Australian sound art in the post-digital age*. London: Routledge, 2016. Print.
Krauss, Rosalind. *The Originality of the Avant-Garde and Other Modernist Myths*. Cambridge, MA: The MIT Press, 1999. Print.
Kristeva, Julia. *Revolution in Poetic Language*. New York: Columbia UP, 1984. Print.
Kumar, Krishan and Herbert F. Tucker. "Introduction". *New Literary History* 48.4 (2017): 609–16. Print.
Ladd, Mike. "9-2-5: The Poetry of Work". *Poetica*. ABC Radio National. 14 January 2012. Radio Program. URL: https://www.abc.net.au/radionational/programs/archived/poetica/925/3740372
Langer, Susanne K. *Philosophy in a New Key: A Study in the Symbolism of Reason, Rite, and Art*. Cambridge, MA: Harvard UP, 1942. Print.
Leavis, F. R. *New Bearings in English Poetry: A Study of the Contemporary Situation*. London: Chatto & Windus, 1961. Print.
Lecercle, Jean-Jacques. *Interpretation as Pragmatics*. London: Macmillan, 1999. Print.
Leleux, Robin. *A Regional History of the Railways of Great Britain, Volume 9: The East Midlands*. Newton Abbot: David & Charles, 1984. Print.
Lilley, Kate. "'Living Backward': Slessor and Masculine Elegy". *Kenneth Slessor: Critical Readings*. Ed. Philip Mead. St Lucia: U of Queensland P, 1997. 246–64. Print

Lippard, Lucy R., ed. *Dadas on Art: Tzara, Arp, Duchamp and Others*. New York: Dover, 1971. Print.
Lloyd, Brian. "Ern Malley and His Rivals". *Australian Literary Studies* 20.1 (2001): 20–32. Print.
Lloyd, Margaret Glynne. *William Carlos Williams's* Paterson*: A Critical Reappraisal*. Rutherford, NJ: Associated U Presses, 1980. Print.
Lonsdale, Roger, ed. *The New Oxford Book of Eighteenth-Century Verse*. Oxford: Oxford UP, 1984. Print.
Lorange, Astrid. *How Reading is Written: A Brief Index to Gertrude*. Middletown, CT: Wesleyan UP, 2014. Print.
——. "Problems are flowers and fade". *Jacket2* (22 November 2011). Web. URL: https://jacket2.org/commentary/problems-are-flowers-and- fade
Lyne, R. O. A. M. *Collected Papers on Latin Poetry*. Oxford: Oxford UP, 2007. Print.
Lysenko, Myron and Kevin Brophy. "Interviewing: Ania Walwicz". *Going Down Swinging* 5 (Spring 1982): 43–8. Print. URL: https://web.archive.org/web/20060824014910/http://www.goingdownswinging.org.au/interview_final.PDF
Macintyre, Stuart. *Australia's Boldest Experiment: War and Reconstruction in the 1940s*. Sydney: New South Publishing, 2015. Print.
Mallarmé, Stéphane. *The Book*. Translated and with an Introduction by Sylvia Gorelick. Cambridge, MA: Exact Change, 2018. Print.
——. *Collected Poems*. Ed. and trans. Henry Weinfield. Berkeley, CA: U of California P, 2010. Print.
——. "Observation Relative au Poème *Un Coup de Dés jamais n'abolira le Hasard*". *Cosmopolis: An International Review* XVII (May, 1897): 417–27. Print.
Malley, Ern. *The Darkening Ecliptic*. Los Angeles: Green Integer, 2017. Print.
——. *The Poems of Ern Malley, Comprising the Complete Poems and Commentaries by Max Harris and Joanna Murray-Smith*. Sydney: Allen & Unwin, 1988. Print.
Marcuse, Herbert. "A Note on Dialectic". *The Essential Frankfurt School Reader*. Eds, Andrew Arato and Eike Gebhardt. Oxford: Basil Blackwell, 1978. 444–51. Print.
Martin, Loy D. "Literary Invention: The Illusion of the Individual Talent". *Critical Inquiry* 6.4 (Summer 1980): 649–67. Print.
Mathews, Harry, John Ashbery, Kenneth Koch, James Schuyler, eds. *Locus Solus 1*. Lans-en-Vercors: Locus Solus Press, Winter 1961. Little Magazine.
Matra, James. "A Proposal For Establishing a Settlement in New South Wales". *Historical Records of New Zealand. Volume 1*. Ed. Robert McNab. Wellington: John Mackey, 1908. 36–41.
McAuley, James. *Collected Poems*. London: Angus & Robertson, 1971. Print.

———. *A Map of Australian Verse: The Twentieth Century*. Melbourne: Oxford UP, 1977. Print.
McCredden, Lyn. "Transgressing Language? The Poetry of Ania Walwicz". *Australian Literary Studies* 17.3 (May 1996): 235–43.
McKenna, Mark. *The Captive Republic: A History of Republicanism in Australia, 1788–1996*. Cambridge: Cambridge UP, 1997. Print.
McKenzie, Geraldine. "Review of *Calques*, by Javant Biarujia". *Jacket2* 23 (August 2003). Web. URL: http://jacketmagazine.com/23/mckenz-biaru.html
McQueen, Humphrey. *A New Britannia: An Argument Concerning the Social Origins of Australian Radicalism and Nationalism*. Sydney: Penguin, 1980. Print.
Mead, Philip. "Chapter 9 1944, Melbourne and Adelaide: The Ern Malley Hoax". *The Edinburgh Companion to Twentieth-Century Literatures in English*. Eds, Brian McHale and Randall Stevenson. Edinburgh: Edinburgh UP, 2006. Print.
———. *Networked Language: Culture and History in Australian Poetry*. North Melbourne: Australian Scholarly Publishing, 2008. Print.
Mead, Philip and John E. Tranter, eds. *The Penguin Book of Modern Australia Poetry*. Ringwood: Penguin Books, 1991. Print.
Meillassoux, Quentin. *The Number and the Siren: A Decipherment of Mallarmé's* Coup de Dés. Falmouth: Urbanomic, 2012. Print.
Miller, Tyrus. "Avant-Garde and Theory: A Misunderstood Relation". *Poetics Today* 20.4 (Winter 1999): 549–79. Print.
———. *Singular Examples: Artistic Politics and the Neo-Avant-Garde*. Evanston, IL: Northwestern UP, 2009. Print.
Mirrlees, Hope. *Paris: A Poem*. Richmond: Hogarth Press, 1919. Print.
Mitter, Partha. *The Triumph of Modernism: India's Artists and the Avant-garde, 1922–1947*. New Delhi: Oxford UP, 2007. Print.
Moore, Dashiell. "The Rally is Calling: Interview with Lionel Fogarty". *Cordite Poetry Review* (1 February, 2019). Web. URL: http://cordite.org.au/interviews/rally-moore-fogarty/
Moore, T. Inglis. *Social Patterns in Australian Literature*. Berkeley: U of California P, 1971. Print.
Morris, Tracie. *BAX 2016: Best American Experimental Writing*. Middletown, CT: Wesleyan UP, 2017. Print.
Muecke, Stephen. *Ancient and Modern: Time, Culture and Indigenous Philosophy*. Sydney: U of New South Wales P, 2004. Print.
Munro, Craig and Robyn Sheahan-Bright. *Paper Empires: A History of the Book in Australia, 1946–2005*. St Lucia: U of Queensland P, 2006. Print.
Murray, Les. *Collected Poems*. Carlton: Black Inc., 2018. Print.
———. *The Daylight Moon: Poems*. London: Angus & Robertson, 1987. Print.
———. *Fivefathers: Five Australian Poets of the Pre-academic Era*. Manchester: Flyfield Books, 1994. Print.

Nash, Roderick Frazier. *The Rights of Nature: A History of Environmental Ethics*. Madison: U of Wisconsin P, 1989. Print.
Neale, Margo and Lynne Kelly. *Songlines: The Power and Promise*. Melbourne: Thames & Hudson, 2020. Print.
Negarestani, Reza. *Cyclonopedia: complicity with anonymous materials*. Melbourne: re.press, 2008. Print.
New, W. H. "Short Notes on Tall Tales: Some Australian Examples". *The Art of Brevity: Excursions in Short Fiction Theory and Analysis*. Eds, Per Winther, Jakob Lothe and Hans H. Skei. Columbia: U of South Carolina P, 2004. 106–27. Print.
Nielsen, Aldon Lynn. *Integral Music: Languages of African American Innovation*. Tuscaloosa: U of Alabama P, 2004. Print.
Noland, Carrie and Barrett Watten, eds. *Diasporic Avant-Gardes: Experimental Poetics and Cultural Displacement*. New York: Palgrave Macmillan, 2009. Print.
Ono, Yoko. *Grapefruit*. Tokyo: Wunternaum Press, 1964. Print.
O'Sullivan, Maggie. *Palace of Reptiles*. Willowdale, ON: THE GIG, 2003. Print.
Ouyang Yu. *Flag of Permanent Defeat*. Waratah: Puncher & Wattmann, 2019. Print.
Page, Geoff. Page, Geoff. "Obscurity in Poetry – A Spectrum". *Southerly* (November 2014). Web. URL: http://southerlyjournal.com.au/2014/11/12/obscurity-in-poetry-a-spectrum/
Pascoe, Bruce. *Dark Emu: Black Seeds Agriculture or Accident?* Broome: Magabala Books, 2014. Print.
Pasquier, Étienne. *Oeuvres Choisies*. Vol. II. Ed. Léon Feugère. Paris: Firmin Didot, 1849. Print.
Pender, Anne. "The Mythical Australian: Barry Humphries, Gough Whitlam and 'New Nationalism.'" *Australian Journal of Politics and History* 51.1 (2005): 67–78. Print.
Pendleton, Adam. *Black Dada Reader*. London: Koenig Books, 2017. Print.
Perec, Georges. *53 Days*. Trans. David Bellos. New Hampshire: David R. Godine, 2000. Print.
Perelman, Bob. "My Avant-Garde Card". *New Literary History* 41.4 (Autumn 2010): 875–94. Print.
——. *The Trouble with Genius: reading Pound, Joyce, Stein, and Zukofsky*. Berkeley: U of California P, 1994. Print.
Perloff, Marjorie. *Unoriginal Genius: Poetry by Other Means in the New Century*. Chicago: The U of Chicago P, 2010. Print.
Philip, M. NourbeSe. *Zong!* Middletown, CT: Wesleyan UP, 2008. Print.
Phillips, A. A. "The Cultural Cringe". *Meanjin* 9.4 (Summer, 1950): 299–302. Print.
Π.O. *Heide*. Sydney: Giramondo, 2019. Print.
Π.O., Peter Murphy, Alex Selenitsch, eds. *Missing Forms: Concrete, Visual and Experimental Poems*. Melbourne: Collective Effort, 1981. Print.

Piper, Adrian. "Ian Burn's Conceptualism". *Art in America* (December 1997): 72–9. Print.

Prichard, Katherine Susannah. "Hoax Renders Service to Literature". *Communist Review* (March 1945): 456–7. Print.

Quartermain, Peter. *Stubborn Poetries: Poetic Facticity and the Avant-Garde*. Tuscaloosa: The U of Alabama P, 2013. Print.

Rasula, Jed. *Acrobatic Modernism From the Avant-Garde to Prehistory*. Oxford: Oxford UP, 2020. Print.

——. *Destruction Was My Beatrice: Dada and the Unmaking of the Twentieth Century*. New York: Basic Books, 2015. Print.

Read, Herbert. *The Meaning of Art*. London: Penguin Books, 1951. Print.

Reed, Brian. *Nobody's Business: Twenty-First Century Avant-Garde Poetry*. Ithaca: Cornell UP, 2013. Print.

——. "Sherwin Bitsui's Blank Dictionary: Navajo Poetics and Non-Indigenous Readers". *The Fate of Difficulty in the Poetry of Our Time*. Eds, Charles Altieri and Nicholas D. Nace. Evanston, IL: Northwestern UP, 2018. 188–99. Print.

Regan, Jayne. "A Cosmopolitan Jindyworobak: Flexmore Hudson, Nationalism and World-Mindedness". *JASAL* 15.3 (2015): n.pag. Web.

Reik, Theodor. *Mystery on the Mountain: The Drama of the Sinai Revelation*. New York: Harper & Brothers, 1959. Print.

Reynolds, Henry. *Forgotten War*. Kensington: New South Books, 2013. Print.

——. *The Other Side of the Frontier: Aboriginal Resistance to the European Invasion of Australia*. Sydney: U of New South Wales P, 2006 [1981]. Print.

Reznikoff, Charles. *Holocaust*. Nottingham: Five Leaves, 2010. Print.

——. *Testimony: Complete Edition*. Los Angeles: Black Sparrow Press, 2015. Print.

Rix, Robert W. "The Poetics of Penal Transportation: Robert Southey's Botany-Bay Eclogues". *Eighteenth-Century Studies* 53.3 (Spring 2020): 429–46. Print.

Rothenberg, Jerome. *New Selected Poems*. New York: New Directions, 1986. Print.

——. *Technicians of the Sacred: A Range of Poetries from Africa, America, Asia, Europe & Oceania*. First Edition. New York: Doubleday & Company, 1968. Print.

——. *Technicians of the Sacred: A Range of Poetries from Africa, America, Asia, Europe & Oceania*. Second Edition. Berkeley: U of California P, 1985. Print.

——. *Technicians of the Sacred: A Range of Poetries from Africa, America, Asia, Europe & Oceania*. Third Edition. Oakland, CA: U of California P, 2017. Print.

——. *That Dada Strain*. New York: New Directions, 1983. Print.

———. *Writing Through: Translations and Variations.* Middletown, CT: Wesleyan UP, 2004. Print.
Rundle, Guy. "The Legacy of Ern Malley". *Eureka Street* (31 May 2006). Web. URL: https://www.eurekastreet.com.au/article/the-legacy-of-ern-malley
Ryan, John Charles. "'No More Boomerang': Environment and Technology in Contemporary Aboriginal Australian Poetry". *Global Indigeneities and the Environment.* Eds, Karen L. Thornber and Tom Havens. Basel: MDPi, 2016. 222–44. Print.
Saillens, Emile. "Le Bush Australien et Son Poète". *Mercure de France* (Paris, 1 Octobre, 2010). 431–42. Print.
Salmon, Peter. "'*53 Days*' by Georges Perec: '*C'est l'Australie qui m'a foutu mal!*'" *Sydney Review of Books*. 6 September 2016. Web. URL: https://sydneyreviewofbooks.com/review/53-days-georges-perec-review/
Sartre, Jean-Paul. *"What is Literature?" And Other Essays.* Cambridge, MA: Harvard UP, 1988. Print.
Schechner, Richard. "The Conservative Avant-Garde". *New Literary History* 41.4 (Autumn 2010): 895–913. Print.
Scobie, Ruth. *Celebrity Culture and the Myth of Oceania in Britain, 1770–1823.* Woodbridge: The Boydell P, 2019. Print.
Seita, Sophie. *Provisional Avant-Gardes: Little Magazine Communities from Dada to Digital.* Stanford: Stanford UP, 2019. Print.
Selenitsch, Alex. *Purgatorio Re-Placed.* Summer Hill: Life Before Man, 2017. Print.
———. *Sonnets.* Melbourne: self-made chapbook, 1973. Print.
Serle, Geoffrey. *From Deserts the Prophets Come: The Creative Spirit in Australia, 1788–1972.* Melbourne: Heinemann, 1973. Print.
Sharkey, Michael. *The Poetic Eye: Occasional Writings, 1982–2012.* Leiden: Brill, 2016. Print.
Slessor, Kenneth. *Five bells: XX poems, with six decorations by Norman Lindsay.* Sydney: Frank C. Johnson, 1939. Print.
Smith, Hazel. "hello!!" Message to A. J. Carruthers. 25 February 2017. Email.
———. "The Transformation of the Word: Text and Performance in the Work of Ania Walwicz and Amanda Stewart". *Representation, Discourse and Desire: Contemporary Australian Culture and Critical Theory.* Ed. Patrick Fuery. Melbourne, Longman Cheshire, 1994. 221–38. Print.
Smith, Hazel and Roger Dean. *Improvisation, Hypermedia and the Arts Since 1945.* Hoboken: Taylor and Francis, 2013. Print.
Soldatow, Sasha. "Introduction". *Poet of the 21st Century: Harry Hooton Collected Poems.* North Ryde: Angus and Robertson, 1990. 1–31. Print.
Southey, Robert. "Botany-Bay Eclogues". *The Complete Poetical Works of Robert Southey.* New York: D. Appleton & Company, 1851. 113–18. Print.

Spencer, Baldwin. *Wanderings in Wild Australia, Vol. 1*. London: Macmillan and Co., 1928. Print.

Spivak, Gayatri Chakravorty. *A Critique of Postcolonial Reason: Toward a History of the Vanishing Present*. Cambridge, MA: Harvard UP, 1999. Print.

———. *The Post-Colonial Critic: Interviews, Strategies, Dialogues*. Ed. Sarah Harasym. New York and London: Routledge, 1990. Print.

St. Pierre, Paul Matthew. *A Portrait of the Artist as Australian: L'oeuvre Bizarre de Barry Humphries*. Montréal: McGill-Queen's UP, 2004. Print.

Stark, Trevor. *Total Expansion of the Letter: Avant-Garde Art and Language After Mallarmé*. Cambridge, MA: The MIT Press, 2020. Print.

Stavrinaki, Maria. *Dada Presentism: An Essay on Art and History*. Stanford: Stanford UP, 2016. Print.

Stein, Gertrude. *Lifting Belly*. Ed. Rebecca Mark. Tallahassee, FL: Naiad Press, 1989. Print.

Stephen, Ann, ed. *Artists Think: The Late Works of Ian Burn*. Sydney: Power Publications, 1996. Print.

Stephen, Ann and Andrew McNamara. "The Modern Primitive and the Antipodes: The Visual Arts and Oceania". *The Modernist World*. Eds, Allana C. Lingren and Stephen Ross. New York: Routledge, 2015. 291–9. Print.

Stewart, Amanda. *I/T: Selected Poems 1980–1996*. Sydney: Here and There/ Split Records, 1998. Print.

———. "The Twentieth Century Never Happened". *NZEPC site (All Together Now: A Digital Bridge for Auckland and Sydney, Kia Kotahi Rā: He Arawhata Ipurangi mō Tamaki Makau Rau me Poihākena)*. September 2010. Web. URL: http://www.nzepc.auckland.ac.nz/features/home&away/stewart-sydney.asp

———. "Vocal Textures". *Voice: Vocal Aesthetics in Digital Arts and Media*. Eds, Norie Neumark, Ross Gibson and Theo Van Leeuwen. Cambridge, MA: MIT Press, 2010. 173–90. Print.

Stewart, Amanda, Jim Denley and Nick Ashwood (180°). *submental*. Splitrec, 2019. Album. URL: https://splitrec.com/shopcatalogue/

Stewart, Amanda, and Sasha Soldatow, producers. "The Death of Harry Hooton". *Radio Helicon*. Radio National: Australian Broadcasting Commission. 18 December 1988. Sydney, NSW. Radio.

Stewart, Garrett. *Reading Voices: Literature and the Phonotext*. Los Angeles: U of California P, 1990. Print.

Strehlow, T. G. H. *Songs of Central Australia*. Sydney: Angus & Robertson, 1970. Print.

Suarez, Angelo V. *Philippine English: A Novel*. Oakland: Gauss PDF, 2015. Web. URL: https://www.gausspdf.com/post/111963008170/gpdf158gpdfe011-angelo-v-su%C3%A1rez-philippine

Šuvaković, Miško. "Impossible Histories". *Impossible Histories: Historical Avant-gardes, Neo-avant-gardes, and Post-avant-gardes in Yugoslavia,*

1918–1991. Eds, Dubravka Djurić and Miško Šuvaković. Cambridge: MIT Press, 2003. 2–35. Print.

Tài, Lê Văn. *Waiting the Waterfall Falls: Concrete Poems*. Melbourne: Victoria U of Technology, 1996. Print.

Tedlock, Dennis and Jerome Rothenberg. "Statement of Intention". *Alcheringa: Ethnopoetics* 1.1 (1975): 1. Print.

Thalia. *A Loose Thread*. Melbourne: Collective Effort, 2015. Print.

——. *New & Selected Poems*. Melbourne: Collective Effort, 1998. Print.

Tiffany, Daniel. *Radio Corpse: Imagism and the Cryptaesthetic of Ezra Pound*. London: Harvard UP, 1995. Print.

Toscano, Alberto. "The Promethean Gap: Modernism, Machines, and the Obsolescence of Man". *Modernism/modernity* 23.3 (September 2016): 593–609. Print.

Tranter, John. *The Alphabet Murders*. London: Angus & Robertson, 1976. Print.

——. *Distant Voices*. University of Wollongong. 2009. Doctor of Creative Arts Thesis. Web. URL: https://ro.uow.edu.au/theses/3191

—, ed. *The New Australian Poetry*. St Lucia: Makar P, 1979. Print.

Tsantsanoglou, Maria. "'The Fantastic Tavern' and Other Caucasian Stories". *The Russian Avant-garde, Siberia and the East*. Eds, John E. Bowlt, Nicoletta Misler and Evgenija Petrova. Milano: Skira, 2014. 132–3. Print.

Tzara, Tristan. "A Note on Negro Poetry". Trans. Pierre Joris. *Alcheringa* 2.1 (1976): 76–7. Print.

——. "Maison Aragon". *Bulletin Dada*. Ed. Tristan Tzara, 6 (Paris, February 1920): 4. Little Magazine.

——. *Seven Dada Manifestos*. London: John Calder, 1977. Print.

"The Uluru Statement from the Heart". The Uluru Statement. 2017. Web. URL: https://ulurustatement.org/the-statement/view-the-statement/

Van Toorn, Penny. "Indigenous texts and narratives". *The Cambridge Companion to Australian Literature*. Ed. Elizabeth Webby. Cambridge: Cambridge UP, 2000. 19–49. Print.

Veit, Walter F. "Dada Among the Missionaries: Sources of Tristan Tzara's 'Poèmes Nègres.'" *Migration and Cultural Contact: Germany and Australia*. Eds, Andrea Bandhauer and Maria Weber. Sydney: Sydney UP, 2009. 45–88. Print.

Vickery, Ann. *Stressing the Modern: Cultural Politics in Australian Women's Poetry*. Cambridge: Salt, 2007. Print.

Wakeling, Corey. "Corey Wakeling Interviews Javant Biarujia". *Cordite Poetry Review*. 1 June, 2014. Web. URL: http://cordite.org.au/interviews/wakeling-biarujia/

——. "Lionel Fogarty's Literary Criticism after the Postcolony". *Plumwood Mountain* 3.2 (2016). Web. URL: https://plumwoodmountain.com/lionel-fogartys-literary-criticism-after-the-postcolony/

Walwicz, Ania. "Australia". *The Macmillan Anthology of Australian Literature*. Eds, Ken Goodwin and Alan Lawson. South Melbourne: Macmillan, 1990. 305–6. Print.

———. "Cut Tongue and the Mechanism of Defence (from a work-in-progress)". *Southerly [The Political Imagination: Postcolonialism and Diaspora in Contemporary Australian Poetry]* 73.1 (2013): 89–95. Print.

———. *Boat*. Sydney: Angus and Robertson, 1989. Print.

———. *Elegant*. Sydney: Vagabond, 2013. Print.

———. "Hammer, from *Palaces of Culture*". *Melbourne Spoken Word Showcase at Conduit Arts* (12 June, 2015). Web. Performance. URL: https://melbournespokenword.com/ania-walwicz-hammer/

———. "Look at Me, Ma–I'm Going to be a Marginal Writer!" *Southerly* 56.1 (1996): 58–61. Print.

———. *Palace of Culture*. Sydney: Puncher and Wattmann, 2014. Print.

———. *Red Roses*. St. Lucia: U of Queensland P, 1992. Print.

———. *Writing*. Melbourne: Rigmarole, 1982. Print.

Wang, Guanglin. *Translation in Diasporic Literatures*. Cham: Palgrave, 2019. Print.

Wertheim, Christine. "The Fall and Rise of Ernest Lalor Malley, The Poet Who Wasn't". *Cabinet* 33 (Spring 2009). Web. URL: http://www.cabinetmagazine.org/issues/33/wertheim.php

White, Eric B. *Transatlantic Avant-Gardes: Little Magazines and Localist Modernism*. Edinburgh: Edinburgh UP, 2013. Print.

White, Patrick. *Voss*. New York: Viking Press, 1957. Print.

Whitlam, Gough. *Socialism Within the Australian Constitution: The John Curtin Memorial Lecture (1961)*. Sydney: SOd Press, 2022. Web. URL: https://s0d.info/GOUGH_WHITLAM_SOCIALISM_WITHIN_THE_AUSTRALIAN_CONSTITUTION.pdf

———. *The Truth of the Matter*. Ringwood, VIC: Penguin Books Australia, 1979. Print.

———. "1969 Election Policy Speech". (1 October 1969). Sydney Town Hall. Web. URL: https://whitlamdismissal.com/1969/10/01/whitlam-1969-election-policy-speech.html

Whittaker, Alison. *Blakwork*. Broome: Magabala Books, 2018. Print.

———. "Not As We Know It: *Terra Nullius*". *Sydney Review of Books* (29 August 2017). Web. URL: https://sydneyreviewofbooks.com/review/terra-nullius-claire-coleman/

Williams, W. C. "The Baroness Elsa von Freytag-Loringhoven". *Twentieth Century Literature* 35.3 (Autumn, 1989): 279–84. Print.

———. "The Botticellian Trees". *Poetry* 37.5 (February 1931): 266–7. Print.

———. *The Collected Poems of William Carlos Williams, Volume II • 1939–1962*. Ed. Christopher MacGowan. New York: New Directions, 1991. Print.

——. *I Wanted to Write a Poem: The Autobiography of the Works of a Poet*. Ed. Edith Heal. Boston: New Directions, 1958. Print.

——. "Preface". *Poetry: The Australian International Quarterly of Verse*. Ed. Flexmore Hudson. Adelaide: Economy Press, 1947. 1–12. Journal / Little Magazine.

Winkiel, Laura. "Manifestoes and *Ars Poetica*". *The Routledge Companion to Experimental Literature*. Eds, Joe Bray, Alison Gibbons and Brian McHale. New York: Routledge, 2012. 253–66. Print.

Wright, Judith. *The Moving Image: Poems*. Melbourne: Meanjin Press, 1946. Print.

Wright, Preston. "An Interview with Chris Mann". *American Public Media* (July 2002). Web. URL: http://musicmavericks.publicradio.org/features/interview_mann.html

Youn, Hyejin, Luís M. A. Bettencourt, Deborah Strumsky and José Lobo. "Invention as a Combinatorial Process: Evidence from U.S. Patents". *Journal of the Royal Society Interface* 12.106 (June 2014): 1–22. Web. URL: https://arxiv.org/abs/1406.2938

Young, Mark. "defiant lethargy". *The Last Vispo Anthology: Visual Poetry 1998–2008*. Eds, Nico Vassilakis and Craig Hill. Seattle: Fantagraphics, 2012. 264. Print.

——. "Dolomite Chorus". *The Last Vispo Anthology: Visual Poetry 1998–2008*. Eds, Nico Vassilakis and Craig Hill. Seattle: Fantagraphics, 2012. 265. Print.

Zukofsky, Louis. "Program: 'Objectivists' 1931". *Poetry* 37.5 (February 1931): 268–72. Print.

Index

Aboriginal art, 28–9
Aboriginal avant-gardes
  emergence, 256
  geopolitical poetics, 243
  historical avant-garde and, 243
  the idea of the "native informant" and, 241–3, 251, 262
  temporality and, 243–4
  white time and, 244–8
  see also First Nations; First Nations avant-gardes
Aboriginal language
  in art, 28–9
  "Rainchant" (Spencer), 160–3, 166
  of the Songlines, 18, 20–1
Aboriginal poetry
  African-American experimental writers and, xi
  ethnopoetics, 17–22
  the Jindyworobak movement and Indigenous language, 32–4
  La Première Aventure Céléste de Mr Antipyrine (Tzara), 17–18
  Npala / Garroo cycle (Tzara), 17
  of Oodgeroo Noonuccal, 251–2
  Songlines/Songspirals, 17–18, 23–4, 25, 48, 87
  Songs from Central Australia (Strehlow), 17–21, 25, 197
  Tzara's translations of, 17–18
  see also Fogarty, Lionel
African-American experimental writers, xi, 243, 249
Ah Kee, Vernon, 28–9, 265
Albiach, Anne-Marie, 49
Alcheringa, 32, 33 n.19
Alcheringa, term, 33
Alizadeh, Ali, 250

Anarcho-Libertarian Push of Sydney, 35
Anderson, Jill, 49
Angry Penguins, 34, 110
Angry Penguins, The, 115–16, 119–20, 125, 131–2
anthologies
  anthologisation of Baldwin's anthropological text, 160–3, 166
  Antipodal avant-garde, 75–83, 85, 125, 174–5
  Ern Malley in, 125
  multi-lingual anthologies, 220
  politics of, 77
  sound poetry, 186–7
  women's experimental writing, 77
anti-Imperialism, xi, 249, 250–1, 254–6, 261, 264–5, 273, 276
Antin, David, 222
Antipodal avant-gardes
  anthologisation, 75–83, 85, 125, 174–5
  Australian modernists and, 104–5
  critical lag and, 26–38, 39, 43–4, 64
  difficulty, 307–8
  figures of, xi–xii
  during Gough Whitlam's era, 94
  the "historic" avant-garde and, 9–10, 13
  history and, 36, 86–7, 90–4, 294–6, 317–19
  influences, 285–8
  interrogations of language and media, 28–30
  invention in, 61, 63, 96–8, 313–16, 317–18
  literary history and, x, xii–xiii, 5–6, 13–14
  literary theory and, 118–19

Index   341

the long avant-garde, 308–12, 318
the Malley affair and, 112–13, 122, 126–7
"neo"-vanguard, 178–9, 180, 194
1940s avant-garde, xiv, 32–5, 89–95, 108–9, 150–3
1980s-now, 72, 79–80, 95–9, 294–5
as non-Western, 279
politics of, 35–7
profanities, 80 n.13
readings of, 43–4
recognition by the international avant-gardes, x, 25–6, 72–3, 129–30
reinvention of poetic language, 96–8
remote avant-garde, xiii, xiv, 27–8, 30–1, 246
scholarship, 27–8
trans-Pacific dialogue, xi, 100–1, 112, 128–9, 135–7, 174–5
Antipodal poetry
the Antipodean imaginary in America, 135–6
Australian poetics criticism, 202–4
as Commonwealth poetry, 13
entrepôt and, 36
invention in, 67
the larrikin voice, 52–3, 65, 73–4
Mallarmé's influence on, 70–1
Modern Australian Verse, 32
modernism, 110–11
negation of romanticism, 114
New Australian Poetry, 92–3
parodic tradition, 114–15
as settler poetry, 11–14
theories of, 13
travel and inspiration in, 63–4
Apollinaire, Guillaume, 11 n.5, 115, 163, 164
arts
Aboriginal art, xiii, 28–9
Australian culture during the 1970s, 171–3
communism and proletarian culture, 120
cultural impact of Gough Whitlam, 94, 171, 172, 173–4, 175, 178, 184
intersection with politics, 148–9
Symbolism, 64
Ashbery, John, 93, 112, 128–9, 136, 174, 175

Atkins, Russell, 243
Auden, W. H, 176
Austin, Lloyd, 53, 55–8, 84
Australia
the Antipodal City, xiii, 143–4, 304, 305
Assisted Passage Migration Scheme, 184
Bicentennial celebrations, 179, 196–7
"Botany-Bay Eclogues" (Southey), 12, 88–9
bourgeois state violence against Aboriginal people, 255–6, 272
colonial Romanticism, 11–12, 89, 213
Frontier Wars, 11, 24, 89, 105, 179, 229, 240, 246
invasion of, 11–14, 88, 246
Land Rights Conference, 72
literary history, xii–xiii
multiculturalism, 236–7
New Nationalism, 166, 173
non-Anglo-Celtic writers, 218–20
Northern Territory Emergency Response, 30
as a penal colony, 88–9
Republicanism, 36, 87–8, 295
as *terra australis incognita*, 12, 14, 58
as *terra nullius*, 12, 13, 14, 213
Australian International Quarterly of Verse, The, 100
avant-gardes
associated terms, 6–7
conservative avant-garde, 26 n.13
ethnopoetics and, 17–21
experimental poetry and, 86, 89–90, 92
hemispheric understandings, 5–7, 206, 237, 239
the "historic" avant-garde, x, xiv, 8–16, 92, 177
literary criticism and, 177, 221
literary theory and, 220–1
logics of exteriority and interiority, 91
Mallarmé and, 74
manifestos, 244–5
modernism and, x, xii, xiii, 6, 26, 92, 104–5, 110–11
periodicity, 44–6
politics of avant-garde language, 74–5

avant-gardes (*cont.*)
  recognition of the Antipodal avant-garde, x, 25–6, 72–3, 129–30
  revolutionary function, 109
  scholarship, 27 n.14
  term, xiii–xiv, 86

Badiou, Alain, 53, 59
Bakhtin, Mikhail, 85–6
Ball, Hugo, 33, 152, 163
Banner, Stuart, 213, 214
Baraka, Amiri, xi
Baranay, Inez, 313
Barnes, Katherinc, 47–8, 52
Benjamin, Walter, 69–70
Beresford, Bruce, 172
Bernstein, Charles, 6–7, 86
Biarujia, Javant
  as an Antipodal avant-garde figure, 99, 286
  "Spelter to Pewter", 96–7
  Taneraic, 96–8, 310
Biddle, Jennifer Loureide, xiii, 27–8, 30–1, 246
Birns, Nicholas, 37, 38
bissett, bill, 176, 193
Black Dada, 262, 263
Black radicalism, xi, 240, 261
Block, Friedrich, 90
Born to Concrete, 180
Boyd, Arthur, 151
bpNichol, 159, 176, 180, 193
Breeze, Mez (Mezangelle), xi, 310–12, 317
Brennan, Christopher John
  as an Antipodal avant-garde figure, xi
  within Antipodal literary history, 48–9, 92
  Australian readership for, 61, 62, 65
  calligraphy, 84
  dedicatory poems to Mallarmé, 83–5
  Ern Malley and, 49, 52–3, 62–3, 64, 65, 85
  friendship with Dowell O'Reilly, 60–1
  personal life, 51, 53, 61
  Poems, 47, 48, 83
  Stéphane Mallarmé's influence on, 47–8, 49, 52, 57, 63, 64, 71, 72, 85, 98–9
  XXI Poems, 52, 60–1

  see also Musicopoematographoscope (Brennan)
Bright, Colin, 198
Broodthaers, Marcel, 81–2
Brooks, David, 121–2, 129
Brown, Pam, 156
Bulletin Dada, 3
Bürger, Peter, 45
Burn, Ian, 29–30
burns, joanne, 209, 220

Cabaret Voltaire, 16, 17, 18
Cage, John, 86, 222, 285, 286, 287, 288, 289, 302
Călinescu, Matei, 8–9, 12
Chambers, Ross, 5
Chatwin, Bruce, 31
chronometer
  of Antipodal poetics, 99, 136–8
  chronometric readings, 85–6
  critical-historical chronometrics, 294–7
  as an era-glass, 10–11
  marine chronometers, 11
  of *Musicopoematographoscope* (Brennan), 67
  term, 10 n.4, 11 n.5
  Tzara's *chronomètre*, 3, 4
  see also time
Clark, Alex, 60–1, 62, 65
Clemens, Justin, 13, 67, 90, 204, 213 n.2, 285
Cobbing, Bob, xi, 287
Colby, Georgina, 6
Collective Effort Press, 78–9, 180
colonialism
  colonial modernism, 72–3
  colonial Romanticism, 11–12, 13–14, 89, 213
  Critique of Postcolonial Reason (Spivak), 241–3, 248, 262
  postcolonial figure of the "native informant", 241–3, 251, 262
communism, 119–21, 236
conceptualism, 29–30
concrete poetics, 80, 81–3
Cook, James, 11
Cook, Stuart, 249
Cosmopolis, 51, 52, 64
Couani, Anna, 77, 220

Cross, Zora, 107
Cummins, Johnny, 257, 260

Dada
 in Australia, x, 78, 96, 149
 and Australian national culture, 168–9, 171–2
 Black Dada, 262, 263
 "Dadaustralia" (Duke), 78–9, 206, 207
 history of, 7
 Humphries's Dada origins, 166–72, 179
 Melbourne Dada Group, x, 139–40
 neo-Dada internationalism, 160
 Oceanic origins, 160–6
 periodicals, 3–4
 poetic line of, 155
 politics of, 166–7
 prank and provocation of, 168–9, 170–1
 "Rainchant" (Spencer), 160–3, 166
 Ribemont-Dessaignes's manifesto, 65
 Rothenberg's critique of historical Dada, 163–6
 term, 162
 typographic experiments, 68, 69
 see also Duke, Jas H.; Humphries, Barry; Rothenberg, Jerome
Dada Days, 167
Dada I, 17
Dada Manifesto, 100, 163
Dada-Jok, 170
Dante Alighieri, 58 n.3
Davray, Henry, 53
Dean, Roger, 198–9
Derrida, Jacques, 71–2, 74, 220
Desai, Radhika, 235
digital poetics, 90, 96, 204, 310–12
Dobson, Rosemary, 108
Docker, John, 129, 131 n.7
Duchamp, Marcel, x, 29, 46, 106 n.3, 170–1, 285
Duke, Jas H.
 "After Jas H. Duke" (Fanoy), 176–7
 "ALEKHINE AND JUNGE AT PRAGUE", 190
 "An Answer To Those Who Say You Can't Write Poetry In A Cultural Backwater Like Australia", 198–9
 Archduke 4, 193
 "BLACK SQUARES", 187–8
 citational poetics, 187–9
 Collective Effort Press, 78–9
 criticism of the "church" of the avant-gardes, 170, 172, 186–7, 299
 Dada Kampfen um Leben und Tod, 181–2, 183, 184, 186
 Dada performances, x, 160
 "Dadaustralia", 78–9, 206, 207
 "Daily Life" poems, 190
 Destiny Wood, 180–1, 182
 "GOING HOME LATE AT NIGHT", 196
 "HAPPY BIRTHDAY AUSTRALIA", 196–7
 historical-cum-citational narrative poems, 190–3
 "A HISTORY OF EXPRESSIONIST POETRY (1910–1920)", 188–9
 history of the avant-garde, 160, 177–8, 185–91, 194, 207
 Hooton's influence on, 149, 176
 influence on Stewart, 150, 204
 lettristic disruption, 179–80, 193
 literary criticism and, 202–3, 210
 lyricisation of Duke in song, 198
 Missing Forms, 79
 nation and Australianness, 195–200
 on Nicholas Zurbrugg, 186
 notational poetics, 197, 198–9
 "The Nottingham Incident", 190–2
 overseas travel, 182–3, 184–5
 Poems of War and Peace, 185
 poetics and the international avant-garde, 178
 "Scratchticket", 195
 small publications, 180
 the social construction of voice, 200–1
 socio-political contexts, 175–6, 178
 sound poetry, 195, 198–200, 283–4
 translation work, 189 n.3
 as a visualist, 179–80
 "Whitman Sings Again", 195–6
 "THE WONDERS OF SCIENCE", 192

Eastern Europe, x
Edwards, Chris
 as an Antipodal avant-garde figure, 99
 A Fluke, 70–1, 72, 73–4, 76

Eliot, T. S., 85, 116, 130, 138, 146
ethnopoetics, 17–22, 32, 90, 278
experimental, term, 89–91
experimental writing
   African-American experimental writers, xi, 243
   in American poetry, 86
   Australian experimental practices, x–xi, 200–5
   avant-gardes and, 86, 89–90, 92
   by migrant poets, 210–11
   publishing challenges for, 313
   readers of, 6
   transcultural narratives, 182–4
   by women, 77–8

Fagan, Kate, 71, 74, 92–3
Fanon, Frantz, 243, 254, 257, 268–9, 270, 275, 276, 279
Fanoy, Jetje, 176–7
Farrell, Michael, 61, 62–3, 67, 156, 201
Fichte, Johann Gottlieb, 47, 48
Field, Barron, 13, 87, 213–14
Fink, Margaret, 133, 134, 139
First Nations
   bourgeois state violence against, 255–6, 272
   "Decalogues", 21–2
   First Knowledge histories, 23–4
   Frontier Wars, 11, 105, 179, 229, 240, 246, 2489
   Indigenous internationalism, 249
   the Jindyworobaks and, 32–3
   political manifestos, 245–6
   reserves and missions, 31 n.17
   ritual and totemic ancestors, 21–2
   senses of Nation, 239, 269, 272–3, 309
   Songlines history, 18–21, 23–4, 25, 87
   the Stolen Generations, 22, 272
   vision of the desert, 305
   during the Whitlam era, 173
   see also Aboriginal avant-gardes; Aboriginal poetry
First Nations avant-gardes
   historical avant-gardes and, 243
   history of resistance, 24–5
   language, 278–81
   manifestos, 245
   a national literature and, 276–82
   as a response to Tzara, 24–5, 243–4
   see also Aboriginal avant-gardes
Fogarty, Lionel
   "Advance Those Asian And Pacific Writers Poets", 273
   "Alcheringa", 32 n.18
   "Aphorism Wealth Grazier", 248
   as an avant-garde figure, xi, 244, 248–51, 252, 276
   "Biral Biral", 250
   "Capitalism – The Murderer in Disguise", 255
   childhood on a punishment reserve, 31 n.17, 255
   "Decipher", 246–7, 269–70
   "Do Yourself a Favour, Educate Your Mind", 271
   "Encounters Conflicts", 274
   First Nations nationalism, 239, 249, 255, 275–7, 282, 285
   geopolitical anti-imperialism, xi, 249, 250–1, 254–6, 261, 264–5, 273, 276
   guerrilla readings of, 256–62, 270
   "Head Keeper Futures Corridor's Bay", 265, 267
   historical style, 253–6, 259, 261–2, 274–5
   "Historical Upheavals", 273–4
   history and a First Nations sense of time, 137, 246–8, 265–7
   "I am Black, I am Both You and I, Truganini", 260, 271–2
   "Intricacies", 256
   Kargun, 249, 252, 257, 259–60, 271, 273
   language, 29, 244, 245, 257–9, 260–1, 265–7, 269, 285
   liberation poetics, 273–4
   as national-prophetic poet, 268–75
   political style, 240, 244, 245, 253–7, 261–2, 263
   prophetic mode, 270–3, 275
   prosodic dissonance, 265–6
   "SCENIC MAPS PARTS", 266–7
   scholarship on, 277
   "Strangled in War", 254
   "Swift Terrorless", 265–6
   "A-U-S-T-R-A-L-I-A", 264–5

as a visualist, 257, 260, 271
  Yugambeh heritage, 244, 246
Forbes, John, 49
Foster, Hal, 45
Fraser, Malcolm, 94
Freeth, John (Poet Freeth/John Free), 88
Freud, Sigmund, 21, 161
Freytag-Loringhoven, Baroness Elsa von
  cross-gendered escapades, 210
  "Hamlet of Wedding Ring", 106
  neurasthenic modernism and, 106 n.3, 116, 117, 118
  scholarship on, 46
  sound poetry, 187
  W. C. Williams's account of, 104, 106–7, 116
Frye, Northrop, 159, 206, 238
Furaih, Ameer Chasib, 249

Gammel, Irene, 106
Gardner, W. H., 115
Gay'wu Group of Women, 23
gaze theory, 29
geometry
  expansive geometry in Walwicz's works, 227–32
  geometric grammar, 188–9
  "Geometry for Beginners" (Hooton), 141–2
  in the poetic line, 139, 141–2
geopolitics
  of Ania Walwicz's works, 233–6
  geopolitical anti-imperialism in Lionel Fogarty's works, xi, 249, 250–1, 254–6, 261, 264–5, 273, 276
  geopolitical poetics of the Aboriginal avant-garde, 243
  geopolitical space of the Antipodal continent, xii, xiii
German Romanticism, 48
Giles, Paul, 136–7
Gillen, F. J., 161
Gilmore, Mary, 107
Ginsberg, Allen, 135
Gould, Bob, 139
Greer, Germaine, 139
Grenier, Robert, 103, 139, 288
Gunew, Sneja, 77–8, 219, 220, 232–5, 237, 240 n.6

Hage, Emily, 3–4
Harford, Lesbia, 107
Harkin, Natalie
  Archival Poetics, 279–80
  Dirty Words, 261–2, 280–1
  poetics, 282
Harris, Max, 34, 110, 111, 125, 128, 132, 151
Harrison, Martin, 201–2
Hartley, Daniel, 253, 254
Hawke, John, 64, 111
Hentea, Marius, 17
Hernández, Robb, xii
Heseltine, Harry, 26, 95, 115, 154, 175
Heyward, Michael, 112, 125, 126
history
  Antipodal avant-garde and, 36, 86–7, 90–4, 317–19
  First Knowledge histories, 23–4
  mistranslation as historical work, 70–4
holophrases, 16
Hooton, Harry
  Anarcho-Libertarian Push of Sydney, 35
  anarcho-technocracy, 118–19, 121, 132, 135, 139–41, 293
  "Anarcho-Technocracy: The Politics of Things", 135
  as avant-garde social critic, 152–6
  "The Clalendar", 141
  Collected Poems, 154
  The Death of Harry Hooton, 133–4, 293
  "Directions", 148–9, 176
  "Geometry for Beginners", 141–2
  The Golden City, 143–4
  Hootonics, 139, 140, 146, 148
  influence on Duke, 149, 176
  "The Inhuman Race", 145–7
  "It Is Great To Be Alive", 79, 119, 119 n.4, 133–4, 137
  on Joyce, 132
  "For the Last Time", 142–3
  linguistic experimentation, 145–7
  on the Malley affair, 115, 132–4
  the new order of the poetic line, 138–44, 154–5
  "Poetry", 143

Hooton, Harry (*cont.*)
"Poetry and the New Proletariat", 153–4
on Pound, 132
"Promes in Pose", 147
proto-posthuman, 116, 147
"Psalm", 153
scientific criticism, 150–2
as small-press publisher, 133, 134–5
trans-Pacific dialogue, 135–6
"Very Words (NOT A POEM)", 147–8
Hope, A. D., 49, 67, 114–15, 232
Hopkins, Gerard Manley, 87, 103, 115, 116, 275, 281, 311
Hopper, Sabina Paula, 258, 259–60
Hudson, Flexmore, 100, 106
Hughes, Randolph, 47 n.1
Hughes, Robert, 111, 119 n.4, 128, 139
Huirimilla, Paulo, 249
Humphries, Barry
Dada and, 78, 166–72, 179
Dada Manifesto, 169–70
Dame Edna Everage, x, 170–1
Dr Aaron Azimuth, 140, 168, 169
first Dadaist exhibition, 168–9
Les Patterson, 167, 171
Melbourne Dada Group, x, 139–40, 167
Tid, x, 167–8
Wonderful World of Barry McKenzie, The, 171, 172

Indian avant-garde, 35 n.21
Industrial Women Collective, 193, 194
Ingamells, Rex, 32, 33

Jacket, 71
Jameson, Fredric, 131 n.7
Janco, Marcel, 7, 8
Jauss, Hans Robert, 40, 41, 43, 160
Jennings, Kate, 77
Jindyworobak Movement, 32–5, 48, 72, 73, 100, 153
Johnson, Barbara, 71–2
Jones, Amelia, 106 n.3, 116, 117
Joyce, James, 132, 143, 145, 217

Kane, Paul, 113–14, 117–18, 203, 204
Kant, Immanuel, 241–2

Keller, Lynn, 228
Kelly, Lynne, 23, 24
Kermode, Frank, 177
Kerr, Sir John, 36 n.22, 94
Kinsella, John, xi, 6, 179, 252
Kirkpatrick, Peter, 33, 92, 111
Konstanz School, 40, 42
Krauss, Rosalind, 109
Kristeva, Julia, 109

La Coeur à barbe, 15
Ladd, Mike, 80
Langer, Susanne, 298–9
language
Biarujia's Taneraic, 96–8, 310
etymology of 'experiment,' 89–90
of First Nations writing, 278–81
in Fogarty's works, 29, 244, 245, 257–9, 260–1, 265–7, 269, 285
geometric grammar, 188–9
Hooton's linguistic experimentation, 145–7
the Jindyworobak movement and Indigenous language, 32–4
language-sound relationship, 298–9
linguistic boundaries, 187
in Mallarmé, 74–5, 259
Mezangelle, 310–12, 317
mistranslation as historical work, 70–4
phonetic markers, 78
politics of avant-garde language, 28–30, 74–5
"Rainchant" (Spencer), 160–3, 166
reinvention of poetic language, 96–8
sound poetry, 186–7, 195, 198–200
in Stewart's works, 284–5, 293–4
translation/untranslatability, 313–15
the Vernacular Republic, 87–8, 107, 200
in Walwicz's works, 218, 221–2, 238–9
see also Aboriginal language
Lawson, Henry, 108
Leavis, F. R., 115, 129
Lecercle, Jean-Jacques, 25, 122–6, 129, 130, 294
literary history
Antipodal avant-garde, x, xii–xiii, 5–6, 13–14

the avant-gardes and, 91–2
chronometric readings, 85–6
literary criticism and, 159–60, 177
literary theory and, 5–6, 38, 39–40, 118–19, 136–8
periodicity, 44–6
presentism, 40–1
reception of avant-garde texts, 40–4, 92
recuperative frameworks, 5, 40, 133, 138, 152–3, 177
retroactive re-readings, 317–18
texts as the illuminators of, 4–5
Lloyd, Brian, 116, 117
Lyne, R. O. A. M., 109–10

Mac Low, Jackson, 222, 285, 286, 287, 289
McAuley, James
 avant-garde status of, 115–16, 117–18
 "Catherine Hill Bay 1942", 112
 see also Malley, Ern
McCredden, Lyn, 210–12, 218
Machine for Making Sense, 283
Macintyre, Stuart, 108, 116
McKenzie, Geraldine, 98
McNamara, Andrew, 17, 18, 25
Macquarie, Lachlan, 213–14
Malcolm X, 254, 255, 263, 267
Malevich, Kazimir, 80, 97, 187
Mallarmé, Stéphane
 Brennan's dedicatory poems to, 83–5
 Broodthaers's reworking of *Un Coup de Dés*, 81–2
 critical readings, 53–5, 59–60, 74
 defence of Brennan's difficulty, 53
 Derrida's reading of, 71–2, 74
 influence on Antipodal poetry, xi, 70–1
 influence on Christopher Brennan, 47–8, 49, 52, 57, 63, 64, 71, 72, 85, 98–9
 kinship of dream, 49
 language of, 74–5, 259
 mistranslations of *Un Coup de Dés*, 70–4
 notational poetics and prosody, 49–50, 61–2, 68
 "Prose, *pour des Esseintes*", 55–8, 60
 typographic experiments, 69–70, 71–2

Un Coup de Dés, x, 49–50, 51, 52, 54, 69, 70, 71–2, 85
Malley, Ern
 Angry Penguins, 34
 The Angry Penguins, 125, 131–2
 anthologisation, 125
 as an Antipodal avant-garde figure, xi, 33, 35, 98, 122, 126–7, 130–2
 the Antipodal parodic tradition and, 114–15
 Australian modernism and, x, 47 n.1, 49, 52–3, 62–3, 64, 92, 107, 110–18, 121–2, 126, 131–3, 137
 Brennan's poetics and, 49, 52–3, 62–3, 64, 65, 85
 citational poetics, 127–8, 130, 188
 colonial modernism and, 72
 "Culture as Exhibit", 127, 128
 The Darkening Ecliptic, 110, 125, 129
 "Dürer: Innsbruck, 1495", 122–5
 Hooton on, 115, 132–4
 Lecercle's discourse on, 25, 122–6, 129, 130, 294
 the Malley reader, 121–32
 as a manifesto, 116–17
 "Petit Testament", 129
 trans-Pacific dialogue, 112, 128–9
 "Young Prince of Tyre", 100, 117
 see also McAuley, James; Stewart, Harold
Man, Paul de, 42
Mann, Chris, 252, 283, 285, 290, 294
Mao Zedong, 121, 254, 255, 263 n.4, 267, 272
Mead, Philip, 38–9, 44, 125, 201, 258
Meanjin, 134
Meillassoux, Quentin, 53, 54, 56
Melbourne Dada Group, x, 139–40, 167
Mezangelle (Mez Breeze), xi, 310–12, 317
Miller, Tyrus, 118
Minter, Peter, 92–3
Mirrlees, Hope, 85
Missing Forms, 78–81, 83, 174
Mitter, Partha, 35 n.21
modernism
 Antipodal audiences for modernist poetry, 107–8
 in Antipodal writing, 26–7, 35–8, 110–11, 136

modernism (*cont.*)
  appropriative modernism, 32–5
  avant-gardes and, x, xii, xiii, 6, 26, 92, 104–5, 110–11
  colonial modernism, 72–3
  the Jindyworobak movement, 32–5, 48
  the Malley affair and, x, 47 n.1, 49, 52–3, 62–3, 64, 92, 107, 110–18, 121–2, 126, 131–3, 137
  neurasthenic modernism, 106 n.3, 116, 118–19
  patrilinearity, 101, 102, 104, 106–7
  primitivism and, 17
  social readings, 101–7
Moginie, Samuel, 28
Morris, Tracie, 86
MS, 143
Mudrooroo, 257–8, 260, 262 n.3
multiculturalism
  in Australia, 236–7
  literary criticism and, 232–5, 250–1
  white bourgeois nationalism and, 268
Murray, Les, xi, 6, 87–8, 99, 200
music
  180°, 303
  experimental music, 167, 302
  "late" Romantic, 316
  lyricisation of Duke in song, 198
  music-poetry relationship, 50–1, 316–17
  notation in poetry for performance, 288
  Songlines/Songspirals, 17–18, 23–4, 25, 48, 87
  Songs from Central Australia (Strehlow), 17–21, 25, 87, 197
  see also notational poetics
Musicopoematographoscope (Brennan)
  Celtic font, 68–9
  as a chronometric piece, 67
  as critique of the Australian reader, 59, 60–1, 62–3, 65, 75
  notational poetics and prosody, 51, 61–3, 66–9
  pages, 51, 62, 66
  (re)inventions in, 67–8
  temporal presence, 51, 52, 64–7, 68, 85

Un Coup de Dés Jamais N'Abolira Le Hasard and, x, 52, 70, 71

Namatjira, Albert, 29
nationalism
  anticolonial counter-nationalism, 268–9
  developmental nationalisms, 268
  First Nations nationalism, 239, 249, 255, 275–7, 282, 285, 309
  Indigenous senses of Nation, 249, 269, 272–3
  intercultural nationalism, 33 n.19, 72–3
  multiculturalism and, 234–5, 268
  national revelation, 48
  New Nationalism, 166, 173
Neale, Margo, 23, 24
Neoteric poets, 109–10
neurasthenic modernism, 106 n.3, 116, 118–19
New Criticism, 118, 128, 129, 177, 221–2
Nielsen, Aldon Lynn, 243
925, 80, 180
Noonuccal, Oodgeroo, 6, 251–2, 276 n.5
notational poetics
  in Duke's work, 197, 198–9
  Fluxus, 199, 286, 289
  in Mallarmé's work, 49–50, 61–2, 68
  of *Musicopoematographoscope* (Brennan), 51, 61–2, 66–9
  of performance poetry, 288
  in Stewart's work, 284, 288–93
  textuality and, 291
  "The Twentieth Century Never Happened" (Stewart), 291–3
  vocal textures, 301–2
notationality, term, 288

Objectivist poetics, 144–5
Oceania, term, 161
Ono, Yoko, 199, 289
O'Reilly, Dowell, 60–1
O'Sullivan, Maggie, xi, 208
Ouyang Yu
  "A Chinese Sojourner in Australia", 213
  "Fuck You, Australia", 196

as a radical migrant writer, 220, 250
A wáng gǎ, 305
Ya yóu gā, 314–15

Palmer, Nettie, 107
Pasquier, Étienne, 8–9, 12
Pender, Anne, 173
Pendleton, Adam, 262, 263
Penguin Book of Modern Australian Poetry, 26, 95, 125
Perec, George, xiii, 25, 306–7
Perelman, Bob, 40–1, 111
Perloff, Marjorie, 127, 128
П.О.
  anti-academic stance, 262 n.3
  on Duke, 176, 184
  Heide, 151
  migrant experience, 219, 220, 250
  in *Missing Forms*, 79, 80
  performance and, 252
  transnational perspectives, 184
  as a visualist, 81
Picabia, Francis, 80
Piper, Adrian, 29
poetic line
  Antipodal time, 85–6, 99
  Australian modernism and, 105, 108–9, 131, 154
  the Australian new order of, 7, 132, 138–44
  of Brennan's work, 68, 83
  of Dada, 155
  geometry, 139, 141–2
  Hooton's new order of, 138–44, 154–5
  neoteric line, 109–10
  poetic form and, 102–3
  Williams's call for a new order, 102–4, 138, 139, 154, 155
poetics
  Australian experimental practices, 200–5
  Australian poetics criticism, 201–7
  citational poetics, 127–8, 130, 188–9
  concrete poetics, 80, 81–3
  definitions, 38–9
  digital poetics, 90, 96, 204, 310–12
  ethnopoetics, 17–22, 32, 90, 278
  geopolitical poetics of the Aboriginal avant-garde, 243

literary criticism and, 38
Objectivist poetics, 144–5
poetic difficulty, 39
space/time poetics, 240, 248
see also notational poetics
poetry
  Australian experimental practices, x–xi
  of colonial Romanticism, 11–12, 13–14
  development of French poetry, 8–9
  literary criticism and, 201–7
  long poem studies, 228–9
  music-poetry relationship, 50–1, 316–17
  obscurity in, 20–1
  recordings of the poet's voice, 208–9
  Spoken Word poetry, 284 n.2
  see also Aboriginal poetry; Antipodal poetry; sound poetry
politics
  American experimental poetry, 86
  of anthologies, 77
  of Australian Dada, 166–7
  of avant-garde language, 28–30, 74–5
  the Chifley era, 108
  cultural history and, 94–5
  cultural impact of Gough Whitlam, 94, 171, 172, 173–4, 175, 178
  Fogarty's political style, 240, 244, 245, 253–7, 261–2, 263
  geopolitical contexts, 233–6
  Indigenous political manifestos, 245–6
  intersection with art, 148–9
  of the 1970s, 96
  political style in poetry, 253–7, 261–2, 263
  Racial Discrimination Act, 184
  in sound poetry, 195
  the Whitlam Dismissal, 36 n.22, 94, 95 n.20, 96, 175, 178
  of women's experimental writing, 77–8
Poljanski, Branko Ve, 170
Pollock, Jackson, 94
Pound, Ezra
  on Elsa von Freytag-Loringhoven, 104
  Hooton on, 132
  literary relationship with W. C. Williams, 100–1, 102, 105–6

Prichard, Katherine Susannah, 120
prosody
  of G. M. Hopkins, 103, 115
  national prosody, 103
  notational poetics and prosody in Brennan, 51, 61–3, 66–9
  notational poetics and prosody in Mallarmé, 49–50, 61–2, 68
  prosodic dissonance in Fogarty, 265–6
  prosodic dissonance in Walwicz, 142, 221–7
  in W. C. Williams's work, 103
psychoanalytic theory, 21–2
Push Movement (Sydney), 139, 141, 174

Read, Herbert, 119 n.4
readership
  Antipodal audiences for modernist poetry, 107–8, 153
  audiences for great poetry, 104
  for Brennan's poetry, 61, 62, 65
  critical readings, 159–60
  difficulty in the Antipodal avant-garde, 307–8
  of experimental poetry, 6
  guerrilla readings of Fogarty's work, 256–62, 270
  the Malley reader, 121–32
  Musicopoematographoscope (Brennan) as a critique of the Australian reader, 59, 60–1, 62–3, 65, 75
  reception of avant-garde texts, 40–4
  tedium and interpretation, 308–9
  for Walwicz's poetry, 216, 218
Reed, Brian, 45–6
Reik, Theodor, 21–2, 87
Richards, June Walkutjukurr, 28, 31
Rix, Robert W., 88–9
Romanticism
  Antipodal negation of, 114
  colonial Romanticism, 11–12, 13–14, 89, 213
  German Romanticism, 48, 245
  literary theory and, 204
  prophecy, 271
  shift to Symbolism, 92
Rothenberg, Jerome
  Alcheringa, 32

  anthologisation of Baldwin's anthropological text, 160–3, 166
  as an Antipodal avant-garde figure, xi
  critiques of historical Dada, 163–4
  "The History of Dada as my Muse", 164
  the Oceanic origins of Dada, 160–3
  "On Prophecies" (Apollinaire), 164
  That Dada Strain, 163–6
  translation of "Maison, pour Aragon", 3, 15
Rrose Selavy, x, 170–1
Rundle, Guy, 126
Ryan, John Charles, 249

Saillens, Émile, 25
Sanchez, Sonia, xi
Sartre, Jean-Paul, 19–20, 21
Schiller, Friedrich, 263
Schwitters, Kurt, 181
Selenitsch, Alex, xi, 58 n.3, 79, 81–3
Shakespeare, William, 117, 274
Sharkey, Michael, 174–5
Shelley, Percy Bysshe, 10
Slessor, Kenneth, 37, 38, 92, 108
Smith, Hazel, xi, 79 n.11, 91 n.18, 198–9, 288
Soldatow, Sasha, 132, 133, 134, 135
Somerville, Oliver M., 132, 138, 141 n.9
sound poetry
  anthologies, 186–7
  of Duke, 195, 198–200, 283–4
  of Freytag-Loringhoven, 187
  as historical, 299
  language-sound relationship, 298–9
  of Stewart, 283–4, 299–303
  vocal textures, 301–2
Southey, Robert, 12, 88–9
Spencer, Baldwin, 161–2
Spivak, Gayatri, 219, 240 n.6, 241–3, 248, 262, 269
Spoken Word poetry, 284 n.2
St. Pierre, Paul Matthew, 167, 168, 170–1
Stark, Trevor, 59–60
Stavrinaki, Maria, 7
Stein, Gertrude, 41, 116, 143, 145, 208, 209, 216, 217, 222

Stephen, Ann, 17, 18, 25, 29
Stewart, Amanda
  180°, 303
  ", No Person, speaks", 299–301
  as an Antipodal avant-garde figure, xi, 284–6
  compared to Walwicz, 288
  critical-historical chronometrics, 294–7
  "on criticism: THIS", 296–7
  The Death of Harry Hooton, 293
  Duke's influence on, 150, 204
  "Forked Lands", 294–5
  "Haiku for Min Tanaka", 290–1
  "Icon", 304
  improvisatory style, 298
  influences, 285–7
  internationalism, 284, 286
  "IT BECOMES: JULY 1981", 293–4, 295
  I/T: Selected Poems, 284
  "Kitsch Postcards", 304
  language, 284–5, 293–4
  "The Liberated Showroom", 289–90
  Machine for Making Sense, 303
  notational poetics, 284, 288–93
  overseas travel, 182–3, 283–4, 286
  performance and, 252, 284, 298
  sound poetry, 283–4, 299–303
  "The Twentieth Century Never Happened", 291–3
  "vice versa", 301
Stewart, Garrett, 221, 227
Stewart, Harold, 110, 115–16, 117–18, 125, 132; *see also* Malley, Ern
Stieglitz, Alfred, 80
Strehlow, Carl, 16, 18, 22
Strehlow, T. G. H., *Songs from Central Australia*, 17–21, 25, 87, 197
Suprematism, 188
Symbolism, 63, 64, 72, 92, 111–12

Taneraic, 96–8, 310
Thalia, 78, 79, 184, 220
Tiffany, Daniel, 106
time
  in Brennan's
    Musicopoematographoscope, 51, 52, 64–7, 68, 85
  First Knowledge histories, 23–4
  history and a First Nations sense of time, 137, 246–8, 265–7
  prophetic time, 164
  space/time poetics, 240, 248
  white time and the Aboriginal avant-gardes, 244–8
  see also chronometer
Tipper, Henry Alfred (Professor Tipper/Henry Dearing/Harold Deering/H. D.), 151–2
Toorn, Penny van, 251–2
Tranter, John
  as an Antipodal avant-garde figure, xi, 6
  "Desmond's Coupé", 73
  Jacket, 71
  mistranslation of *Un Coup de Dés*, 73–4
  The New Australian Poetry, 92–3, 174–5
  Penguin Book of Modern Australian Poetry, 125
Tzara, Tristan
  "COLONIAL SYLLOGISM", 22
  Dada Manifesto, 100, 163
  ethnological studies, 17–18, 163
  ethnopoetics, 90, 278
  evocation of Australia, 3, 4
  as a key avant-garde figure, xi
  La Première Aventure Céléste de Mr Antipyrine, 17–18
  "Maison, pour Aragon", 3, 4, 10, 14–16
  Npala / Garroo cycle, 17
  pseudonym, 31–2
  Songlines translations, 16–18, 25, 163, 306
  tradition and the avant-garde, 31

United States of America
  African-American experimental writers, xi, 243, 249
  American prosody, 103
  expansion historiographies, 229
  First Nations, 249
  New American Poetry, 92
  trans-Pacific dialogue, xi, 100–1, 112, 128–9, 135–7, 174–5
  "The United States" (Williams), 101–2

United States of America (*cont.*)
   William Carlos Williams and Ezra Pound, 100–1, 102

Vickery, Ann, 107

Wakeling, Corey, 97
Walwicz, Ania
   as an Antipodal avant-garde figure, xi, 98, 210, 215–17
   "Australia", 196, 211–15, 232–3
   Boat, 225, 226, 227, 228, 230
   double-marginal status, 216, 218–19, 243
   expansive *poesis*, 221, 227–32
   geopolitical contexts, 233–6
   language, 218, 221–2, 238–9
   literary criticism and, 210
   "Look at me, Ma.", 216–17
   the migrant experience, 80 n.13, 183, 210–15, 218–19, 243
   multicultural readings, 232–5, 237
   overreadings, 238
   Palace of Culture, 227–8, 230–1, 232, 236
   performance of her poetry, 209–10
   "Poland", 211–12
   prosodic dissonance, 142, 221–7
   readership, 216, 218
   Red Roses, 227
   self-portrait, 211
   social function of the author, 236, 239
   Steinishness, 208, 209, 216, 217, 222
   Stewart compared to, 288
   transnational perspectives, 184, 220, 233–7
   voice recordings, 208–9
   writing process, 222
Wertheim, Christine, 128–9
White, Eric, 104, 154
Whitlam, Gough
   Assisted Passage Migration Scheme, 184
   cultural impact, 94, 171, 172, 173–4, 175, 178
   quip to Mao Zedong on revolution, 272
   the Whitlam Dismissal, 36 n.22, 94, 95 n.20, 96, 175, 178
Whitman, Walt, 100, 103, 104, 105 n.2, 116, 134, 137, 138
Whittaker, Alison, 156, 277–8
Williams, William Carlos
   account of Dada, 106
   "The Botticellian Trees", 145
   call for a new order of the line, 102–4, 138, 139, 154, 155
   on cultural patrilineariety, 101, 102, 104, 108
   on Elsa von Freytag-Loringhoven, 104, 106–7, 116
   invention and poetic form, 102–3
   Kora in Hell, 106
   literary relationship with Ezra Pound, 100–1, 102, 105–6
   Paterson, 6–7, 101, 102, 106
   "The United States", 101–2
Winkiel, Laura, 244, 248
women
   anthologies of experimental women's writing, 77
   Industrial Women Collective, 193, 194
   long poems, 228–9
   negotiation of modernism's paternity, 101, 102, 104, 106–8
   New Woman, 106
   during the post-war reconstruction, 108
   writers of the 1940s, 107–8
Wonderful World of Barry McKenzie, The, 171, 172
Wright, Judith, 6, 108
writing
   graphic practices, 48, 49, 50, 69, 193, 258, 288, 293
   meaning-making, 220
   photocopy writing, 291–3
   temporality, 209
   Walwicz's process of, 222
   see also notational poetics

Yock, Daniel, 255, 272

Zukofsky, Louis, 104, 144
Zurbrugg, Nicholas, 186

EU representative:
Easy Access System Europe
Mustamäe tee 50, 10621 Tallinn, Estonia
Gpsr.requests@easproject.com

www.ingramcontent.com/pod-product-compliance
Lightning Source LLC
Chambersburg PA
CBHW050159240426
43671CB00013B/2187